3.

THE GREENING OF
URBAN TRANSPORT

The greening of urban transport: planning for walking and cycling in Western cities

Edited by

Rodney Tolley

JOHN WILEY & SONS
Chichester • New York • Brisbane • Toronto • Singapore

© Rodney Tolley and Contributors, 1990

First published in Great Britain in 1990 by
Belhaven Press (a division of Pinter Publishers Limited)
25 Floral Street, London WC2E 9DS

Published in February 1995 by John Wiley & Sons Ltd,
Baffins Lane, Chichester,
West Sussex PO19 1UD, England
Telephone National Chichester (01243) 779777
International (+44) 1243 779777

Other Wiley Editorial Offices

John Wiley & Sons, Inc., 605 Third Avenue,
New York, NY 10158-0012, USA

Jacaranda Wiley Ltd, 33 Park Road, Milton,
Queensland 4064, Australia

John Wiley & Sons (Canada) Ltd, 22 Worcester Road,
Rexdale, Ontario M9W 1L1, Canada

John Wiley & Sons (SEA) Pte Ltd, 37 Jalan Pemimpin #05-04,
Block B, Union Industrial Building, Singapore 2057

ISBN 0-471-94778-4

Typeset by Florencetype Ltd, Kewstoke, Avon BS22 9YR
Printed and bound in Great Britain by Antony Rowe Ltd, Chippenham, Wiltshire

Contents

List of figures   vii

List of tables   x

Notes on contributors   xiii

Preface and acknowledgements   xv

The European Charter of Pedestrians' Rights   xvi

Introduction: trading-in the red modes for the green   1
Rodney Tolley

Part 1   Principles

1   A hard road: the problems of walking and cycling in British cities *Rodney Tolley*   13

2   The economic case for green modes *John Roberts*   34

3   The safety of walking and cycling in different countries *Barbara Preston*   47

4   Planning for the green modes: a critique of public policy and practice *Mayer Hillman*   64

5   The principle of environmental traffic management *John Whitelegg*   75

6   Feet first: putting people at the centre of planning *Judith Hanna*   88

7   The pedestrian town as an environmentally tolerable alternative to motorised travel *Otto Ullrich*   97

Part 2   Strategies

8   Traffic and environmental policy in the Netherlands *Martin Kroon*   113

9   Policy issues in promoting the green modes *Rolf Monheim*   134

10   A systematic approach to the planning of urban networks for walking *Anthony Ramsay*   159

11 Why you can't walk there: strategies for improving the pedestrian environment in the United States *Rich Untermann*   172

12 Walking and public transport: two sides of the same coin *Dietrich Garbrecht*   185

Part 3 Practice

13 The Delft bicycle network *Jan Hartman*   193

14 Planning for the bicycle in urban Britain: an assessment of experience and issues *Hugh McClintock*   201

15 The 'Bicycle-Friendly Towns' Project in the Federal Republic of Germany *Wulf Hülsmann*   218

16 Public transport and cycling: experience of modal integration in West Germany *Jürgen Brunsing*   231

17 The evolution and impact of pedestrian areas in the Federal Republic of Germany *Rolf Monheim*   244

18 Safe routes to school in Odense, Denmark *Ole Helboe Nielsen*   255

19 Environmental traffic management strategies in Buxtehude, West Germany *Alice Döldissen and Werner Draeger*   266

Part 4 An Overview

20 Summary and conclusions for policy *John Roberts*   287

Index   303

List of figures

1.1 The pedestrian subway: a urine-scented gallery 15
1.2 Fouling of the pavement by dogs is a common complaint and is increasingly being dealt with by law 17
1.3 An alternative to conventional priorities for walking 20
1.4 50 is too much! Propaganda from a Dutch road safety pressure group seeking 30 km/h limits 21
1.5 Pavement parking in Amsterdam 21
1.6 Cycle tracks in Britain are infrequent and discontinuous 23
1.7 Traffic calming in Holland: a Woonerf in Delft 27
1.8 Integration of modes in place of segregation: a calmed area in Haarlem 28
1.9 City-wide calming in Freiburg includes a pedestrian network and segregated and planted tram tracks, which converge on the car-free centre 30
1.10 Many people have rediscovered the pleasures of strolling in car-free city centres 31
2.1 Turnover and parking provision in ten West German cities 43
5.1 (a–e) Diagrams showing traffic calming in Niedersprockhövel, Nordrhein-Westfalen: a main street (B51) 80–1
5.2 Speed measurements before and after traffic calming in Buxtehude, West Germany 82
8.1 The contribution of road traffic to acidification and photochemical air pollution in the Netherlands 115
8.2 The three-track approach to the abatement of environmental pollution by motor vehicles 118
8.3 Emission performances of current engine technologies for 1.4–2.0-litre cars in the Netherlands 120
8.4 Average emissions as measured, before and after tuning, per technology in g/test for (a) carbon monoxide and (b) nitrogen oxides 131
9.1 The bicycle network of Erlangen, West Germany 149
13.1 The Delft cycle network 198
14.1 Location of the Department of Transport experimental schemes, 1977–89 202
14.2 Diagrammatic map of the Greater Nottingham Cycle Route Network Project (1986–90), showing implementation progress as at spring 1989 204

14.3   A two-way cycle path near the Silverdale roundabout in
        Nottingham, helping cyclists avoid heavy traffic on the
        main road and roundabout   206
14.4   Signalled cycle crossings can open up safer and more direct
        links for cyclists, despite constraints of space in city centres:
        Canal Street, Nottingham   207
15.1   Waiting areas for cyclists making indirect turns on crossroads
        in the 'Bicycle-Friendly Towns' Project   224
15.2   Cycle route with right of way for the cyclist in the
        'Bicycle-Friendly Towns' Project   224
16.1   Evaluation of bike-parking facilities   234
16.2   Bicycle cages   234
16.3   Bicycle transport facility in suburban rapid rail   236
16.4   Bike bus in Braunschweig   238
16.5   The interior of a re-designed bus in Braunschweig   238
16.6   A bicycle trailer   239
16.7   Bicycle transport in Bonn   241
17.1   Munich: pedestrian precincts, traffic arrangements and
        retail trade   250
18.1   The process of developing safe routes to school in Odense   259
18.2   A raised area and soft landscaping on a safe route to
        school in Odense   260
18.3   An example of road narrowing in the 'Safe Routes to
        School' Project   261
18.4   An example of a traffic island in the 'Safe Routes to
        School' Project   262
18.5   Separate foot and cycle paths for schoolchildren on a
        safe route to school   262
19.1   Environmental traffic management in Buxtehude: land use
        and the 'direct connection network'   269
19.2   A cycle path against a one-way street in Buxtehude   272
19.3   A well-designed cycle and pedestrian subway under the
        railway in Buxtehude   272
19.4   Environmental traffic management in Buxtehude:
        the cycle and pedestrian route network   273
19.5   A pleasantly designed direct pedestrian route to
        Buxtehude town centre   273
19.6   A pedestrian precinct open to cyclists ('Radfahrer frei').
        The hare and the hedgehog are well-known figures in a
        famous Buxtehude fable   274
19.7   A bicycle street in Buxtehude with limited access for cars
        and lorries   274
19.8   A road narrowing on the Konopkastrasse in Buxtehude with
        raised paving of crossing point of main pedestrian and
        cycle route   276

19.9   Speed-reducing paving design in Buxtehude (optical
        'narrowing' and 'shortening' of the carriageway) and
        road narrowings allowing cyclists to pass freely   277
19.10   The junction of Altländerstrasse with Dammhauserstrasse
        in Buxtehude with provisional narrowing of entrance using
        large flower pots (1984)   277
19.11   The junction of Altländerstrasse with Dammhauserstrasse
        in Buxtehude after final redesigning had been completed
        (1987)   278
19.12   Viverstrasse in Buxtehude, with the cycle lane crossing
        the free right-turn lane (right) and a cycle path against the
        one-way street (left)   280
19.13   Raised and redesigned paving for pedestrians and cyclists
        crossing the free right-turn lane at a junction of two main
        roads in Buxtehude   280
19.14   A direct left-turn cycle lane in Buxtehude   281
19.15   Accidents involving cyclists in the Buxtehude project area,
        before and after environmental traffic management   283

List of tables

2.1   Some shopping and modal splits   37
2.2   Selected results from the West Midlands turnover/mode
      survey   38
2.3   Per capita spending by mode in Bromley, East Ham and
      Kensington High Streets in 1987   39
2.4   Urban rail transport and shopping turnover for selected
      West German cities   41
3.1   Definitions of road death in those countries where it is
      not defined as 'death within 30 days of the accident'   48
3.2   Pedestrians killed per 100 000 population in different
      countries   50
3.3   Pedal cyclists killed per 100 000 population in different
      countries in 1985   51
3.4   Cyclists killed per million cycles in different countries   51
3.5   Death and injury rates per 100 million kilometres
      travelled for pedestrians and for cyclists in Britain
      and the Netherlands   52
3.6   Percentage of the total number of pedal cyclists injured,
      by country and age group in 1985   53
3.7   Pedestrian deaths, actual and predicted, as a percentage
      of total deaths in different countries   55
3.8   Death rates for child pedstrians by age groups in
      different countries   57
3.9   Death rates for pedetrians aged 25–64 years in countries
      with different urban speed limits in 1985   60
3.10 A comparison of the death rates for all modes of travel in
      Sweden, Japan and South Africa in 1977 and 1986   62
4.1   Percentage of journeys on foot or cycle in Great Britain,
      by age and sex, 1975–76 and 1985–86   66
4.2   A comparison of journeys by mode in Great Britain including
      and excluding journeys of under 1.6km, 1985–86   68
4.3   Percentages of journeys in Great Britain by all modes
      and by walking and cycling over distances of less than 1.6km,
      by age and sex, 1985–86   68
5.1   *Verkehrsberuhigung* measures organised by type of street   78
5.2   Summary of the main features of *Verkehrsberuhigung* in
      three pioneer schemes in Germany   79

5.3	Development of speed: percentage travelling over 30 km/h in selected streets in Dortmund before and after the introduction of Tempo 30 measures	83
5.4	Consequences of *Verkehrsberuhigung* for the safety of children: the example of Berlin	83
5.5	Accident counts on streets in Dortmund before and after the application of *Verkehrsberuhigung* measures	85
6.1	Main problems for pedestrians (prompted and unprompted) in the National Consumer Council's survey	89
8.1	Emissions from road traffic in the Netherlands, in tonnes and as a percentage of emissions from all sources	115
8.2	Transport emission targets in the NMP (National Environmental Policy Plan, 1990–94) and percentage reductions over 1986	117
8.3	Exhaust gas standards established by the 1985 Luxembourg agreement	119
8.4	Trend in the number of car kilometres in the Netherlands	130
9.1	Modal split, West Germany, 1982	136
16.1	Evaluation of the combination of bike/public transport and likelihood of use	233
17.1	Pedestrian areas in Nordrhein-Westfalen according to municipality size, 1988	248
17.2	Pedestrian areas and traffic-calmed shopping streets in centres in Bavaria according to municipality size, 1985	249
18.1	Number of accidents in Odense between motor vehicles and children aged 0–14 years, on foot on bicycle, measured over a three-year period (1975–77)	256
18.2	Number and percentage of accidents in Odense to child pedestrians and child cyclists, recorded and not recorded by the police, 1975–77	257
18.3	Mode of transport in Odense of children of different ages, from both school and other activities	258
18.4	The use of bicycles in Odense	263
19.1	The German interministerial research programme on environmental traffic management schemes: the six project areas	268
19.2	Percentage modal split according to journey purpose, Buxtehude project area	270

Notes on contributors

Jurgen Brunsing has studied in Vienna and Dortmund, was visiting Research Associate at the University of Lancaster in 1989 and since 1990 has been a research assistant in the Department of Transportation Planning at the Universität Dortmund. He is a consultant in the transport planning field, with particular interests in pedestrian and cycle transport, and in the relationship between these non-motorised modes and public transport.

Alice Döldissen has a background in study and research in town and regional planning. Since 1981 she has been working for the German Federal Environmental Agency in Berlin, where she is responsible for noise abatement in town and transportation planning and, in particular, inner-city environmental traffic management schemes.

Werner Draeger studied civil engineering in Aachen and lectured at the Rhineland-Westphalian Technical University. From 1977 to 1989 he was employed at the Bundesanstalt für Straßenwesen (Federal Institute for Road Research), responsible for advising the Federal Ministry of Transport in the fields of traffic restraint, cycle and pedestrian traffic and parking policy. He now works for an independent consulting office in Bonn, specialising in integrated environmental, city and transport planning.

Dietrich Garbrecht has been a designer and planner with architectural firms in several countries and, since 1978, has been a freelance consultant. He continues to edit, write, lecture and consult in the fields of architecture and planning. In 1982 he was awarded the German Cities and Communities Foundation Award for the promotion of urban knowledge for his book *Gehen (Walking)*.

Judith Hanna is Assistant Director of Transport 2000, the environmental pressure group campaigning for an integrated transport policy for Britain. She co-ordinates T2000's Feet First work, in addition to work on a range of other transport issues. She is a frequent pedestrian and public transport user, an occasional cyclist and a very occasional motorist.

Jan Hartman has worked for the Dutch Ministry of Transport since 1983. Until 1988 he led research projects on policies for bicycle infrastructure and the re-design of residential areas. Since then he has been deputy head and research co-ordinator of a road aesthetics section concerned with visual quality of roads, perception and driving behaviour.

Anthony Ramsay lectures in town planning at the University of Strathclyde. He researches, speaks and writes regularly about provision for walking internationally, striving for equity *vis-à-vis* other forms of traffic and for recognition of the special needs *qua* pedestrians of the very young, the very old and the badly disabled. He is the Secretary-General of AESOP, the Association of European Schools of Planning.

John Roberts, with qualifications in the fields of architecture and transport, founded Transport and Environment Studies (TEST) in 1972 and directed it until his death in 1992. He taught at Oxford Polytechnic and University College London, and spent eight years with the Greater London Council and three with Llewelyn-Davies, Weeks and Partners.

Rodney Tolley is a Senior Lecturer in Geography at Staffordshire University, a consultant to local authorities and others on transport matters and is a member of the Chartered Institute of Transport. As a committee member of the Transport Geography Study Group of the Institute of British Geographers, he convened the conference at Coventry Polytechnic in January 1989 on which many of the chapters in this book are based. He is the author of *Calming Traffic in Residential Areas* (1990) and spent 1990–1 on secondment to the University of Zimbabwe.

Otto Ulrich lives in Berlin and is a member of several political advisory commissions on the subjects of technology, work, energy and traffic. He has published on these themes as well as on industrial sociology and history, and is the author of *Technology and Government Authority* (1979).

Rich Untermann, educated at Berkeley and Harvard, has been Professor of Landscape Architecture, Urban Planning and Environmental Studies at the University of Washington in Seattle since 1971. His major consulting, research and teaching interests concern the creation of 'liveable environments' and strong 'sense of community'; he is the author of five books, including *Accommodating the Pedestrian* (1984).

John Whitelegg is a Lecturer in the Department of Geography at Lancaster University. He has worked extensively in Germany on transport and traffic projects and is the author of *Transport Policy in the EEC* (1988).

Preface and acknowledgements

Each January at the conference of the Institute of British Geographers, the Transport Geography Study Group convenes its own symposium, with a topic for the papers relevant both to that of the theme and location of the parent conference that year. The 1989 conference theme was 'Managing our environment' and the venue was Coventry, historic home of the British cycle industry and with a place in the pantheon of post-war pedestrianisation in Britain. It was most appropriate then for the Group to choose for the first time a theme related to walking and cycling and to discuss it under the title of 'Planning for the green modes'.

This book is not the proceedings of that symposium, but some of the chapters have grown from contributions originally presented there. Most, however, have been commissioned subsequently in order to target the work specifically at Western urban milieux and to draw on the work of specialists in fields other than geography and those from mainland Europe whose published work is in a language other than English. Thus although the book is, as it should be, the responsibility of the contributors and editor, it owes much to the Transport Geography Study Group under its then Chair, Richard Knowles of Salford University. It goes without saying that Iain Stevenson at Belhaven provided valuable support and indispensable guidance.

A debt of gratitude is owed to many others who contributed in their various ways. On the production side, cartographic matters were handled with great skill and care by Paul Taylor of the Cartography Unit in the Department of Geography and Recreation Studies at Staffordshire Polytechnic. Kerry Summerfield did sterling work in interpreting and typing, as well as in coping with the complexities of shuttling drafts between various countries. Joan Goulden was as ever a cheerful and willing aide in the Department, whilst Peter Butler of the Computing Service Unit provided invaluable advice and technical help in translating a variety of computer discs into a standard format.

For the text itself, thanks must go to Terry Postings for his meticulous translation work and to Sue Major and John Whitelegg for additional help. Many European contributors assisted by writing in English or providing translations and all are to be thanked for their equanimity in meeting editorial demands. Particular thanks are due to John Roberts for his helpful comments and for the additional work involved in writing the summary chapter. Lastly, thanks are due to my family for accepting my disappearances into the study when other demands could have been made on my time, notably to go out riding the bikes rather than writing about them.   *Rodney Tolley, March 1990*

The European Charter of Pedestrians' Rights adopted by the European Parliament in 1988

I.   The pedestrian has the right to live in a healthy environment and freely to enjoy the amenities offered by public areas under conditions that adequately safeguard his physical and psychological well-being.

II.   The pedestrian has the right to live in urban or village centres tailored to the needs of the motor car and to have amenities within walking or cycling distance.

III.   Children, the elderly and the disabled have the right to expect towns to be places of easy social contact and not places that aggravate their inherent weakness.

IV.   The disabled have the right to specify measures to maximise their independent mobility, including adjustments in public areas, transport systems and public transport (guidelines, warning signs, acoustic signals, accessible buses, trams and trains).

V.   The pedestrian has the right to urban areas which are intended exclusively for his use, are as extensive as possible and are not mere 'pedestrian precincts' but in harmony with the overall organisation of the town, and also the exclusive right to connecting short, logical and safe routes.

VI.   The pedestrian has a particular right to expect:

(a) compliance with chemical and noise emission standards for motor vehicles which scientists consider to be tolerable;

(b) the introduction into all public transport systems of vehicles that are not a source of either air or noise pollution;

(c) the creation of 'green lungs', including the planting of trees in urban areas;

(d) the fixing of speed limits and modifications to the layout of roads and junctions as a way of effectively safeguarding pedestrian and bicycle traffic;

(e) the banning of advertising which encourages an improper and dangerous use of the motor car;

(f) an effective system of road signs whose design also takes into account the needs of the blind and deaf;

(g) the adoption of specific measures to ensure that vehicular pedestrian traffic has ease of access to, and freedom of movement and the possibility of stopping on, roads and pavements respectively;

(h) adjustments to the shape and equipment of motor vehicles so as to give a smoother line to those parts which project most and to make signalling systems more efficient;

(i) the introduction of the system of risk liability so that the person creating the risk bears the financial consequences thereof (as has been the case in France, for example, since 1985);

(j) a drivers' training programme designed to encourage suitable conduct on the roads in respect of pedestrians and other slow road users.

VII. The pedestrian has the right to complete and unimpeded mobility, which can be achieved through the integrated use of the means of transport. In particular, he has the right to expect:

(a) an ecologically sound, extensive and well-equipped public transport service which will meet the needs of all citizens, from the physically fit to the disabled;

(b) the provision of facilities for bicycles throughout the urban areas;

(c) parking lots which are sited in such a way that they affect neither the mobility of pedestrians nor their ability to enjoy areas of architectural distinction.

VIII. Each Member State must ensure that comprehensive information on the rights of pedestrians and on alternative ecologically sound forms of transport is disseminated through the most appropriate channels and is made available to children from the beginning of their school career.

Introduction: trading-in the red modes for the green

Rodney Tolley

Why promote the green modes? and why now?

The consequences of increasing congestion in Western cities are becoming intolerable. Much of this is due to reliance on a flawed mode of transport with severe environmental and social side-effects, and one whose resource demands are not sustainable in the long term. Many trips currently made by car could be made on foot or by cycle, but these 'green modes', though environmentally benign, are the ones most deleteriously affected by motorised traffic. Their use is thus declining in the face of increasing danger, lengthening trips, worsening facilities and escalating pollution. A rational society must sooner or later recognise that energy-efficient and non-polluting modes of transport will eventually dominate city movement if the cities themselves are to survive. This book examines policies and strategies for the achievement of that new order and reviews progress towards it in a variety of geographical circumstances and policy environments.

Given that the sustainability of urban life is a timeless topic, some explanation for the timing of this book is perhaps needed. First, urban renovation was in vogue in the 1980s, as cities attempted to retain high-income groups, attract modern jobs, achieve glamorous images and re-spond competitively to the growth of out-of-town shopping. In this struggle the provision of high-quality pedestrianised town centres has been a key weapon. In Britain, this is not necessarily a fundamental change of heart or direction, for many such areas have been constructed with encircling roads and car parks that have made walking and cycling access to town centres more difficult, not less. Nevertheless, the dramatic resurgence of car-free shopping and strolling in British cities has reminded many of the pleasure to be gained from urban walking when planning and designing are done well. As Monheim says in Chapter 16 about Germany, which is undoubtedly the world leader in city centre pedestrianisation, 'a town without representative pedestrian areas now appears hopelessly antiquated'. Thus have pedestrian areas become fashionable and the quality of walking environments a matter of public interest, so that proposals to improve such qualities in other city districts are likely to be favourably received.

A second justification for this collective work is that the reduction of car use that would result from more walking and cycling would be accompanied by falls in local, national and global pollution levels. These are matters of great – and growing – public interest. There is a thirst for environmental discussion at present and much concern over the specific atmospheric consequences of the transport that we use. In other words, these ideas will be offered to an audience which is increasingly ready for them.

There are three levels at which this environmental concern can be seen to be influential. At the macro scale, there is much greater appreciation of the global nature of pollution problems, of the need for urgent action, and of the role of motorised transport in contributing to transboundary phenomena such as acid rain and global warming. Opinion surveys for the DoE in 1986 and 1989 revealed a fourfold increase in the percentage of people feeling that environment or pollution issues should be among the most important on the Government's agenda (*Guardian*, 1990a).

At a national and regional level, there is a burgeoning public debate over road congestion and growing consciousness of the relationships between traffic and environmental degradation. By the late 1980s Britain's urban and inter-urban roads were severely congested, a consequence of growing private affluence, continued subsidy for company motoring, repeated cuts in support for the railways and for urban mass transport, and rapidly sprawling urban functions, particularly the explosion of out-of-town shopping and leisure complexes. The government's response in 1989 was a proposal to raise the investment target for the road-building programme from £6 billion to £12 billion, based on forecasts for traffic volume increases of up to 142 per cent by the year 2025 (Department of Transport, 1989a).

Whilst this was predictably welcomed by the road lobby, the degree of public scepticism was unprecedented, with widespread critical comment and the then Secretary of State for Transport, Cecil Parkinson, lampooned in the press, in numerous cartoons and biting editorials. The Department of the Environment could scarcely conceal its opposition to what it saw as 'unacceptable' proposals and the D.Tp., attempting to justify its position, caused even greater incredulity with its claim that as pollution was caused by congestion, the solution was to build more roads. By early 1990, no longer was opposition to road building simply of the NIMBY variety: the wider appreciation of the connection between motoring and pollution problems was becoming evident in the thinking of opposition parties, to the extent that the Prime Minister felt the need to defend the 'car economy' and to attack the 'airy fairies' who disagreed with her (*Guardian*, 1990b).

Rising levels of environmental conciousness can also be seen at the local level. Again in Britain, a study in early 1989 found strong public support for more pedal cycle facilities, for the provision of complete cycle networks, for more pedestrian facilities and for a recognition of the need for more surface pedestrian crossings (Department of Transport, 1989b). In terms of city traffic congestion, there was a feeling that positive steps would have to be taken to restrict car use, provided that this was part of a package that included improvements in public transport and some reallocation of road space, such as new cycle or bus facilities, extra space for pedestrians or residents' parking. The virility of this nascent environmental movement was confirmed in March 1990, when consultants' proposals for road building in London were abandoned by the Department of Transport in the face of massive public opposition and demands for investment instead in public transport, cycle lanes and traffic calming.

At each of these levels, there is growing, if reluctant, appreciation of the need for restraint of car use, even if public acceptance of the need to dampen ownership levels has yet to become widespread. So long as trips remain lengthy, car restraint must result in transfer to public transport, so that many British cities are now contemplating the introduction of some form of light rail. However, should trip length be reduced by careful planning that places destinations within easy reach of origins, many journeys could be made on foot or by cycle, thereby re-creating a traditional urban form cemented by traditional forms of movement.

It may seem paradoxical that most of the justifications for this book on walking and cycling are couched in terms of the need to restrain motorised traffic. The virtues of the green modes could of course be extolled – their role in health promotion for example – but for the most part they are self-evident. Besides, it is the fact that cars defile the environment, not that walking and cycling do not, that is at the root of the environmental crisis in the cities, so the emphasis on restraint of motorised traffic should not surprise. However, the key issue here is that there is no point in promoting the green modes unless the car is restrained. For example, the health benefits of cycling are well known and this has played a part in the current boom in cycle sales. Yet rising ownership is not being matched by rising use for everyday travel, mostly because of the well-justified fear of conflict with increasing volumes of motorised traffic. This will not be the only place in this book that the point will be made that encouraging the green modes is futile without discouragement of the principal 'red' one, the car.

What is this book about?

A series of innovative experiments in mainland European towns in the past decade has shown that dramatic increases in the amount of walking and cycling are possible (Tolley, 1990). Yet there is still much to do, for car ownership continues to rise and the gains for the green modes in some localities are more than offset by the losses everywhere else. In other

Western countries there is interest in these developments but little knowledge or direct experience, so there is much to be learned about the promotion of the green modes and more sensible use of the car. In this, Britain will be aided enormously by its closer integration with the mainland, parts of which are now a decade ahead of the rest of the world in experience of traffic restraint and green mode promotion. Things may not be so easy for the United States with its car dependence and remoteness from innovative practice, where Roberts (1988) speculates that 'the merest whispers of traffic restraint probably lead to the unbuttoning of holsters, and the removal of safety catches'.

Much then is known but a good deal of the accumulated knowledge is in inaccessible form, in working papers, research memoranda and government reports in different languages. The object of this book is to bring together the key areas of research, to introduce the principles of planning for the green modes, to analyse the strategies for their application, and to examine the state of the art in a variety of approaches and locations. Three groups of chapters – on principles, strategy and practice – occupy the first three sections of the book, whilst the last section contains a single chapter, a summary, to which readers should turn for an overview of the book. In this introduction only the briefest outline will be provided.

The principles section begins with two chapters that concentrate on environmental/social and economic issues respectively. The first outlines the problems of walking and cycling and examines methods of calming traffic in order to diminish the impacts of motor traffic on the environment in which the green modes operate. Roberts in Chapter 2 demonstrates that pedestrianisation has been economically healthy for Western European cities and concludes that as a good physical environment is a good economic environment, the encouragement of the green modes is consonant with city renovation. But there is widespread ignorance of the particular experience of the green modes, not least the way in which the increasing danger of walking and cycling is concealed in the aggregate statistics usually used, as Preston shows in Chapter 3. Support is provided by Hillman's contribution, which shows how these modes are ignored in information-gathering and decision-making, and argues that pedestrians and cyclists are discriminated against in public policy.

In Chapter 5, Whitelegg moves the debate on by analysing the extension of the traffic calming principle into one of integrated traffic and transport planning, whereby the goal is to restrain traffic over wide areas, including main traffic arteries. Hanna in Chapter 6 also takes the broad view, stressing that in order to encourage the green modes, the principle must be one of locating facilities in ways which enhance their accessibility, thereby in future putting the needs of people before those of reducing the friction of travel. In contrast, past transport planning has conventionally addressed the 'problem' of mobility, producing the detrimental effects of motorised travel on the environment detailed by Ullrich in Chapter 7. He argues that policy should be aimed at achieving tolerable levels of environmental intrusion, chiefly through reclaiming space from the car and restructuring settlements in order to shorten trips.

The second section of the book focuses on strategies for encouragement of the green modes. The way in which a pro-green mode policy fits with general environmental policy is examined by Kroon in Chapter 8, using Holland as a test case. He makes the point that attempts to cut pollution by clean car technology alone will be overwhelmed by rising car numbers, so the strategy has become one of planning in addition for a reduction in car use. Success in Holland with these approaches is of critical importance, for it will set the guidelines for other Western countries to follow. Monheim indicates the kind of policy obstacles that are likely to be encountered. He analyses, in a German context, the circumstances that have led to the continuing failure to adopt large-scale, comprehensive, environmentally sound city transport, despite the efforts of various national and regional government agencies and pressure groups. However, if these barriers can be overcome there will be a need to plan the networks for the green modes which will become the town's arteries. Ramsay's contribution in Chapter 10 considers geometrical, topological, aesthetic, social and psychological perspectives in the design of the ideal networks for walking.

Though success for the green modes has yet to appear throughout Europe, there are at least encouraging prospects. In contrast, Untermann reviews pedestrian facilities in the United States, or rather the lack of them, describes how this has come about and outlines what strategic alterations in the planning system are required if walking is to become pleasant, or even feasible, in the US city. Garbrecht's insistence on the need for planned integration of public transport and walking is not specific to any particular continent, though: indeed, his speculation of how this might be achieved uses a mythical city and is not perhaps strictly strategy, but provides an enchanting vision of what might be.

The third group of chapters assembles experience and results of green mode encouragement and thus functions as a review of the state of the art in the late 1980s. Hartman begins the section by describing the conception, design and realisation of the Delft cycle network. This crucial and keenly anticipated piece of research shows that coherent networks of cycle tracks can arrest the modal switch from bike to car in medium-sized towns. By contrast, McClintock's critical review of cycle planning in the United Kingdom shows how little has been achieved in a country that sees the bike as either a toy for children or as a problem for adults. The facilities that are required to promote cycling must be seen in a wider context encompassing matters of traffic danger, trip length and the climate created by transport and environmental policies.

Between the extremes of the widespread encouragement of cycling in the Netherlands and its effective discouragement in Britain lies the German approach, described by Hülsmann in Chapter 15. The West

Germans have adopted an innovative approach to releasing the latent demand for cycling by creating 'bicycle-friendly towns' as demonstration projects, in the expectation that other towns will be stimulated to act themselves. These approaches are expected to go hand in hand with environmental traffic management measures described in Chapters 1 and 5 to achieve a transport system which is compatible with the needs of the environment and therefore with those of society. Just as Garbrecht argued for the need for integration in such a system between walking and public transport, so here does Brunsing examine the experience in Germany in helping cyclists to use buses, trams and trains.

Examination of practice in providing for walking and cycling continues with a contribution from Rolf Monheim that describes the experience and consequences of pedestrianisation in West Germany and notes its catalytic effect on urban renaissance. The focus shifts northward in Nielsen's chapter, in which the 'Safe Routes to School' Project in Odense is described. This project is of great relevance to other Western cities, where fear of traffic danger generates parental journeys in the role of chauffeurs to children. In Britain, for example, one-third of all women's driving is for escort purposes, prompting the thought that women are escaping from bondage to the kitchen sink only to become chained to the steering wheel. Although safe routes to school are not specifically incorporated in the comprehensive German experiments in environmental traffic management described in Chapter 19, many of the other approaches seen in this 'practice' section are put into operation there. The goals and conduct of the experiments are examined by Döldissen and Draeger and the particular measures and outcomes in one project town analysed. The prognosis is very positive, provided that measures to slow motorised traffic are used simultaneously to give protection and priority to those on foot and cycle.

The book's final chapter provides an overview, as Roberts pulls together common themes from preceding chapters, identifies main conclusions and proposes policy directions.

What are the obstacles to greening urban transport?

There should be no underestimation of the size of the task ahead if walking and cycling are to become ubiquitous. Because suppression of motorised traffic is a *sine qua non* of encouraging walking and cycling, ranged against the green modes will be the 'system of motorisation' described by Ullrich in Chapter 7. This is pervasive, extensive and immensely influential: just for a start it includes the ten largest companies in the world, all of which sell either oil or cars.

Moreover, there is evidence now that the road lobby is greening its image and subtly changing its stance, but without any fundamental shift away from its principal goal of encouraging more traffic. One could, for example, point to the catalytic converter as a technological fix provided by the motor industry and which, in the words of Roberts (1989), 'has affinities with the philosopher's stone: it permits continuous use of the car and ownership growth, while reducing air pollution emissions' (though of course it increases the production of the principal 'greenhouse' gas, CO_2). Monheim in Chapter 9 shows how insidious has been the opposition of the road lobby to progressive traffic planning in West Germany. Indeed, it is not unreasonable to speculate that traffic calming in that country may have been an elaborate confidence trick perpetrated by the road lobby to get the environmentalists off their backs, for parallel to the growth in calming has continued the secular upward trend in car sales and use. Roberts, in his summary (Chapter 20) even wonders whether traffic calming itself has actually resulted in an increase in car parking space in calmed areas, thus sanctifying the cult of car ownership and use.

As well as these obstacles which are present in all Western industrialised countries, in Britain there are additional major barriers to the encouragement of the green modes embedded in current official attitudes to transport policy. Not only is there a lack of direct encouragement of walking and cycling – even active discrimination against them according to Hillman in Chapter 4 – but there is a continuing drift in British cities towards piecemeal and reactive market-governed practice, a vacuum in urban transport policy from which attempts to domesticate the car seem unlikely to emerge. The only saving grace is that it seems increasingly likely that it will be the environment that will set the agenda for transport planning in the future, with plentiful indications that the public are way ahead of the Department of Transport on this issue.

A particular problem in Britain is the trend-bound transport planning which has characterised the post-war years, a system which interprets 'trend' as 'destiny' and thus sees traffic growth as inevitable and uncontrollable, like rainfall. This has led to road building to meet anticipated increases in traffic and has, in a classic self-fulfilling prophecy, generated the traffic to fill the new road space. It is a system which is anathema to the success of promoting the green modes and is fundamentally antipathetic to the environmental and social goals which permeate the philosophy of traffic calming.

It is also increasingly out of step with the most progressive thinking in mainland Europe. The contrast was highlighted dramatically in May 1989 when, coincidentally, both the British and Dutch governments made major policy statements on future transport investment. The doubling of the British investment in the road-building programme has already been described. Though faced with similarly horrific forecasts, the Dutch responded with plans that are diametrically opposed to those in Britain. They decided to combat the trend underpinning the forecasts and to take the first step towards 'sustainable development' by the year 2010. This entails a

new strategy for environmental policy in the 1990s, involving the investment of some six billion guilders per annum to reduce exhaust emissions,
principally through reducing car use and applying environmental traffic
management in cities (Ministry of Housing, Physical Planning and
Environment, 1989).

As Kroon makes clear in Chapter 8, there are immense obstacles to the
achievement of the Dutch goals. Learning to reduce dependence on cars is
untrodden ground and the response of the car lobby is unlikely to be
passive. Nevertheless, the Dutch have plotted a new course for transport
and the environment for the opening of the twenty-first century; the British
have accelerated their own journey in the opposite direction, adding a
further twist to the disastrous spiral of environmental degradation, rising
mobility expenditure and road building.

At the risk of repetition, one fundamental point needs to be emphasised.
Although the title of this book implies an emphasis on encouraging walking
and cycling, there are in fact as many chapters in it that deal with the
myriad problems of discouraging motorised traffic. That balance is deliberate, for, without question, extolling the virtues of the green modes will be
futile without the simultaneous and concomitant reduction in car use and
eventually in ownership. The traffic light can show red, as at present, or
green: it cannot show both at once.

References

Department of Transport, 1989a, *Roads for prosperity*, HMSO, London.
—— 1989b, *Traffic regulation in urban areas: the public view*, Traffic Topics 1, Traffic Advisory Unit, D.Tp., London.
Guardian, 1990a, 'Pollution permeates public conciousness', 15 February.
—— 1990b, 16 March.
Ministry of Housing, Physical Planning and Environment, 1989, *Nationaal milieubeleidsplan (National environmental policy plan): to choose or to lose*, The Hague.
Roberts, J., 1988, '*Genius loci*: how is it retained or revived?' *Proceedings, Ninth Annual Pedestrian Conference*, Boulder, Colo, ed. City of Boulder.
1989, *User Friendly cities: what Britain can learn from mainland Europe*, TEST, London.
Tolley, R.S., 1990, *Calming traffic in residential areas*, Brefi Press, Tregaron.

PART 1
Principles

1 A hard road: the problems of walking and cycling in British cities

Rodney Tolley

The natural form of locomotion for a human being is walking. Humans on foot are thermodynamically more efficient than any motorised vehicle and most animals, yet humans on bicycles surpass them, able as they are to go three to four times faster and yet use five times less energy in the process. Equipped with a bicycle, man is more efficient than all machines and all animals too.

Humans using their feet for transport are inherently equal. What is more, walking and cycling have no impacts on the environment and consume virtually no energy. One person walking or cycling has no effect on the opportunity surface of others, or on the choices that others can make. In short, using your feet allows you to move without interfering with anyone else's freedom. The contrast with car use, where no-one can save time without forcing others to lose it, is marked.

Walking and cycling, the green modes, are thus ideal ways of travelling from the point of view of energy conservation, environmental impact and social equality. However, topography and climate may pose particular problems for such modes of movement that rely on muscular effort in exposed conditions, and might represent a deterrent to their use. But such considerations are secondary: the fact that Sweden, in spite of its climate, has cycle ownership rates nearly four times those of Britain, points to the existence of other factors in the environment which are not the product of natural forces but nevertheless condition the relative attractiveness of the green modes.

The most important such factor is the use of motorised transport, what one might call the 'red' modes. Specifically, the car has a series of impacts on the environment – some direct, some less so – that deter walking and cycling. Unpackaged travellers are endangered by those encased in metal and moving at higher speeds, their air is poisoned and their journeys made noisy and uncomfortable. Moreover, use of the car causes facilities and services to become more widespread, often to the point where they are beyond the range of green mode users. As Illich puts it, 'motorised vehicles create new distances which they alone can shrink. They create them for all, but they can shrink them for only a few' (Illich, 1974).

Not surprisingly, then, the attraction of the green modes goes down as red mode use goes up. It is the contention of many contributors to this book that any attempt to raise green mode use without attempting to depress travel by the red modes will at best hold the line at current travelling conditions and modal splits, and at worst will fail.

This contribution opens the debate by establishing levels and trends of green mode use and identifying current problems, particularly danger on the road. Because green modes are essential in a civilised city, yet conditions for them are currently grossly unsatisfactory and getting worse, the case for positive planning for walking and cycling will be made. Though the macro-level impacts of motorised traffic will be left to subsequent chapters, the micro-level effects of motor traffic on the green modes in their street environment will be discussed. Finally, methods of reclaiming streets for the green modes will be outlined in support of the view that encouragement of walking and cycling can only succeed in conditions where motorised traffic is restrained.

Walking as a problem

What role does walking play?

A pro-walking policy would have to start with the recognition of the vital role that walking plays in everyday life, yet this role is at present often ignored in transport policies. Admittedly, walking behaviour differs greatly between people of different age, class and gender and between journeys for different purposes, so that generalisation is often unhelpful. Nevertheless, it is useful to remember that children walk more than any other age group and women walk more than men. Moreover, walking varies greatly in importance depending on trip purpose. In Britain some 60 per cent of education journeys and 43 per cent of shopping and personal business trips are made on foot, with one-fifth and one-third of all walk journeys respectively being made for these purposes (Mitchell and Stokes, 1982).

Walking in fact involves two separate transport modes, since travel on foot to access other modes such as car or bus is different in almost all respects from walking the whole way. Such 'ancillary' walks are of course shorter than 'primary' walk journeys, representing nearly one-third of all walk stages but less than one-fifth of all walked kilometres. They also incorporate different participants. It is noticeable that the group that in general is in control of the transport system (i.e. males aged 25–60) has the lowest percentage making 'primary' walk journeys, and uses walking to

Figure 1.1. The pedestrian subway: a urine-scented gallery

meet less of its travel requirements than any other age and gender group. Thus many in this group will be familiar with easier, shorter 'ancillary' walks than those such as women, children and the elderly who have over-average representation in the 'primary' walk journey category.

It is not surprising therefore that walking is very much taken for granted by transport decision-makers, a familiarity that has two consequences. Firstly, walking is not perceived as a serious form of transport. Most trips involve a certain amount of walking and most people can walk, with 97 per cent of the population able to go out on foot. Walking, it seems, is just something that we do, like breathing. Transport only happens, apparently, when a motor is started. The implicit view is that walking is irrelevant to city transport problems because it does not cause pollution, or accidents, or noise, or congestion: it is not a problem as such. The notion that it is extremely relevant precisely because it does none of these things seems to go unappreciated in official circles.

The second consequence of the failure to accord to walking the dominant role in urban transport that its trip share warrants is that facilities for it are either absent or neglected (Figure 1.1). Overall, in Britain, more than one in three of all journeys are made door-to-door on foot and pedestrian journeys of 0.8 km or less make up one-sixth of total personal transport demand. Yet official data continue to stress that walking only accounts for three per cent of all mileage. The inference from this is, as Hillman says in Chapter 4, 'that longer journeys are considered far more pertinent to policy and therefore more worthy of attention and public investment'. Under these circumstances, it is scarcely surprising that walking in Britain is of diminishing importance, with total distance walked decreasing as is the percentage of all journeys that are made on foot.

What do walkers need? and have?

The potential for increasing the safety and attractiveness of walking is enormous, as may be seen if the needs of walkers and the facilities provided are even crudely compared. These needs and facilities are both part of the pedestrian's environment, which might be defined as the interface between the walker's personal ability to cope with environmental challenge, the location and accessibility of destinations, and the characteristics of the environment en route (TEST, 1976). The interaction of these three elements leads to discordances and complaint, as when a frail person's destinations are too distant, or when buggy-pushing parents encounter narrow pavements.

In terms of needs, pedestrians prefer to walk on the level and by direct routes. They are sensitive to rain, heat, cold and splash from roads. They attempt shorter distances when conditions are unfavourable and walk further when surroundings have been made visually attractive by artwork, shop windows and the like. They avoid places where they perceive the risk of assault to be high. They are extremely vulnerable to impact by vehicles, although they will trade off this risk against increased journey length: it is not unusual to see people clambering over or through barriers designed to force them to cross roads away from junctions (Hitchcock and Mitchell, 1984).

The most common infrastructure provided for pedestrians comprises a segregated footpath, hard-surfaced and drained, kept reasonably free of rubbish and loose obstructions. In Britain these surfaces are inspected at least quarterly for projections, cracks and rocking slabs, and the highway authority has a clear duty to maintain these facilities to provide unobstructed and free passage. The quantity of facilities provided for the exclusive use of pedestrians is significant, particularly when compared to the low level of provision available for the other green mode, cycling.

The main impediments to the free flow of people are those placed there to facilitate the free flow of motorised traffic, particularly road-crossing barriers, signs embedded in the footway and steps and ramps to carry the walker over or under the roadway. The volume of complaint about the difficulties encountered by pedestrians is certainly high and has been recorded in a number of surveys in recent years. The Consumer Concerns survey carried out by the National Consumer Council (NCC) in 1979–80, for example, revealed a quarter of all respondents encountering problems walking in the previous year, over half of which were considered serious. The principal objection was the condition of the pavements, particularly

Figure 1.2. Fouling of tho pavement by dogs is a common complaint and is increasingly being dealt with by law

broken and uneven surfaces, car parking on pavements, dog fouling and pavement cycling (Figure 1.2). The second concern was the shortage of pedestrian crossings. In general the survey revealed that 'the declining state of the environment was a major worry to a large number of people' and led the NCC to commission a further, more detailed, investigation of pedestrian problems in 1986, described by Hanna in Chapter 6 (National Consumer Council, 1987).

Other surveys have identified the walking problems of the handicapped, for whom accessibility to shops and services is so frequently a problem. A Coventry survey of the registered disabled showed that a half or more experienced difficulty with hills, ramps, steps and crowds, a third with crossing roads, a fifth with uneven or narrow pavements, and a tenth with kerbs (Feeney *et al.*, 1979). Particular varieties of handicap bring their own specific problems, such as, for the visually impaired, obstructions in the footway and crossing roads, or, for the mentally handicapped, dealing with crowds or directional information.

In identifying the needs of the disabled, we must avoid thinking solely of those with the most visible disabilities. Although the registered disabled comprise a substantial proportion – some 12 per cent – of the population of Britain, only two to three per cent of them are chairbound and only four per cent of the registered blind have a guide dog. It is more helpful to think in terms of 'the fragile' or 'the traffic-vulnerable' rather than 'the disabled' *per se*. For example, many non-disabled people can become temporarily vulnerable, such as parents pushing buggies or carrying children, normally fit people with broken limbs, or shoppers with large parcels. Others with walking limitations are not immediately identifiable, such as stroke or epilepsy victims, those with circulatory defects, or the drug- or alcohol-dependent. Indeed in a 'traffic-vulnerable' category we would have to include the very young and very old, so that it could comprise 30–50 per cent of the population depending on age definitions. Given that the proportion of over-75s in the population will rise by 14 per cent in the 30 years from 1981, the needs of the traffic-vulnerable will inevitably become more insistent.

How safe is walking?

Many of the complaints about the pedestrian environment arise because of their implications for personal safety. Walking is the most dangerous travel mode next to motor cycling, and walkers make up one-third of all road deaths. Per billion traveller-km in Britain in 1987, five car users were killed, 64 pedal cyclists and 78 pedestrians (West-Oram, 1989). What is more, the trends indicate increasing danger: amongst the indicative 10–14-year-old group (whose walking pattern has changed little through the years), the number killed or seriously injured (ksi) per 100 000 in the age group rose from 32 in 1954 to 68 in 1987.

Some people are more likely to have an accident than others, with the young and the elderly being particularly vulnerable, as Preston points out in Chapter 3. Over half of all casualties are under 19 and this proportion is increasing. The 10–14-year-olds are the group most at risk, with the under-14s more than three times as likely as adults to be injured on any particular foot journey. Those aged above 60 have a pedestrian casualty rate per head of population which is nearly double that of the 20–39 age group, whilst their greater likelihood of dying from a particular accident gives them a fatality rate six and a half times higher. The reliance of elderly people on walking as a mode of transport increases their exposure to risk, whilst declining mental awareness and physical agility reduce their ability to avoid potential or actual conflicts (TEST, 1976).

There are, of course, particular danger spots in the pedestrian environment. Over half of all casualties, for example, occur at junctions. When

NCC survey respondents were asked to identify the problems of a particular danger spot known to them, one-third cited junctions and around one-quarter pointed to traffic volume, traffic speed and lack of pedestrian facilities. They overwhelmingly reported the roads to be more difficult to cross than five years previously, the change being ascribed to increased volumes of traffic (89 per cent) and faster traffic (28 per cent) (National Consumer Council, 1987). Ramsay (1989) has likened the situation in many towns to that of a castaway on a tropical island. Just as the castaway is limited to a coastal path around the jungly interior, so is the urban walker restricted to the quadrilateral of footpath around each block. To get to the next section of footway the pedestrian has to risk death by collision in the road reserved for motoring, analagous to the castaway having to swim the shark-infested waters to reach the next island (Figure 1.3).

The likelihood of collision and the severity of the consequences both increase with rising speeds. In most streets in Britain where a 30 mph limit is in force, there are no physical obstructions to prevent speeding. Adherence to the limit tends to be checked only by chance observation from police cars or by targeting a specific street about which residents have complained. It is not reasonable to expect the police to be able to enforce rigorously a large-scale, blanket speed limit and it is apparent that they do not try to do so. The efficacy of speed limits thus depends on drivers' self-discipline: with powerful cars, no physical obstacles and with the knowledge that legal retribution is unlikely, it is not surprising that the limit in residential areas is exceeded by 50 per cent of the vehicles on 50 per cent of the roads (Plowden and Hillman, 1984).

A second problem is that even if a motorist – despite all the odds – actually adheres to the recommended limits, all the evidence points to the fact that he or she is still driving too fast for the safety of those on foot or bike. An emergency stop from 50 km/h (30 mph) takes 33 metres, which, in a situation where a driver may be confronted at any moment by a dashing child, is clearly far too much (Figure 1.4). At 30 km/h the braking distance is reduced to 16 metres. Not only does this make collision avoidance more likely, but it also dramatically reduces the severity of the consequences for the pedestrian. Swiss research has shown, for example, that at collision speeds of below 25 km/h only three per cent of pedestrians are severely injured, whereas at over 50 km/h less than 10 per cent survive (Kraay *et al.*, no date).

Horrendous though the road accident statistics are, they do not include the very large number of pedestrians who are injured in 'pavement accidents' by trips, slips and falls where no vehicle is involved. Because no records of these are kept, the number of victims is unknown, but it is thought that nearly 200 die in street falls per annum in England and Wales. It is estimated that there are 6.5–8.5 million pavement accidents per annum, many more than road accidents. Though the proportion of road accident victims requiring medical attention is higher, the absolute number

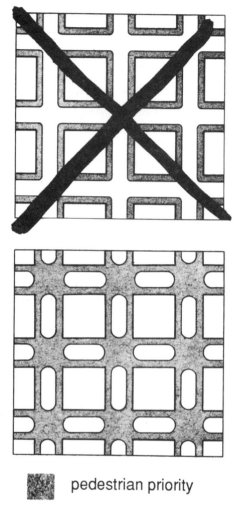

pedestrian priority

Figure 1.3. An alternative to conventional priorities for walking

of pavement accidents resulting in injury is far greater, perhaps by as much as 11 to 1 (National Consumer Council, 1987).

About a third of these accidents result from damaged pavements. Much footway damage is natural deterioration, of course, but it has been estimated that overriding by vehicles is implicated in over half of the cases where planned maintenance work is carried out. Not only then do about a quarter of respondents to the NCC survey in 1986 see pavement parking as one of the problems for pedestrians, in that they object to the loss of pavement space to the vehicle and the obstruction caused by it, but they are then subjected to considerable accident rates as a result of the broken slabs and uneven surfaces that result (Figure 1.5).

30 km per uur in de bebouwde kom

voorlichtingsboekje over de 30 km maatregel

een uitgave van het komitee 50 is teveel

Figure 1.4. 50 is too much! Propaganda from a Dutch road safety pressure group seeking 30 km/h limits

Figure 1.5. Pavement parking in Amsterdam

Overall, given these problems of poor facilities, inadequate recognition of (and planning for) walking, and rising danger levels from motorised traffic, the experience of being a pedestrian in the 1980s is, in the words of the Chairman of the National Consumer Council (1987), 'a walking disaster'. Walking has always been the principal method of human transport, yet during the current motorised interlude those that cannot or do not ride must step aside – literally – for those that do. The walkers are expected to be grateful for the left-over street space that is allocated to them and not to object when more is taken for road widening and corner-shaving, or when motorists use the remainder of the footway to park on. Humans on foot must step over the broken flagstones and around the car paraphernalia which are implanted in the footpath so as not to obstruct the motorised flow. And when it comes to crossing the traffic, designated places are set aside, a limited time is given to cross, and some, perhaps through their own lack of judgement, will be unlucky and be run over. Lest we are in any doubt about where responsibility for pedestrian casualties lies, propaganda on pedestrian accidents is aimed at the pedestrian, rarely at the motorist: as one 'public information announcement' puts it, 'One false move and you're dead'.

The cycling 'problem'

Many of the benefits – and the problems – of walking are shared by cycling. The bicycle is cheap to buy and run and is in urban areas often the quickest door-to-door mode. Road and parking capacities are increased tenfold if bicycles are used instead of cars, so that urban space can be used much more efficiently. Moreover, the cycle is a benign form of transport, being noiseless, fuel-efficient, non-polluting and non-threatening to most other road users. A cycling population would be fitter, healthier and more egalitarian than one reliant on privileged personal access to a car. Because facilities for cycles are simple and inexpensive, achieving mobility through cycling is cheap for society and for the individual.

However, in many countries, cycling is dangerous and getting worse. In Britain, for example, the ksi (killed or seriously injured) rate for pedal cyclists per billion vehicle-km has risen by 80 per cent from 1954 to 1988 to a level some 20 times that for car drivers, whose ksi rate halved over the same period (West-Oram, 1989). Very little is spent on cycling facilities (Figure 1.6): in 1984–6 the cycling budget of the D.Tp. totalled £160 000, less than one-thousandth of the £180 million granted for local road expenditure in 1987–8 (McClintock, 1987). Under these circumstances it is hardly surprising that the official view of cycling in Britain is that it is 'another problem . . . rather than a partial solution to environmental problems' (Davies, 1984).

Figure 1.6. Cycle tracks in Britain are infrequent and discontinuous

This negative view of cycling and the reluctance to spend public money on facilities for it lead to exhortations to cyclists to do something about their own safety. It is implied that if they continue to be careless enough to have collisions with cars, then it is only reasonable to demand that they should wear helmets, a view which is now being heard with increasing frequency. Thus is the victim blamed, the obstacles to cycling as a 'normal' activity increased and the negative stereotype of the cyclist as either hard-up or a half-wit reinforced. Finch (1985), for example, has shown how strong now is the anti-cycling culture in England, with many considering cycling as an 'untrendy', and principally childhood, activity. Two-thirds of those that persist with cycling in this climate of discouragement are male, with fear preventing large numbers of women from cycling and many parents from permitting children to use on the roads the bikes that nearly all of them own. Where cycling is given such a negative image it is women and children who suffer most.

The impact of motorised traffic on the environment of walkers and cyclists

To be classed as a walker or a cyclist, it is not necessary to be going somewhere: neighbours chatting in the street or children playing on their bikes outside their homes are included too. Providing for the green modes therefore involves not just route provision, but also creating acceptable conditions for their use in streets where people live. But the environment of such streets is impaired by motorised traffic, with effects described as 'subtle, complex and, in many instances, very destructive' by Appleyard and Lintell (1975) in their pioneering work.

These environmental problems associated with traffic in housing areas affect very large numbers of people. Around a half of all people claim to be bothered by noise, a third by dirt, a half by fumes and a quarter by vibration (Morton-Williams, 1978). The general importance of 'street-related' issues in people's appreciation of the quality of life is clear. There is, as one study concluded, 'an overwhelming desire to shop and live in conditions free from disturbance and interference from traffic' (Hoinville and Prescott-Clarke, 1972).

What are these environmental impacts of motorised traffic on street environments? Next to the danger from traffic already described, noise is one of the most widespread concerns, whether stemming from a background rumble or the occasional roar of a high-revving car or motor bike. Brake and tyre squeal, together with banging of unsecured loads or loose bodywork, causes as much disturbance as engine noise and probably more anxiety. Stationary vehicles may cause considerable nuisance, through having doors slammed, sound systems overamplified or starter-motors repeatedly engaged, especially when this happens late at night or early in the morning.

The air pollution that is associated with car use has been more popularly understood in recent years. The effect of lead compounds on children, of other emissions on human health, of carbon dioxide on the 'greenhouse effect' and sulphurous and nitrous emissions on acid rain, have all become matters for widespread discussion – and are addressed here by Ullrich and Kroon in Chapters 7 and 8. The types of air pollution that cause the greatest annoyance for local movement and living, however, are the traffic fumes, smell and dust which penetrate houses, discolour exterior paintwork and make walking and cycling unpleasant.

Even when it is at rest, silent and apparently non-polluting, the car continues to have environmental impacts. It reduces visual amenity by blocking views, and impedes and endangers movement by cluttering open space and damaging pavement surfaces when parked. In front gardens, lawns are paved over for off-street parking space and in the road more intrusion and obstruction results from signs, barriers and other traffic-related street furniture. Much litter is related to vehicles too, whether thrown from them in passing or resulting from their roadside cleansing or repair.

Not only does motorised traffic have safety and environmental impacts on the environment of walkers and cyclists, but there are social consequences too. Appleyard and Lintell's (1975) research in San Francisco showed how residents' privacy diminished in heavily trafficked streets, their network of acquaintances shrank, their sense of personal territory was restricted, and their interest in the street was curtailed by its streams of motorised traffic.

To many the street now has a negative connotation, as phrases such as 'street crime' and 'on the street' might indicate. The word 'street' is used as a metaphor for what is aberrant and fearful in the light of social norms (Anderson, 1978). Yet a living street is a multi-functional place, with its interest provided by its contrasting uses. It is, for example, a public space and yet a private one too, as an extension of the adjacent buildings. Again, it is a canal for all kinds of transport and yet is a bridge to the outside world, providing access. With respect to these many functions, 'creating and recreating a living street is finding the balance appropriate to the circumstances' (De Boer, 1986). It is evident that in many of our urban areas no such balance any longer exists, for the street has been given over entirely to motorised traffic, with other functions now expected to be subordinate to it.

Transport has, in the words of De Jong (1986), 'differentiated and killed the street' in a sequence of events through time. First came the banishment of pedestrians to pavements and the widening of surfaces by demolition and the infilling of water courses. Later the addition of a third dimension in the form of cables and pipes sterilised the overlying surface, as did the laying of rails to facilitate rapid movement by tram. The final destruction of the road's equilibrium took place when it was given over to high speed travel by car. As De Jong says, 'One single purpose has attained predominance, has acquired the monopoly for which everything is sacrificed; the others have been driven out, either totally or into special roads.' Among the casualties of the process that he lists are animals, nature, street trades, professions at the edge of the street, celebrations and recreation, official and military displays, processions and parades, and children and children's games.

If safety and comfort are to be regained for the green modes, a balance in the use of streets must be restored. In particular, there is a need to give priority to the street's primary use, for the residential street environment is a matter of continual concern to residents, but of only fleeting interest to the passing driver. Justice demands therefore that it be designed primarily for living, not travel. Moreover, those who have greatest need of the street should have at least an equal right to its use, so that children and elderly people, for example, should not have their links with the outside world severed by traffic flows past their doors. It is thus not fanciful to claim, as

De Boer has done, that the social motives of protecting 'liveability' in residential areas demand nothing less than 'recapturing the street from the automobile' (De Boer, 1986).

Traffic restraint

Traffic calming

The previous section has shown that the conditions for walking and cycling as travel modes are deleteriously affected by motorised transport and that the environmental and social qualities of the street in which these modes operate have also been badly impaired. It is true that there are various street layouts that have been designed to avoid these problems, such as Radburn layouts, SCAFT guidelines in Sweden, and Buchanan's environmental areas in Britain (Tolley, 1990). But such designs have not protected the majority of green mode users nor enabled most people to live in 'liveable' streets. For example, such approaches have only been applied to new housing areas, or have failed to deal with problems caused by local traffic, or caused greater environmental problems as a result of lengthened journeys and higher speeds in one-way streets, and so on.

However, beginning in the Netherlands in the 1970s, a suite of policies and practices has grown to address these issues, paying particular attention to making streets safer for the green modes, ameliorating the adverse impacts of motorised travel on the environment, and improving living conditions for residents. Such approaches have come to be known as 'traffic calming'. As Döldissen and Draeger show in Chapter 19, calming has been put to practical use in several mainland European countries and produced enormous environmental benefits in housing areas: car speeds and pollution levels are lower and accidents have been reduced to fractions of their previous levels. The streets are not only safer, but are greener and quieter and belong once more to the residents, not to passing drivers (Figure 1.7). The measures are enormously popular: in town after town in Denmark, for example, authorities cannot keep up with the public demand for redesigning the streets, even though residents, in many cases, have to pay for it themselves.

The distinctive features of these new approaches, discussed in greater depth by Tolley (1990), need to be outlined here. First, they represent a different philosophy of 'traffic management' in that they are not designed to get the best out of the street system for traffic, which has been our understanding of the term in the past, but instead are designed to manage the traffic for the benefit of residents and the environment. Second, the approach is based on a reappraisal of the relationship between the pedestrian and the vehicle. Put simply, it is no longer accepted that the only way

Figure 1.7. Traffic calming in Holland: a Woonerf in Delft

to protect one from the other is to separate them. Instead, many of the new applications of traffic calming involve an acceptance of various levels of traffic-mixing – of cars and people – but under radically different assumptions about their relationship, which will henceforth be one of equality rather than one of car dominance. This approach thus applies principles of traffic 'integration' in contradistinction to the more familiar traffic 'segregation' (Figure 1.8).

Last, because calming individual streets diverts many drivers to an alternative route and thus to some degree transfers the problem, the practice of treating whole networks of streets, on an area-wide basis, has evolved. The benefits from restraining the traffic are thus spread widely across areas and reach large numbers of people, rather than the favoured few in the isolated schemes used in the past. This area-wide application of traffic calming is proving immensely popular and effective in dealing with traffic-related problems in extensive residentaal areas; motorised traffic is lower in volume and calmer in behaviour, so that living conditions are better and the green modes can flourish once again.

Environmental traffic management

The problem with area-wide traffic restraint is that there is still some traffic diversion from residential to arterial roads, just as there was in Buchanan's

Figure 1.8. Integration of modes in place of segregation: a calmed area in Haarlem

'environmental areas' approach of 30 years ago. Though this may be beneficial for the newly quietened 'cells' concerned, it will not solve the safety and environmental problems of the city as a whole. The fundamental issue here is that Buchanan's goal of finding civilised ways of accommodating ever-increasing volumes of traffic is not achievable. As Plowden (1980) has argued, the only way in which environmental areas start to make sense is in the context of a general policy of traffic restraint under which traffic volumes are reduced throughout the urban area. Under these circumstances any extra traffic decanted on to the boundary roads from calmed environmental areas would be offset by the overall reduction in traffic that would result from general traffic restraint.

The reform implied in such 'city-wide traffic restraint' or 'environmental traffic management' (ETM) is much more fundamental than the likely achievements of the 'area-wide' approaches described so far. In this more radical view, infrastructural works are combined with spatial, economic, legal, psychological and educational approaches into a coherent policy. Monheim (1986), for example, talks of it in terms of a 'new framework for transport planning', one that 'tries to reduce car traffic in general by changes to other transport modes', and one that acts as 'an important instrument of urban development planning . . . sensitive to the relationships between speed, accessibility, environmental quality and urban development'.

All of the five principal strands of policy which are necessary for the achievement of ETM are discussed in this book and two – the encouragement of pedestrian and bicycle traffic – are central to it. The remaining three – the promotion of public transport, the 'domestication' of the car, and traffic-reducing town planning – may be outlined here so that planning for walking and cycling may be seen in the context of the wider demands of environmental traffic management.

First, much car traffic, particularly that used for shopping and commuting, must transfer to public transport if city-wide traffic restraint is to be successful. Specifically, there should be an aggressive fares policy, with 'customer friendliness' the principal criterion in interaction with the consumer. The rail-based modes should be spatially extended to all major settlement areas, with the bus used as a supplementary distributive system. In densely populated areas, the network density must be concomitantly increased to reduce access distances to customers. Stops must be closer together, well placed with respect to local demand, and designed to protect and entertain their users.

Second, a corollary of these pro-public transport policies must be the 'domestication' of the car. The strategy here is for the car's demand for space to be restricted and for its speed to be restrained. Many streets now carry as much traffic as they are able in a technical sense, but much more than they can carry without environmental degradation. The environmental limit should become the controlling force, with capacity cut down by reducing green times on traffic lights, the number of parking spaces and the number of lanes, particularly turning lanes at junctions. Speeds may be lowered by the same measures used in residential areas, such as 'bottlenecking' speed tables, shared space, 30 km/h limits and the like. 'Domesticating' the car means taming it to the needs of the city, not the city to it. The critical step is to reduce the space set aside for its use, whether for its circulation or parking, for any additional space will increase car volume or speed or both and thus counteract the goals of restraint.

Last, in this consideration of how ETM can be achieved, there is a need to use town planning to reduce traffic. The way that Western cities have grown since the 1930s has lengthened journeys by increasing distances between necessary functions. The resultant dispersed, segregated, low-density town is in part consequence, and in part generator, of unrestrained car use and is one that by its spatial separation discourages the green modes and by its low density undermines the viability of public transport. Monheim (1986) argues that traffic restraint must be associated with conscious re-urbanisation, via a reduction of suburbanisation, a utilisation of available city land, a discouragement of segregated uses and avoidance of concentrations of traffic generators. By the manipulation of land uses in this way, so may accessibility be accentuated and trips shortened. This will have a great number of beneficial effects, not the least that shorter trips will encourage a transfer to soft modes and will produce less deleterious

Figure 1.9.   City-wide calming in Freiburg includes a pedestrian network and these segregated and planted tram tracks, which converge on the car-free centre

side-effects from the trips that remain motorised, since these will now be fewer and shorter. Whatever motorised traffic remains after implementation of these approaches should be calmed, using legal and infrastructural measures in combination.

A cornerstone of ETM is that motorised traffic is suppressed. In other words, as areas are treated, much traffic disappears *but does not reappear elsewhere*. This may be because calming has specifically encouraged drivers to change to public transport, or to walk or cycle. However, it is also likely that, post-calming, many trips will simply not be made at all. Inessential, discretionary, motorised trips, which in the past have not been discouraged by traffic policies that have been favourable to the car, under ETM would be deterred by traffic strategies that make journeys less effortless.

This is such a critical point that it bears repeating. Just as many have argued for some time that road building to ease congestion is futile because new roads generate traffic to fill the space available, so is the corollary being set out here: if roads are taken away, traffic volume will shrink to fit the space available. In simple terms, building roads *generates* traffic, removing them *degenerates* traffic. This proposition has yet to be conclusively demonstrated, but the evidence from city-wide calming in places such as Odense and Freiburg is beginning to appear in the form of clear indications of the reduction in car use that follows ETM measures (Figure 1.9).

Figure 1.10. Many people have rediscovered the pleasures of strolling in car-free city centres

Conclusions

Quite apart from society's moral obligation to maintain, as far as possible, an individual's quality of life through accessibility to necessary functions and services, there is a public economic interest too in so doing. For example, if facilities for the elderly and disabled are poor, the fear of walking may lead many to become house-bound or institutionalised and, once so dependent, the cost of public service provision to the individual rises very sharply. If wider costs were to be considered, as they should be, one could also look to savings from reduced pollution, energy consumption and accident rates, quite apart from the health maintenance benefits of a walking and cycling population. What is more, recapturing the city for humans using their feet would bring immense improvements in the ambiance of the city and thus in the quality of urban life.

For such gains to be made, it must be understood that encouragement of the green modes does not just involve building special facilities for them. In terms of cycling, for example, it is vital for policy-makers to come to appreciate that greater gains are likely to come from environmental traffic management as a means of restraining motorised travel than from engineering to protect the dwindling band of determined cyclists from the growing number of cars. It follows that the abandonment of former piecemeal opportunism in cycle planning is essential if modal behaviour is to change and if individuals are to make long-term locational decisions, such as where to live or work, in the light of that changed behaviour. The low level of capital investment in a cycle is such that it is easily left at home if facilities deteriorate or if whole journeys cannot be made in safety and comfort.

In many city centres the creation of an attractive walking environment through pedestrianisation has undoubtedly increased both retail turnover and pedestrian flows (Figure 1.10). In most of those same cities, the task of creating safe and attractive walking and cycling conditions in other parts of the city has scarcely begun. A thorough commitment to a positive policy of encouraging the green modes throughout the city and restraining motorised traffic is inescapable if streets are to be seized from the dominance of 'canned' humans and given back to the 'fresh' ones.

References

Anderson, S. (ed.), 1978, *On streets*, MIT Press, Cambridge, Mass., vii.
Appleyard, D. and Lintell, M., 1975, 'Streets: dead or alive?', *New Society*, 3 July, 9–11.
Davies, D.G., 1984, 'A survey of county council cycle planning in Britain', *Traffic Engineering and Control*, April, 182–5.
De Boer, E. (ed.), 1986, *Transport sociology: social aspects of transport planning*, Pergamon Press, Oxford, 73.
De Jong, R., 1986, 'The recapture of the street?', in De Boer, E. (ed.), *Transport sociology: social aspects of transport planning*, Pergamon Press, Oxford, 77–91.
Feeney, R.J. *et al.*, 1979, *Travel and the handicapped: a project summary*, Report SR 480, TRRL, Crowthorne.
Finch, H., 1985, *Attitudes to cycling*, Research Report 14, TRRL, Crowthorne.
Illich, I., (1974), *Energy and equity*, Calder and Boyars, London.
Hitchcock, A. and Mitchell, C.G.B., 1984, 'Man and his transport behaviour, Part 2a: Walking as a means of transport', *Transport Reviews*, **4**, 2, 177–87.
Hoinville, G. and Prescott-Clarke, P., 1972, *Traffic disturbance and amenity values*, Social and Community Planning Research, London.
Kraay, J.H., Mathijssen, M.P.M. and Wegman, F.C.M., no date, *Towards safer residential areas*, Institute for Road Safety Research SWOV/Ministry of Transport, Leidschendam, 15.

McClintock, H., 1987, 'On the right track? An assessment of recent English experience of innovations in urban bicycle planning', *Town Planning Review*, **58**, 3, 267–91.

Mitchell, C.G.B. and Stokes, R.G.F., 1982, *Walking as a mode of transport*, Report LR 1064, TRRL, Crowthorne.

Monheim, H., 1986, 'Area-wide traffic restraint: a concept for better urban transport', *Built Environment*, **12**, 1/2, 74–82.

Morton-Williams, J. *et al.*, 1978, *Road traffic and the environment*, Social and Community Planning Research, London.

National Consumer Council, 1987, *What's wrong with WALKING?*, HMSO, London.

Plowden, S., 1980, *Taming traffic*, André Deutsch, London, 109.

—— and Hillman, M., 1984, *Danger on the road: the needless scourge*, Policy Studies Institute, London.

Ramsay, A., 1989, '*A systematic approach to the planning of urban networks for walking*', paper presented to the Transport Geography Study Group Symposium on Planning for the Green Modes, Institute of British Geographers Conference, Coventry Polytechnic, January.

TEST, 1976, *Improving the pedestrian's environment, Volume 2: Literature review*, TEST, London, 19.

Tolley, R.S., 1990, *Calming traffic in residential areas*, Brefi Press, Tregaron.

West-Oram, F., 1989, 'Measuring danger on the road', *Traffic Engineering and Control*, November.

2 The economic case for green modes

John Roberts

Introduction

This chapter's aim is to describe certain indicators suggestive of the kind of broad economic achievement which can flow from a continuum, or 'economic chain' of changes in the urban centre. That is, if you reduce inessential (mainly car) traffic, and facilitate 'green' traffic, an environmental improvement will follow. From that, one can expect an enhanced economy in the area so transformed. The economic indicators include retail turnover, turnover by mode of transport used, rents, land values, employment, employer and employee satisfaction, and the enthusiasm of urban inhabitants to arrive and multiply – in urban centres – their activities, combining shopping with walking, visits to parks, libraries, town halls, pubs and restaurants, cinema and theatre, and so on. This concept, of improving the economy by reducing vehicular traffic, was considered to be heretical until TEST published a cross-European study *Quality streets* (TEST, 1988). That report is drawn on here. Because it has limitations of national goals, culture, language, operation, system and other differences between countries, the reader should therefore not be surprised to find that this chapter reflects those differences.

'Economic' is used immodestly and unmathematically here. This chapter is also not comprehensive. There are probably good methods in search of an author who could apply them to city-wide conditions, but this author has had enough trouble just examining the relation between green modes and city centre economies without needing to place himself more at risk. Continuing with definitions, the concept 'inessential car use' is more easily addressed through its opposite: essentiality has been defined, not entirely satisfactorily, by Bayliss *et al.* (1979) as:

— having to make many trips during a working day;
— having to carry freight (tools, samples, ladders etc.) connected with work;
— working unsocial hours;

— there not being an adequate public transport alternative;
— movement of those with a disability;
— when carrying more than one child under three years.

Several of these beg the question: why isn't public transport adequate? But that is another story.

Finally, a 'good physical environment' is one where you will not be threatened by motor vehicles, where you can hear what someone walking with you is saying, where you do not have to breathe noxious fumes, and where vehicles do not impair your access to things you need to reach safely, easily and quickly. These are the essentials. If you have got that far, why not have buildings which are pedestrian-friendly, trees and flowers, good lighting, interesting walking surfaces, somewhere to sit and chat, somewhere to drink and eat outside if it is a nice day? Does this sound too imprecise? What is a 'pedestrian-friendly' building? Well, it might be within a totally artificial environment, whose air and light and sound are controlled mechanically, natural phenomena clearly performing inadequately; after all, only plastic flowers hold their shape and colour indefinitely. Or it might be outdoors, full of the hazards of reality, arcaded as in Bologna or Turin, or there might be a canopy projecting all the way round a building, protecting pedestrians from rain. Or it might be a matter of scale, of welcoming doors, lighting just above one's head, groups of seats around a fountain set in the building's wall. Of course, there would also be ramps for the disabled, handrails, textured surfaces . . .

From where did all those concerns arise? TEST, among others, has investigated pedestrian precincts over many years. It has also extensively considered issues of access to such precincts, on foot, by bus and by car. Out of these parallel streams emerged the dilemma common to many local authorities: is it possible simultaneously to improve the environment of a street or area by pedestrianisation, and still retain a high level of access to it? A particular problem arises with buses; they are bulky and dominant and often are excluded from pedestrianised areas for those reasons, even though streets were amply wide enough to accommodate them. With cars it is different. Conventional wisdom says they *have* to be accommodated, or the traditional city centre loses trade to out-of-centre shopping. This point will be returned to later, but now we need to recall the Department of Transport's repeated statements (1978, 1987) that access to shops by bus should be at least as good as it is by car.

And from that follows TEST's (1987) report on spending by mode in traditional London High Streets in the town centres of Bromley, East Ham, and Kensington: this will be discussed in detail below, but here we should note that of the total spending recorded in each locality on a Tuesday and Saturday, public transport users alone accounted for between 19 per cent and 45 per cent, the average being 36 per cent. Over both days in all three localities public transport users alone spent 59 per cent of the amount spent by car users, who were a distinct minority everywhere except Bromley on the Saturday. Overall, those reaching these centres by bus and on foot were, cumulatively, of far more importance than car users. While these results may have less application to many smaller cities and towns in Britain, most traditional centres attract a large proportion of shoppers who come and go on foot, and the larger cities are still highly bus- (occasionally rail-) dependent.

This chapter is structured by variables rather than by locality. It draws heavily on TEST's work in many mainland and offshore European cities – first on the hypothesis that a good physical environment is a good economic environment (TEST, 1988), and second from comparisons of retail location policy in Britain and Germany (TEST, 1989a).

Access issues: spending by mode

This important topic has had scant treatment in the literature. What we need to know in a book on green modes, and a chapter on their economic potential, is how people reach places where they can dispose of income residuals, and what proportion of these get there on foot, by bicycle and (slightly off the green wavelength on the spectrum) by public transport. Then we need to know which mode-user spends what. Most work has been done on shopping, as a trip purpose, though clearly it would be interesting to know about leisure trips as well (Jansen-Verbeke (1987) discusses women, shopping and leisure).

A review of modal splits for shopping purposes is a suitable starting point, and Table 2.1 shows a selection. These shopping modal splits are not intended to be either exhaustive or representative: doubtless there are examples elsewhere which show quite different results. The *National travel survey* ones are given to show the effects of nationwide generalising; they show a misleadingly small proportion of public transport use and at the same time a misleadingly high proportion of walkers. The 1985–6 *National travel survey* (Department of Transport, 1988) obfuscates the situation, for in this survey shopping is not listed as a separate journey purpose, but as one among others for 'personal business'.

Presented in the more specific form of Table 2.1 we can see the importance of walking and public transport use and, to a lesser extent, of cycling. Through all the examples there are only three instances where car use exceeds 50 per cent, and the German cities are generally, and surprisingly, less car-dependent than the British centres. Where two weekdays were examined, Saturdays invariably have higher car use at the expense of public transport. Cycling is generally subsumed under 'other', though Freiburg includes a remarkable 28.9 per cent, and all the Hanover 'other' percentages are for bicycles.

Table 2.1 Some shopping modal splits (%)

		Pub.Trans.*	Car,van	Walk(<50 m)	Other private
National Travel Survey	Tuesday	16	24	58	3
	Saturday	17	41	40	2
Birmingham**		68.0	29.7	1.6	0.7
Croydon**		43.6	46.2	9.2	1.0
Halifax**		47.2	41.7	10.4	0.6
Paisley**		38.9	43.1	16.6	1.3
Rochdale**		33.9	29.1	33.6	3.5
Slough**		15.5	55.9	16.2	2.1
Bromley (1)	Tuesday	39	41	19	1
	Saturday	29	58	13	0
East Ham (1)	Tuesday	37	15	45	3
	Saturday	43	22	35	0
Kensington (1)	Tuesday	48	14	34	3
	Saturday	49	22	25	4
Freiburg, early 1980s (2)		25.1	13.9	29.2	31.7
Hanover to CBD, 1984 (2)					
	Thursday	57.8	22.4	12.3	7.0
	Saturday	44.7	32.9	13.1	8.0
Hanover Hinterland to CBD, 1984 (2)					
	Thursday	55.7	41.3	0.7	1.0
	Saturday	37.4	58.0	0.2	1.6
Stuttgart, 5 Dept. stores, 1984 (2)					
	Thursday	62.6	25.1	9.5	1.1
	Saturday	45.5	42.7	8.5	1.8

* Bus, all types of rail
** TEST's 'space-sharing' studies, 1986–9; all in town centres on Saturdays
(1) TEST's 'spend-by-mode' studies, 1987; traditional London High Streets
(2) Data from TEST (1988)
Sources: Department of Transport, 1983; TEST, 1987, 1988, 1989b.

The West Midlands Passenger Transport Executive in 1979 surveyed shoppers in various centres of the West Midlands County. A selection of results is shown in Table 2.2. The first two figures are per cent modal contribution to turnover, with the figure in brackets being the per cent of the modal split; the third is the per capita spend in £. The table is ranked according to non-car modes used to reach the centres. Birmingham is a regional shopping centre, with Coventry as a sub-regional centre. The others are of lesser significance. Per capita incomes and car ownership are higher in Stourbridge and Sutton Coldfield than in the other localities.

Table 2.2 Selected results from the West Midlands turnover/mode survey

Location	Bus		Car		Other, inc. rail	
	Turnover (modal split) %	Per capita spend £	Turnover (modal split) %	Per capita spend £	Turnover (modal split) %	Per capita spend £
Birmingham	46 (56)	3.86	33 (19)	7.55	21 (25)	3.82
Walsall	44 (51)	6.53	40 (29)	10.50	16 (20)	6.03
Coventry	44 (54)	2.52	44 (29)	4.63	12 (17)	2.16
Dudley	46 (51)	7.76	40 (34)	10.15	14 (15)	7.39
West Bromwich	41 (51)	8.36	47 (35)	13.62	12 (14)	8.45
Stourbridge	22 (26)	6.14	55 (45)	8.64	23 (29)	5.85
Sutton Coldfield	19 (23)	6.42	65 (55)	9.22	16 (22)	5.84

Source: West Midlands Passenger Transport Executive, 1979.

If we look first at the modal split figures in brackets there is a wide range in car use from only 19 per cent in Birmingham to 55 per cent in Sutton Coldfield. In the 'other' category, Birmingham's 25 per cent includes 9 per cent rail; the high 'other' figure of 29 per cent for Stourbridge probably reflects a smaller community in which many can walk to the shops.

In terms of turnover, the contribution of public transport is interesting: for Birmingham it was 56 per cent (46 per cent from bus plus 10 per cent from rail). Apart from the two wealthy localities, bus users contributed at least 41 per cent. Per capita spending by bus users was generally 50–70 per cent of car user spending (compared with a mean of 59 per cent for the TEST studies described below). Unfortunately, the stronger greens of walking and cycling are not clearly presented, being combined with rail.

The West Midlands study was an innovative breakthrough. Others have followed, though they are few. The London Borough of Brent (1986) examined a superstore's effect on an existing supermarket, through which some spending-by-mode information was achieved. Between May 1985 (before the new store opened) and September 1985 (after it had) there was a fall-off in per capita spending in each mode. So, bus users reduced from £8.30 to £6.57 per person, car users from £20.33 to £18.01, and walking from £7.91 to £7.07. In fact, the *number* walking increased, as did its proportion of the modal split (from 35 per cent to 42 per cent). Carver (1984) referred to a study in Romford, Essex, which showed that the 39 per cent of shoppers who arrived by car accounted for 45 per cent of food spending and 61 per cent of non-food spending. And Hallsworth (no date) studied an Asda store near Portsmouth; 71 per cent of his respondents came by car, cycle and motorcycle, 13 per cent by bus, and the residual 16 per cent on foot. Unfortunately, so few pedestrians answered the 'amount

Table 2.3 Per capita spending by mode in Bromley, East Ham and Kensington High Streets in 1987

		Per capita spending (£)		
		Walk	*Public transport*	*Car*
Bromley	Tuesday	5.45	11.99	19.35
	Saturday	13.06	15.68	29.22
East Ham	Tuesday	12.68	11.28	10.47
	Saturday	8.21	10.42	14.07
Kensington	Tuesday	12.13	10.98	29.97
	Saturday	14.74	16.12	26.96
	Mean Tuesday	10.09	11.42	19.93
	Mean Saturday	12.00	14.07	23.42
	Mean Tue.–Sat.	11.05	12.75	21.68

Source: TEST, 1987.

spent' question that their mean spend of £35.00 per head is probably distorted. Yet bus users spent £27.44 against car users' £31.02, a very high bus:car relationship.

TEST (1987) carried out a specific spend-by-mode study for London Regional Transport in the three London High Streets listed in Table 2.1. Table 2.3 shows the results. The means show that a pedestrian's spending is not greatly different from a bus user's. Public transport spending averages about 60 per cent of car user spending, but this has to be seen in terms of the modal split. The data were grossed up for a six-day week. In the outer London borough of Bromley, with high car ownership, 64 per cent of the week's spending was by car users. In Kensington there was quite a different picture: 43 per cent of the total week's spending was by public transport users, 28 per cent by those walking all the way, and only 29 per cent by car users. In the much poorer East Ham, 44 per cent of the week's spending was attributable to those on foot, 38 per cent to public transport users, and a mere 18 per cent to car users. Yet, East Ham's High Street had all the normal multiples, evidently not dissatisfied with their turnover. This raises interesting questions about the number of cars that should be accommodated in traditional centres, a point which will be returned to later.

Preventing adversity and promoting equanimity

Having looked at the contribution of green modes *in access terms* to shopping turnover, we can now turn to some other economic measures which reflect their *influence* upon the layout of urban centres, most notably the Central Business District (CBD). In other words, not simply how you reach such a centre, but what you find when you get there, and the influence it has had on the economy of the centre. A range of measures has been used which might be grouped as *preventive* and *promotional* ones.

A *preventive* measure encourages the removal of heavy commercial vehicles from all-traffic streams, for example, to facilitate a better noise environment and/or remove intrusive vehicles from locations where they can scarcely fit, physically. Similarly, vehicles are *prevented* from achieving their full accident potential by the imposition of speed limits or physical obstructions. Haphazard and obstructive parking is minimised by *preventive* measures. Self-interest is so great in societies that none of these actions would occur if requested by governments – they have to be enforced by law. While these measures are *preventive*, they still contribute positively to a better environment.

Perhaps we feel happier about *promoting* certain actions. Thus we can encourage people to walk by widening footways, making road crossing safer and pedestrianising densely used streets. We can help safer children's play by traffic calming certain streets, usually residential ones. We can stimulate cycling by providing segregated tracks and signal-controlled crossing points. We can extend the use of public transport by integrating it with other modes and the urban fabric, by giving it priority over other traffic, by making it more comfortable, cheaper and efficient, and by making people realise the absurdity of each driving themselves, to the threshold where the congestion they create not only brings them to a wholly uneconomic standstill, it adversely affects green mode users too. Unlike the preventive measures, some of these promotional ones can actually be achieved by groups of people agreeing amongst themselves they want certain things to happen, and being prepared for some constraints on their lives as well as positive gains. And, lest we forget, none of the devices in this paragraph makes much sense if people cannot easily and safely gain access to the things they want to reach.

Land-use policies

In the longer term, we can reintroduce rationality to land-use planning. For thousands of years we have accepted tightly knit urban communities, where much travel was on foot and the rich used horses and carriages. Immigration from rural areas, improved health and extended lives, and therefore populations, all contributed to increased size of urban areas. Public transport was then introduced to accommodate some necessarily longer journeys. Then the irrational was invented – the car. This was not needed to accommodate the longer journeys caused by the factors above, it *generated* them: urban sprawl and rural infiltration, without an economic

Table 2.4 Urban rail transport and shopping turnover for selected West German cities

	Retail expenditure per capita 1984 (DM)	rail metres per capita	Urban rail transport kilometres of:			
			S-Bahn	U-Bahn	Light Rail	Tram
Bonn	8 949	0.17			25.5	22.8
Bremen	8 940	0.10				56.9
Cologne	9 142	0.36	191.5		41.6	121.6
Essen	8 616	0.35	143.9		10.1	71.1
Frankfurt	12 925	0.49	186.0		41.8*	81.2
Freiburg	11 415	0.13				22.5
Hamburg	12 274	0.15	148.3	97.7		
Hanover	10 845	0.17			69.0	26.0
Munich	11 172	0.42	418.2	41.7		87.4
Stuttgart	10 698	0.46	150.2		35.7	77.4

* includes one U-bahn line

Sources: TEST, 1988; UITP, 1985; VoV, 1989.

purpose, were the results. Either stimulated by, or riding on, this wave was the other phenomenon – concentration of services. So retailing, leisure, education and health facilities were redistributed on a coarse grid, away from the fine one that accompanied tightly knit communities: additional mechanised movement was an essential corollary. If we were able to revert to the tightly knit model, a fascinating range of economic benefits, and few disbenefits, would arise.

Major traffic restraint measures and broad effects on the economy

Public transport improvements

It is not possible to attribute economic improvements to a CBD solely to improved public transport, but the level of investment in public transport can be demonstrated for those cities whose central shops have done well in turnover terms. Table 2.4 shows a range of large cities within an S-bahn network, and some smaller ones. Bremen (534 000 population) and Freiburg (175 000) only have trams and Hanover has light rail and trams. No city has all four types of rail and Hamburg has neither light rail or tram: there is thus a wide variation in provision.

In terms of metres of rail track per capita, Frankfurt, Stuttgart, Munich, Cologne and Essen are the best performers, Freiburg and Bremen the worst. It is unlikely to be coincidental that Frankfurt, with an elaborate public transport network, also has the highest retail expenditure per capita, and Stuttgart and Munich are not far behind. The anomalies occur between the relatively low rail provision of Freiburg, Hamburg and Hanover and their high spending. The explanations may be that Freiburg has above average walking and cycling within the modal split and extensive traffic calming city-wide; Hamburg has many buses; and Hanover encourages walking and cycling to its city centre.

Effects of car parking provision

It is a transport and planning convention that the more car parking spaces that are provided in shopping centres, the better the retail trade. In fact, it appears as if there is some threshold of parking provision in city centres above which turnover per square metre declines. While the threshold has not yet been determined, TEST (1988) studied 10 West German cities' car parking provision and retail turnover. A scattergram then plotted turnover per square metre against square metre of retail floorspace per car parking space. While it would have been imagined a best-fit curve would have connected low parking provision + low turnover with high parking provision + high turnover, no such relationship emerged (Figure 2.1). Apart from Munich, extraordinarily placed with high turnover + low car parking provision (but very high public transport accessibility), the other nine cities all tended to have a similar turnover irrespective of car parking provision.

Pedestrianisation and traffic calming

There is now a wealth of evidence to show that pedestrianisation, unless it is mis-designed or located, benefits retail turnover. This is probably attributable to three phenomena: pedestrian flows increase by at least 50 per cent; pedestrians are more relaxed when freed from the hassles of vehicular traffic; they can more easily compare what is on offer and, in fact, see things they would probably have missed in a traffic-congested street. At one time traders had to be persuaded to accept pedestrianisation; now many chambers of commerce actively clamour for it, and this particularly applies to streets which have not been converted but are near ones that have. It is perhaps enough to quote supportive evidence from twelve years ago: OECD's (1978) study of the effects of pedestrianisation in over 100 of its member countries' cities. World-wide, turnover increased in 49 per cent of the cities, remained stable in 25 per cent, decreased by 10 per cent in 18 per cent of the cities, and by 25 per cent in the remainder. The best increases were in Austria (71 per cent), Germany (63 per cent), and Scandinavia (67 per cent).

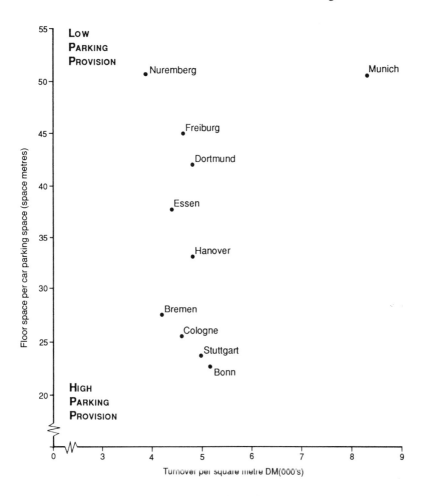

Figure 2.1. Turnover and parking provision in ten West German cities

Traffic calming – when used to mean quietening all-traffic streets in which no vehicle's speed is supposed to exceed walking pace – is less applicable to city centres than pedestrianisation. The Dutch have a number of *Winkelerven* or 'shopping yards', and in most German cities the concept of *Verkehrsrsberuhigung* (from which 'traffic calming' was a literal translation) is being applied close to city centres – Bonn, Hanover and Stuttgart are cases in point. Similarly, Oslo has some streets of this kind close to but not in the city centre. London's Neal Street is traffic calmed though you would not know it: there is no legal entry sign for it in Britain, despite its use throughout the real Europe.

Attitudes to cycling in city centres differ from country to country. Britain tends to exclude cyclists from precincts, while much of Germany, Bonn in particular, permits them free movement within precincts. Denmark and the Netherlands are reasonably relaxed. Access to the centre depends *inter alia* on the provision of cycle networks: though Germany has some way to go to compete with cycleway provision in the Netherlands, Hamburg has 1500 km, Munich 690 km, Bremen 460 km and Bonn 300 km. It is reasonable to assume that facility provision for this green mode will have a similar effect on pedestrianisation, even though the numbers adopting it will be less.

Some other effects of traffic restraint

Land values and rents

Pedestrianisation can induce landlords to increase rents well beyond realistic levels. This is an adverse effect of traffic restraint in the minds of all but the landlords; in some areas high rents mean frequent bankruptcies, but the attractiveness of a pedestrian street can be such that others will take up the remains of a lease, perhaps to go the same way. While it is not known whether lessees found these increases within their trading means, South Molton Street in London's Mayfair incurred rent increases from £145 a week to £1250 in one case, and a 625 per cent increase in another (Sudjic, 1980). The pedestrianisation of Stonegate in York led to rent increases from £215 to £860 per square metre. What is the effect of traffic restraint on offices? Insignificant, according to Goddard (1973); he concluded that restraint would not impair the efficiency of Central London offices. On the contrary, many employees' efficiency would increase, as their environment, and thus their job satisfaction improved.

Employment

Over the years 1972–80, during which CBD traffic restraint was implemented, Gothenburg experienced a slight increase in CBD jobs. In Hanover, 1970–76, the city as a whole lost 34 000 jobs (eight per cent), while the CBD only lost 1000 (1.2 per cent); in services, it gained five per cent. The very core of Vienna lost 12 per cent of its retail employment between 1973 and 1981, but its hotels, restaurants and banks each gained nine per cent of employment during that period. The core is the pedestrianised area and, if it is compared with the larger 'Vienna 1' within the Ringstrasse (which experienced an overall loss of 23 per cent in the three employment categories of the core), is the part best served by new public transport.

Attraction of the city centre

The sheer attractiveness of a reborn city centre, resulting from less vehicular traffic and concomitant environmental improvements, can introduce less tangible benefits. It will become a magnet for tourists. It will be a better place for working, so employees and employers will have greater satisfaction. It will permit on-street entertainment, political meetings, concerts – all contributing not only to a better quality of life, but also to economic enhancement. New buildings will arise and old ones will be renovated, shop fronts will be renewed or repainted. And it will be a mecca for green travellers – a good place to walk, cycle and perhaps tour round in a minibus. There is an interactiveness about all these events, one stimulating another.

Conclusions

To many people's astonishment, the motor car is not the economic grail that they have been led to expect. Vanke's (1988) work demolishes the case for road building as an economic stimulant, while this chapter has demonstrated persuasive connections between the economic buoyancy of city centres oriented towards the bright green modes of walking and cycling and the more staid green of public transport. Even though the message is clear, it seems that peer group pressure and advertiser's hype will only be overcome by unavailability or unaffordability of vehicle fuels; rationality does not seem to be wholly adequate as a cause for change.

References

Bayliss, D., Blide, D., May, T. and Miyazaki, T., 1979, 'London: case study', in *Managing transport*, OECD, Paris.
Carver, J., 1984, *Shopper's mode of travel*, London Transport TN160, London.
Department of Transport, 1978, *Notes on the preparation of pedestrianisation schemes*, Local Transport Note (LTN) 2/78, London.
—— 1983, *National travel survey: 1978/79 report*, HMSO, London.
—— 1987, *Pedestrian zones: getting the right balance*, LTN1/87, London.
—— 1988, *National travel survey: 1985/86 report*, HMSO, London.
Goddard, J.B., 1973, *Office linkages and location*, Pergamon, Oxford.
Hall, P. and Hass-Klau, C., 1985, *Can rail save the city?*, Gower, Aldershot.
Hallsworth, A.G., no date, 'Trading patterns, Asda, Waterlooville', Department of Geography, Portsmouth Polytechnic.
Jansen-Verbeke, M., 1987, 'Women, shopping and leisure', *Leisure Studies*, **6**, 1, January, 71–86.
London Borough of Brent, 1986, *Tesco, Neasden: a study of the retail impact*, Brent.

Organisation for Economic Cooperation and Development, 1978, *Results of questionnaire survey on pedestrian zones*, OECD, Paris.

Sudjic, D., 1980, 'Quality street on the rack', *Sunday Times*, April 27, London.

TEST, 1987, *Big spenders by bus*, report for London Regional Transport, TEST, London.

—— 1988, *Quality streets: how traditional urban centres benefit from traffic-calming*, TEST, London.

—— 1989a, *Trouble in store? Retail locational policy in Britain and Germany*, report for the Anglo-German Foundation, TEST, London.

—— 1989b, *Options for Paisley High Street*, report to Strathclyde PTE, TEST, London.

UITP, 1985, *UITP handbook of public transport 1985–86*, 3 vols, UITP, Brussels.

Vanke, J., 1988, 'Roads to prosperity?', *The Planner*, December, 41.

Verband offentlicher Verkehrsbetreibe, 1989, *VoV statistik '88*, Cologne.

West Midlands Passenger Transport Executive, 1979, *Mode of travel/shopping turnover survey*, WMPTE, Birmingham.

3 The safety of walking and cycling in different countries

Barbara Preston

Introduction

The way people travel is not the same in all countries and the safety measures that have been introduced also differ. For instance, a great many people cycle in the Netherlands, whereas few adults cycle in the United States. Again, in Sweden great attention has been paid to the safety of child pedestrians, whereas in Britain recent safety measures have largely been of benefit to those in vehicles. It is, therefore, of interest to try to see how these differences in travel patterns in different countries and the safety measures used affect road casualties. Specifically, if the green modes are to be encouraged, those countries that have established the safest conditions for them need to be identified in order to assist policy formulation elsewhere.

International comparisons are fraught with difficulties. First, the definition of injuries and deaths varies; in some countries very slight injuries may be recorded, in others only those requiring hospital treatment. Also, not all injuries are recorded in the official statistics and the error of under-reporting will, almost certainly, vary between countries. For these reasons it is usually accepted that international comparisons based on total casualties are not valid, though they can be used for rough comparisons of the age distributions of accidents within countries.

Deaths can be compared, but the definition of a road death is not the same in every country. The international definition, used by most countries, is a fatality due to a road accident when the death occurs within 30 days of the accident. Not all countries conform to this standard; the main exceptions are shown in Table 3.1. To make comparisons with these countries it is necessary to adjust the number of deaths to the number that would be expected to occur within 30 days. This will depend on the medical and ambulance facilities available, the age of the casualty and the type of injury, which may depend on the mode of travel. It is perhaps not surprising that the standardising factors that are used vary from time to time and

Table 3.1   Definitions of road death in those countries where it is not defined as 'death within 30 days of the accident'

Country	Period after the accident in which the death must occur to be classified as a road death
Portugal	at the scene of the accident
Spain & Japan	within 24 hours
Greece & Austria	within 3 days
France	within 6 days
Italy	within 7 days
Canada & Switzerland	within 1 year

Source: Department of Transport, 1988a.

in different statistical and written sources, which can be confusing. It is generally considered that if the total road deaths occurring within countries are being compared, the standardising factors are reasonably adequate, except for Portugal, which, for that reason, has not been included in this chapter. However, when the death rates of pedestrians and of pedal cyclists are of interest, as is the case here, these may be distorted by the different definitions of a road death.   The second problem is the rate used. When deaths by all modes of travel are quoted they may be given per 100 000 population, per 10 000 motor vehicles or per 100 million vehicle kilometres. As the number of people killed on the roads in any country will depend on the population at risk, the number of vehicles and how far they travel, none of these rates is perfect for comparisons.

Smeed suggested a formula for the expected number of deaths in any country that included both the size of the population and the number of vehicles (Smeed, 1949). It is however somewhat complicated:

$$D = 0.0003 \, (N.P^2)^{1/3}$$

where D is the expected number of deaths, N is the number of motor vehicles and P the population. If countries are to be compared, the percentage difference between the number of deaths and the expected number has also to be given and this figure, though less biased than the rates generally given, is not usually published.

The rate per 100 000 population is often used in international comparisons. It is easy to interpret, though it does vary with the number of motor vehicles in a country and is therefore very low for the developing countries with few vehicles compared with a country such as the United States. However, using the rate per 10 000 motor vehicles gives even more distortion. The countries with many motor vehicles per 1000 population appear erroneously to be safer than countries with fewer vehicles. For instance, the United States appears to be a very safe country if the rate per 10 000 vehicles is used, with 2.6 road deaths compared with 2.4 in the safest countries, Norway, Sweden and Japan. If, however, road deaths per 100 000 population is taken, the United States has a much poorer record at 19.0 compared with 10 or less for Britain, East Germany, Czechoslovakia and Japan. Giving the rate per 100 million vehicle kilometres may distort the picture even more. If we are considering the death rates of vehicle occupants, then the rates per 10 000 vehicles or per 100 million vehicle kilometres are the best rates to take. If, however, other road users are considered they are not suitable rates to use, since they could show an apparent decrease in the death rate even though the risk for any individual pedestrian or cyclist had increased because the roads were more over-crowded and more dangerous.

If these biases are realised, any suitable rate can be used but the worry is that sometimes the rates per 10 000 motor vehicles or per 100 million kilometres are quoted as simply death rates – without specifying which rate is being quoted – and this can result in a very biased presentation of the safety records of countries with fewer vehicles. It is odd, too, that these death rates are always given per HUNDRED thousand population but per TEN thousand vehicles; it makes motor vehicles appear less lethal on first sight, but is there any other reason?

Comparisons of cyclists' death rates

In this chapter the death rates of pedestrians and pedal cyclists will be considered for every country on which information is available, with the exceptions of Portugal and those very small countries with few fatalities. These death rates are given, per 100 000 population, in Tables 3.2 and 3.3. These rates, particularly those given in Table 3.3 for cyclists, are mislead-ing since they do not allow for the distance travelled, which will not be the same in different countries. For pedestrians the amount of walking will depend partly on the number of motor vehicles. This is not, however, a simple relationship. If there are very few motor vehicles there will be few pedestrians killed, but when car ownership is higher, as in the Western countries, the number of pedestrians killed will be lower in countries with more cars because fewer people will walk. Ideally we need to know the distances walked by people in different countries; but this is not available.

Most people, in most countries, will do some walk journeys, but when it comes to considering cyclists the problem is much more acute since in some countries many people do not cycle at all. The differences in the distance cycled may be very large and so comparison of the cycle death rates per 100 000 population is misleading. For instance, cycling is very popular in the Netherlands and much has been done for the safety of cyclists, yet, as shown in Table 3.3, the death rate for cyclists per 100 000 population is

Table 3.2   Pedestrians killed per 100 000 population in different countries

Country	Death rate per 100 000 population	
	1976	1986
Netherlands	3	1.5
Sweden	3	1.8
Italy	4	2.2
Canada	5*	2.2
Norway	4	2.4
Denmark	4	2.6
Finland	4	2.7
USA	3	2.8
Japan	4*	2.9
Switzerland	5	2.9
East Germany	4	3.0
Czechoslovakia	6	3.1
France	5	3.2
Australia	5	3.3
Belgium	6	3.3
Great Britain	4	3.3
New Zealand	3	3.4
West Germany	6	3.4
Irish Republic	5	3.5
Austria	7	3.7
Spain	5	3.9
Greece	4**	4.6
Poland	8	5.7
Hungary	6	5.9
Yugoslavia	7	5.9
South Africa	N/A	15.3

* 1975
** 1977

Sources: Department of Transport, 1978, 1988a; Republic of South Africa, 1988.

higher in the Netherlands than in other countries. This could be simply because more people cycle, and cycle for longer distances, in the Netherlands than they do in other countries.

Data on the number of cycles are not available in many countries, but for the countries where they are published the number killed per million cycles is given in Table 3.4. Some of the estimations of the number of cycles may not be trustworthy. Can cycling in Turkey be so very much more dangerous than it appears to be in other countries? The figure for Britain is based on the number of cycles per person given in the *National travel survey* (De-partment of Transport, 1988b). Apart from doubts about the accuracy of the table, there is still the problem of how much people use their cycles.

Information on the distance travelled on foot and cycle in Britain and the Netherlands is available (Department of Transport, 1988b; Netherlands,

Table 3.3   Pedal cyclists killed per 100 000 population in different countries in 1985

Country	Death rate per 100 000 population	Country	Death rate per 100 000 population
Greece*	0.3	Poland*	1.0
Spain	0.4	Czechoslovakia	1.1
USA	0.4	Irish Republic	1.1
UK	0.5	Sweden	1.1
Romania	0.6	South Africa**	1.2
France	0.8	Austria	1.3
Norway	0.8	West Germany	1.3
Switzerland	0.9	Yugoslavia	1.4
East Germany	1.0	Belgium	1.9
Italy*	1.0	Finland	1.9
		Denmark	2.0
		Hungary	2.1
		Netherlands	2.2

* 1984
** 1986

Sources: United Nations, 1987; Republic of South Africa, 1988.

Table 3.4   Cyclists killed per million cycles in different countries

Country	Cyclists killed per million cycles, 1984
Turkey	729
Belgium	57
Switzerland	32
Netherlands	31
France	30
Finland	25
West Germany	23
Japan	22
Great Britain*	21
Sweden	19
Norway	9

*1985

Sources: Organisation for Economic Cooperation and Development, 1987; Department of Transport, 1988(a) and (b).

Table 3.5 Death and injury rates per 100 million kilometres travelled for pedestrians and for cyclists in Britain and the Netherlands

Country	Pedestrians		Cyclists	
	death rate	injury rate	death rate	injury rate
Britain	6.8	223	7.2	665
Netherlands	3.7	80	3.2	127

Sources: Department of Transport, 1988a, b; United Nations, 1987; Netherlands, 1983.

1983), so the death and injury rates per 100 million kilometres travelled can be compared in these two countries as shown in Table 3.5. For cyclists the death rate in the Netherlands per 100 million kilometres travelled is less than half the death rate in Britain; for walking it was just over half the British death rate. So it seems that both cycling and walking are safer in the Netherlands than in Britain when the distances travelled are considered. This is important as it has sometimes been suggested that the low pedestrian death rate in the Netherlands has not been caused by the safety measures for pedestrians which have been introduced there, but that it might be merely because people walk less if they cycle more. The low pedestrian death rate in the Netherlands cannot be explained in this way. Apparently both walking and cycling are much safer in the Netherlands than in Britain when the distances walked and cycled are taken into account. It also highlights how important it is to consider whether the rate used is meaningful before drawing any conclusions. Unfortunately, information on the distance cycled, or walked, was not available for other countries.

It might appear from Table 3.5 that accidents to people on foot are much more likely to be fatal than cycling accidents. Part of this difference will be due to the age of the victims. Older people are more likely to die as a result of an accident than younger people and younger people are more likely to cycle than older people. In Britain in 1987 there were 15 918 pedestrian and 11 199 pedal cyclist casualties in the age group 10–19 years, but for those aged 70 and over there were 6668 pedestrian and only 622 cyclist casualties. In Britain, for the age group 10–14 years, 1.1 per cent of the pedestrian casualties were fatal and 0.96 per cent of the cycling casualties; and for those aged 70 years and over 9.6 per cent of the pedestrian casualties were fatal and 5.8 per cent of the cycling casualties; it may be at this age that only the younger and fitter over-70s cycle while the older and frailer people walk.

The proportion of the total number of pedal cyclists injured at different ages, for the countries considered, is shown in Table 3.6. This is of interest as it indicates the different patterns of cycle usage in different countries, though it will also be influenced by the safety measures introduced to make cycling safer, especially for children. In some countries over half the

Table 3.6 Percentage of the total number of pedal cyclists injured, by country and age group in 1985

Country	Age group (years)		
	6–14	*25–64*	*65 and over*
Austria	24	39	11
Belgium	23	36	10
Czechoslovakia	27	42	10
Denmark	20	41	10
Finland	16	51	15
France	28	38	9
East Germany	23	46	12
West Germany	25	37	9
Greece*	42	24	11
Hungary	19	53	15
Irish Republic	30	21	4
Italy	21	39	22
Netherlands	22	36	12
Norway	37	26	8
Poland*	21	51	16
Romania	5	47	6
Spain	30	31	5
Sweden	17	46	13
Switzerland	26	41	7
UK	29	30	4
USA	37	22	1
Yugoslavia	10	53	9

* 1984

Source: United Nations, 1987.

injuries are to cyclists aged 25–64 years. This is the case in Finland, Hungary, Poland and Yugoslavia, and though the last three have low car ownership this does not apply to Finland. In most countries between 20 and 30 per cent of the injuries are to children aged 6–14 years, but in Greece, Norway and the United States over 35 per cent are children. One can only guess at the reasons for this. Norway and Greece are mountainous, which may be a deterrent to adult cycling – only a quarter of those injured in these countries were aged 25–64 years – and in the United States the reason may be the very high car ownership. The proportion of those injured who were aged 65 or over varied from one per cent in the United States to 22 per cent in Italy.

Comparisons of pedestrians' death rates

The pedestrian death rate, per 100 000 population, is not quite so difficult to interpret since nearly everyone walks. Though the distance walked will not be the same in all countries, the differences will not be as great as they are for cycling. The amount of walking will depend to some extent on the level of car ownership. In Britain, people in households without cars walk further than those in households with a car; on average people in Britain walk 8.7 kilometres per week but those in households without cars walk 10.6 kilometres (Department of Transport, 1988b).

As car ownership and use increase, people walk less and drive more. Per distance travelled it is much safer to be in a car than walking. In Britain in 1987 the pedestrian casualty rate was 264 per 100 million kilometres while the car user rate was 35 (Department of Transport, 1988a). Between 1977 and 1987 the use of cars and taxis – measured by 100 million kilometres travelled – increased by 45 per cent. Pedestrian casualties over the same period decreased by 13 823 or 19 per cent and, as people transferred in large numbers to cars, driver and passenger casualties increased by 7958 or five per cent, despite this being a safer mode of transport. In 1977 the proportion of the total casualties who were pedestrians was 20 per cent, whilst 44 per cent of the total casualties were in cars; by 1987 pedestrians comprised 18 per cent of the total casualties and 51 per cent were in cars.

It would be expected, therefore, that in countries with high car ownership a small percentage of the total road deaths should be pedestrians. This can be checked by seeing if there is a relationship between the number of cars per 1000 population and the percentage of the total road deaths who were pedestrians. For the 21 countries for which this information is available there is a strong relationship between the percentage of the total road deaths who were pedestrians and the number of cars per 1000 population. The correlation is –0.80. The percentage of road deaths that would be expected to be pedestrians for a country with a given number of cars per 1000 population can be calculated from the regression equation:

$$y = -0.07x + 43.44$$

The number of cars per 1000 population, the percentage of the road deaths that were pedestrians, the percentage that would have been expected and the difference between the percentage expected and the percentage that occurred are shown in Table 3.7.

The dangers of walking in different countries might be better compared, with a reasonable degree of reliability, if the distances walked were known. Here, however, the level of car ownership is used as a very rough approximation to level out the presumed differences in the distance walked. Even assuming that this has been achieved, the percentage of the total fatalities who were pedestrians will also depend on the safety measures that have been introduced both for pedestrians and for other road users. South Africa, Britain and the United States were the worst three countries when the difference between the expected and the actual percentage of deaths who had been pedestrians was considered. South Africa has a poor road

Table 3.7 Pedestrian deaths, actual and predicted, as a percentage of total deaths in different countries

Country	Cars per 1000 population	Pedestrian deaths as per cent of total road deaths	Per cent expected from regression equation	Difference between per cent found and per cent expected
Austria	334	20.6	21.7	−1.1
Belgium	350	18.0	20.6	−2.6
Denmark	306	16.3	23.5	−7.2
Finland	316	23.3	22.9	+0.4
France	379	14.9	18.7	−3.8
W. Germany	428	21.3	15.6	+5.7
Great Britain	314	33.2	23.0	+10.2
Greece	130	25.2	35.0	−9.8
Hungary	135	37.6	34.6	+3.0
Ireland	202	33.7	30.3	+3.4
Italy	392	17.7	17.9	−0.2
Japan	230	27.8	28.5	−0.7
Netherlands	338	13.0	21.4	−8.4
Norway	364	17.2	19.7	−2.5
Poland	98	43.6	37.1	+6.5
South Africa	107	47.7	36.5	+11.2
Spain	240	20.9	27.8	−6.9
Sweden	377	14.0	18.9	−4.9
Switzerland	402	21.0	17.2	+3.8
USA	539	15.5	8.3	+7.2
Yugoslavia	125	31.9	35.3	−3.4

Sources: United Nations, 1987; International Road Federation, 1987; Japan, 1988; Republic of South Africa, 1988.

safety record for other modes of travel as well as walking, whether the death rate per population or per motor vehicle is considered. There are therefore no extenuating circumstances for the very poor record for pedestrian deaths. This will be discussed again in the final section of this chapter. Britain, with the second worst difference between the observed and expected percentage of pedestrian deaths, has done a great deal in recent years for the safety of vehicle occupants so it can be considered that this is partly responsible for the high percentage of the total deaths who were pedestrians. Similarly a great deal has been done to improve vehicle safety in the United States. It is the relative safety of walking compared with other modes of transport that is shown here rather than the absolute safety. From the point of view of the effectiveness of the safety measures that have been introduced in various countries this relative safety is important.

Accidents involving child pedestrians

All pedestrian casualties do not, of course, occur to people intentionally walking from one place to another. Many children are injured while they are playing, not going to any specific place (Preston, 1972, 1976). The importance of safe play space for children was perhaps first shown when Play Streets were introduced in Salford in the 1930s (Godfrey, 1937). In 1929 Major Godfrey, the Chief Constable of Salford, said that if there were children and traffic on the same streets then children would be injured, but he added that to remove the children was obviously quite impossible so that the only logical alternative was to remove the traffic instead. Some countries endorse this view whereas others, such as Britain, consider that it is the parents' duty to see that children do not go out without adult supervision. In some countries it is recognised that children need to play outside with other children, for both physical and mental health. Psychologists advise that children should be allowed to explore their surroundings and play, unsupervised, with other children. Many parents instinctively feel this to be true. For people who live in houses with reasonably large gardens there is no conflict; the children can play out in safety in the gardens with their neighbours and can play in their neighbours' gardens. For those in flats or houses without adequate gardens there is a dilemma; parents worry about the child's safety if the child plays outside and about the child's welfare if the child is detained indoors unable to learn how to get along with other children in the natural way that children once did.

Play Streets certainly worked. Between 1931 and 1936 the number of children (aged 0–14 years) injured in Salford was nearly halved and the number killed was reduced from eleven in 1931 to one in 1936. Play Streets were not the only safety measures introduced at that time, so it cannot be claimed that these remarkable reductions were entirely due to the provision of Play Streets, but they were probably the main factor. They were effective then, but they cannot be recommended now. The police cannot enforce access-only orders. Nowadays very little is done in Britain to improve residential areas for the safety of young children, though a start has been made in a very few areas (Beth and Pharoah, 1988; Tolley, 1990).

In Sweden motor traffic is completely banned from many residential areas so that children can play out in safety (Thulin, 1986). Cars must be parked some 100 metres from the houses and there is a safe network for pedestrians and pedal cyclists, without motor traffic, linking these residential neighbourhoods with schools, shops, etc. In the Netherlands, *Woonerven* have been created in suitable residential areas to which traffic is allowed access, but is restricted to very low speeds by physical means (Royal Dutch Touring Club, 1980).

These measures would be expected to be of the greatest benefit to young children who do not go far from home. The death rates per 100 000 children for the age groups for the countries considered are given in Table 3.8. As these rates are very low in some countries the average for 1984 and 1985 are given, except for Italy and Poland where only the 1984 figures were available. For the youngest age group, Finland and Sweden, with

Table 3.8 Death rates for child pedestrians by age groups in different countries

Country	Death rate per 100 000		
	<6 years	*6–9 years*	*10–14 years*
Austria	3.0	3.7	1.5
Belgium	2.5	4.3	2.0
Czechoslovakia	1.3	3.0	1.1
Denmark	2.5	2.5	2.3
Finland	0.6	2.3	2.3
France	2.2	3.2	2.0
East Germany	1.4	3.3	1.4
West Germany	2.8	3.2	1.0
Hungary	1.9	3.8	2.1
Ireland	4.5	4.0	2.2
Italy	1.3	1.3	0.7
Netherlands	1.4	1.5	0.8
Norway	1.5	3.3	2.1
Poland	3.3	4.2	1.9
Romania	3.7	4.0	1.7
Spain	1.9	2.2	1.6
Sweden	0.8	1.0	0.9
Switzerland	2.2	3.3	0.7
UK	2.1	4.2	3.5
USA	2.0	2.6	1.6
Yugoslavia	3.9	7.7	3.4

Deaths are averages for 1984 and 1985, except Italy and Poland (all 1984 only)
Source: United Nations, 1987.

death rates of less than one child per 100 000 children under 6 years of age, were the safest countries, and Ireland and Yugoslavia were the most dangerous with death rates of 4.5 and 3.9 respectively. In the Netherlands the death rate was 1.4 and in the United Kingdom it was 2.1.

From the ages of 6 to 14 years the dangers of the journey to school are also important. Again, both Sweden and the Netherlands pay special attention to the safety of the route to school. As Nielsen describes in Chapter 18, some communities in Denmark now have 'safe routes to school' projects, though the improvement in safety that these have brought is too recent to be reflected in Table 3.8. In Britain although School Crossing Patrols are provided on busy roads outside some primary schools the criteria required for both the amount of traffic and the number of children crossing mean that children only have this protection at the busiest crossing points. For the age group 6–9 years the safest countries are Sweden, Italy and the Netherlands with death rates of 1.0, 1.3 and 1.5 respectively. The death rate in the United Kingdom is 4.2 and Yugoslavia is the most dangerous country for children of this age with a death rate of 7.7 per 100 000 children.

For the age group 10–14 years, Italy, Switzerland, the Netherlands and Sweden all have death rates of less than one per 100 000 children, whereas the death rate in the United Kingdom is 3.5. The United Kingdom has the highest death rate for this age group of the 21 countries considered, slightly worse than Yugoslavia with a death rate of 3.4, reflecting the fact that very little is done for the safety of secondary school children in Britain. There seems to be no doubt that the countries renowned for their policies of providing safe residential areas for children to play and safe routes to school have much lower child pedestrian death rates than the United Kingdom.

The influence of speed limits

Another very important factor for the safety of pedestrians is the speed of the traffic. In Britain 95 per cent of the pedestrians injured are in built-up areas so that pedestrian safety is largely an urban problem. For many years it has been accepted that speed limits are essential in urban areas and all the countries considered have urban speed limits. When these speed limits were first introduced they were very effective in preventing casualties (Preston, 1954; Smeed, 1960, 1961; Newby, 1962). Stopping distances depend on the square of the initial speed of the vehicle, so if a driver attempts to stop to avoid an accident the speed that he is travelling is very important. Perhaps even more important is the fact that if an accident does occur, the severity of the accident, other things being equal, will again depend on the square of the speed at impact. The severity of the accident will also depend on whether the person is protected by being inside a vehicle, or is a more vulnerable unprotected road user, a pedestrian or cyclist. The severity will also depend on the age of the person injured.

Ashton (1982) has studied this for pedestrians. A very young child hit by the front of a vehicle may receive a head injury which is lethal, or may be knocked forward, run over and stuck under the wheels of the vehicle, which may also be very serious. The proportion of fatal and serious casualties that are fatal is therefore higher for those under three years of age than for the middle-aged. For taller people the initial impact will be to the legs and so will be less serious than a head injury, though depending on the speed the pedestrian may then swing forward on to the bonnet and the second impact may be against the windscreen. The driver will then slow down and as the car stops the pedestrian will not and will be thrown forward on to the ground where a third impact will occur. The seriousness of this type of accident increases with age as the elderly are more likely than younger people to die from any specific injury. Ashton reported that for adults an increase in age of 2.5 years was roughly comparable to an increase in impact speed of one km/h in affecting the severity of an injury.

Pedestrians as a whole, ignoring age effects, are likely to survive impact speeds of less than 50 km/h (31 mph) while speeds greater than 55 km/h (34 mph) are likely to be lethal. For those over 60 years of age the comparable critical speed is 7.5 km/h (5 mph) less.

All of the countries considered have urban speed limits of 50 or 60 km/h. The proportion of the pedestrians killed who are young or who are elderly will influence the overall death rates and this proportion varies in the different countries. To compensate for this, the death rates only for pedestrians aged 25–64 years of age can be considered: these are shown in Table 3.9 for countries with urban speed limits of 50 km/h or less and countries with urban speed limits of 60 km/h. (Denmark is not included in this table as the speed limit was reduced from 60 to 50 km/h during 1985.) The average death rate in 1985 for this age group was 2.3 per 100 000 population for the countries with the lower speed limits and 3.3 for those with 60 km/h speed limits, a difference which is statistically significant at the 0.05 probability level, for a one-tailed 't' test.

Fieldwick and Brown (1987), using a sophisticated multiple regression analysis for all road deaths in 22 countries, predicted that a change in urban speed limits from 60 km/h to 50 km/h might reduce the number of fatalities by up to 28 per cent. The Danish speed limit in urban areas was reduced from 60 km/h to 50 km/h in October 1985. Engel and Thomson (1988) studied the effect of this and reported that the number of fatalities was reduced by 24 per cent and the number of injury accidents by nine per cent. Again, this was for all road users not just pedestrians. In Britain just over half of those killed in built-up areas are pedestrians and, as this 10 km/h change in speeds is particularly critical to the severity of pedestrian casualties, these reductions would apply particularly to pedestrians.

In recent years West Germany has used 'traffic calming' methods to reduce the speed of traffic in urban areas (TEST, 1988, Tulley, 1990) and the number of pedestrians killed decreased from 3095 in 1980 to 1790 in 1985. The change in the pedestrian death rate per 100 000 pedestrians for different countries between 1976 and 1986 is shown in Table 3.2. There has been a decrease in nearly all the countries for which figures are available: the change in West Germany was not markedly different from that in most other countries, though these aggregate figures conceal significant and accelerating decreases at the lower level, as Whitelegg (Chapter 5) and Döldissen and Draeger (Chapter 19) show in this volume. Slower speeds are particularly important for the safety of pedestrians and other road users but speed limits are difficult to enforce. They are unpopular with drivers and despite the accumulated evidence over the years, many people appear to convince themselves that exceeding the speed limit is merely a technical offence. Risk compensation theory (Adams, 1985) suggests that most safety measures are useless because drivers compensate for the added safety by driving more dangerously to keep the perceived level of risk the same. There is much truth in this theory, though it does not apply to all

Table 3.9   Death rates for pedestrians aged 25–64 years in countries with different urban speed limits in 1985

Speed limit 50 km/h or less		60 km/h speed limit	
Country	Death rate per 100 000 population	Country	Death rate per 100 000 population
Norway	0.64	Switzerland	1.53
Sweden	0.76	Belgium	2.20
Netherlands	0.81	France	2.33
Italy	1.64	Spain	2.41
E. Germany	1.79	Czechoslovakia	3.24
W. Germany	1.81	Romania	3.46
UK	1.94	Hungary	5.66
Finland	2.23	Yugoslavia	5.73
USA	2.57		
Ireland	2.78		
Austria	3.14		
Greece	3.28		
Poland	6.15		
Mean	2.3	Mean	3.3

Source: United Nations, 1987.

safety measures. It does not apply to speed reduction because, if this is enforced, the driver cannot increase the risk in the way that is easiest, by driving faster. This may explain why speed limits, if they are enforced, are so unpopular.

Conclusions

The aim of this chapter has been to show that countries which have introduced specific safety measures for different types and ages of road user have been successful in reducing the relevant death rates. The countries which have done most for the safety of pedestrians are Sweden and the Netherlands with pedestrian death rates per 100 000 population of 1.5 and 1.8 respectively. The country which has probably done least is South Africa with a pedestrian death rate of 15.3 per 100 000 population (Republic of South Africa, 1988).

The Netherlands and the Scandinavian countries have had a very good record for road safety for all modes of travel for many years whereas South Africa has had a poor record, whatever rates are used for comparison. Moreover, the overall death rate in Scandinavia and the Netherlands has continued to improve, whereas the death rate per 100 000 population in South Africa has increased in recent years, though the death rate per

10 000 vehicles has improved as the number of vehicles has increased. The death rates for Sweden, Japan and South Africa in 1977 and 1986 are shown in Table 3.10.

It has been suggested that the differences in the road death rates in different countries are due to differences in national character, rather than specific road safety measures. There is probably some truth in this theory. Maybe the Scandinavians and the Dutch are inherently more careful and law abiding than, for instance, the South Africans, where death rates vary among the racial groups in South Africa. The death rates per 100 000 population for pedestrians in South Africa is very different for the different population groups: in 1987 it was 3 for the whites, 7 for the Asians, 19 for the blacks and 23 for the coloureds. (There were 150 white pedestrians and 3816 black pedestrians killed.) But the theory that the differences between countries with consistently good and consistently bad safety records is dependent on national characteristics rather than safety measures, and is therefore unlikely to be changed if safety measures are introduced, has been disproved in Japan (Preston, 1981; Japan, 1988).

In 1970 Japan had a very poor accident record; there were 21 795 people killed on the roads (correcting for those who would have died within 30 days). Japan then introduced a five-year plan and by 1975 the number killed had been reduced to 14 030. The second five-year plan was then introduced and deaths were reduced to 11 387 by 1980. The five-year plan included a great many safety measures for all road users (Mamantoff, 1980). Cycling is encouraged in Japan and cycle tracks with special provisions for crossing main roads have been introduced. There are very low speed limits, 40 km/h (25 mph) in towns, and even lower speed limits, 30 km/h (19 mph) near schools, and there are also bridges or subways for pedestrians to cross the road in safety. Since the end of the second five-year plan, road deaths have risen again; 12 112 people were killed on the roads in 1986. Between 1980 and 1986 the number of fatal traffic accidents between a motor vehicle and a pedestrian continued to decrease slightly, while fatal accidents between motor vehicles increased. The number of motor vehicles registered in Japan increased from 18.6 million in 1970 to 50.3 million in 1986.

Japan's success rate in accident prevention has been spectacular. The death rate per 10 000 motor vehicles decreased from 11.7 in 1970 to 2.4 in 1986 and the death rate per 100 000 population decreased from 21.1 to 10. In Japan in 1986 only one pedestrian death was attributed to playing on the road and there were no deaths under the heading 'infants walking alone' – and that in a country with a population of 121 million.

The countries that have done most for the safety of pedestrians and particularly for the safety of child pedestrians, the Netherlands and Sweden, are the countries with the lowest pedestrian death rates; the country that does least for many of its pedestrians. South Africa, has a very high death rate for these pedestrians. Japan has proved that this is not

Table 3.10 A comparison of the death rates for all modes of travel in Sweden, Japan and South Africa in 1977 and 1986

Country	Death rate			
	per 100 000 population		per 10 000 motor vehicles	
	1977	1986	1977	1986
Sweden	12	10	3	2.4
Japan	12	10	3	2.4
South Africa	23	33	20	17.5

Sources: Department of Transport, 1978, 1988a; International Road Federation, 1987; Republic of South Africa, 1988.

entirely due to some immutable national characteristic by showing what can be done, in a comparatively short period of time, when extensive safety measures are implemented.

References

Adams, J.G.U., 1985, *Risk and freedom*, Transport Publishing Projects, Cardiff.
Ashton, R.F., 1982, 'Vehicle design and pedestrian injuries', in Chapman, A.J., Wade, F.M., and Foot, H.C. (eds), *Pedestrian accidents*, John Wiley, Chichester.
Beth, L. and Pharoah, T., 1988, *Adapting residential roads for safety and amenity*, South Bank Polytechnic, London.
Department of Transport, 1978, *Road accidents Great Britain 1977*, HMSO, London.
—— 1980, *Road accidents Great Britain 1978*, HMSO, London.
—— 1988a, *Road accidents Great Britain 1987*, HMSO, London.
—— 1988b, *National travel survey 1985/1986 Report: Part 1*, HMSO, London.
Engel, U. and Thomson, L.K., 1988, *Speeds, speed limits and accidents*, Technical Report 3/1988, Danish Council for Road Safety Research, Copenhagen.
Fieldwick, R. and Brown, R.J., 1987, 'The effect of speed limits on road casualties', *Traffic Engineering and Control*, December, 635–40.
Godfrey, C.V., 1937, *Roadsense for children*, Oxford University Press, Oxford.
International Road Federation, 1987, *World road statistics 1981–1985*, New York.
Japan, 1988, *Statistics bureau yearbook*.
Mamontoff, B., 1980, 'La sécurité routière au Japon', *Transport Environment Circulation*, 38, Paris.
Netherlands, 1983, *Statistical year book 1982*, The Hague.
Newby, R.F., 1962, 'Speed restrictions', *Traffic Engineering and Control*, **4**, 156–77.
Organisation for Economic Cooperation and Development, 1987, *Statistical report on road accidents*, European Conference of Ministers of Transport, OECD, Paris.
Preston, B., 1954, *Focus on road accidents*, Public Affairs News Service, London.

—— 1972, 'Statistical analysis of child pedestrian accidents in Manchester and Salford', *Accident Analysis and Prevention*, **4**, 323–32

—— 1976, *Child pedestrian accidents in Manchester and Salford*, Manchester Polytechnic, Manchester.

—— 1981, 'Road safety: international comparisons', *Transport Reviews*, **1**, 1, 75–100.

Republic of South Africa, 1988, *Bulletin of statistics*, **22**, 2, 13, 42.

Royal Dutch Touring Club, 1980, *Woonerf*, ANWB, The Hague.

Smeed, R.J., 1949, 'Some statistical aspects of road safety research', *Journal of the Royal Statistical Society*, A 112, 1, 1–23.

—— 1960, 1961, 'The influence of speed and speed regulations on traffic flow and accidents', *Roads and Road Construction*, **38**, 456, 395–7; **39**, 457, 15–24.

TEST, 1988, *Quality streets: how traditional urban centres benefit from traffic-calming*, TEST, London.

Thulin, H., 1986, 'Safety neighbourhoods in Sweden', in *Road safety: what next*, Proceedings of conference, October 1985, Policy Studies Institute, London.

Tolley, R.S., 1990, *Calming traffic in residential areas*, Brefi Press, Tregaron.

United Nations, 1987, *Statistics of road traffic accidents in Europe 1980–1985*, United Nations, New York.

4 Planning for the green modes: a critique of public policy and practice

Mayer Hillman

When judged from the viewpoint of the wider *public* interest, the balance of advantage over disadvantage is heavily tipped in favour of the green modes – walking and cycling – as the most desirable of all transport modes. They incur by far the lowest expenditure: provision for them is very cheap and, for the individual, capital and 'running' expenses are exceptionally low. In marked contrast to the owner of a car who generally has to rely on a garage for maintenance or repairs, most cyclists can 'do it themselves' – mend a puncture or adjust the brakes. The efficiency of the two modes is very high, their environmental impact is negligible and their use of finite fuels almost zero. Given the fact that they cause no pollution nor add to global warming, they could be seen as an ideal answer to some of today's environmental concerns.

Walking is almost universally 'available', and cycling has more scope for wide use among the general population than any of the other mechanised modes, the prerequisites for use of which, of adequate age and capability, are much more limiting. Finally, travel by either of the green modes contributes to general physical fitness which is a key element in any programme of public health promotion: a significant proportion of the population could engage in regular exercise such as brisk walking or cycling on their daily journey to school or work and, in this way, reduce the risk of heart and respiratory diseases, and protect themselves against the risk of bone fracture in old age.

In these circumstances, one could have expected that every effort would be made through the medium of public policy and practice at national and local authority level to encourage walking and cycling. Instead, the environment that would best conduce this has been allowed to deteriorate steadily, largely as a result of the growth of car ownership and of motorised traffic.

This has led to all road users, particularly pedestrians and cyclists, having to exercise greater care and having to adopt preventive behavioural responses in the more dangerous environment. Campaigns are mounted regularly to alert pedestrians to the seriousness of the risks that they run daily. Indeed, it could be hypothesised that a major reason for the fall in road accidents in the last 20 years is attributable to the success of these campaigns, the public being obliged to travel in ways that, given a safer environment, they would avoid, and in some instances only being prepared to travel if the journey is essential.

Many old people are frightened by the speed and volume of traffic, and children, who tend to be careless, impulsive and unpredictable, have difficulty in coping with it. Because of their fear of the risk of accident, this generation's parents are more disposed towards denying their children the opportunity of travelling on their own, especially by the children's preferred mode, the bicycle, and feel it necessary to accompany them on all their children's journeys.

The level and ubiquity of noise and air pollution which affect the quality and attractions of the green modes have continued to increase. For instance, the level of nitrogen oxides in London's air over the last ten years has risen by one-half – the great majority from motor vehicles – and safe levels of carbon monoxide regularly exceed World Health Organisation guidelines (London Scientific Services, 1988).

At the same time, changes in land use – lower residential densities, the wider geographical spread of facilities, and so on – have led to more dispersed patterns of activity and thereby to the erosion of the quality of travel opportunities by the non-motorised modes because of the greater distances that have to be covered in the course of a typical day. In turn, these changes have exacerbated the main disadvantages associated with the green modes, namely their limited range and increased exposure to the adverse impacts noted above.

As a consequence, in so far as an understanding can be gained from official survey sources of changes over the last 20 or 30 years in patterns of travel, the use of walking as a transport mode continues to decline, and the use of bicycles has fallen dramatically. Indeed, whilst there are about 13 million bicycles in Britain, the *National travel survey* shows that only one in four is used in an average week (Department of Transport, 1988a), a marked contrast to the ownership and use of cars. (The recent mini-renaissance of cycling is far more a reflection of its appropriateness as a transport mode to cyclists even in a distinctly hostile environment than of recognition in public policy of that appropriateness.)

Table 4.1 shows the change in the proportion of personal journeys made on foot or cycle from the *National travel surveys* conducted in the mid-1970s and the mid-1980s. It can be seen that their use has fallen significantly, but it should be noted that, in spite of the increasing availability of cars and, for the majority of the population, a reasonable level of public

Table 4.1 Percentage of journeys on foot or cycle in Great Britain, by age and sex, 1975–76 and 1985–86

	Children 0–15	Elderly 60+	Women 16–59	Men 16–59	All
NTS 1975–76*	62	50	43	26	43
NTS 1985–86**	51	43	36	26	37

*special tabulation from the D.Tp.'s National Travel Survey, 1975/6 Report (Department of Transport, 1979)
** special calculations from published figures in Department of Transport, 1988a.

transport, they still cater for over one in three of all journeys. They account for a half of all children's journeys – though the great majority of children live in car-owning households – for over two in five of the journeys of everyone over the age of 60, and even for a quarter of the journeys of men of economically active age – a proportion which has not changed during the decade that has elapsed between the two surveys.

What is the explanation for this overall decline in walking and cycling? This chapter argues that the reason stems from a lack of appreciation of the relevance of these modes to a sane, equitable and sustainable transport policy and from the inadequacy of the lobby to promote them. It derives too from a lack of appreciation of the latent demand for the green modes, especially cycling, and a lamentable perception of the benefits of such an approach.

The omission of walking and cycling from public policy

The significance attached to walking and cycling in public policy in recent years can be established by checking through the numerous official documents on transport in which it could be expected that they would feature. Such an examination reveals that few of these documents mention them, and those that do typically categorise them as 'also rans'.

Reference to the two modes is rare, particularly in the context of planning. Where it is made, evidence of their role and discussion of this tend to be limited. It is almost as if those who draw up policy, or compile documents in which such reference would be highly appropriate, consider that they have to do so but that it has very little bearing on today's transport realities and needs.

Forecasts made in the process of determining plans for meeting future transport demand and expenditure on these plans extraordinarily exclude walking and cycling. It would appear that only motorised travel is worthy of consideration. Yet the relevance of this process and its reliability would be considerably improved, and the focus of policy sharpened, if it were simply acknowledged that in the year for which predictions were made, close on 100 per cent of the population will be able to walk. Almost certainly, too, the majority will be able to cycle, and would welcome wider opportunities for doing so if proper provision were made. In this way, a future role for walking and cycling would be recognised and policy adjusted accordingly.

The Report on the European Community Ministers of Transport Round Table 75 *Research relevant to trends in transport* (ECMT, 1987) incorporated a set of papers on demand for future vehicular travel but only one of them referred to walking or cycling. Furthermore, the Secretary of State for Transport's 1989 *Statement on Transport in London* 'Approach towards the operation and development of London's transport systems' consigns cyclists and pedestrians to eight paragraphs in Appendix 8, even though one of these paragraphs cites the significant finding that 'over one third of all the journeys undertaken in London are made on foot' (Department of Transport, 1989).

National statistics incorporating walking as a transport mode in the overall pattern of travel were not available in published form until 1979. These were set out in the report of the findings of the *National travel survey of 1975/76* (Department of Transport, 1979). However, any attempt to monitor the changes that have occurred since then have been rendered comprehensible only to the most astute observer owing to the fact that all the main analyses in the most recent report of the *National travel survey of 1985/86* exclude journeys of under 1.6 kilometres (one mile) – the distance within which the great majority of walking trips are made (Department of Transport, 1988a).

The justification for this decision is that the principal uses to which the findings of the survey are put is in order to be able to recognise changing trends in the demand for travel. For this reason, it concentrates on travel distance. In an easily overlooked note prefacing the (*National travel survey*, 1985/6), it is pointed out that journeys of under 1.6 km only account for three per cent of all personal travel distance and that 'most of these are walks' – with the implication that they are of little consequence.

However, the omission of these 'very short' (*sic*) journeys leads to a very different image of the distribution of journeys by mode. Table 4.2 compares this distribution for each of the main modes including and excluding journeys of under 1.6 km. It can be seen that their omission results in the significance of the non-motorised modes, particularly those on foot, being seriously under-represented.

Moreover, as Table 4.3 shows, over a third of the journeys that people made were over distances of under 1.6 km. It can be seen too that, again, nearly half of the journeys of children and nearly two-fifths of those of people over the age of 60 years were made over this distance. The table

Table 4.2 A comparison of journeys by mode in Great Britain, including and excluding journeys of under 1.6 km, 1985–86

| | Journeys of under 1.6 km: | |
| | included | excluded |
Mode	(per cent)	(per cent)
Walk	34	11
Cycle	3	2
Bus	9	11
Car	51	69
Other	4	7
All	100	100

Source: special calculations from published figures in Department of Transport, 1988a.

Table 4.3 Percentages of journeys in Great Britain by all modes and by walking and cycling, over distances of less than 1.6 km, by age and sex, 1985–86.

| | Journeys under 1.6 km | | | | |
	Children 0–15	Elderly 60+	Women 16–59	Men 16–59	All
Per cent of all journeys	45	38	33	22	33
Per cent of these on foot or cycle	78	78	79	69	76

Source: special calculations from published figures in Department of Transport, 1988a.

also shows that roughly three-quarters of this significant proportion of journeys were made on foot or by bicycle.

It can be inferred from this spurious decision that longer journeys are considered far more pertinent to policy and therefore more worthy of attention and public investment. However, this effectively leads to discrimination against those whose patterns of activity are more contained and who use walking and cycling as their predominant means of travel – the modes that the introduction to this chapter suggests are the ones that it would be in the public's interest to promote.

To compound this error of judgement, the most widely used sources of data on patterns of travel, such as the current volume of *Transport statistics: Great Britain* (Department of Transport, 1988b) and *Social trends*, Section 9 (Central Statistical Office, 1989), do not incorporate figures on these shorter trips, thereby providing meaningless and distorting bases for consideration and for the formation of a sensible transport policy.

Against this background, it is not surprising to note that the *Government's expenditure plans* setting out the aims and objectives of transport policy make no reference to walking or cycling, other than obliquely in the context of road safety (H.M. Treasury, 1989). This could be interpreted as very surprising given that one of the main aims of government is to cut public expenditure, and that the more people can be enabled to make their journeys on foot or by cycle, the lower are the public costs in catering for their travel. Clearly, the problem stems from the fact that provision for these modes is too cheap to warrant mention and, therefore, their role is overlooked. As a result, spending on the provision for cycle tracks is only a very small fraction of that for roads and capital spending by local authorities on cycle facilities in recent years has been only about 0.2 per cent of their total transport expenditure.

The inadequacy of provision for cycling is apparent from a comparison of the ownership and use of cycles with the ownership and use of cars, noted earlier. Such a comparison reveals both the considerable latent demand for cycling and the fact that observed patterns of travel, and changes observed in them in recent years, are not necessarily reliable indicators of public preference as they reflect the way in which people are encouraged in their personal decision-making on transport to discount the external costs for the community of those decisions. For these reasons, they should not be used as the primary source for formulating transport planning for the future.

The diversion from reality that this oversight of the role of walking and cycling leads to can be further illustrated by reference to the recent *Planning policy guidance: major retail development* (Department of the Environment, 1988). This document, which is aimed at directing local authorities towards public interest decisions on patterns of shopping provision within their area, relies on the main *National travel survey* figures which exclude journeys of under 1.6 km. It therefore reports on walking having only a very minor role, and shopping journeys having more than doubled since 1965. In this way, it overlooks the fact that nearly half of all shopping trips are made on foot.

Having incorrectly over-rated the significance of car trips, the document then emphasises for the authorities the importance of providing sufficient parking space for car-borne shoppers. It goes on to give policy guidance for large stores and the 'now well-established form of retail development, clearly meeting strong customer demand for convenient car-borne weekly household shopping'.

The justification for this wholly distorting approach appears to be a desire to enable comparisons to be made with *National travel surveys* carried out since 1965 – which largely ignored walking as a transport mode – and an implicit judgement that, in any case, shorter journeys are not very significant as the 'journeys of under a mile account for only three per cent of all mileage'. Again this leads to the very reverse of what could be categorised as the desirable 'public interest' modal split.

Public policy decisions clearly need to be made on the basis of an understanding of the scale of external costs that the use of each transport mode entails. Yet, no comprehensive record is kept on changes in the quality of the environment in which pedestrians and cyclists have to circulate. There are no nationwide statistics of levels of danger nor of pollution and noise on roads, and those measures which would allow monitoring of success or failure in this regard are poor. Changes in the levels of traffic noise are currently recorded in terms of 'complaints per million of the population'; changes to the level of risk to pedestrians are given in terms of traffic mileage without reference to pedestrian mileage or to changes in the speed and acceleration of motor vehicles. Further, no appreciation is shown of the extent to which children have to be denied the opportunity of getting about on foot or cycle on their own because of the increasingly dangerous traffic environment.

The effect of paying scant regard to the green modes is evident too in the panoply of central and local government practices which affect their users in their daily lives. It can be inferred also from the findings of the 1987 National Consumer Council survey which revealed widespread dissatisfaction with the pedestrian environment to the extent that 94 per cent expressed concern about its quality (National Consumer Council, 1987).

A conspiracy to discriminate against pedestrians and cyclists?

One might conclude from this review of current policy that the outcome is almost akin to a conspiracy to discriminate against pedestrians and cyclists, effectively classifying them as 'second class' citizens, and to do injustice to those who choose to travel by these modes, including putting their lives at high risk and damaging their health. It is as if there is a plan to do so.

For the policy on spoiling their environment, the air they breathe is polluted. Advantage can be taken of the fact that toxic exhaust fumes stay suspended in the air for a time before settling by positioning the great majority of exhaust pipes at the rear of vehicles on the left-hand side in such a way that the fumes are expelled at low level and in the direction most damaging to health. Only those vehicle owners who make the fumes visible run the risk of prosecution. Suggestions made to colour vehicle exhausts as a warning of the toxicity of the fumes can be rejected on the grounds that the necessary pigment could slightly damage the engines of vehicles. Examination of the toxicity of exhaust emissions from the annual MOT test is excluded even though, with existing technology, this would be quick and reliable. The level of vehicle noise is allowed to spread by area and time of day, and no record of changes in this is kept.

For the policy on making the environment as unsafe as possible, especially for children, the following measures are taken. The pedestrian network is interrupted at every road intersection, and pedestrians are obliged to detour – in the interests of their own safety, of course – by footbridges and underpasses which are rarely cleaned or policed. A blind eye is turned to the widespread misuse of pavements and of kerbs at road junctions for car parking. The surfaces used by pedestrians are allowed to deteriorate and, where possible, the utilities – gas, water, electricity, cables for television – are obliged to run their services under pavements. Street furniture is located to restrict the widths of pavements. The minimum of attention is paid to potholes which damage cycle wheels and cause cyclists to swerve, and no record is kept of the consequential high incidence of accidents among pedestrians and cyclists. Vehicle speeds which inculate fear among pedestrians and cyclists are set and poorly enforced, and then pedestrians are often blamed for not taking sufficient care in the event of an accident. Vehicles which are capable of very high acceleration and speeds well in excess of the top limit are allowed to be manufactured. When accidents do occur, all traces are removed immediately, and any suggestion that plaques be erected to mark the incident is treated as too harrowing a proposition for the bereaved.

For the policy on disguising the significance of walking and cycling, and to encourage the general public to believe that the alternative to the car is public transport, as has been seen, the majority of walking and cycling journeys are omitted from the principal published national surveys on people's travel patterns, and reference to the existence of pedestrians and cyclists is left out of forecasts employed in planning for the future.

In order to discourage appreciation of the far greater cost-effectiveness of investment in provision for pedestrians and cyclists compared with that for motorised travel, no meaningful figures on the costs of provision for them are collated; and if some local authorities actually recognise the benefits of such an approach, they are rate-capped or abolished.

For the policy on making use of the non-motorised modes less convenient, planning proposals must rarely consider the consequences for pedestrians and cyclists. Instead the 'goal posts' (the destinations that can be easily reached on foot), are allowed to be moved on the grounds of economies of scale so that the distances people have to walk or cycle – the only effectively limiting characteristic of the green modes – are increased and the distances become unacceptable. At the same time, the ownership of cars is promoted and when they are used drivers are obliged to discount the externalities of this use by ensuring that they only have to pay a very low marginal cost for each kilometre travelled.

Finally, in order to ensure that no national policy on walking is developed, it is important that no Consultation Paper on this subject be published (even though one is promised), and for only a few civil servants to be assigned to 'handling cyclists and pedestrians' as *Civil Service year book* phraseology puts it (Cabinet Office, 1989).

In 1979, the Policy Studies Institute published a report entitled *Walking is transport* which called for walking 'to be included in tests of social, environmental, financial and energy performance, and judged on the same criteria as the motorised modes' (Hillman and Whalley, 1979). It concluded:

Are people in fact better off or worse off if they make more of their journeys by motorised means rather than on foot, or if their daily travel needs are met over increasing distances? Or would the community benefit from people being encouraged to adopt life styles which become more walk-oriented? Indeed, how can transport and planning policy be appropriately determined without establishing the advantages and disadvantages both to the individual and to the community of all the major methods of travel as well as of changes in the balance of people's patterns of travel – including walking.

A parallel study on cycling could well have drawn the same conclusion.

Some of us may draw comfort from the gradual 'greening' observable in statements and actions over the last few years by Department of Transport ministers, reflecting a growing recognition of the importance of the green modes. Peter Bottomley has been quoted as stating that 'for too long, people on foot have been the "Cinderellas" of road users, in spite of the large number of journeys that involve walking'. Technical guidance is now given to local authorities on how to improve conditions for pedestrians and cyclists, and more funds have been allocated to some authorities which have introduced 'cycle innovatory schemes', urban cycle networks and cycle paths on disused rail lines.

But the necessary measures that need to be taken properly to reflect their importance – pedestrian and cycling impact statements, continuous green mode networks, uninterrupted at road intersections, the imposition and proper enforcement of much lower speed limits, and so on – require a far more ambitious approach than has been seen to date. A precursor to such an approach, with these measures forming part of an overall policy on the subject, must be a government green paper.

At a conference at Policy Studies Institute in 1980, the Right Hon. Norman Fowler, the then Secretary of State for Transport, acknowledged that 'walking undoubtedly serves all and that is going to be an increasingly important central Government objective' (Policy Studies Institute, 1980). He stated his department's intention of taking 'a real interest in policy for pedestrians . . . to see what changes or improvements might be made . . . and hope that later this year we shall be able to produce a discussion paper on pedestrian policy'.

The following year he repeated his intention to produce such a policy paper, but in 1983 Mrs Lynda Chalker, the Under-Secretary of State in the department at the time, decided not to do so 'in view of the lack of significant new data on the subject which are likely to be of interest to the public'. In a letter to the Chairman of the Pedestrians' Association, she said: 'Although the Department attaches great importance to the interest of pedestrians generally . . . we are not yet ready to get in a public debate.' The evidence cited in this paper suggests that it is timely for that debate to begin. It would be difficult to find a better start for it than to adopt the 1988 European Charter of Pedestrians' Rights, suitably expanded to embrace also the rights of cyclists (European Parliament Session Documents, 1988). This Charter adopted by the European Parliament is reproduced in full as the frontispiece to this volume and includes the following clauses which are particularly pertinent:

I. The pedestrian has the right to live in a healthy environment and freely to enjoy the amenities offered by public areas under conditions that adequately safeguard his physical and psychological well-being.
II. The pedestrian has the right to live in urban or village centres tailored to the needs of human beings and not to the needs of the motor car and to have amenities within walking or cycling distance.
III. Children, the elderly and the disabled have the right to expect towns to be places of easy social contact and not places that aggravate their inherent weakness.
IV. The pedestrian has the right to urban areas which are intended exclusively for his use, are as extensive as possible and are not mere 'pedestrian precincts' but in harmony with the overall organization of the town.

References

Cabinet Office, 1989, *The Civil Service year book 1989*, HMSO, London.
Central Statistical Office, 1989, *Social trends 19*, Section 9, HMSO, London.
Department of Environment, 1988, *Planning policy guidance: major retail development*, PPG 6, HMSO, London.
Department of Transport, 1979, *National travel survey 1975/76 report*, HMSO, London.
— 1988a, *National travel survey: 1985/86 report: Part 1, An analysis of personal travel*, HMSO, London.
— 1988b, *Transport statistics: Great Britain, 1977–87*, HMSO, London.
— 1989, *Statement on transport in London*, HMSO, London.
ECMT (European Community Ministers of Transport), 1987, *Research relevant to trends in transport over the coming decade*, Round Table 75, Paris.
European Parliament Session Documents, 1988, *Report on the protection of pedestrians and the European Charter of Pedestrians' Rights*, Document A2–0154/88.
H.M. Treasury, 1989, *The Government's expenditure plans 1989–90 to 1991–92*, HMSO, London.
Hillman, M. and Whalley, A., 1979, *Walking is transport*, Policy Studies Institute, London.
— 1983, *Energy and personal travel: obstacles to conservation*, Policy Studies Institute, London.

London Scientific Services, 1988, *London-wide monitoring programme: third report*, London Scientific Services.

National Consumer Council, 1987, *What's wrong with WALKING? A consumer review of the pedestrian environment*, HMSO, London.

Plowden, S. and Hillman, M., 1984, *Danger on the road: the needless scourge*, Policy Studies Institute, London.

Policy Studies Institute, 1980, *Report of the proceedings of a conference on walking*, June, PSI, London.

Transport 2000, 1988, *Feet first*, Transport 2000, London.

5 The principle of environmental traffic management
John Whitelegg

Introduction

It is paradoxical that Germany has embraced innovative transport concepts so enthusiastically. It is a country still without a speed limit on its 8200 kilometres of motorway and with a car industry which is more powerful and economically significant than any other national car market in Europe. The significance of the car for the economy is matched by its psychological significance as a manifestation of personality and ego (Sachs, 1984). In the mid-1980s Germany possessed 25 million passenger cars to Britain's 16 million and these cars covered 314×10^9 vehicle kilometres compared to Britain's 221.8×10^9. The population differential between the two countries (an FRG:GB ratio of 1.1:1) cannot explain these differences.

In the period 1967–87 (inclusive) Germany killed 294 145 and injured 10 047 313 on its roads compared to Britain's achievement in the same period of 135 976 killed and 6 957 000 injured.

In both countries the cumulative effect of air pollution through exhaust emissions, health effects of air pollution, disruption and disturbance caused by noise, community severance, fear and insecurity, and loss of life represent considerable burdens imposed on society for the illusory benefits of motorised transport. Germany is not alone in having made a serious start to resolve some of these problems and has made a great deal of progress with policies designed to improve living environments and the conditions for cyclists and pedestrians. This chapter looks at the measures taken and the progress which has been made and assesses how far this progress has made a dent in the inexorable growth of motorisation and its damaging consequences.

The scale of the problem

Motorised transport imposes a considerable burden on society which is easily perceived but difficult to measure. In 1985 the global total for deaths in road traffic accidents was more than 200 000. In Germany alone in 1987 more than 420 000 were injured and almost 8000 killed in road traffic accidents. In Cologne the lifetime risk of becoming a fatal or a serious casualty in a road traffic accident is 1 in 19 for a child under the age of 14 (Whitelegg, 1989).

Emissions of carbon dioxide and nitrous oxides continue to rise, with serious implications for human health. Carbon dioxide emissions in Germany amount to approximately 120 million tonnes per annum, making a substantial contribution to the greenhouse effect and world climatic change. Diesel emissions contribute to an increased cancer risk and noise to increased stress and psychological impairment. In Germany more than one million people are exposed to day-time noise levels of above 65 dB(A).

In cities people are exposed to cumulative hazards of noise, stress, accident danger, poor air quality and visual pollution. Traditional 'solutions' in Britain have clearly failed to hold these hazards in check, and the May 1989 announcement of a doubling in the road programme budget from £6 billion to £12 billion over ten years promises an increase in pollution and congestion well into the next century.

In Germany there is an awareness of the seriousness of these problems and of the necessity to take radical action (Ahrens and Beckmann, 1989). There is an emerging consensus on the types of action which should be taken. These include the following measures:

- 30 km/h speed limits in all residential areas;
- 50 km/h speed limits on main streets in towns;
- reduction of street capacity for motorised vehicles in favour of increased capacity for bus, rail, pedestrians and cyclists;
- reduction and eventual elimination of short-term car parking in cities;
- detailed improvements to pedestrian, cyclist and public transport facilities and a fusion of these separate interests into a coherent whole;
- fiscal penalties for the production of damaging emissions;
- the de-commissioning of streets to remove them completely where this will improve quality of life for residents or solve particularly bad traffic problems, e.g. Elbealle in Cologne, which has been decommissioned and replaced by a park.

Detailed proposals such as these stem from clear principles which can be articulated:

- Motorised means of transport, and particularly cars and lorries, are unwelcome in cities. They are unfriendly to the environment and to people and they should be removed.
- Residential areas must be improved as a combined process of housing improvement, improvement in street design, environmental improvement and reduction in motorised traffic.

— Public transport must be improved to offer a clearly better alternative to the car, particularly for shopping journeys and journeys to work.

The concept of *Verkehrsberuhigung* (traffic calming)

The main way in which such principles are applied is through the concept of *Verkehrsberuhigung* or traffic calming. The concept and principles are well explained in BBU (1984), Bundesminister für Raumordnung, Bauwesen und Stadtebau (1986), and Arbeitskreis Verkehr und Umwelt (1988). There is not very much material available in English, although a complete issue of the journal *Built Environment* (Hass-Klau, 1986) provides a good introduction to the subject and Tolley (1990) has contributed a comprehensive review. *Verkehrsberuhigung* is not without its opposition in Germany, particularly from the equivalent of British chambers of trade and commerce. Their arguments are summarised in Industrie und Handelskammer zu Köln (1988).

What is Verkehrsberuhigung?

Tables 5.1 and 5.2 summarise *Verkehrsberuhigung* and are taken from a study of the city of Dorsten (Kommunalverband Ruhrgebiet, 1986a). Table 5.1 shows the relationship between type of street, type of problem and the measures taken. The principal elements are the reduction of vehicle speeds by a variety of measures including 'Tempo 30' (30 km/h) regulation and physical changes to the street geometry as well as large reductions in the space formerly allocated for vehicles. The reclamation of formerly wide streets for parks, gardens, shared and segregated pedestrian and cycle space is an important feature of these plans. Table 5.2 shows the results of such schemes in three important areas in Germany where the idea has been pioneered.

Traffic calming can take place on streets of any size and function, though there are serious problems with main streets. These are not insurmountable (ILS, 1986). For example, the plans in Figure 5.1 illustrate some of the details of a main street *Verkehrsberuhigung* scheme in Niedersprockhövel in Nordrhein-Westfalen (NRW). (Kommunalverband Ruhrgebiet, 1986b). Bielefeld (also in NRW) has successfully traffic-calmed a main street. To be most effective, traffic-calmed streets need to be part of an area-wide approach as has been implemented in the areas mentioned in Table 5.2 and to a lesser extent (though very successfully) in smaller cities such as Darmstadt (Institut Wohnen und Umwelt, 1986).

It is difficult to estimate how many such schemes have been carried out in Germany but in NRW there are approximately 4 000 areas (Monheim, 1987). Since this state has pursued these policies with more enthusiasm

Table 5.1   *Verkehrsberuhigung* measures organised by type of street

---

Main traffic streets with business and public functions

Problems
High traffic density, too many lorries, speeds too high, serious crossing problems, unfavourable conditions for pedestrians and cyclists, no possibilities of enjoying the street as a social space, inappropriate parking

Package of measures
Traffic lights with variable timings to control speed and flow, implementation of parking ban on footpaths, 'tree-gates', marked crossing areas for pedestrians and bikes, construction of cycleways, use of planting and bollards to create safe spaces where people can linger

Main traffic streets with many living areas

Problems and *Package of measures*
Much the same as above except the addition of a protection zone between the traffic and pedestrians

Main collecting/distributor streets with public functions

Problems
Occasional high traffic density, inappropriately high traffic speeds, crossing problems, danger for cyclists, illegal parking

Package of measures
Speed limitation, severing of through-routes, overtaking forbidden, regulation of non-moving traffic, construction of multi-purpose lanes for slow traffic, broadening of footpaths, 'humping' of crossing areas, taking driving lanes for pedestrians and cyclists, creation of green areas on former road space, installation of street furniture.

Residential streets

Problems
Traffic density too high for area function, crossing problems, insufficient cycleways and pathways, rat-running, parking pressure, not enough public space

Package of measures
Speed restrictions, through-route severance, reduced turning opportunities from main streets, overtaking forbidden, lorry bans, parking controls, humps, broader paths, road narrowing, 'tree-gates', creation of play areas, traffic zig-zags, creation of one-way streets

---

Source: Kommunalverband Ruhrgebiet, 1986a, pp. 55–6. (tr. J. and M.E. Whitelegg).

than any other figure cannot be generalised across other Länder. Traffic calming has been developed to a high standard of design and experience in NRW and currently (1989) it has a programme covering 126 different schemes in 94 cities and towns, costing of these projects is 160 million DM (£60 million) (Fiebig et al, 1988). In NRW a 1989 study puts the number of areas with traffic calming measures at 8 147 (Akopian/Planlokal, 1989).

Table 5.2 Summary of the main features of *Verkehrsberuhigung* in three pioneer schemes in Germany

---

Buxtehude

Measures
Zonal speed limitation (Tempo 30), street markings to reduce width of driving space, use of plants and planting tubs, speed advice through flashing lights, road humps at entrances to streets, 'tree-gates', traffic islands

Results
Reduction of speeds by 10 km/h, creation of uniform speeds and no speeds higher than 80–90 km/h, noise levels down by 7dB(A), improvements in air quality through reduction in emissions, though increase in energy consumption. The schemes were approved by 39 per cent of residents before construction and 71 per cent after

Berlin-Moabit

Measures
Specific selective construction measures. Narrowing of lanes through planting, humps especially at T-junctions, crossings in the vicinity of public facilities, increased areas of planting

Results
Reduction of 35 km/h in speeds, drastic reduction in personal injury and damage in road traffic accidents, noise down by 7dB(A), no change in emissions. The schemes were not welcomed initially because of reduction in parking places. More approval came later as space for socialising became used and the street became the place for lingering and interaction

Berlin-Charlottenburg

Measures
Reconstruction and modification of streets to provide more space for people and less for cars. Extensive use of humps and street design to force cars from one side to the other. Speed limitation

Results
No research into speeds, accidents down by between 40 and 80 per cent depending on type. No research into noise or emissions

---

Source: Kommunalverband Ruhrgebiet, 1986a, pp. 54 (tr. J. and M.E. Whitelegg).

Measuring the benefits of *Verkehrsberuhigung*

There is something of a growth industry in Germany in research into the effects of traffic-calmed areas (see especially Bundesforschungsanstalt für Landeskunde und Raumordnung, 1988). The research is very detailed and empirical and is mainly concerned with noise, speeds and accidents. Speed is the important variable since noise and accident levels will both rise as

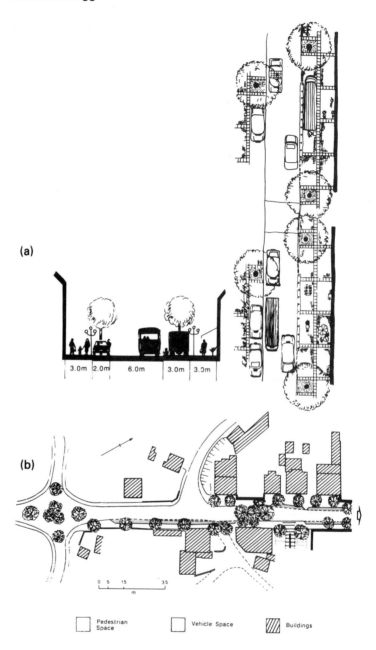

Figure 5.1   Diagrams showing traffic calming in Niedersprockhövel, Nordrhein-Westfalen: a main street (B51). The profile and model allocation all shown in (a); plans of two sections of the street are shown in (b)–(c) and (d)–(e).

(c)

(d)

(e)

Pedestrian
Space

Vehicle Space

Buildings

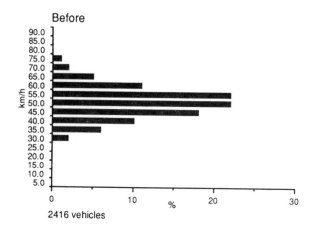

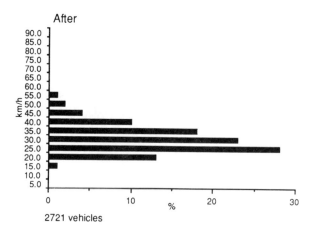

Figure 5.2 Speed measurements before and after traffic calming in Buxtehude, West Germany

Source: Bundes forschungsanstalt für Landeskunde und Raumordnung, p. 26 (1988)

speed increases. There is extensive evidence on speed reduction effects which can be summarised in diagrammatic form in Figure 5.2. Table 5.3 summarises the results from a study of several streets in Dortmund where Tempo 30 measures had been introduced (ILS, 1988).

The results show real gains which, though not spectacular, have implications for safety which should not be underestimated. More dramatic reductions in speed were reported in the Darmstadt study (Institut Wohnen und Umwelt, 1986) but results are highly variable and dependent on a large number of external factors. Flade and Müller (1988) report reductions in accidents to children following the introduction of *Verkehrsberuhigung*. Table 5.4 shows the results.

Table 5.3 Development of speed: percentage travelling over 30 km/h in selected streets in Dortmund before and after the introduction of Tempo 30 measures

Location	Before Tempo 30	After Tempo 30	Difference
Büttnerstrasse			
Büttnerstr/Schule	92.9	78.8	−14.1
Büttnerstr/Sportplatz	84.0	79.5	− 4.5
Färberstrasse	84.6	65.3	−19.3
Helenenbergweg			
Helenenbergweg 25	96.1	90.0	− 6.1
Helenenbergweg 41	92.7	92.3	− 0.4
Solbergweg 38	90.3	89.6	− 0.7
Pulverstrasse 8	95.0	90.9	− 4.1
Grüningsweg			
Grüningsweg 11	91.7	89.4	− 2.3
Grüningsweg 61	80.7	71.5	− 9.2
Grüningsweg 148	91.3	93.0	+ 1.7
All streets	89.9	84.0	− 5.9

Source: ILS, 1988, Table 5, p. 19.

Table 5.4 Consequences of *Verkehrsberuhigung* for the safety of children: the example of Berlin

	Child-injury accidents per 1000 children	
	1977–79 (before)	1982–84 (after)
Berlin-Charlottenburg (with VB)	11.2	4.0
Berlin-Moabit (without VB)	7.6	11.3
Berlin West (total)	8.6	7.1

VB = *Verkehrsberuhigung*
Source: Flade and Müller, 1988, Table 5, p. 11.

In the Dortmund study referred to above (ILS, 1988) the before and after situation for road traffic accidents was also monitored. Table 5.5 summarises the main results. They show very clearly the benefits of *Verkehrsberuhigung* in the area of road safety, particularly for children and unprotected road users. Similar results have been obtained for other *Verkehrsberuhigung* areas and these are discussed in some detail in Bundesforschunganstalt für Landeskunde und Raumordnung (1988) for both Buxtehude and Borgentreich. *Verkehrsberuhigung* also provides significant environmental benefits, including a 17.5 per cent reduction in CO, a 10.4 per cent reduction in HC, and a 31.8 per cent fall in NOx (Verkehrs Club Schweiz, 1989).

Towards a general traffic concept

It is possible to view recent German experience as a series of improvements to urban areas through pedestrianisation, traffic calming of residential and larger streets, speed limitation through Tempo 30, and the provision of segregated cycling facilities. These things have happened but equally there has been a development of integrated traffic and transport planning (*Verkehrsentwicklungsplanung* or VEP) which embraces an overall concept of what should happen in the city and how environmental and social gains can be achieved from policies which encourage pedestrians and cyclists. Measures to improve the immediate environment of residential areas involve the elimination or reduction of traffic volumes and traffic speeds. This produces benefits in the form of safer streets, more play space and circulation space for residents, less noise and pollution, and, importantly, a better feeling for urban living.

VEP embraces the physical improvement of streets and also the support and development of public transport systems, the provision of adequate access for all groups in society to a range of facilities which includes recreational and free-time facilities, and the needs of specific groups such as women and children. Most importantly, it embraces a concept of alternative transport futures to that which would be achieved if historical trends in the growth of car ownership and use were to be projected and satisfied by new road construction and city remodelling to satisfy the demands of the car. VEPs now exist for many cities in Germany but this is not to imply that they are all of a uniformly high standard or have grasped the central point of departing from the environmental and fiscal cul-de-sac of the car-friendly city.

Conclusion

The achievements of German transport planning are impressive. Any visitor from a British city to a German city of comparable size cannot be

Table 5.5 Accident counts on streets in Dortmund before and after the application of *Verkehrsberuhigung* measures

| | Locations (see key) | | | | | | | | | | | |
| | A | | B | | C | | D | | E | | Total | |
	a	p	a	p	a	p	a	p	a	p	a	p
Number	20	23	13	11	10	6	10	14	8	14	61	68
Seriously injured	3	0	0	0	0	1	0	0	0	0	3	1
Lightly injured	2	0	2	0	5	0	0	0	0	0	9	0
Cyclists	3	0	1	0	1	1	0	0	0	0	5	1
Pedestrians	1	0	0	0	0	0	0	0	0	0	1	0
Under 14s	3	0	0	0	0	0	0	0	0	0	3	0

a = ante and refers to a period one year before the measures were introduced
p = post and refers to a period one year after the measures were introduced.

A = Nienberge; B = Heedbrink; C = Grüningsweg; D = Helenenbergweg; E = Am Surck.

Source: ILS, 1988, Table 12, p. 26.

left unimpressed by the public transport systems, facilities for interchange between public transport modes, and facilities for pedestrians and cyclists. There are, however, major unresolved problems. The growth of car owner-ship and the acquisition of second and third cars fuels a growth in volume which nullifies many gains made by policies which encourage non-motorised modes. The sheer volume of traffic in German cities and the insatiable demands for parking on any available space including pavements render the physical environment of many places very poor indeed. The same authorities that are pursuing *Verkehrsberuhigung* are in many cases also pursuing the construction of additional car parking in city centres and the construction of more road space. This is the case in Dortmund: it is difficult to see how both policies can usefully co-exist.

The casualty rate in German cities is a source of concern. In a compari-son of Cologne and Manchester at the level of local government wards and their German equivalent (Whitelegg, 1989), casualty rates in Germany for pedestrians and cyclists were twice as high as in England. The conditions for pedestrians outside *Verkehrsberuhigung* areas are very poor indeed with noise, pollution and danger at a high level and physical problems of crossing roads and negotiating blocked pavements much worse than in British cities. Whilst *Verkehrsberuhigung* represents a major improvement for residents in traditional inner city areas it is not a policy which brings general improvements for pedestrians as a group. Their needs are heavily outgunned by the well-armed car lobby.

The future for Germany, as for all industrialised and over-motorised nations, lies in the recapture of streets for pedestrians and cyclists as living and social spaces and the relegation of a polluting and life-damaging technology to the marginal role it deserves. Germany has shown more vigour in its support of alternative transport policies and concepts than has Britain, but this has not dented the parasitic dominance of the car and its ability to exterminate person-friendly alternatives.

Verkehrsberuhigung itself has reached a critical point in its development. Its achievements are clear and impressive and the example of the city of Cologne shows that the gains have not simply been achieved by moving the problem around (Rowohlt, Reinbeck bei Hamburg, Stadt Köln, 1987). In Germany the debate has advanced to the next stage and the question now to be resolved is the extent to which traffic calming can continue to be implemented in its present form or should be replaced by a new approach. There are still many areas to be calmed but there is also an awareness that calming particular streets or areas does not solve the central problem. The city of Frankfurt under the influence of the Greens is now producing plans to calm the whole central area. If such a thing is possible then a real quantum breakthrough will have been achieved and the car will have passed a critical threshold in its disastrous relationship with people and places.

References

Ahrens, G.A. and Beckmann, K., 1989, 'Verkehrsinfarkt: Chance für Stadt und Umwelt, Bauwelt', *Stadtbauwelt*, 10/12, 24 March, 554–7.

Akoplan/Planlokal, 1989, Dokumentation zum stand der verkehrsberuhigung im der gemeinden Nordrhein-Westfalens, Institut für Landes- und Stadtentwicklungforschung des Landes Nordrhein-Westfalen, Dortmund.

Arbeitskreis Verkehr und Umwelt e.V., 1988, *Lärm-Minderung durch prinzipielle Verkehrs-Beruhigung*, Berlin.

Bundesforschungsanstalt für Landeskunde und Raumordnung, 1988, Tagungsband 4 Kolloquium, *Forschungsvorhaben Flachenhäfte Verkehrsberuhigung Ergebnisse aus drei Modellstadten*, 26/27 May, Buxtehude.

Bundesminister für Raumordnung, Bauwesen und Stadtebau, 1986, *Stadtverkehr im Wandel*, Bonn.

BBU, 1984, *Prinzipielle Verkehrsberuhigung. Ein Verkehrspolitisches Programm*, Bundesverband Burgerinitiativen Umweltschutz, Argumente 8.

Fiebig, K.H. *et al.*, 1989, *Umweltverbesserung in der Städten: Ein Wegweiser durch Literatur und Beispiele aus der Praxis*, Heft 5, Stadtverkehr, Deutsches Institut für Urbanistik, Berlin.

Flade, A. and Müller, P., 1988, *Kinderverkehrsunfalle: Eine Analyse am Beispiel Darmstadt und Massnahmenvorschläge*, Institut für Wohnen und Umwelt, Darmstadt.

Hass-Klau, C., 1986, 'New ways of managing traffic', *Built Environment*, **12**, 1/2, Alexandrine Press, Oxford.

ILS, 1986, 'Haupt (verkehrs)strassen und Verkehrsberuhigung', *Bausteine für die Planungspraxis in Nordrhein-Westfalen*, No. 6, Institut für Landes- und Stadtentwicklungsforschung des Landes Nordrhein-Westfalen, Dortmund.

—— 1988, *Wirksamkeit von Tempo 30*, Schriften 13, Institut für Landes- und Stadtentwicklungsforschung des Landes Nordrhein Westfalen, Dortmund.

Industrie- und Handelskammer zu Köln, 1988, *Problematik der Verkehrsberuhigung: Negative Auswirkungen der Kommunalen Verkehrspolitik*, Cologne.

Institut Wohnen und Umwelt, 1986, *Tempo 30: Modellversuche in Darmstadt*, Darmstadt.

Kommunalverband Ruhrgebiet, 1986a, *Gesamtstädtische Verkehrsberuhigung Dorsten*, Essen.

—— 1986b, *Verkehrsberuhigung Niedersprockhövel: Flachenhäfte Verkehrsberuhigung und stadtbauliche Integration der Hauptstrasse* (B51), Essen

KONTIV, 1976 and 1982, durchgefuhrt von Socialdata GmbH, Munchen, and quoted in Erl, G.E., *Wird das Fahrrad im Stadtverkehr dominierenin Fahrrad Stadt Verkehr*, ADFC Hessen, Griesheim, 8–12.

Monheim, H., 1987, *10 Jahre Verkehrsberuhigung in Nordrhein-Westfalen: Bilanz und Ausblick*, Planungsburo Richter-Richard, Aachen.

Paven-Höppner, U. and Höppner, M., 1988, *Einfluss von verkehrsberuhigung: Massnahmen auf der verkehrsablauf*, in Forschungsvorhaben 'Flachenhäfte verkehrsberuhigung', Ergebnisse aus drei Modellstadten, Bundesforschungsanstalt für Landeskunde und Raumordnung, Bonn.

Sachs, W., 1984, *Die Liebe zum Automobil: Ein Ruckblick in die Geschichte unserer Wunsche*, Reinbeck bei Hamburg.

Rowohlt, ⌐nbeck bei Hamburg, Stadt Köln, 1987, *Verkehrsberuhigung in Köln: Ziele, Manahmen, Erwartungen, Kritik, Wirkungen*, Beratungsstelle für Schadenverhutung des HUK-Verbandes.

Tolley, R.S., 1990, *Calming traffic in residential areas*, Brefi Press, Tregaron.

Verkehrs Club Schweiz, 1989, *Lust auf Tempo 30*, VCS, Postfach, 3360 Herzogenbuchsee.

Whitelegg, J., 1989, *A comparison of road traffic accidents and injuries in Manchester and Köln*, Institut für Landes- und Stadtentwicklungsforschung des Landes Nordrhein-Westfalen, Dortmund.

6 Feet first: putting people at the centre of planning

Judith Hanna

As a pressure group seeking to represent the needs and wishes of ordinary people, Transport 2000 has become concerned to increase the awareness of the importance of walking as a transport mode, the need for a better pedestrian environment, and the technical options which can be used to improve access on foot in the areas where people live, shop, work and play. Accordingly, the 'Feet First' campaign was launched in 1988 (Transport 2000, 1988).

There is welcome evidence of growing interest in this country in pedestrianisation and traffic calming measures among local authorities and planners (e.g. Department of Transport 1987c; IHT, 1989; Rigby, 1989; Griffiths, 1989; Swann, 1989). Improved conditions for cyclists can, and should, be part of this. Almost every sizeable town now seems to have one or two pedestrianised shopping streets and the benefits in increased retail turnover as a result of increased attractiveness are widely recognised. But few schemes extend beyond one or two streets. Those that do exist account for a minute proportion of road space, mere islands in an ocean of motor traffic (TEST, 1981). Much more is needed in order to provide networks of strategic pedestrian routes that allow people to reach destinations on foot from home, public transport stations, or parking areas.

In Western Europe over the past twenty years, pioneering schemes have demonstrated a variety of successful approaches to rescuing city and town centres from motor traffic domination. *Quality streets* (TEST, 1988) and *New life for city centres* (Hass-Klau, 1988) contain useful surveys of such schemes. Traffic calming adaptations to residential streets reallocate road space from motorist priority to pedestrian and cyclist priority, relying on self-enforcing street design and engineering measures to eliminate rat-running and reduce speeds to safe levels below 30 km/h (15 mph) (Tolley, 1990).

But in the United Kingdom, road programmes still concentrate on building expensive road space to accommodate ever-increasing levels of motor traffic, with pedestrian safety an afterthought, and pedestrian access still further behind. The reduction in the quality of the walking environment which this causes is shown by the problems which, according to a

Table 6.1 Main problems for pedestrians (prompted and unprompted) in the National Consumer Council's survey

	Total	Sex		Age					Socio-economic group			
		men	women	16–24	25–34	35–54	55–64	65+	AB	C1	C2	DE
Base (weighted)	2,034	967	1,067	403	358	599	285	389	349	453	629	603
Problem:	%	%	%	%	%	%	%	%	%	%	%	%
cracked or uneven pavements	**46**	39	52	38	44	43	53	54	40	44	46	51
dog dirt	**42**	39	44	32	43	40	45	50	42	40	41	43
too much traffic/busy roads	**37**	35	39	35	36	39	35	40	42	38	34	37
uncleared snow/ice/leaves	**32**	31	32	33	32	30	33	31	30	32	32	31
vehicles parked on pavements	**24**	21	26	20	24	22	26	27	16	26	25	25
no pedestrian crossing	**23**	23	23	25	26	24	17	20	22	24	22	24
bicycles ridden on pavements	**19**	19	20	15	17	17	21	29	17	18	19	23
litter/uncleared rubbish	**17**	17	17	12	13	19	21	21	18	19	15	18
pavements dug up/ being repaired	**13**	12	14	13	14	13	14	13	15	12	11	16
poor/broken street lighting	**13**	12	13	16	15	13	10	8	12	10	15	12
narrow pavements	**11**	11	12	11	14	11	11	11	16	11	10	11
overhanging trees/hedges	**11**	9	13	8	8	12	16	14	15	10	10	12
too little time at pelicans	**10**	8	12	6	10	10	11	15	8	12	9	12
no pavements	**7**	8	6	6	7	9	7	5	10	6	7	6
weeds/overgrown hedges	**6**	6	6	5	4	6	7	9	8	6	5	6
no street lighting	**6**	6	6	8	9	6	6	2	5	5	7	7
kerbs too high	**5**	5	5	7	5	4	3	7	4	5	5	7
obstructions on pavements	**4**	5	4	4	3	5	5	5	4	5	4	6
need to use over/under passes	**3**	3	3	3	3	4	3	3	3	3	3	4
other	**17**	17	16	15	18	17	19	15	20	19	15	15
D/K	**2**	3	2	2	2	3	1	3	3	2	2	3
none—no problems	**6**	8	5	8	4	7	5	7	7	5	7	7

Source: National Consumer Council, 1987.

National Consumer Council survey (reproduced as Table 6.1), affect 96 per cent of pedestrians.

To change this situation requires rethinking several conventional assumptions. This chapter will elaborate on six which are particularly problematic. They are: elasticity of travel demand; the assumption that 'road user' means 'motorist'; 'normal' accessibility standards; approaches to safety; rational location of facilities; and consulting the 'experts'.

How much motor traffic can we cater for?

The key criterion in planning for pedestrians must be improving access, to which both safety and environmental conditions contribute (Myerscough, 1975). At present the built environment is so dominated by motor traffic that much of what needs to be done to benefit pedestrians and people at large requires restraining traffic – not seeking to ban it, for cars and lorries have essential uses at times, but changing the terms of the relationship so that pedestrian and cyclist do not suffer curbs on mobility and risk of injury in order not to interfere with either mobility or risk for motorists. At present the relationship, in terms of both risk and mobility, is unfairly imbalanced in favour of the might of the speeding tonne of metal on the one hand, whatever the rights or wrongs of the tens of kilos of flesh on the other. The terms 'risk' and 'mobility' require emphasis here because the interdepartmental review *Road safety: the next steps* (Department of Transport, 1987a) called for safety policy to achieve a balance between them (see also Department of Transport, 1987b).

In the government's own terms, then, the case can be made for restraint of motor traffic in favour of pedestrian mobility and safety. Restraining traffic *speeds* is necessary to improve safety for the 'vulnerable road user', the pedestrian or cyclist. Restraining traffic *volume* will reduce the environmental burden of pollution, the nuisance of noise and the expense of land-take for roads and parking, which are in competition with other uses of public open space. Moreover, reduced traffic levels can (but do not automatically) improve safety. Such reductions need to be accompanied by self-enforcing street engineering measures (chicanes, junction narrowing, speed humps, etc.) to make it impossible for the careless or frustrated motorist to continue in his or her reckless habits.

Despite evidence from Buchanan (1963) to Mogridge (1985, 1989) that it is not feasible to build enough road space to accommodate car traffic demands, planners from central and local government have shrunk from the need to manage traffic demand, whether by such 'carrots' as encouraging modal transfer, or encouraging rational siting of facilities to reduce travel distances, or by the 'stick' of road closures, rationing of parking space, and even road pricing.

The manifest demand for travel shows strong elasticity – it can increase rapidly to fill extra road space made available, as shown by the case of the instant congestion on the newly built M25 around London. The converse implication, that demand could (and should) equally be managed to per-suade it to shrink to more manageable dimensions, has hardly been tested in this country. But overseas, traffic calming schemes such as that in Copenhagen (TEST, 1988) have produced reductions in motor demand, as has Oxford's Park and Ride scheme.

As elected bodies, councils and ministers look to 'political will', that is, a balance between protest and support, in deciding the terms of the debate and their priorities for the resources they administer. Inertia, the force of precedent which is the product of habitual thinking and practice, keeps the status quo coasting along until forcibly derailed. It is thus vital that pressure groups such as Transport 2000, as well as sympathetic academics, planners and activists, continue to highlight the success of schemes on the continent as well as the relatively few ambitious examples in the United Kingdom in order to show what has been done to tackle various conditions, how schemes have worked, and how popular the changes in user priority have proven.

The pedestrian as majority road user

As Hillman and Whalley (1980) have pointed out, most of the journeys people make are short and most short journeys are on foot. Pedestrians may be endangered, but are not a minority. Almost 100 per cent of the population walk, even if just from parking place, rail station or bus stop to destination. Many local journeys are thought of not as travel but as 'just popping out', part of the fabric of normal life. It is a truism that in busy shopping streets, and in residential areas, pedestrian activity can be expected to outnumber motor vehicle activity, i.e. pedestrians are the majority road users.

Yet the design and layout of most residential and shopping streets still give dominance to motor traffic – the assumptions remain that roads are for cars, pedestrians belong on footpaths, and, of course, pedestrians must give way to cars. (Do many motorists even *know* that Item 65 of the Highway Code gives pedestrians legal right of way over turning traffic?)

Statements that roads have multiple uses (such as by Buchanan (1963)) are given lip-service by government and planners. But pedestrian move-ments or activities are not routinely counted, nor does road planning cater for them unless pedestrians pose a problem as casualty statistics or by interfering with motor traffic. That motor traffic routinely poses problems for pedestrian access is so pervasive it is ignored – pedestrians learn to expect to have to wait for traffic, to be directed towards inconvenient detours or intimidating underpasses in order to cross busy roads, and become resigned to giving up desired trips as too difficult or dangerous to tackle on foot.

Traffic calming measures – which do not exclude traffic, but are designed to moderate speeds, enrich the visual environment and encourage pedestrians (and cyclists) as the main users of the area – need to become common practice in Britain before the myriad potential uses of streets, which are in many areas the only public open space, become safely and enjoyably possible (Tolley, 1990). Appleyard's (1978) work in San Francisco shows the loss in neighbourhood activity and people's alienation from local streetscape as traffic levels increase.

'Normal' accessibility and mobility handicap

How do we, in the present context, define 'normal'? 'Normal' would seem to mean an able-bodied, unencumbered person with good eyesight and hearing, paying undistracted attention. That definition excludes children under 12 (perceptual studies suggest they cannot adequately judge traffic risks) and many people over 50 (normal ageing effects include loss of hearing and visual acuity, slower reactions and less agility). Too bad if your leg is in a plaster cast (perhaps as a result of a motor vehicle impact?) or you are carrying a suitcase or heavy box or shopping bags. 'Wheeled pedestrians' in wheelchairs, or pushing baby buggies or shopping carts are even more affected by difficulties of access that inconvenience all pedestrians.

In effect it is those who are most dependent on walking and least likely to have access to their own car – such as the elderly, children and women – who are disproportionately affected by the unnecessarily demanding standards of 'normal' accessibility that are assumed (Hanna, 1988). Moreover, the Disabled People's Transport Advisory Committee estimates that one in seven of the population at any time will be suffering some form of mobility handicap (DPTAC, 1988). Yet as John Mitchell of the National Consumer Council has pointed out, barriers are designed into new construction when it would be just as cheap and often simpler to design for the absence of barriers to mobility (Mitchell, 1988). After all, who actually needs a step down into a railway station lavatory? Likewise, using maintenance and renovation programmes to upgrade design towards increased accessibility should achieve much-needed improvements at minimum cost and labour.

As walking conditions improve, walking and cycling may be expected to increase, an elasticity of demand cheaper to cater for than that of the motor car and less environmentally damaging too. The improvements called for in Transport 2000's 'Feet First' campaign may, for an old person or wheelchair user, make the difference between being housebound and dependent or being able to live independently. For a parent, they mean the difference between not daring to let a child out alone and that child being able to play outside or run or cycle alone to and from school, sport and friends' homes.

Safety

In the context of transport, safety is normally looked at in terms of casualties caused by vehicles striking people. The problem is seen as the people who are injured, and the desired solution is to eliminate such incidents. There are two underbellies to this notion of safety. The first is, as John Adams (1985, 1988) and Frank West-Oram (1989) have pointed out, that casualty statistics do not measure how safe people feel, or the risks they run, but only record reported consequences of misjudgements. Since not all injuries are reported, and recording categories are unreliable, the statistics are an unreliable record even of those. In particular, they provide no record of risk deterrence: journeys forgone because, for instance, crossing London's Archway Road has become too dangerous a venture. In turn such deterrence of pedestrian trips generates new journeys, sometimes motorised, such as the continuing increase in women's journeys escorting others, many of these trips to drop off children at school.

If conditions become safer and people consume the safety benefit in extra trips (i.e. extra exposure), paradoxically casualties may increase, giving a statistical picture that suggests less safety. Measures of exposure against casualty rates are needed. Also needed are perception studies of how safe people feel, how much they feel in control of the risks their local environment poses, and (given that total elimination of risks is impossible and perhaps undesirable) what levels of risk are acceptable.

The second major aspect of pedestrian safety is public street safety, that is, the risk of assault by other people, for not all pedestrians are 'good guys'. Initial key considerations are such environmental requirements as good lighting, clear sight-lines (i.e. no dark hiding places for muggers), and good maintenance. Encouraging safe levels of activity both deters anti-social behaviour and offers the reassurance of help at hand if hassled.

From this point of view, there must be some reservations about segregating motor traffic from pedestrians, for its presence can contribute to a safe activity level, especially during the evenings and weekends. Encouraging residential provision in city centres and the opening of restaurants, pubs, cafés, theatres and other night life is helpful in keeping shopping or office areas alive after dark. Location and layout of public transport stops also need attention, such as having all bus services concentrated in a small well-lit area at quiet times, rather than spread around a vast, dark bus station.

This aspect of street safety is particularly vital for women and the elderly, who feel especially vulnerable to attack. A 1989 MORI survey found that 90 per cent of women interviewed were afraid to go out on their own at night and 70 per cent avoided going out alone after dark unless absolutely necessary. So much forgone activity may well be a more meaningful measure of street safety than the relatively low incidence of actual attacks. Nor is this a problem only for women, for men also feel intimidated by dark, deserted streets prowled by the occasional, possibly predatory, male, and say they find the presence of people, particularly women, reassuring.

Rational location of facilities

The evidence for elasticity in demand for travel has already been noted. Many trips are inessential and often the journey purpose could be achieved by substituting a closer destination, thus making the use of a green mode of transport more likely. When people are asked what makes a 'good neighbourhood', having facilities within walking distance emerges as a key indicator of local quality of life.

Travel is not necessarily a benefit; it is equally a cost, in time and energy. The benefit is access, rather than mobility, that is, the ease of reaching a destination, not the amount of travel. The less distance and time required to do so, the better. The Department of Transport's COBA (cost benefit analysis) road-building model partially recognises this by its emphasis on the need to speed traffic flows to save motorists' time. From the pedestrians' perspective, given that an individual's walking pace is fairly constant, time savings are achieved by minimising distances to be travelled. It follows that it is the rational location of facilities that is the environmentally sound, minimalist solution. When such services as hospitals, schools and shops are 'rationalised' into larger, centralised units with reduced running costs, the costs of increased travel borne by the users is seldom taken into account. In locating facilities there are thus two potential losses in forgone but desired, or in generated but unnecessary, journeys.

Consulting the experts

There are two kinds of expert, both of whom need to be involved from the earliest stages. On the one hand, there are those conversant with the technical options for analysing transport problems and with the range of engineering or regulatory measures which may be applied. On the other hand, there are those familiar with the particular area under consideration, its patterns of use and problems of access, environment and so on – that is, the residents, office- or shop-workers, visitors and other users. Different segments of the community perceive different, even incompatible, needs. A successful scheme needs to realise and address, even if it cannot fully satisfy, the range of concerns.

Nor should consultation stop once an initial design has been selected. Ongoing monitoring and evaluation of the effects of the changes is desirable in order to prove the benefits, or to correct any problems that emerge. The more local the involvement, the more acceptable the scheme: not only is it likely to be technically better because of better identification of the problems and needs involved, but residents who have been involved in consultation feel more personal investment in the changes, in addition to understanding what is being done and why.

Conclusion

At present transport planning is driven by the problem of meeting the increasing demand for expensive and environmentally damaging motor transport. The green modes, being less expensive and damaging to cater for, have presented a less politically problematic profile. If an environmentally and socially sound transport policy is to be achieved, conventional assumptions about 'the problem' transport policy should address, and the terms in which the debate is conducted, must be changed along the lines indicated in this chapter. This is every bit as important as implementing road design and engineering standards that meet the needs of pedestrians and cyclists.

References

Adams, J., 1985, *Risk and freedom: the record of road safety regulation*, Transport Publishing Projects, Cardiff.
—— 1988, 'How safe?', *Transport Retort*, **11**, 2, August.
Appleyard, D., 1978, *Liveable streets*, University of California Press, San Francisco.
Buchanan, C., 1963, *Traffic in towns*, Penguin, London.
Department of Transport, 1987a, *Road safety: the next steps*, consultation paper, HMSO, London.
—— 1987b, *Road safety: the detailed review*, HMSO, London.
—— 1987c, *Measures to control traffic for the benefit of residents, pedestrians and cyclists*, Traffic Advisory Unit leaflet 1/87, London.
Disabled People's Transport Advisory Committee (DPTAC), 1988, *Finance for extra markets for public transport*, D.Tp., London.
Hanna, J., 1988, 'Equal opportunity travel', *Transport Retort*, **10**, 10, Jan./Feb.
Hass-Klau, C. (ed.), 1988, *New life for city centres: planning, transport and conservation in British and German cities*, Anglo-German Foundation, London.
Hillman, M. and Whalley, A., 1980, *Walking is transport*, Policy Studies Institute, London.
Griffiths, J., 1989, 'Pedestrian planning in Hertfordshire', in *Transport and the pedestrian*, Transport 2000/City University, London.
Institute of Highways and Transportation (IHT), 1989, *Guidelines for pedestrian areas*, London.

Mitchell, J., 1988, 'The invisible pedestrian', in *Positive steps forward*, Institution of Civil Engineers, London.

Mogridge, M., 1985, *Jam yesterday, jam today and jam tomorrow*, University College London, London.

—— 1989, *Interaction between road and public transport policy in urban areas*, Rees Jeffreys discussion paper, Transport Studies Unit, Oxford.

Myerscough, C. (ed.), 1975, *Feet first: a pedestrian survival handbook*, Wolfe for Pedestrian's Association, London.

National Consumer Council, 1987, *What's wrong with WALKING?*, HMSO, London.

Rigby, J., 1989, 'The footstreets scheme in the city of York', in *Transport and the pedestrian*, Transport 2000/City University, London.

Swann, P., 1989, 'A better pedestrian environment', in *Transport and the pedestrian*, Transport 2000/City University, London.

TEST, 1981, *Pedestrian precincts in Britain*, TEST, London.

—— 1988, *Quality streets: how traditional urban centres benefit from traffic-calming*, TEST, London.

Tolley, R.S., 1990, *Calming traffic in residential areas*, Brefi Press, Tregaron.

Transport 2000, 1988, *Feet first: the case for a campaign*, Transport 2000, London.

West-Oram, F., 1989, *Green mode travel safety: the real facts*, paper presented to the Institute of British Geographers' Transport Geography Study Group conference on 'planning for the green modes: walking and cycling', Coventry Polytechnic, January.

7 The pedestrian town as an environmentally tolerable alternative to motorised travel

Otto Ullrich

Motorised travel as systems technology

When the theme of 'the car and the environment' is discussed, as a rule the examination is limited to the technical end-product, the car. The car is categorised as an isolated consumer article whose effects are seen as limited to traffic and depend principally on the user. As far as problematical consequences for the environment are concerned, only a few vehicle-specific emissions come to prominence: the 'standard' air pollution and noise, together with passing references to emissions into water and the earth. Accordingly, as long as this remains the dominant view, the measures for protection of the environment will be restricted to possible improvements in vehicle technology, complemented by suggestions for expansion in road construction.

In industrialised countries, however, the car is not a normal consumer article with a typical market economy cycle from manufacture, sale, usage, to waste management. Today, very extensive and powerful service and user infrastructures are associated with the car. This 'system of motorisation' embraces the car industry; an unknown number of suppliers from the chemical and metal industries; the oil industry; roads suitable for cars; the road construction economy; the filling station network; repair operations; accident hospitals; traffic police; traffic courts; insurance; car lobby associations; car scrap dealers; car graveyards and so on. Thus motorised individual transport is actually an infrastructure-forming system and hence consideration of the theme requires an examination of the whole motorised transport system and its consequences for the environment. It follows that in this discussion about environmentally tolerable traffic not only must improvements of details within the car system itself be examined, but also an alternative system to motorisation.

Environmental pollution: effects and limits

Detrimental effects of the motor vehicle system

A suitable starting point is the need for a comprehensive stocktaking of the detrimental effects of the motorised system, for the measures and alternatives which are taken depend upon an adequate perception of the problem. At present, traffic-produced pollution tends to be played down: for example, CO_2 is still scarcely discussed as a pollutant from vehicles, although changes to the earth's climate have been known for many years to result from massive burning of fossil fuels. Similarly, the space-destroying effects of car traffic systems are rarely discussed publicly. As this chapter concentrates on suggestions for environmentally tolerable traffic in towns, the most important groups of producers of damage in the system of mass motorisation will be summarised.

The most scandalous effect of pollution by motorised individual transport (MIT) is the killing and maiming of people on a warlike scale. In the Federal Republic of Germany since the Second World War about half a million people have been killed on the roads. In the last ten years alone, about 1.6 million people have been seriously injured in traffic accidents, usually resulting in lifelong disablement. In the same period, 15 000 children under 15 died because of the car in West Germany. Presumably it will remain a puzzle to later generations how a society could come to terms with a technology which demands human sacrifice in such vast numbers. It would be contemptuous or perverse to categorise a transport technology as environmentally friendly if it did not fare considerably better than this in terms of injury causation.

Likewise, high rates of mortality amongst animals have been caused by MIT. In the Federal Republic many millions of animals are killed by being run over: indeed, for many individual species such as the barn owl, death from cars is a prime cause. Further, because of the isolation of biospheres, whole species of animals are threatened with extinction. Through indirect effects, such as forest dieback or oil pollution in seas and water bodies, an unknown number of animals are dying and their death is increasingly attributable to motorised traffic.

A detrimental effect of mass individual motoring that has long been played down (and one also caused by planes and fast trains) is noise pollution in towns, villages and whole areas. The health of a very high percentage of the population is impaired by it, insidiously but permanently, an effect which is now being researched thoroughly for the first time. It can be argued that the present position of traffic noise in West Germany is not just unacceptable, but in fact constitutes a noise crisis (for a comparison with the international position, see Ullrich, 1987).

Motorised traffic produces about half of the 'classical' pollution. In addition, CO_2 must also be considered as a pollutant. Moreover, the large amount of hydrocarbons emitted from motorised vehicles cause particular concern for human health. The long-term effects of these are not sufficiently researched: for some there is no acceptable threshold for they can be carcinogenic in the smallest doses. As an example, Benzole (Benzypren) has been identified as a toxic substance with fatal effects, but it nevertheless streams out of the exhausts of motorised vehicles at a rate of over 50 000 tonnes per annum in West Germany (for source material and for a further development of this theme, see Holzapfel, Traube and Ullrich, 1988). What dangers lurk in lead substitutes and in other additives to fuels and motor oils is, to date, unknown.

The massacre of the land through avalanches of industrial pollutants, though extremely threatening, is only slowly coming to public consciousness in West Germany, because the effects are not directly experienced and also because there is a considerable backlog of research efforts, for instance through the Federal Environment Office. The number and quantity of pollutants that are transmitted from motorised vehicles into the ground and water is tremendous: each year in West Germany, for example, 100 000 tonnes of synthetic fine dust are created by tyre-rub, about 1.5 million tonnes of road salt are distributed, and one millimetre of the surface is rubbed off from the entire road network. Millions of leaking installations and consumption processes emit asbestos, organic substances, BSB5, CSB, grease, oils, phosphate, nitrite, nitrate, rubber, lead, chrome, copper, nickel, zinc, cadmium, etc. The emission of many of these substances should be immediately and completely banned.

One very dramatic type of pollution of the environment is the detrimental effect of motorised individual transport (MIT) on space: it is, for example, the greatest consumer of the countryside in the Federal Republic. MIT claims extensive areas to facilitate easy and flowing traffic, makes town planning more difficult, gives rise to 'road landscapes', and complicates the organisation of space. It needs to be understood that car-justified investments brutally destroy towns and landscapes, making them unpleasant to live in and indescribably ugly. Moreover, adjoining areas suffer an unreasonable loss of function through MIT.

Finally, it must not be forgotten that the motor transport system gobbles up about half of the Federal Republic's oil imports. That is not only extremely irresponsible towards future generations but also a great environmental threat, because about half of the pollution caused by the mineral oil industry (e.g. sea pollution by tanker accidents and spillages, drilling-rig leaks and accidents, etc.) is attributable to motorised traffic.

The violation of basic rights by traffic

There is no other single technological system which produces such dramatic damage in so many dimensions as motorisation. Naturally, there are some advantages. The car makes it possible to go anywhere at effortless speed, protected from the weather at all times. It lengthens the operating radius for reconnaissance, contact and relaxation. It transports and protects goods which have been bought and prevents the female traveller from being annoyed by men. It provides compensation for those lacking in confidence by strengthening their technical ability, demonstrating superiority and improving status. It stabilises economic structures by uniting national economic resources and it gives the state an ideal means of taxation for road building. The characteristics of MIT, such as confidence in progress, economic freedom, product decay and its role as a technically coagulating symbol of the industrial dynamic, produce an extremely convenient dream-child for the industrial and capitalist economy and consumer society (See Sachs, 1984).

At this stage it is necessary to scrutinise MIT and compare it with that of alternative transport systems. Just as for other technical systems in which society has become blindly involved – for instance, in the realms of energy, industrialized agriculture or synthetic chemistry – it is essential to do this in order to be able to decide politically on the appropriate solutions. This could range from an improvement of the technical system, a completion of its development, a reorganisation, a partial reduction of commitment, or an abandonment of the technology in question.

In the technological system of motorisation there is a whole range of detrimental effects which are not capable of compromise and therefore cannot be erased by any positive effects. Constitutional status must be conceded to such natural sources of relief as the right to undisturbed sleep, clean water and pure air, for such bases of human existence are under the special protection of state authority. Thus with the establishment of the Federal Office for the Environment in 1973 in Germany the minister responsible at that time formulated the model for environmental protection as a constitutional brief for the protection of the dignity of man. Only in this way can the difficult exercise of defining anew the safeguarding and structuring of the environment as the main focus of state trade be achieved (Genscher, 1973, p. 306).

Limits of tolerance

Any adoption of newly defined environmental goals for decent living must produce a fundamental new direction for transport policy. In the first instance, the desires for expansion of the motor world would no longer have priority over the tolerable thresholds of stress endured by man and nature. Thus for the fundamental right of undisturbed sleep and clean air there are medically supported levels which should not be exceeded, such as the night-time threshold value of 25–30 decibels for noise in populated areas. It should be noted that there is a considerable difference between the environmental impacts of traffic requirements and those that result from meeting the mobility needs of people.

Defining what might be called 'limits of tolerance' here could establish broad outlines for more person- and environmentally tolerable urban traffic policy, as pioneered by the German Institute for Urban Studies in Berlin (DIFU) (See Apel and Brandt, 1982). According to road types – whether in populated areas or business districts – there is a need to indicate critical levels of pollution and frontiers of reasonableness for such variables as noise emission, air pollution, ground pollution, land-take, and for separate effects such as ease of crossing for pedestrians, safety and suppressing of social functions of the road.

There is a need, too, to establish by how many vehicles a street can be burdened per hour and how fast these vehicles may travel. Because of the present density of vehicles in the town and the speed at which they travel, it is evident that there is a need to reduce to a fraction not only the number of cars, but also their maximum speed. In effect, at least in the most densely populated areas, the system of individual mass motorisation must be replaced by different traffic concepts and systems, because reasonable thresholds of pollution cannot be attained by improvements to the car system alone.

Perspectives on an environmentally tolerable traffic policy in towns

Limits to technical improvements to vehicles

One can see the inadequacy of possible technical improvements to motor vehicles by calculating, for each of the known causes of pollution, the rate of reduction which is technically possible. Thus the most effective environmental protection technique against emission from petrol engines is the catalytic converter and, if all cars were equipped with it, the emission from this class of vehicle for classic pollution would be reduced by some 60–80 per cent. However, even just for air pollution from motorised vehicles this would still be far from an environmentally tolerable solution, for the reduced level of air pollution when multiplied by the many millions of cars would still in total be much too great. For example, there would still be at least 200 000 tonnes of nitric oxide emitted from motor vehicles per year in the Federal Republic. Moreover, the damaging CO_2 discharge and use of oxygen by motor vehicles would still remain with the installation of a catalytic converter, whilst for the diesel vehicle there is still no satisfactory and practicable way of preventing the emission of soot.

Even if the building of a car system which emitted no pollution were to succeed, the other pollutants produced by mass motorisation would more or less remain. As for noise, the sound of tyres even at low speeds sets clear barriers of technical feasibility, while as far as space-consumption issues are concerned, technical improvements in vehicles (making them very small and slow) offer no prospect of solution because of the huge number involved. With regard to emissions into water and the earth, even very expensively insulated vehicles – producing from their various sources the lowest feasible level of emissions – would still release an unacceptable stream of pollutants, only to be multiplied by the millions of vehicles. In addition there are the emissions from wear and tear and friction, not to mention the great piles of wrecked cars. Thus, in terms of acceptable levels of pollution, almost all the possible technical improvements to the individual vehicle are counteracted by the mass effect.

To responsible practitioners of town planning and urban policy it has been clear for many years that a so-called environmentally friendly car as a mass means of transport in the town has no future. Thus, for instance, the internationally experienced town planner Dietrich Garbrecht summarises:

Years ago we believed it was possible to rebuild towns in such a way that they were appropriate to man and vehicles. Now we must state precisely the incompatibility of what is right for car and man: even when car traffic is appreciably reduced, parked cars remain continually incompatible to playing children, cars parked on pavements restrict passers-by, and they restrict standing around and sitting around. Clearly it is impossible to so organise a town that it is satisfactory to men and to the immoderately driven car at the same time. Clearly also, a town cannot be so equipped that it will be appropriate to men and parked cars. The number of cars must be reduced! (Garbrecht, 1981, p.184)

As early as 1970, the lord mayor of the car-ruined Munich stated that 'every billion that is put into road construction in a town leads it nearer to its death' (Vogel, 1972). He considered the present flood of cars so menacing that he did not shy away from radical political consequences, at least verbally: 'I consider the deification of cars, and the fact that the rate of increase of the automobile industry here is virtually taboo, as a cancer in our community. Where production is harmful it must be forbidden with the powers at the disposal of this society, and that means legislation.'

The basis for the creation of a system of environmentally tolerable traffic may be simply outlined. First, the fact that direct use of the feet would be the most important means of locomotion – about half the population in everyday life relies on walking – must be acknowledged and supported through appropriate measures. Second, conditions for the indirect use of feet should be improved by realising the potential for the use of the cycle. Only in third place would public transport be discussed as an alternative to the car and even then only as an intensive, integrated concept which is orientated towards supporting the pedestrian and cyclist. This integrated urban transport system of pedestrian ways, a cycle network and public transport would be so designed that it would not increase motorised traffic but supersede it. The key headings therefore for a person- and nature-tolerable urban transport system are the pedestrian town, the cycle infrastructure and public transport. For the transition period, measures must be taken for the speediest possible easing of the pollution effect of motorised individual transport through the reduction of maximum speed and the creation of areas of traffic calming. Additionally there must be measures enacted for a well-ordered exit from motorisation, such as the management of car parking and the internalisation of external costs of car usage.

Pedestrian town

There is a great deal to be said for the fact that master builders and planners of old towns

were better sociologists, psychologists and economists than those who take the decisions nowadays. The town was understood as an entity, psychologically and physically, individually and socially. This was expressed in the local and temporal mixing of social functions and in planning of the use of an area which subordinated private activities to the safety and well being of the town. Much points to a planning maxim of decentralisation as much as possible and concentration as much as is needed. (Heinze and Drutschmann, 1977, p.58)

The pedestrianised town can be seen as the ideal model of an urban traffic system which retains human dignity and is tolerable to nature. Through this the best conditions are created for people to live in close proximity and for the marking of the identity of a place, which is one of the conditions by which a dwelling place can be turned into a home (Mitscherlich, 1965). Above all other means of transport, feet are the ones which cause the least damage to the environment.

The planners and builders of the modern town adopted quite different principles of use of space. Starting from the new opportunities offered by mechanised transport driven by fossil energy, for them the spatial functioning of living, working, shopping and leisure became the ideal planning principles of a town. The dominant formations of the modern town became concentration, a preference for large developments, a hierarchical arrangement of spaces, a preference for the far rather than the near, and a removal of service installations from the proximity of living accommodation. In addition, on the basis of privatisation of original common property, came reckless land speculation benefitting profiteering economic interests. Finally there was the ruining of the towns by car traffic.

More recently, a more careful but far-reaching learning process has been taken up by a series of town planners, architects, traffic engineers and politicians, who are striving to find human standards again through a new orientation of urban and traffic policy. They have abandoned the planning of monstrous hospitals, schools, offices, etc. by recognising that there are socially critical sizes for buildings and developments which should not be exceeded. They are committed to cautious redevelopment and the evolution of coherent living arrangements, in place of the 'planning by clearance' previously felt to be progressive. In order to avoid motorised traffic as much as possible, they demand neighbourhood quality, easy access to important buildings, and carefully planned districts with a variety of functions. Thus there is now a plethora of publications, plans, initiatives, experiments and redevelopments, which collectively attempt to mitigate past urban development sins, particularly of the period up to the 1970s. For some town and traffic planners the pedestrian town is again becoming an important model, producing a habitat which is more worthy of people and more tolerable to the environment (see Peters, 1977).

In order to win back a pedestrian town, the most appropriate starting point is a new distribution of space, a reinstatement of areas. As a result of the extremely high space needs of individual motorised traffic, claimants to the use of public urban space such as pedestrians, cyclists and others are literally up against the wall. These unbearable conditions have been created through an insidious process of addiction to car-preferential policy. Indeed, 'if the present day measure of disadvantage to pedestrians and cyclists had arisen in one blow, people would scarcely have let it happen' (Monheim, 1979).

It is estimated that with an average occupancy of 1.4 people, the space needs of a car are around 11 m^2 when parked and 169 m^2 at a speed of 50 km/h. The average living space of citizens of West Germany is about 35m^2 and there is about 0.5 m^2 of public open space per head. So the burden on space from motor vehicles is extremely high. In larger towns in 1971 it was between 10 and 20 million vehicle km/km^2 per year with local concentrations of more than 250 million vehicle km/km^2 per year.

The demand on space made by traffic installations amounts to 25 per cent of inhabited areas and even as much as 60 per cent of the total area in heavily built-up districts. As the traffic area can in no way be expanded, a reallocation of space to pedestrians, cyclists, residents, plants, animals, and public transport systems can thus only be carried out at the expense of the traffic areas which are now mainly used by vehicles.

The new distribution of user rights and claims on the space for traffic in urban regions should be based on the following principles. First, the area needed by roadside trees must be set aside and kept clear from access by traffic and pedestrians. For free-standing rooted trees, bands 2.5–4.5 metres wide are needed, depending on variety. As a guiding principle, about one-third of the present traffic areas in town should be reinstated with trees and green areas. By this means the quality of life of the towns would be noticeably improved.

About half of the remaining traffic area must be at the disposal of pedestrians. Footpaths should be four metres wide at least, though they would be more adequate at five or six metres. The other half of the remaining traffic area must be shared by moving traffic, cyclists, trams, buses, public service vehicles and those few cars (principally taxis) that would still be tolerated. On safety grounds vehicles must be restricted to a maximum of 20–30 km/h, at which speed bicycle and motor traffic can be mixed if there is not room for a separate cycle track.

Thus the areas available to motor traffic must in general be reduced by more than half. This needs to be done in order to recognise the rights of residents (in the sense of winning back the streets as living areas), whilst the number of vehicles must also be limited on account of the pollution criteria for noise, exhaust emissions, opportunities for pedestrians to cross roads and so on.

In order to complete the reinstatement of areas for non-motorised travel and the creation of a pedestrian town fit for people, a coherent network of paths for pedestrians is important. Such a network must not be interrupted by motor traffic and steps for under- and overpasses – especially escalators – are to be avoided because they are so pedestrian-unfriendly.

So that areas may be reinstated and the privileges of car traffic reduced, a fundamental reorientation of car park supply is vital. At present the huge number of parked cars curtails the rights of other users of the space. They impede children, pedestrians and cyclists and to a considerable extent they ruin the image of the town. Moreover, the most important prerequisite for the decision to make a car journey is the anticipated parking area at the destination. Therefore no parking spaces at all should be identified in, and in the vicinity of, the city core. Thus everyone will know with certainty that at the destination there will be no parking place and they will thus not undertake the journey there by car. At the same time, the traffic which is simply circulating in search of a parking space – which is around 25–40 per cent of workday car traffic in towns today – will disappear. It would mean a return to the old principle which prevailed before the introduction of the car, that no unmanned or unwomanned vehicle may be left around.

Increase in cycle usage

In order to emphasise the significance of cars, lovers of these vehicles use a means-orientated definition of mobility by equating it with vehicle kilometres. By this means it is maintained that with the spread of the car the mobility of people has also increased. However, this measure is unreasonable and misleading for the quantifying of mobility needs. Indeed, if one examines the only sensible definition of mobility – namely, the accessibility of specific destinations such as work, shopping, visiting friends, etc. – then it can be established, surprisingly, that mobility by means of the car has not increased but in urban areas has in fact, actually diminished.

The number of trips or changes of place per inhabitant per day varies in accordance with social particulars such as age, sex and work potential. For all destinations together, on average each inhabitant makes something over three trips on workdays and about three if weekends are included. These averages have not changed between 1960 and 1980 even in a period of intense increase in car traffic. The conclusion must be that in this period there has not been an increase in mobility, but a change of means of transport instead. The change has been to car journeys, principally from cycle and foot journeys, and from public transport to a lesser degree. Even the 'car availability' variable has little or no influence over frequency of journeys, and thus on real mobility (Apel and Ernst, 1980).

The problem of transportation is thus not the often-emphasized mobility of industrial society but car traffic. Therefore, as there has not been an increase in mobility but only a shift in choice of means of transport, then again a return to feet, the cycle and public transport could follow. Against this it could be objected that through reorganisation of the settlement structure in recent decades, journeys have become longer and thus pressure towards use of the car has been produced.

It is indeed true that many trips have lengthened as a result of the facets of modern planning that have already been mentioned, such as spatial differentiation of function and concentration of land uses. Because of cutbacks in public transport, for many the only option has become the use of the car. But in spite of this existing lengthening of journeys as a consequence of the restructuring of settlements (whose reorganisation to desirable forms of settlement again will cost much money and time), it cannot be overlooked that most of the trips undertaken by car are still very short. Thus, for example, three per cent of all journeys by car drivers are no greater than 500 metres! One-third of all car journeys are no further than three kilometres, one-half no more than five kilometres (which is still a feasible cycle journey), and around two-thirds of all car journeys are no more than 15 kilometres. These figures refer to the whole Federal Republic. In the towns the proportion of short journeys made by car is even greater.

Thus without any structural reorganisation of settlements (though depending on the number of paths), one could transfer at least half of the car journeys (considerably more in towns) to walking or cycling, without those affected being seriously restricted in their mobility. Thus the debate is not about mobility or essential car journeys but is about the comfort of some, an accustomed thoughtless, button-pressing comfort in moving, which some permit themselves at the expense of others. Research establishments such as Socialdata, the German Institute for Economic Research, and the Federal Office for the Environment have demonstrated great potential for the use of the cycle. In recent years, cycle usage has again increased, but for a real breakthrough for possible cycle usage as an everyday means of transport decisive improvements for the cyclist are lacking. The most important conditions for this have already been mentioned: they include the reduction of the maximum speed of motor vehicles to 30 km/h in the town as a whole and to walking pace in purely residential areas, reinstatement of areas to cyclists and considerable diminution of car traffic. Tempo 30 for the whole town (which recently has been demanded by the organisation of German town governments) would be the remaining most favourable immediate measure for the reduction of damage caused by motorised transport. The number of deaths among pedestrians in such schemes would be reduced by about two-thirds and that of sacrificed cyclists and motorists by at least one-third. Contrary to earlier assumptions and prejudices, even emissions of noise and exhaust have decreased considerably through Tempo 30, as the studies of the Federal Office for the Environment in the Tempo 30 test areas have shown (see the chapter by Döldissen and Draeger in this volume). At present cycle usage is, by a long way, the most important environmentally friendly means of locomotion, but it is endangered by motorised traffic in an intolerable fashion, as well as being obstructed to a degree that makes it virtually impossible at times.

Quite apart from improving the basic conditions for cycle usage, a determined renunciation of car-preferential traffic policy would create cycle infrastructure for the environmentally friendly city as in, for example, a coherent network of cycle tracks. In West Germany, the present separated cycle ways on pavements serve the interests of car drivers and not cyclists and pedestrians. Thief-proof and weather-proof parking places and a network of repair and service stations are needed. With these goals in mind detailed plans have been worked out over many years by cycle initiatives, the environment office and the German Cycle Club (ADFC). With existing small improvements in the cycle climate, cycle usage is increasing and through it car traffic is cut. This is shown by some pioneering West German towns but more especially, however, by Dutch and Scandinavian models, as shown by the thorough study by Apel (1984).

Public transport

If the known polluting effects of motorised individual transport (MIT) are compared with those of motorised public transport (MPT), then MPT comes out of it considerably better. Buses use space some 15 times more efficiently than cars, and trams use it at least 30 times better. Similarly in the case of many environmentally harmful emissions, the levels emitted from MPT are much more favourable than those from MIT, whilst comparing deaths and injuries shows the greater safety of public transport. In other words, as the external costs borne by the national economy are patently higher as a result of the use of the car than from the use of the bus, tram or train, then it should be accepted that the state, as administrator of general well-being, can only promote and support one system of transport: the integrated system of public transport, pedestrians and cycle usage. The fact that all federal governments so far have supported motorised individual transport simply demonstrates that up to now traffic policy has principally given way to the private interests of the strongest lobby in the state.

In the large towns, well-established local public transport systems exist but their usage is completely unsatisfactory. Since these towns built wider and faster roads for car drivers, they saw no necessity to change to public transport or use feet or cycle. The urban traffic planners who, in the main, were themselves car users, proceeded from the erroneous concept that only through the improved attractiveness of public transport could and should the car driver be urged to change. Now, however, the realization has become widespread that car drivers can only be moved to use environmentally more favourable means of transport if the measures begin to curtail their unauthorised privileges in the use of space.

In many respects the MPT system may still be improved, such as in organisation, co-ordination and especially in possible improvements in emission standards. The present-day widespread diesel bus is noisy and soot-producing. Trams are patently more favourable for passengers and the environment, but even they often need to be quietened. However, the tram, though favourable to traffic technology, has itself become a sacrifice to car-preferential policies, since it is argued that the streets must be kept free for cars. For lorries and goods transport in the towns, public systems ought to be tested, for amongst other things the present high levels of empty journeys could be reduced. Moreover, the concept of electric vehicles for delivery should be put to the test, such as for post and home deliveries.

In sum, systems of public transport are, for the environment, far more favourable than the mass of private cars. But, nevertheless, public motorised traffic generates emissions and pollution of many kinds. A policy for environmentally tolerable traffic in towns thus should ensure that the MPT system does not get out of hand and does not become a burden on urban mobility in the same way as individual motorised locomotion has done.

However, how far and how quickly a kinder traffic system to mankind and to the environment is implemented will depend probably on the political activity of those deleteriously affected by car traffic. Studies, concepts and scenarios of traffic-calmed futures are now in abundance, but the car lovers still rule the field and try to equate their interests with the general good. New political forums are essential, for these would not only be seen as further development of democratic discussion, but would also bring into the discussion an effective consideration of the interests and rights of children, young people, the unemployed, women, the elderly and future generations.

Summary

The burdens on ecology and health from motor traffic in the town have clearly been exceeded. No diminution of the detrimental effects of traffic can be expected from technical improvements to transport and road construction alone. A fundamental new direction in traffic policy is essential. Such an environmentally tolerable transport policy in the towns must in the first instance support and extend the direct use of the feet. Secondly, the conditions for the indirect use of the feet through the use of cycles must be improved. Only then, in third place, should public transport be discussed as an alternative to the car; moreover, it must be seen as an intensive, integrated concept which is orientated towards and supports walking and cycling. This integrated urban transport system of pedestrian ways, cycle networks and public transport should be so conceived that it does not complement motorised traffic but replaces it.

References

Apel, D. 1984, *Urban traffic planning: Part 3: Redistribution of urban personal transport, foreign and home experiences with urban tolerable traffic planning*, DIFU, Berlin.

—— and Brandt, E., 1982, *Town streets: environmental demands and structuring of roads. Urban traffic planning in DIFU*, Part 2, Berlin.

—— and Ernst, K., 1980, *Urban traffic planning: Part 1: Mobility bases for the development of urban personal transport*, DIFU, Berlin.

Garbrecht, D., 1981, *Walking: a plea for life in the town*, Beltz Verlag, Weinheim and Basel.

Genscher, H.D., 1973, 'Basic social constitutional rights for a healthy environment', *Bulletin*, 34, Press and Information Service of the Federal Government.

Heinze, G.W. and Drutschmann, H.-M., 1977, *Space, traffic and settlement as a system set out by the example of the medieval German town*, Vandenhoeck and Ruprecht, Göttingen.

Holzapfel, H., Traube, K. and Ullrich, O., 1988, (2nd ed) *Car traffic 2000: ways to an ecologically and socially tolerable road transport*, Verlag C.F. Müller, Karlsruhe.

Mitscherlich, A., 1965, *The inhospitability of our towns*, Suhrkam Verlag, Frankfurt.

Monheim, H., 1979, 'Outlines for an alternative town planning', in Duve, H. (ed.), *Traffic in a cul-de-sac*, Rowohlt Verlag, Reinbek.

Peters, P., 1977, *Pedestrian town: town planning and formation for the pedestrian*, Callwey Verlag, Munich.

Sachs, W., 1984, *Love for the car: a retrospective view in the history of our wishes*, Rowohlt Verlag, Reinbek.

Ullrich, O., 1987, *Influence of traffic-steered and traffic-controlled measures on the noise emission of motorised vehicles: measures for the promotion of noise 'mean' transport*, research report for the Federal Office for the Environment, Berlin.

Vogel, H., 1972, quoting Dollinger, H., *The total car society*, Carl Hanser Verlag, Munich.

PART 2
Strategies

8 Traffic and environmental policy in the Netherlands

Martin Kroon

Introduction

Never before in a Western European country has a government fallen over an environmental issue, let alone a question related to the reduction of car use. Yet on 2 May 1989 the seven-year-old Lubbers government, being a coalition of centre Christian Democrats and right-wing Liberals, split over the question of curtailing tax benefits for car commuters in the Netherlands. Surprisingly, it was not the Cabinet itself that split. After weeks of inter-ministerial negotiations, the Cabinet had finally reached agreement on a Dfl 650 (£200) million commuter tax reform that would create a funding basis for several environmental and public transport programmes. But the mere rumour of a tax reform caused great concern among the Liberal Party's members and representatives. So it was that just one of the great many projects under the new National Environmental Policy Plan 1990–1994 caused a political crisis for a largely successful coalition.

It is worthwhile examining what environmental problems and traffic policy concerns are at stake in the Netherlands, and which measures are being developed under environmental and traffic policy responsibilities. This contribution describes current policy developments in the Netherlands for the reduction of pollution due to motorised traffic.

Traffic and environment

In the Netherlands, transport and communication activities represent more than seven per cent of gross national product, even surpassing the agricultural sector in economic output. The negative effects of road transport activities mainly include accidents, congestion, air pollution and noise, waste, soil pollution by spilled fuels, energy consumption, and consumption of land, space and other resources for infrastructure and vehicle use. The non-internalised social costs of road transport probably amount to several per cent of the gross national product. Emissions from the transport sector represent a high share of overall man-made emissions, and a contribution which is increasing relative to that of other sectors.

Road traffic is the largest single source of air pollution and noise nuisance. More than six million motor vehicles travel a total of about 100 billion kilometres a year (1988), producing 723 000 tonnes of carbon monoxide (CO), 198 000 tonnes of hydrocarbons (HC), and 299 000 tonnes of nitrogen oxides (NOx). Its CO_2 output of 25 million tonnes represents over 15 per cent of the Netherlands' contribution to global warming. Furthermore, road traffic represents by far the largest source of environmental pollution in urban areas, not only for the compounds mentioned above but also for particulates, asbestos, SO_2, and noise nuisance. Table 8.1 shows the volume of air pollutants that are predominantly produced by road traffic in the Netherlands.

The effects of vehicle emissions can be distinguished between those concerning human health and those affecting the environment as a whole. Those affecting human health are:

— nuisance: noise, odour, haze and decrease in visibility due to mild smogs;
— irritation: of respiratory systems, eyes, skin, etc. by nitrogen oxides, surphur oxides, oxidants, particulates;
— toxic systematic action: carbon monoxide, lead compounds, certain hydrocarbons;
— mutagenic/carcinogenic action: particulates, asbestos and certain hydrocarbons (polycyclic aromatic hydrocarbons, dioxins, benzene).

Recently, hot and still weather in Mexico City, Athens and Barcelona has demonstrated the lethal effects of road traffic air pollution. High concentrations of these air pollutants are mainly found in urban areas and near busy motorways. High ozone concentrations due to transboundary pollution and domestic traffic emissions occurred several times in the Netherlands in the hot spring and summer of 1989.

Apart from the widespread ecological damage and general land-use effect, the long-term/long-range environment effects of road traffic may well be illustrated through its share in acidification and photochemical air pollution (ozone formation). In the Dutch situation, road traffic contributes substantially to both forms through its share of over 55 per cent of NOx emissions and of 45 per cent of HC emissions (Figure 8.1).

Acidification and photochemical oxidation are transboundary phenomena with strong damaging effects on nature, forests, agriculture and man-made goods such as monuments and archives. What goes up must come down: more than 50 per cent of acid deposition on Dutch soils and waters originates from abroad, and more than half of Dutch SO_2/NOx emissions is raining down on Scandinavia, Germany and over the North Sea.

Table 8.1 Emissions from road traffic in the Netherlands, in tonnes and as a percentage of emissions from all sources

	Tonnes (1970)	Tonnes (1988)	Per cent of all emissions
Lead	950	340	80
CO	1 360 000	723 000	70
NOx	134 000	299 000	<55
HC	200 000	198 000	45
Asbestos	n/a	480	35
Particles	n/a	36 000	20
CO_2	n/a	c.25 000 000	<15

Source: Netherlands Central Bureau of Statistics.

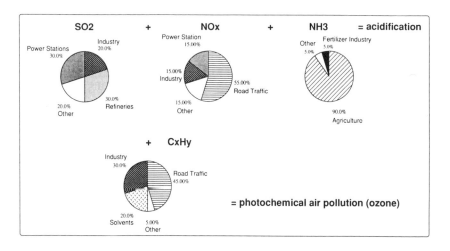

Figure 8.1 The contribution of road traffic to acidification and photochemical air pollution in the Netherlands

Today there is enough scientific evidence to show that both pine and deciduous forests in the Netherlands are among the most severely threatened by acidification in Europe. Despite its green and healthy image the Netherlands can be said to be the most heavily polluted country in Western Europe. The Netherlands is, in the industrialized world, number one in terms of population density and car density, energy consumption and conversion, and agricultural production (per km^2). Chemical waste and soil pollution scandals, the pollution of the River Rhine and large-scale air pollution in the Rotterdam area created considerable public awareness of environmental problems in the 1970s and early 1980s. More recently, 'acid rain' and the long-term consequences of global warming, such as rising sea levels, brought the environmental issue to the top of public interest and concern. Contemporaneously, the government's environmental policy shifted towards a more effect-oriented approach, resulting in stricter emission reductions goals and a solid scientific foundation for stricter products/process-emission standards.

The publication of *Our common future* (World Commission on Environment and Development, 1987) and the report *Concern for tomorrow* (National Institute of Public Health and Environment Protection, 1989) set the terms for a more fundamental discussion on the environment issue from a global and long-term perspective. Also the government itself initiated political discussions on the problems of traffic planning and environment and on far-reaching emission reductions (70–90 per cent) for acidifying substances. The time was ripe for the environment to become a cornerstone of public policy. On 25 May 1989 the Lubbers government issued the 'NMP', its National Environmental Policy Plan 1990–94 (Ministry of Housing, Physical Planning and Environment, 1989) which is a first step towards the implementation of 'sustainable development' between now and 2010 and the strategy for a new environmental policy in the 1990s. This plan will add more than six billion guilders (£1.9 billion) a year to the costs of environmental investments and expenditures.

New emission reduction targets and abatement policy

New and stricter reduction goals and abatement measures concerning acidification and all 'contributing' sources have been laid down in the NMP. Total acid depositions (averaging 5200 acid equivalents per hectare per annum are to be reduced in the long run to 400–700 equivalents in order to prevent any ecological damage. This implies emission reductions (for SO_2, NH_3, NOx and HC) of a magnitude of 70–90 per cent, which are goals that cannot be met by the year 2000. So a set of maximum achievable emission reduction targets has been laid down in the NMP for the year 2000, resulting in 50–80 per cent reductions compared to 1986 emissions (Table 8.2.) Together with parallel reductions of transboundary sources (especially from Germany) this may result in an average yearly deposition of 2400 equivalents in the year 2000. Sadly enough, this will only slow down the continued dying of Dutch forests and the continuation of other forms of damage. Eighty per cent of forests in the Netherlands will still be in danger.

Additional and stricter emission-reduction targets are to be expected under the new government coalition of Social Democrats and Christian

Table 8.2 Transport emission in the NMP (National Environmental Policy Plan, 1990–94) and percentage reductions over 1986

Emission	1986	1994	2000		2010	
NOx passenger cars, 000 tonnes pa	163	100	40	(−75%)	40 (−75%)	
NOx lorries, buses, 000 tonnes pa	122	110	72	(−35%)	25 (−75%)	
HC passenger cars, 000 tonnes pa	136	n/a	35	(−75%)	35 (−75%)	
HC lorries, buses, 000 tonnes pa	46	n/a	30	(−35%)	12 (−75%)	
CO2 total road traffic, 000 tonnes pa	24 000	24 000	24 000	(0)	21 600 (−10%)	
Noise, passenger cars[1]	80	n/a	74		70	
Noise, lorries/buses[1]	81−88	n/a	75−80		70	
Noise nuisance, serious[2]	260 000	190 000	130 000	(−50%)	n/a	
Noise nuisance to any degree[3]	2 000 000	1 900 000	1 800 000	(−10%)	1 000 000 (−50%)	

[1] target values for the maximum noise production of vehicles in dB(A)
[2] number of dwellings exposed to an unacceptably high noise level, reduced by 50 per cent in 2000 through measures at source and in the transmission zone
[3] dwellings subject to noise loading of more than 55 dB(A)

n/a not available

Source: Ministry of Housing, Physical Planning and Environment, 1989.

Democrats. In its first declaration the new government intended to bring out a supplementary plan in 1990 and expressed its intention to reduce total CO_2 emissions within four years by eight per cent, compared to the autonomous growth that would have been expected. For road traffic this might imply a ten per cent CO_2 reduction by 1994.

Other goals and objectives

The use of carcinogenic or other harmful substances in vehicles must be reduced by the year 2000 to a level where the risks are negligible, and the quantity of reusable materials must be raised to 85 per cent.

In terms of land use, further 'scatteration' in rural areas will be prevented. If new communication links are absolutely necessary, compensatory measures will be taken where possible so that, on balance, fragmentation does not increase. The problem of soil and air pollution at petrol stations will shortly result in legislation on new and existing facilities regarding sanitation, vapour-return, etc.

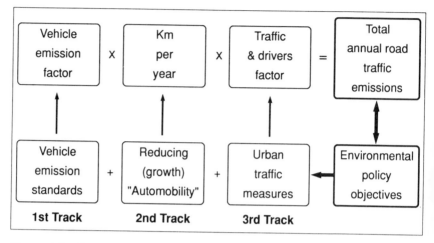

Figure 8.2 The three-track approach to the abatement of environmental pollution by motor vehicles

The policy conducted will be regularly checked to see whether it is effective. Calibration points are given for 1994 to see whether the reduction in the environmental impact in the period prior to 2000 is proceeding according to plan (Table 8.2). If the calibration point for 1994 is not achieved this will result in the timely preparation of supplementary policy.

Main abatement policy lines

Environment pollution by road traffic is produced in a three-step process, involving (1) the vehicle emission factor, (2) the 'automobility' volume factor, and (3) the traffic/driving behaviour factor. The Dutch environmental policy towards road traffic is set up along parallel lines as shown in Figure 8.2. Specifically, the objectives of the NMP for traffic and transport have been formulated as follows:

— vehicles must be as clean, quiet, economical and safe as possible, and made of parts and materials which are optimally suitable for refuse;
— the choice of mode for passenger transport must result in the lowest possible energy consumption and the least possible pollution. On the basis of anticipated technical developments this means a preference for public transport and bicycles for the coming decades. Great attention must also be paid to reducing energy consumption and environmental pollution in freight transport;
— the locations where people live, work, shop and spend their leisure time will be co-ordinated in such a way that the need to travel is minimal.

These objectives lead to a three-track approach to environmental pollution reduction, those of technical vehicle standards, reducing 'automobility' and instigating urban traffic measures.

Technical vehicle standards (the first track)

Target standards

The first track approach is followed throughout the world as a natural and effective means of reducing car pollution 'at source' through regulations limiting air pollution and noise per (new) vehicle. Step by step over a certain period of time, car makers have been persuaded to start research and produce cars – with electronic engine management and catalytic converters – that emit up to 90 per cent less air pollutants than similar cars in the past.

Undoubtedly the United States and Japan are far ahead of the European Community in regulating exhaust gases. It should be realised that the EC – being a supranational body with 12 member states – has an almost exclusive legislative power regarding technical standards for products to be marketed within the Community. In doing so the EC establishes a harmonised regulatory framework in order to protect the free flow of products within the EC market. As a consequence, EC directives mark the limits within which member states may set standards for air pollution, noise, etc. As a member state, the Netherlands participates in negotiations regarding pollution standards and tries to reach agreements on the highest possible levels of abatement and control.

In 1985 the so-called Luxembourg agreement established more stringent EC exhaust gas standards for almost all categories of passenger cars (see Table 8.3). In June 1989, again in Luxembourg, the European Council of Ministers of the Environment agreed upon even stricter standards for cars of under 2-litre engine capacity as from October 1992. Thus from that date all new cars entering the EC market will comply with standards equivalent to current US standards established in 1983.

Table 8.3 Exhaust gas standards established by the 1985 Luxembourg agreement

Engine Capacity	Date of implementation	CO	Gram per test HC + NOx	NOx	present share new car sales (per cent)
>2 000cm³	1–10–88/89	25	6.5	3.5	c. 7
>1 400 and <2 000	1–10–91/93	30	8		c.40
<1 400 cm³	1–10–90/91	45	15	6	c.53
Present standards '15/04'		58–110	19–28		

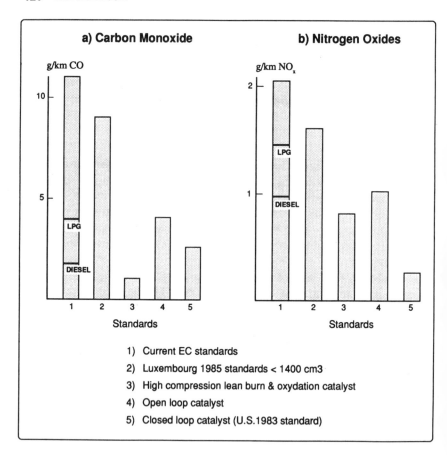

Figure 8.3   Emission performances of current engine technologies for 1.4–2.0 litre cars in the Netherlands

From the Netherlands' Clean Car Research Programme a clear view on emission performances of current engine technologies has evolved in terms of grams (in CO and NOx) per kilometre in conformity to standard test procedures (see Figure 8.3). A parallel – and even more interesting – picture appears from the 'conformity of production' testing of vehicles-in-use, combined with a high-speed cycle test and engine tuning according to manufacturer's specifications (Figure 8.4 see p. 129). It may be concluded that both in practice as well as in laboratory conditions the closed-loop catalyst technology represents the state-of-the-art in air pollution reduction.

Considerable progress still has to be made in a wide variety of issues to be covered by EC standards before all these regulations can be said to be equivalent to state-of-the-art technology. Reducing the total air pollution of road traffic requires constant screening of those factors that influence the real exhaust gas composition of all categories under all 'real life' driving conditions. In 1989 and 1990 new EC standards will be established for the following items: light commercial vehicles; a high-speed test cycle and high-speed emissions; diesel emissions of particles and gaseous compounds; evaporation losses of petrol-engined cars; and enforcement and lifespan reduction standards for catalyst and other reduction equipment.

Measures in the Netherlands

As from 1 April 1986, several measures entered into force in the Netherlands in order to promote the introduction of 'clean' cars. Leaded regular gasoline was replaced by unleaded regular, and fiscal benefits were provided for the purchase of 'clean' cars that comply with the new EC standards. As a result, by the end of 1989 about 75 per cent of all newly sold cars were (US 1983 standard equivalent) catalyst-equipped. This approach – using economic incentives to compensate for additional costs of catalyst and other emission-reduction equipment – has proved to be an effective way of 'cleaning up' the passenger car fleet long before it could be done by compulsory measures alone.

In 1988 a publicity campaign on 'clean' cars, catalytic converters and unleaded gasoline was organised. The campaign sought both to remove some of the misunderstandings surrounding these topics and to promote the sale of cars fitted with catalytic converters. This campaign was set up in close co-operation with the Dutch petroleum industry and car importers.

In February 1989, it was decided to adapt fiscal regulations in such a way as to provide maximum benefits only in respect of those vehicles that comply with US 1983 standards. Until the new EC standards enter into force, compensation will be provided for the purchase of 'clean' cars (that comply with the new standards) at a rate of Dfl.1700 (£520) for closed-loop catalyst technology and Dfl.850 (£265) for open-loop or any other (non-catalyst) technology that complies with milder EC standards. This regulation came into force on 13 March 1989. Within five months, one in three of newly sold cars conformed with US 1983 standards!

In order to guarantee that cars do not cause more air pollution and noise than strictly necessary during their life, general periodic car inspections will be extended to cover environmental aspects. In addition, an extended random-sample inspection programme is being undertaken over a five-year period to check the anti-emission devices in use in terms of their effectiveness, durability and their conformity to production standards.

Cleaner lorries and buses

In addition to the introduction of cleaner passenger cars, the rapid introduction of cleaner lorries is also desirable. A 'gentleman's agreement' signed with the manufacturers and importers on 29 September 1987 represents the first step in this direction, establishing a 10–15 per cent NOx reduction per vehicle for 80 per cent of all newly sold lorries as from 1988. With regard to noise reduction, the same incentive approach has been successfully applied through subsidies for investments in lorries that meet future (stricter) noise standards.

The Dutch government is a strong supporter of a 50 per cent tightening-up of exhaust gas standands in the coming years within the EC, thus making maximum use of current technological options. The government will also endeavour to reach agreement in the EC by the rapid introduction of cleaner vehicles, if necessary by anticipating new stricter EC standards. For this purpose the environmental investment subsidy programme will be raised by Dfl.90 (£28) million per year. The amount, which will be funded through an increase in diesel excises, will be raised gradually from 1 January 1991 onwards because cleaner vehicles will not immediately be available in great numbers on the European market. The programme will be terminated once the European norms, involving a 50 per cent reduction, become effective.

It is expected that this policy, given the expected autonomous growth in freight traffic from 17 billion km to 26.4 billion km in the year 2010, will lead to about 30 per cent lower emissions of nitrogen oxides and hydrocarbons in 2000. Furthermore, measures to prevent unnecessarily high emissions of smoke and soot from lorries will be investigated, with an enforcement system to be developed and implemented similar to that in Germany.

Of equally great importance is the development of even cleaner lorries and buses. By 2010 a 75 per cent reduction in the emission of harmful substances must be achieved, although the technology for this is still unknown. In 1989 the Ministry of Housing, Physical Planning and Environment and the Ministry of Transport and Public Works together with the lorry industry embarked on broad international research into promising new technologies.

Transport in cities will serve as a spearhead in demonstrating and applying clean technologies. A wide range of possibilities is available, examples being alternative fuels (natural gas), electric vehicles, hybrid vehicles, storage of braking energy, use of particle filters, etc. Many of the options can be applied simultaneously. In view of the specific circumstances the optimal solution will differ from case to case. An attempt will be made in the next few years to ensure that public transport in cities is provided with clean vehicles. An annual amount has been set aside to support this development, running to Dfl.30 (£9.4) million in 1994.

Reducing car use (automobility, the second track)

Future levels of air pollutants emitted by traffic will be determined by the average vehicle emission factor (emission per vehicle per km) and total distance travelled by all vehicles.

$$(\text{VEHICLE EMISSION FACTOR}) \times (\text{KM PER YEAR})$$
$$= (\text{TOTAL ANNUAL EMISSIONS})$$

It follows that the growth of automobile use of three to five per cent a year if policy remained unchanged would inevitably consume a large part of the emission reductions resulting from the 'clean' car programme, thus frustrating environmental objectives for emisson reduction on both an (inter)-national and an urban scale. Indeed, growth rates of about six per cent would lead to actual increases of emissions, despite the successful introduction of 'clean' cars. For example, in 1988 all emissions rose compared to 1987 due to the high traffic growth, with NOx up by 5 per cent in a year. Furthermore, the 'clean' car programme cannot solve the problems of noise nuisance, land-use and CO_2 emissions that are expected to increase with traffic growth.

Considering the severity of the effects of acidification and ozone formation, which is reflected in reduction goals of a magnitude of 70–90 per cent, urgent action is needed. Also, it takes too long a period (from now to about 2000) before the total car population will be replaced by maximum feasible 'clean' cars. This demonstrates how imperative it is to take adequate measures soon. One must also realise that the issue at stake is an adjustment in a socio-economic trend, which is no easy task and should not be delayed any longer.

Thus it is that the Second Traffic and Transport Structure Scheme (SVV II) in 1988 seeks a balance between individual freedom, accessibility and environment. It has been concluded that the only way of doing sufficient justice to all these aspects is to control the use of cars. Consequently, a set of new measures and improvements in current approaches are to be developed to tackle the 'automobility' problem. They may result in a drop in the growth of automobility from 72 per cent to 56 per cent by 2010.

It may be deduced from the above that the volume of traffic is an independent factor, the effect of which on total emission levels increases in relation to the failure to introduce stricter emission standards, or the delay involved in introducing them. In the long term, the proportion of growth in Dutch traffic volume accounted for by freight traffic assumes an even more important role. Thus the growth factor reinforces the necessity for the EC to do all it can to minimise the vehicle emission factor, the more because all EC members countries expect high growth rates at least until 2010.

The second track brings about a fundamentally different approach from the 'classical' approach in both traffic and environmental policy. However, even for reducing traffic jams a substantial reduction of car use is thought to be justified and effective. Thus both environmental and traffic policy goals may be reached simultaneously through the same instrument, reduction of car use.

In 1989, a specific task-force, supported by McKinsey & Co., developed a series of economic and traffic measures to curb congestion in the crowded Randstad of Holland, not only by constructing new infrastructure, but also by raising the cost of car use and parking. Several other proposed measures should pull car drivers into public transport or even on to the bicycle saddle. This 'Randstad Mobility Scenario' report provoked much applause from some interested parties, but even more criticism from car-related businesses and driver organisations.

Undoubtedly, any substantial reductions of traffic volume can only be realised when both parliament and society as a whole are willing to change ther balance of interest between environment and unlimited mobility.

Limits to the reduction of car use

To what extent may car use – or at least the growth of kilometres travelled – be limited without disturbing the economy or society as a whole? Several studies show that a considerable part of car use in the Netherlands is not 'essential': indeed, an estimated 30–40 per cent of all car rides may be judged as having a reasonable substitute in public transport, telecommunications or the bicycle. Nearly half of all car movements are performed within reasonable cycling distance (five km) or even walking distance (two km). With regard to air pollution, both long-distance daily travelling (producing high NOx output), and frequent, short, cold, start-and-stop trips by car (shopping, commuting, social and educational visits, with relatively high CO and HC emissions) should be substituted as a matter of priority.

The Netherlands has the most effective and ecological answer to the needs for short distance mobility: 12 million bicycles. Moreover, public transport is relatively well developed. On the other hand, a great many factors structurally favour car use: the autonomous growth in car owning/driving age groups, the psycho-social benefits of car ownership, the physical distribution of housing and employment locations, growing job mobility, rising job participation for married women, fiscal and other incentives, and – last but not least – the inherent advantage of cars in terms of speed, convenience, privacy and freedom. Undeniably, the Dutch and their political representatives show a strong aversion to governmental interference in private behaviour, especially when such measures are unconventional or burdensome or both. In fact, it may be expected that government measures that raise the cost of car use in order to influence present drivers' behaviour will meet strong opposition from various parts of society. The recent government crisis proves the strength of such opposition and its political determination.

Various measures for reducing car use

Evidently under current social and political circumstances there are no simple measures that can have direct and major effects on the volume of traffic. This is because the guiding principles in the current decision-making process assume no limitation of car ownership; guarantees for freedom of mobility for social, business and distribution purposes; and the superiority of a market-oriented approach over regulation.

Given the importance of the automobile in modern society, substantial limitation on its use requires fundamental measures, capable of influencing people's choice of mode of transport. Only a wide-ranging package of measures which complement each other can have any significant effect. Perhaps even a cultural revolution might be necessary. Certainly, within the last three years the issue of 'automobility' has developed from one of taboo into a political battleground and a widely recognized problem. Consequently, government papers on traffic and physical planning and environment reveal a steadily developing set of policy goals and decisions, the latest (NMP) always more elaborate than its predecessors (Fourth Physical Planning Memorandum, SVV II).

'Sustainable development' in traffic and transport means that a shift will have to occur in modes of transport towards modes that are less energy-consuming and less polluting. The following changes need to occur as regards choice of mode of passenger transport:

— for short distances (up to 5–10 kilometres) a shift from using cars to using bicycles, with a considerable increase in the number of kilometres covered by non-motorised transport;
— a shift from using cars to public transport with, as a result, twice as many passenger kilometres being covered by public transport by 2010;
— a shift from travelling by air for distances up to 1000 kilometres to travelling by high-speed train.

For that purpose:

— a great improvement will be made in facilities for public transport and for cyclists as an alternative to using the car, notably for commuter traffic;
— pricing and incentive instruments will be used to influence the choice of transport mode in passenger transport;
— information and stimuli will be provided to all those involved, notably businesses, municipal authorities and individual members of the public;

— encouraging the use of public tranport has to be coupled with discouraging the use of cars, otherwise no contribution will be made to sustainable development.

None of these options can be realised overnight; some of them require amendments to legislation, while the precise advantages and disadvantages of others still need to be studied carefully.

To be effective, a balanced package will have to include the following elements:

— a strong increase in variable (driving) costs, possibly in combination with a reduction in fixed costs through 'variabilisation', road pricing, taxation, etc.;
— reducing parking facilities for commuter traffic through action on volume and regulation;
— increased attractiveness of public transport by improving capacity and infrastructure, service and comfort, speed and price, etc.;
— optimum use of physical planning via concentration and public transport orientation of land uses.

Increasing variable car costs

Variable car costs affect the use of cars while fixed costs principally affect car ownership. If the variable costs are raised, use diminishes and it is thus an effective instrument of policy on mobility. The most direct method of achieving this is to increase fuel prices.

The level of excise duty on petrol in the Netherlands is approximately at the proposed harmonisation level of the European Commission. This proposal allows no scope for a substantial increase on excise duty on petrol. On the other hand, excise duty on diesel and LPG is relatively low or absent. Therefore costs for users of diesel and LPG cars will increase by Dfl.540 (£169) million from 1 January 1990 by way of an increase in diesel excises (of 6.3 cents (2p) per litre) and an increase in the LPG surcharge in the motor vehicle tax.

This NMP provides for a further increase of Dfl.190 (£59) million in diesel excises with which to finance the programme for accelerating the introduction of cleaner lorries (Dfl.90 (£28) million) and cleaner buses (Dfl.30 (£9) million), as well as improvements in rail and waterway facilities on behalf of freight transport (Dfl.70 (£22) million). This total of 190 million guilders corresponds to about 4.3 cents (1.4p) per litre of diesel.

Road pricing will be introduced as the key instrument for controlling traffic growth. It is an instrument which charges car traffic for variable costs by time and place. Road pricing will be developed and introduced as quickly as possible, at the latest by 1996. A test project will be started in 1992 in anticipation of the large-scale introduction of the system. A modern electronic (in-vehicle) 'chip-value card' system is being tested already.

Commuter traffic (standard tax deduction)

In order to discourage the use of single passenger private cars for commuting in favour of other forms of transportation such as car-pooling, group transport and public transport, or to encourage people to live closer to where they work, the existing standard tax deduction for commuter traffic will – in phases – be abolished and transformed into policies directed at reducing the environmental burden and improving accessibility. The new Cabinet will formulate a position regarding the allocation of the revenues generated after hearing the opinion of a specially established working party. Amongst other possibilities, a reduced fare pass for those who use or will use public transport will be examined. Car-pooling and private group transport should receive much more emphasis because they provide for more intensive use of existing cars without a heavier burden on public transport capacity.

Increased attractiveness of public transport

Improving and extending service by public transport could include the following:

— automobile kilometre reduction plans;
— investments in public transport infrastructure;
— investments in bicycle facilities;
— fare and ticket integration;
— contribution to public transport operating costs deficit;
— encouraging co-operation between transport regions;
— research and public information.

Altogether this would involve an extra Dfl.250–75 (£78–86) million per year.

Kilometre reduction plan. Companies and (government) institutions will be asked to draw up kilometre reduction plans to screen commuter traffic and commercial traffic to and from the company or agency and examine all possibilities of reducing the number of vehicle kilometres. In 1990 such plans will be drawn up on a voluntary basis with a subsidy from central government. In the long run, the drawing up of kilometre reduction plans will be part of the internal environmental responsibility of enterprises and agencies and an annual report will be drawn up by government bodies giving the results which have been achieved.

Investments in public transport infrastructure. Additional investments are necessary in the urban district networks for a further improvement in the quality of public transport in the four major urban districts (Amsterdam, Rotterdam, The Hague and Utrecht). Extra measures are being anticipated in the other urban districts to improve the regularity and streamlining of bus services and to improve stopping accommodation. Outside the urban districts a further improvement in the infrastructure for intraregional transport will be needed. During the planning period (until 2010) an additional investment is required to accelerate improvements to the Dutch railway infrastructure which includes doubling the amount of track, grade-separated junctions and other measures to improve speed such as TGV and 'intercity-plus' trains.

Investment in bicycle facilities. The use of bicycles will be encouraged and extra infrastructural measures for bicycle traffic will be taken for this purpose. Ways of doing this include the provision of separate bicycle routes in and around towns, notably in commuter corridors, as well as routes to and from stations and bicycle parking facilities.

Encouraging co-operation between transport regions. Regional co-operation between those involved in transport and traffic, such as municipal authorities and public transport companies, is indispensable for solving the complex problems of accessibility and environment. Central government can provide funding if a transport region draws up a co-ordinated plan to solve the traffic and environmental problems in an integrated way. The plan must aim at reducing unnecessary car traffic, improving accessibility and reducing local environmental problems. The plan may involve parking arrangements, promoting public transport, promoting bicycle traffic, integration of taxis into the transport chain, planning measures, public information and educational activities, etc. Notably, no new institutional body is envisaged: transport regions shall be developed by co-operation between existing authorities.

Tightening up physical planning policy

Physical planning policy will concentrate on discouraging labour-intensive business and amenities attracting numerous visitors in locations which are less readily accessible by public transport. Physical planning and environmental policy instruments will be deployed to prevent buildings being constructed in unsuitable locations. The municipal authorities are being asked to view existing building plans in this light and possibly reconsider them.

Improving freight transport by rail and water

In order to raise the percentage of freight transport travelling by rail and water in the future, the competitive position of these branches must be strengthened. This means giving additional attention to the infrastructural bottlenecks in the rail and waterway networks. Additional money will be made available through the increase in diesel excises already described,

The investments provided for in SVVII will be carried out with greater speed. The total investment involved is about Dfl.40 (£12.5) million per year in the period up to 2000. An advisory commission has made recommendations to the Minister for Transport and Public Works on the strategy to be pursued to strengthen substantially the position of freight transport by rail into the next century. Several billion guilders (!) are to be invested in new and existing rail infrastructure in order to triple the annual tonnage transported by 2010.

The infrastructural bottlenecks in the waterways network will be resolved at an accelerated pace. About Dfl.30 (£9) million per year is involved in stepping up the improvements planned in the SVVII up to the year 2000. The higher excise duty on diesel fuel may also result in some shift towards freight transport by rail and water.

Further research is due to start shortly into the factors that affect choice of transport and particularly into the motives of shippers in choosing a particular mode. In the course of 1990 a detailed study will be completed into reducing the environmental impact of freight transport and into the reduction of energy consumption in this sector. The study will also examine the possibilities of restricting the number of goods vehicle kilometres by a more efficient use of vehicles.

Effects of measures

The mobility measures are part of a package; it is not possible to judge their effectiveness individually. The effectiveness of the whole set of measures is expressed in a curbing of the growth in the use of cars in relation to the forecast for unchanged policy and the proposed policy in the SVVII (Table 8.4).

Given current know-how in vehicle technology and the trend in car use, the objectives for NOx in 2000 and 2010 can just be achieved (with regard to passenger cars). As regards CO_2 emissions, it is expected that these will diminish by 2010 by approximately five per cent. Thus the CO_2 objective

Table 8.4 Trend in the number of car kilometres in the Netherlands

	1994	2000	2010
SVVII forecast (unchanged policy)	124	140	172
SVVII policy	120	126	156
With NMP packages *	117**	120	148

1986 = 100
* It has been assumed that measures can be taken in 1990.
** 1989: 116 already!

cannot be achieved. The same refers to the reduction objectives for 2010 for noise nuisance and NOx/HC emissions by lorries.

Total investment in roads may diminish as a result of the lower growth in car traffic. These savings will first occur in the second half of the SVV plan period since there are currently backlogs which have to be caught up to reach the level of completion intended. Savings on municipal and provincial roads cannot currently be estimated. It is expected that the new Cabinet will substantially reduce the road infrastructure budget in favour of public transport and bicycle infrastructure investments.

Urban traffic measures (third track)

Due to the problems of noise nuisance, air pollution, visual pollution, traffic safety and lack of space, the quality of the urban environment has seriously deteriorated. This is particularly the case in the big cities, where motorised traffic is the main cause of pollution. Most of the air pollutants present at street level originate from motor vehicles, including, in a busy street, 90 per cent of the CO, 60 per cent of the NO_2, 30 per cent of the SO_2 and 98 per cent of the lead.

Air pollution through carbon monoxide, lead and nitrogen dioxide mainly originate from passenger cars. In over 1000 urban streets in the Netherlands with intensities of over 10 000 vehicles per day, the concentration of these pollutants is in excess of the ambient air quality standards for CO, Pb and NO_2, set in 1987. For benzene and particles the same will be so, although air quality standards are not set yet for these substances.

Excessive levels of air pollution and noise nuisance cannot entirely be eliminated by tougher emission standards alone. In addition to the above-mentioned general measures designed to reduce the use of cars, the following measures would help to alleviate the problem at a local scale:

— stricter enforcement of parking restrictions;
— traffic management influencing driver's choice of routes;

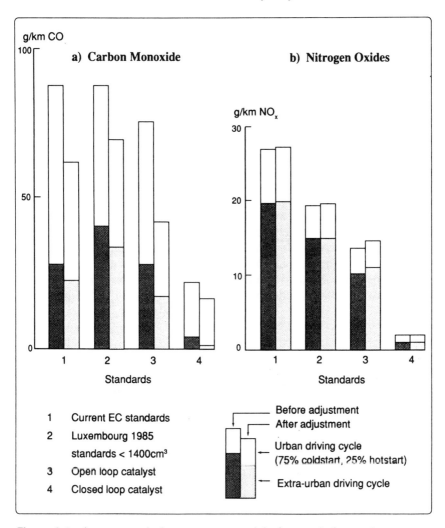

Figure 8.4 Average emissions as measured, before and after tuning, per technology in g/test for a) carbon monoxide and b) nitrogen oxides

— route signs for freight through-traffic;
— traffic-dosaging on approach roads to city centres;
— publicity designed to influence local people's driving habits;
— introduction of low-speed zones;
— circulation schemes to calm traffic and to spread it more evenly over the road network.

This kind of approach combines environmental protection with road safety. The implementation of the policy outlined above will, in the first instance, be the responsibility of the municipalities, although some elements of the policy are more within the realm of central government. To this end the newly amended Road Traffic Act will make it legally possible to implement traffic measures solely or partly on environmental grounds.

Central government grants for municipal infrastructure will be directed more towards reducing the environmental effects, for example, on the basis of 'traffic pollution maps'. Air pollution and noise levels are indicated on these maps and can be directly associated with the traffic flows that cause them by using different colours, the shades indicating the seriousness of the situation. Problem areas become immediately apparent, they can be localized and further assessed. The processing of input data as well as the actual drawing of such maps is computer-aided. A digitised traffic network and a traffic model form part of the system. Modifications and the effect on air pollution and noise can immediately be visualised until an optimal solution is found. About 20 'pilot study' municipalities are preparing such a map. For this purpose the Ministry of Housing, Physical Planning and Environment has allocated four million guilders (£1.25 million) per year, in addition to 15 million guilders (£4.7 million) per year for traffic measures.

Conclusion

Mobility is an essential requirement of our society, as is the protection of the environment. To combine the conflicting demands of traffic and environment in the best possible way is a demanding task from which administrations at local, provincial and state level cannot flinch. The execution of the task is not going to be easy. In particular, it remains to be seen whether the automobility-reduction approach can be realised without the help of a new oil crisis or a new wave of environmental concerns resulting in a real culture shock. If is *is* achieved, then knocking down the Berlin Wall will, in comparison, appear to have been absolutely no problem at all!

For the time being, four major uncertainties remain:

— Will there be enough political support for the unpopular measures that effectively raise the cost of car use and reduce automobility?
— Will such measures really provoke the mass behaviour response amongst motorists as necessary?
— Can we stay away in the long run from more dictatorial ways of influencing people's choice of transport mode and of activity locations?
— Can we slow the growth rate of lorry mileage through influencing the freight transport modal split without embarrassing (the Dutch position in) international transport and distribution?

One thing is for sure: technology can solve a great many of the problems discussed above, but 'behaviour' remains a key factor when traffic and the environment are to be sustainably developed into the next century. The (car) key is in our own hands . . .

References

Ministry of Housing, Physical Planning and Environment, 1989, *Nationaal milieubeleidsplan (National environmental policy plan): to choose or to lose*, The Hague.

National Institute of Public Health and Environmental Protection, 1987, *Zorgen voor morgen (Concern for tomorrow)*. Bilthoven.

World Commission on Environment and Development (Brundtland Committee), 1987, *Our common future*, Oxford University Press, Oxford.

9 Policy issues in promoting the green modes

Rolf Monheim

Many traffic engineers still defend the fiction that traffic planning has to rely on technical and scientific principles that are free of politics. However, the manual of traffic planning published in Germany by the Research Institute for Roads and Traffic has refuted this, establishing that traffic planning requires the input of goals and concepts which depend on the value and interests that underlie change and conflict. The manual rightly infers that it is the politicians who have to decide about the exertion of influence on traffic development, and thus on such issues as the impact of traffic on different social groups and the utilisation of resources (Forschungsgesellschaft für Strassen-und Verkehrswesen, 1985a). This understanding, however, is only making slow progress in traffic planning, principally because this political character also exists in the control of decision-making by interest groups – and hence in power structures. Examples of the consequences of political goals on research and on the planning of traffic are given by Monheim (1989).

The treatment of 'policy issues in promoting the green modes' in this chapter thus concentrates on the analysis of the structures and activities of the participating groups in the decision-making process: the federal and state ministries, local municipalities, alliances and political parties, associations and citizen initiatives. Without question, knowledge of these activities is an important prerequisite for the understanding of the development of the green modes. (A more detailed report on experiences and strategies in bicycle traffic policy has been given by Bracher, 1987; a useful bibliography has been edited by Arbeitsgruppe Fahrradforschung, 1985). First, though, the actual experience of the green modes in the Federal Republic of Germany should be examined.

Users of the green modes

A key to understanding traffic policy lies in the structure of the users of the various means of transport. Policy-makers and planners are principally users of cars and their experiences and interests thus lead to a well-known 'windscreen perspective' of traffic planning and policy. The green modes, on the contrary, are used predominantly by the less influential groups such as women, children, old people, the disabled, the unemployed, the poor and foreigners. The differences in the modal choice among the population groups for the Federal Republic in 1982 are shown in Table 9.1.

Of all journeys made by Germans over 10 years old, 27 per cent were made on foot, 11 per cent by bicycle and 13 per cent by public transport. As some 37 per cent drove a car, and a further 10 per cent were passengers in one, about half of all journeys were by environmentally friendly means of transport and half by the environmentally damaging car. Differences according to sex are clear. Men completed only 42 per cent of their trips by environmentally friendly means compared to 60 per cent completed by women. In particular, great differences between walkers and drivers appear here: only 20 per cent of men can be seen on the footpaths compared to 34 per cent of women, and behind the wheel sit 49 per cent of men but only 24 per cent of women.

The differences according to age are even clearer. People either under 18 or over 65 years old completed most environmentally friendly journeys (79 per cent and 75 per cent respectively) and people between 24 and 41 the least (33 per cent). Accordingly, those over 65 years old constituted the greatest proportion of pedestrians (50 per cent) and 10–17-year-old groups the highest ratio of cyclists (28 per cent); moreover, these two groups were the largest users of public transport.

The influence of ownership is very great. Those who had a car and licence made only 26 per cent of their journeys by environmentally friendly means; those who had no car in the family did this for 84 per cent of journeys (45 per cent on foot). The trip purpose, likewise, had considerable influence on the mode of transport. The environmentally friendly modes achieved only 37 per cent of journeys to work, 51 per cent of the travel for leisure purposes, 61 per cent of the shopping trips and 77 per cent of the educational trips. Thus shopping expeditions achieved the highest pedestrian participation (38 per cent) and educational travel the highest proportions of cyclists and users of public transport (19 and 38 per cent). Personal criteria and trip purpose overlap. The car-driving constituents are principally middle-aged, car-owning men making journeys to work, whilst older women without cars in the household do almost all of their journeys on foot.

It is frequently believed that pedestrians and cyclists are only of significance in smaller towns. A classification according to types of settlement, however, shows that the proportion of pedestrian and cycle trips is similar whatever the scale of the urban area, the reason being the dominance of short journeys. Even in towns with over 0.5 million inhabitants, 24 per cent of all journeys are one kilometre at most, with a further 22 per cent up to three kilometres, and an additional 13 per cent up to five kilometres. In

Table 9.1   Modal split, West Germany, 1982 (per cent)

Population group	On foot	Cyclists	Motor-cyclists	Car drivers	Car passengers	Public transport	Total
All groups	27	11	2	37	10	13	100
Sex							
male	20	11	3	49	6	11	51
female	34	12	1	24	15	14	49
Age							
10–17	28	28	6	1	14	22	15
18–23	18	10	6	39	12	14	11
24–29	21	7	2	52	11	6	11
30–41	21	8	1	55	9	5	20
42–53	24	9	1	48	9	7	19
54–65	33	10	1	34	9	11	13
>65	50	6	0	15	7	19	9
Car availability							
personal	17	5	1	68	5	5	45
household	31	18	4	13	19	15	38
no car	45	12	3	7	6	27	17
Journey purpose							
work	14	8	2	55	6	15	22
education	20	19	4	12	7	38	9
shopping	38	12	1	30	8	11	29
recreation	31	12	3	30	16	8	34
Type of settlement							
big centres (>500,000 population)	28	9	2	32	8	20	17
main centre in highly concentrated area	28	9	1	36	11	15	7
medium-sized centre in highly concentrated area	27	13	3	38	11	8	18
remaining main centres/medium-sized centres (>50,000 population)	30	11	2	35	9	12	13
remaining communities	26	12	2	38	11	9	46

fact, there is even more reliance on foot travel than Table 9.1 shows, as many interviewees did not mention their short journeys, especially those made within a multi-stage trip. A case study in Bayreuth showed that 32 per cent of all journeys that started at home were made on foot, but of all the journeys between the several and various destinations in one outing, walking claimed some 54 per cent (Monheim, 1985).

Up to now, many planners and politicians have failed to recognise these modal splits, maintaining that everyone owns and uses a car. In fact, 32 per cent of all households in Germany – and indeed 68 per cent of one-person households – did not possess a car in 1982 (Brög, 1985). Given this importance of the green modes, it is clear that traffic policy should always incorporate social policy.

Even though walking has a much higher share of all trips than cycling, political and planning activities consider walking a much less relevant mode of transport than the use of bicycles (although an important exception is Garbrecht, 1981). Because this chapter is an analysis of such activities, there will be an element of bias towards the bicycle here, although this does not imply acceptance of an imbalance in the relative importance of the two modes.

Actors in urban traffic policy

The traffic development of towns is subject to manifold influences and correspondingly those who participate in it are equally numerous. There are those whose function affects traffic directly, such as those involved with traffic networks, guidelines for traffic planning, transport legislation, financing means of transport, and environmental and social consequences. Additionally, there are those who are concerned indirectly, especially through the development of settlement structure, as journeys become longer to larger but fewer schools, shopping and leisure centres. To date the trends in the structure of settlements, economies and populations have produced car traffic growth, which is accelerated by feedback and self-reinforcement.

A political turning point began at the end of the 1960s as part of a general euphoria of reform; it has been strengthened since 1973 by the oil crisis and growing awareness of the environment, encouraged by the pressure of citizen initiative groups. In the course of the 1970s leading politicians, special commissions about 'the car and the environment'(BM-Bau, 1980) and municipal councils increasingly took a critical approach to car traffic. To diminish the problem, investment was recommended almost exclusively in public transport (Der Rat von Sachverständigen für Umweltfragen, 1973; BMBau, 1974).

However, road building, the construction of multi-storey car parks and, above all, car-orientated traffic planning continued almost unchanged. The isolated measures for environmentally friendly means of transport served rather as an alibi to silence the critics. Even in the 1980s, in spite of fine-sounding principles, declarations of intent and specific initiatives solely for the green modes, the obstinate opposition of the car lobby has persisted.

In the perception of problems and possibilities for change, the accent has shifted in the course of time. Political achievement is dependent upon, not least, whether a suitable time-window can be found for an initiative to 'land' successfully, a process which is comparable to the timing of space flights. For example, at the moment arguments about exhaust pollution seem to be particularly successful, whilst the points of view that stress social justice issues – such as the reduction of accessibility through the one-sided orientation towards cars, or the consequences of accidents – have been displaced. A chance of gaining the necessary support for a change in traffic policy can be seen from the experience of 'traffic suffocation' (Ahrens and Beckmann, 1989).

The emphasis of this chapter is on the activities of the administrations. However, these should not be presented as the principal actors because the previous efforts of politicians, associations, citizen initiatives or individual personalities are frequently necessary preconditions for administrations to take problems on board. This political background, however, is often difficult to grasp.

Federal ministries and their research agencies

Responsibilities and basic research

In the federal government a policy directly concerning the green modes is pursued particularly through ministries responsible for traffic (BMV), town planning (BMBau) and the environment (BMU, initially BMI), together with agencies assigned to them, namely, the Federal Institute for Road Systems (BASt), the Federal Research Institute for Regional Studies and Land Usage (BfLR), and the Federal Office for the Environment (UBA). These display quite different attitudes towards non-motorised traffic.

The transport ministry (BMV) is traditionally concerned with motorised traffic and in addition it supports traffic-accident research. From 277 research items that were commissioned between 1967 and the beginning of 1980 by the BMV for the improvement of traffic in urban areas, only four dealt with pedestrian movement and none with cycling. In relation to traffic calming, there were just two studies that referred to environmentally tolerable traffic planning (BMV, 1981b).

Because of the growing importance of two-wheeled vehicles in road transport and their high accident numbers, the BASt commissioned basic research on small mopeds (mofas) and mopeds, but without any transport policy commitment (BASt,1977). The BMV, in order to acquire statistical data on traffic accidents, commissioned a survey on modal choice and the duration and length of trips made by each mode of transport. This survey, called KONTIV, was conducted from 1975 to 1977 by Socialdata, a private institute of social research specialising in traffic/transportation behaviour. The results refuted the planners' belief that no one still travelled on foot: in 1976, 30 per cent of all trips were made on foot and 10 per cent by cycle, whilst the car accounted for 47 per cent. This was given prominence first in 1978 in a publication about traffic calming by the Federal Ministry for Regional Planning, Building and Urban Development (Schwerdfeger, 1979). The BMV published the results as late as 1981 (Schwerdfeger, 1981). In 1982 the KONTIV was repeated, but the two volumes containing much statistical data for 1976 and 1982 were never published by the BMV. Part of the data is available in English in Brög (1985).

Promotion of cycling

In the mid-1970s, the BMBau and the associated BfLR recognised the significance of traffic to the quality of life in the towns. This newly claimed political authority was demonstrated first by research, commissioned in 1975 and published in 1978, which attempted to discover 'what measures would support a more positive use of the bicycle in local traffic'. The study advocated greater recognition of the bicycle in communal traffic planning (BMBau, 1978)

In 1979 the UBA intervened in the traffic discussion. To support the use of cycles, it started an initiative on 'the cycle and the environment' (Der Bundesminister des Innern, 1983). This recognised the fact that whilst both traffic planning and town planning imply planning for the environment, in reality they fail to take environmental points of view adequately into account (Umweltbundesamt, 1980). Even though institutions and groups representing cycle traffic met several times to discuss cycling and the environment, the attempt to promote cycle traffic using a cycling grant organisation that was not directly dependent on the state (similar to foreign models) failed because of the lack of economic commitment.

At the end of 1979, the Federal Republic advertised a 'model "cycle-friendly town" plan' for towns with between 30 000 and 100 000 inhabitants, as the article by Hülsmann in this volume describes. The towns of Detmold and Rosenheim were chosen from 131 applicants. In nine further towns certain aspects of cycle traffic were promoted. The course of the experiment shows the difficulties raised by a new direction in traffic planning. Often these problems could not be overcome, even in the framework of the model plan. The results were correspondingly sobering. Although the length of the cycle track network was increased and supporting measures were taken (such as public relations work and the opening of cycle offices), only in Rosenheim could a considerable increase of cycle usage be achieved, in this case from 23 per cent to 26 per cent of all journeys. In Detmold, largely pre-existing deficiencies prevented great progress (Clarke, 1988). In both cases, there was no question of the emergence of a general new direction of planning.

The 'cycle-friendly town' model, just like the later demonstration projects on traffic-calmed areas, went beyond the model towns. For this purpose research was financed, such as that on 'cycling and public transport' and 'bicycles in foreign countries'. Particularly important was that on cycle law (Gersemann, 1982; 1984), which dealt principally with the regulations which discriminated against cycle traffic. Even after its amendment in 1988, the Road Traffic Ordinance (StVO) contained many regulations which impeded – and even, to a degree, threatened – the cyclist. In spite of all the official statements, the regulations of traffic law and financing show clearly that the weaker forms of transport are still disadvantaged.

On the basis of a report from the UBA, a programme for the relief of the environment through promotion of cycle traffic was developed in 1982. At the interministerial working group, a large number of bodies were involved, including the Federal Ministries for the Interior (at that time responsible for the environment); for Transport; for Regional Planning, Building, and Urban Development; for Food, Agriculture and Forestry; for Employment and Social Order as well as for Youth, Family and Health. In addition UBA, BfLR and BASt co-operated, as did the research officers of the Federal Institute for Nature Conservancy and Landscape Ecology. This large number of participating institutions shows the many-sided nature of the problems involved. It might, however, also be one of the reasons why the programme was not effectively realised.

Traffic calming

Parallel to the encouragement of cycle traffic and the battle against individual traffic problems, the commitment since the second half of the 1970s has been focused on increasingly extensive plans for widespread traffic calming. Foreign examples gave impetus to this, notably a conference of the OECD on *Better towns with less traffic* in 1975 (OECD, 1975), as well as the model of the *Woonerf* developed in the Netherlands. Such widespread traffic calming was an important prerequisite for extensive encouragement of pedestrian and cycle traffic and for curbing car usage.

The BMBau, as well as the state of Nordrhein-Westfalen, played a leading role in the realisation of new concepts, using research and model projects as basic tools. In a volume, already mentioned, entitled *Traffic calming: a contribution to urban renewal*, the BMBau embraced these new concepts of traffic planning (BMBau, 1979) that were orientated towards a policy for urban development. The traffic-calmed street, a vital instrument in promoting environment and town friendly traffic, was introduced in 1980 into the Road Traffic Ordinance, after a major experiment conducted by the province of Nordrhein–Westfalen in 1977–8. It is indicated by a new traffic sign (no. 325/6 StVO). The BMBau simultaneously drew up an illustrated magazine on residential streets of the future, showing the use of traffic calming for the improvement of the residential environment (BMBau, 1980). Many impressive photographs were used to illustrate such town friendly traffic planning, so that planners, politicians and citizens would be helped in their struggle against the car lobby. In addition, a planning primer for traffic calming was published in 1982, as was a survey of the costs of traffic calming in 1983 (BMBau, 1982, 1983). Due to the great demand for information about the new planning principles, many publications of the BMBau were out of print after a short time; therefore the BMBau in 1985 published a reader collecting together the most important contributions (BMBau, 1985b).

The BMBau continued its commitment to town friendly traffic even after the change of government in 1982. In 1986 it published an illustrated magazine called *Urban traffic in change*, which gave clear prominence to the whole town-changing character of the new traffic policy (BMBau,1986b). As a result, even stronger counter-reactions of interest groups were provoked and this must have contributed to the withdrawal of the publication two years later.

In order to reorientate municipal traffic planning, a revision of the guidelines for road and traffic planning (which were principally car-orientated) was necessary. These had always been worked out by the Research Institute for Road and Traffic Concerns (FGSV), a private institution, which was supported by the institutions connected with the motor and road-construction industries. The official institutions then took over its guidelines and considered them with regard to financial subsidies and what was legally permitted in road construction.

In 1979 the BMBau and BASt agreed to work together on the revision of recommendations for the design of access roads. For that purpose, in 1981 BASt presented revised guidelines (RAS-E-81) and in 1982 the BMBau issued 'recommendations for the design of access roads' (EAE-82) as a result of a research assignment. From these separate approaches, the 'recommendation for the design of access roads' (EAE-85) emerged in 1985 (Forschungsgesellschaft für Strassen- und Verkehrswesen, 1985a). To supplement it, the BMBau issued an introductory publication *Roads in town and village, 1985* (BMBau, 1985a). The integration of town traffic into future town development was clarified simultaneously in a specialist conference organised by BMBau on 'new tasks for town planning' (BMBau, 1986a).

Politically more controversial was the revision of the guidelines for major roads, since the existing guidelines were especially designed to aid 'traffic' flow and did not take into account that these roads frequently produced heavy pedestrian and cycle traffic and were important locations for retail trade and public facilities. A problem analysis was produced in 1984 on the integration of urban main roads into town planning (BMBau,

1984) and since 1985, a commission has been working on new guidelines for the design of main roads compatible with the needs of the urban environment (EAHV). Without waiting for its results, numerous towns have already remodelled major roads according to these principles.

These 'attacks ' on the main road network have aroused violent counter-reactions from the traditional planners. They assume that the principle of the car-friendly town might be replaced by the car-free or car-hostile town, with the result that the complex organisation of the town may suffer damage (Baron, 1988; Kuhn *et al.*, 1988). This, however, is not correct, as can be clearly seen from relevant publications (e.g. Eichenauer *et al.*, 1988).

Widespread traffic calming has been tested by the federal government since 1981 in a trial plan. Using the example of six urban areas, each with a different structure, the possibilities and consequences of traffic calming were investigated. The concepts and overall results of the projects were discussed in five meetings between 1980 and 1990: the chapter by Döldissen and Draeger in this volume provides the details for this model.

For the green modes the model project has achieved a special significance, because the three ministries concerned with traffic, and the agencies assigned to them, worked intensively together. Moreover, the commissions for planners and researchers, as well as the seminars, strengthened such groups and encouraged them to support new models. On the other hand, numerous difficulties manifested themselves in carrying out this project: since the federal government has no immediate competence for local planning and citizens' participation form an important element in these concepts – discussions with local planners, politicians and those affected needed a great deal of time. Often the concepts had to be altered, even when this led to problematic compromises. Nevertheless, the commitment of the local planners in most cases made impressive results possible and produced broad agreement of the citizens, especially in the model area of Buxtehude.

At first, traffic calming was mainly introduced by the 'traffic-calmed street' sign (325/6 StVO). However, the introduction of calmed streets was slow, partly because of the high costs for the remodelling of the roads (which was regarded as a prerequisite for their use with equal rights by all road users), and partly due to the narrow range of the permitted number of vehicles. It was also a consequence of the resistance of the car lobby. As an alternative, zonal restriction of the permitted maximun speed to 30 km/h was proposed, but the car lobby ensured that the restricted zones were authorised only experimentally from 1985 to 1989. (From 1990 they have been established definitively.) Moreover, in many towns, this control depended on an application by the residents and their majority agreement.

The administrative authorities in most towns were inundated by a flood of applications from the population for 30 km/h zones, although the authorities themselves often remain disapproving (especially in Bavaria).

Meanwhile, the German town authorities demanded speed limits of 30 km/h as a general regulation for built-up areas, with higher speeds only authorised on specified main traffic routes. The BMV and the ADAC (German Automobile Club), representing the interests of car drivers, likewise approved speed limits in residential areas, but argued for these to be established on a restricted basis ; the ADAC even preferred a 40 km/h speed limit (ADAC, 1986).

The growing sensitivity to environmental problems from the mid-1980s on led to stronger intervention in the discussions on traffic policy by the newly created Federal Ministry for the Environment (BMU). By the end of 1988 (finally!), a closer co-operation with the BMV had been established. In addition, federal–state committees discussed plans to diminish traffic-caused pollution, as will be seen in the next section. The BMU intends to establish a working group on traffic and the environment in order to be able to introduce its ideas better into the political decision-making process. Also in the UBA the relevant organisational structures are to be created, since up to now its authority has not been adequate for the support of an environment friendly traffic policy.

Despite its lack of direct authority, the BMBau has been the strongest of the federal ministries in supporting more environmentally tolerable traffic, a strength which derives from its large number of research commissions and publications. As a result, pedestrian and cycle traffic have become respected as parts of comprehensive plans.

States

Through the federal structure of Germany, the states have extensive jurisdiction over traffic, urban development and the environment, in particular in the implementation of laws and measures. Consequently, states in which the parliamentary or administrative structures are more favourable to an environmentally friendly traffic policy have taken on the role of pilot, whilst others have followed at a distance. In this chapter all states cannot be considered and only some activities will be shown as examples. There are close interrelationships with the initiatives of the federal government: indeed, on many questions the ministries of the states and the federal government have formed working parties. Amongst the states, Nordrhein-Westfalen has repeatedly been the pacemaker in the promotion of environmentally friendly traffic. The reasons lie partly in the political culture, for the Rhine-Ruhr, as the most densely urbanised area in the Federal Republic, has environmental problems typical of a large population concentration, but which are intensified by the consequences of disorganised industrial development. The improvement of the urban environment is an important condition for future economic welfare. This provides a greater awareness of problems regarding environmental pollution from traffic.

The state of Nordrhein-Westfalen has, since 1971, maintained an Institute for State and Town Development Research (ILS), and within this, in support of an environmentally and urban friendly traffic policy, an 'area of responsibility for traffic' was set up in 1986. The increasing importance of town and regional planning led in 1976 to the concentration of relevant departments into a Ministry for State and Town Development. Following the pattern of the BMBau, this soon became involved with urban traffic planning and especially with calming traffic. In 1985 it received jurisdiction for traffic, which previously had been assigned to the Ministry for Economic Affairs, thereby enhancing the possibilities for the achievement of an urban friendly traffic plan.

With regard to construction of pedestrian areas, Nordrhein-Westfalen played a leading role: there were the two oldest and most famous pre-1970s pedestrian areas, in Cologne and Essen, and it also boasted the greatest profusion of pedestrian areas in the FRG. In 1975 the Interior Minister of Nordrhein-Westfalen ordered a study of how 'space for pedestrians' could be achieved and organised in the town as a whole. The findings were published in 1977 and 1979 (ILS, 1977, 1979). In one of these volumes on 'ways through the town', pedestrians were treated as a separate type of traffic and suggestions were made for their consideration in urban development plans.

In 1976, increasing demands for traffic calming in urban areas from the media and from civic initiatives – including 30 from the Ruhr area alone – led the minister responsible for traffic in Nordrhein-Westfalen, in cooperation with the HUK (the Association of Legal Liability, Accident and Motor Traffic Insurers), to undertake a major study on *Traffic calming in residential areas*. It became a milestone in the new traffic policy (Der Minister für Wirtschaft, Mittelstand und Verkehr des Landes Nordrhein-Westfalen, 1979). Using the example of 30 areas with environmental and traffic problems, the effectiveness of various traffic-calming measures was tested. There were very positive results, particularly in safety, with 44 per cent fewer injury accidents on calmed streets than on other urban roads in the state and 53 per cent fewer accidents causing severe injuries. This improved traffic climate gave rise to a positive attitude amongst residents: virtually no one wanted to reverse the moves towards traffic calming.

In part parallel to the major experiment, in part because of the positive results, numerous other states and even many municipalities have correspondingly produced initiatives, especially since 1979. As Nordrhein-Westfalen made use of traffic calming principally to improve the quality of life, in 1981 it changed the financial emphasis of municipal building support to reflect this new aim (Der Minister für Landes- und Stadtentwicklung, 1982). In support of the new concept, the Nordrhein-Westfalen Minister for Land and Town Development organised a competition in 1983, 'Quiet living – safe streets'. Some 44 municipalities and 19 action groups, including three cycling associations, took part. The results were published in 1984 in order to encourage others to imitate (Der Minister für Landes- und Stadtentwicklung, 1984). To combat the accident danger to cyclists, the Minister for Urban Development, Housing and Transport of Nordrhein-Westfalen published a brochure in co-operation with the German Cycling Club (ADFC), *Safety on the cycle* (Der Minister für Stadtentwicklung, Wohnen und Verkehr des Landes Nordrhein-Westfalen, 1988b). Complaints from administrators and citizens about disturbance of pedestrian areas by cyclists, and also about obstructions to environmentally friendly cycle traffic, prompted the Niedersachsen social minister to initiate a study into cycle traffic in pedestrian areas (Der Niedersächsische Sozialminister, 1983). It showed that, as far as possible, forbidding cycling in pedestrian areas should be avoided, principally because – in practice – problems sort themselves out after a while. It proposed measures by which potential conflicts can be avoided or defused.

In order to fit traffic planning into the aims of urban revival and environmental protection, Nordrhein-Westfalen released in 1988 a guide to principles for better integration of urban renewal and urban traffic (Der Minister für Stadtentwicklung, Wohnen und Verkehr des Landes Nordrhein-Westfalen, 1988a). On this basis, more and more towns reworked their existing general traffic plans. In 1989 a supporting programme on cycle friendly towns and communities was passed. The example of measures for the bicycle-orientated city of Münster and the respective ordinance of the state ministry are shown in Wacker and Wolters (1989). Whilst the state governments (as well as the federal government) have no direct authority in urban traffic planning, they are themselves planning representatives for main federal and state roads and can directly promote new goals in traffic policy. For that reason Nordrhein-Westfalen altered the state road construction regulations of 1980. Thereafter, special emphasis was to be given to the urban friendly modification of state roads which pass through built-up areas, the minimisation of land usage in road construction and the installation of cycle ways (Der Minister für Stadtentwicklung, Wohnen und Verkehr des Landes Nordrhein-Westfalen, no date).

In spite of the prototype experiments, support programmes and decrees from federal and state governments, as well as rhetorical declarations of politicians over practical traffic and urban development policy, car-orientated forces have maintained a dominant influence. However, decisive opposing forces could emerge from environmental policy in the future if the intention to set legal limits for maximum exhaust pollution is pushed through. Thus, for example, in 1989 the prime ministers of the states instructed the responsible ministers at the conference for environment and traffic to develop proposals for the reduction of exhaust emission caused by traffic. Both the federal environment ministry and the UBA were involved in the working party. It was acknowledged that technical measures on the vehicle and incentives for owners to use less polluting vehicles were not sufficient to achieve the target values and that alterations in the modal split and extensive traffic calming were necessary. The working party saw the potential for modal split changes principally in terms of the shifting of individual motorised movement to travel by public means of transport, whilst suggestions for the promotion of non-motorised traffic were deferred.

Towns and cities and their organisation

Traffic calming and the promotion of the green modes must actually be carried out by the towns and municipalities, so that the achievement of an environmentally friendly traffic policy depends upon them. The variety of their political and administrative structures opens up great flexibility, through which individual towns can relatively easily assume the role of precursor. Moreover, the municipalities influence political processes through the leading organisations, Deutscher Städtetag (DST) and Deutscher Städte- und Gemeindebund, which they support at the state and federal level. Additionally, for consultations and applied research, they support the German Institute for Urban Studies (DIFU). Finally, there are regional planning-orientated mergers as, for example, in the most densely concentrated area in the Federal Republic, the Municipal League of the Ruhr (KVR). These institutions have repeatedly been important innovators for an urban friendly traffic policy.

The DST has furthered the cause of the green modes via the exchange of information between the towns on their experiences as well as through resolutions. As early as 1961 it has called for the introduction of pedestrian areas and in 1972 the planning conference of the town authorities put out models and information for pedestrian areas (Ludmann, 1972). In 1984 the central commission of the DST adopted a new 'traffic policy concept', after long and controversial discussions (DST, 1984; Muthesius, 1984). In contrast to the concept drawn up a decade earlier, it looked at the extension of roads and expensive public transport more critically and supported cycle traffic, which had not been mentioned at all in 1974. It called for the reduction of accidents and the speed of car traffic.

In 1988, as a consequence of the positive results of the trials with Tempo 30 (30 km/h zones), the municipal authorities promoted a three-tier system for the regulation of traffic speeds in cities:

— the principal traffic routes (the 'reserved network') would be designated as roads with right of way for vehicles, with normal maximum speeds of 50 km/h, but with the possiblity of special regulations, such as 40 or 60 km/h;

- for the remaining traffic roads there would be a general maximum speed of 30 km/h without the need for individual road signs;
- for streets where the residential function is more important than moving traffic, walking pace would be the norm and there would be mixed usage by all street users with equal rights (i.e. there would be no separation between carriageway and sidewalks). They would be designated by a special traffic sign as traffic-calmed streets.

Taking into account the political heterogeneity of the member towns and the rejection of speed restrictions amongst conservative politicians, this resolution is remarkable (Kiepe, 1989). However, in spite of support by the BMBau, the towns could not at first carry it through with the BMV. (The DST has collected the articles which had been published on Tempo 30 in its journals from 1986 to 1989 into a special volume (DST, 1989).)

The DIFU has supplied fundamental help in the argument through documentation and research for an environmentally and urban friendly traffic policy; because of their special importance, some of these contributions will be briefly considered here. First of all, in a series about town traffic planning, the fundamental facts on mobility in towns were drawn up and critically evaluated (Apel and Ernst, 1980). This led to considerations of altering the choice of means of transport in favour of the more environmentally friendly means (Apel, 1984). Important conclusions for traffic policy came to light by comparing towns with regard to accidents, which were found to be considerably fewer in urban areas abroad than in even the best-performing German towns (Apel *et al.*, 1988). Serious personal injuries were more frequent the greater the number of main traffic routes there were in a town, the more extensively it was built up, the higher its degree of motorisation and the more trips that were made by car. Greater proportions of cycle traffic did not give rise to an increase in the risk of accidents; instead, the danger to individual cyclists on their trips diminished. The smallest number of accidents occurred in compact urban structures with short routes and moderate development of major traffic networks.

As an example of the scope for the sort of urban traffic that cares for the environment and is safe, the DIFU drew up a model plan for the development of traffic, in co-operation with the town of Lahr (Apel and Lehmbrock, 1985). Additionally, the Communal Association of the Ruhr (KVR) supported the town of Dorsten by the preparation of plans for traffic calming the whole town (KVR, 1986). Again, since the achievement of an environmentally tolerable traffic plan is often obstructed by lack of information, and the towns themselves can scarcely review the relevant publications and practical examples, the DIFU drew up a comprehensive guide (Fiebig *et al.*, 1988).

As far as cycle usage is concerned, there are extremely large differences between communities. Obviously the cultural, social and political climate of a town plays a fundamental role, much more than bad weather. Above-average increases in cycle usage in a city are connected with its readiness for innovation, the process being a self-intensifying, circular one. Counts show that even in large cities astonishing increases are possible, such as the increases in Munich from 1980 to 1988 of 171 per cent on the Isar bridges and of 288 per cent on the bridges close to the town centre. In Nuremberg cycle traffic on the Pegnitz bridges rose by around 95 per cent from 1980 to 1984, during which time there were only three per cent more cars. These increases in bicycle traffic in large cities are most likely to be facilitated by their special disposition towards innovation.

Erlangen is the best known example of politically achieved promotion of cycle traffic as part of a broader approach to an environmentally compatible town planning (Grebe, 1982). There, in 1972, a young candidate won the election for mayor through, *inter alia*, the promise of an urban-friendly traffic policy. However, the general traffic plan proposed – on account of forecast increases in car traffic – more roads, and referred only in passing to bus routes and cycle ways, since those modes would have a reduced share of the traffic. (Stadt Erlangen, 1977a). The city rejected this concept, because it had not examined, firstly, whether the advantages of such planning concepts for the flow of car traffic outweighed the disadvantages for urban structure and quality of life, and, secondly, whether the level of change to road capacity was so great that it would actually be preferable to reduce the forecast needs (Stadt Erlangen, 1977b). It was decided that for the protection of the city it would be necessary to prevent the forecast from becoming reality by shifting car journeys to public transport, cycle and pedestrian movement. To do this, road building was stopped and there were massive improvements in public transport and cycle traffic, as Figure 9.1 shows. In this way, the use of cars was reduced by 35 per cent from 1974 to 1980 and the use of cycles increased by 26 per cent, so proving impressively that trend is not destiny.

In spite of these sucesses the car lobby fought against this policy. The principal opposition came from the inhabitants of the surrounding countryside who demanded that more roads be built in the city, but in the interests of quality of life Erlangen was not willing to do this. Indeed, an investigation of traffic policy in Erlangen by six independent experts in 1987 upheld the planning of the city. In sum, the process of planning and (non–) decision-making in Erlangen typifies the problems of altering deeply rooted structures. (For a more extensive description of this case, see Vereinigung der Stadt-, Regional- und Landesplaner, 1988; and Monheim, 1990.)

Political parties

The conduct of the political parties in relation to green modes is inconsistent. When it is a matter of general demands they are mostly positive;

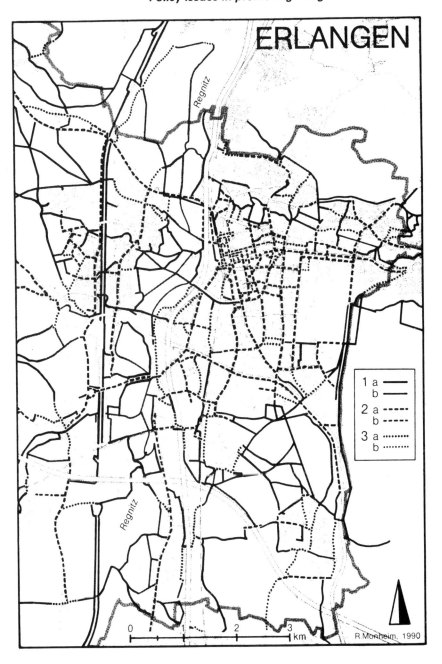

Figure 9.1   The bicycle network of Erlangen, West Germany

a = existing solution   b = planned expansion
1 independent bike path
2 bikepath parallel to a road or in a traffic calmed/pedestrian street
3 connections in the bike network with a low volume of road traffic

however, as soon as car drivers' privileges come into question or cost-effective measures need to be enacted, not much is done, However, there are examples of awakening commitment in the parties.

In 1983 the CDU (Christian Democratic Party), in a working paper on cycle infrastructure in inner cities, issued by the Konrad Adenauer Foundation, called – though with some scepticism – for the courage to give political priority to unconventional measures for cycle traffic (Institut für Kommunalwissenschaften, Konrad-Adenauer-Stiftung, 1983). Münster is the best example of a bicycle-orientated city governed by a majority of the CDU (Wacker and Wolters, 1989). Within the SPD (Socialist Party of Germany) federal parliamentary group, a working party made suggestions in 1985 for the encouragement of cycling (Burghof and Stolterfoth, 1985). As an example of the local involvement of SPD politicians, Erlangen has already been discussed. For the 'Greens' the encouragement of environmentally tolerable means of transport and the battle against domination by the car is a central matter of concern on all political levels (DIE GRÜNEN, 1985, no date).

The transport policy activities of the parties towards the green modes do not lend themselves to simple black and white categorisation, since within the CDU/CSU occasional representatives of environmentally friendly means of transport are to be found and many SPD politicians remain car-faithful. Uncomfortable decisions against the car lobby are most likely today to come from socialist – green coalitions. Thus, in 1989 in Berlin and Frankfurt after a change of government, a complete new orientation of traffic policy was agreed in order to achieve greater respect for the environment.

Citizen initiatives and associations

The fact that citizen initiatives and associations are dealt with last in this chapter does not imply that they have any less importance for the green modes. On the contrary, it is often they that press the institutions to act. In the Federal Republic over 2000 action groups have formed against the burden of traffic; many fight individual problems, but others also see wider connections, and take more and more part in traffic policy. Klewe and Weppler (1982) have, through case studies, analysed the working of citizen initiatives in their attempts to achieve traffic calming.

For a policy orientated towards traffic compatibility with other urban functions, the necessary conditions include organisation of the exchange of information and co-ordination of action. One platform, since 1972, has been the registered Federal Association of Citizen Initiatives for Protection of the Environment (BBU). In 1980 it drew up, with the support of the UBA, a 'cycle primer' *Change to the cycle* (BBU, 1980), which set out the most important elements of cycle policy. In order to improve co-ordination, a traffic committee working group was formed. It published two booklets, *Citizens for the bicycle* and *Sidewalks in cities* (Arbeitskreis Verkehr im Bundesverband Bürgerinitiativen Umweltschutz, 1980, 1981). This group belonged to the BBU until 1985 and since then has been independent as a working committee for traffic and the environment (UMKEHR).

Some cyclist initiatives (especially from Hamburg and Berlin) have combined themselves under the description of 'Green Cyclists' and some pedestrian initiatives have become the 'Pedestrian Protection Society'. Nevertheless, they still also take part in the working committee for traffic and environment. The co-ordination of traffic initiatives is managed by a Berlin citizen initiative which was formed in 1974 against the building of a further urban freeway. Since 1980 it has published a traffic newsletter called *Information service on traffic* (Arbeitskreis Verkehr und Umwelt, no date); brochures on traffic problems, e.g. footpaths, cycles, town traffic, children and traffic (Arbeitskreis Verkehr und Umwelt, 1985); and materials for public relations work.

In addition, mutual operations have been stimulated, such as the 1982 cycle demonstrations which took place in over 100 cities on the 'Day of the Environment', involving 200 000 cyclists. The traffic initiatives have, since 1978, promoted a 'Citizen Initiatives Traffic Congress'; it took place for the seventh time in 1989.

The citizen initiatives have also joined up in the states and formed working groups for traffic. One example is the State Union of Registered Citizen Initiatives for Environment Protection in Niedersachsen (LBU), which for the state parliamentary elections in 1985 published a special issue of its journal *Environment information for Niedersachsen* on 'Traffic in Niedersachsen' (LBU, 1985). Whilst the citizen initiatives are committed principally to their own respective places of residence and only work together loosely, environmental groups consider a wider representation of the interests of environmental protection to be essential. To this end, the environmental associations which had existed in many parts of Germany for a long time (e.g. in Bavaria since 1914 and in Bremen since 1916) combined in a central League for Environment and Nature Protection in Germany (BUND). In addition, to combat environmental problems caused by traffic, they formed a working group which presented a fundamental programme of traffic policy in 1983 (BUND, 1983).

In 1979 the General German Cyclists' Club (ADFC) was founded, modelled on the ADAC (General German Automobile Club) (ADFC, 1989). Through a large membership, service can be offered to cyclists and their interests represented in planning, policy and the cycle industry, and public opinion can be influenced. Within 10 years the ADFC reached 36 000 members. Since 1980 the new publication *Cycling* has served as the instrument of public relations work (ADFC, no date). Its appearance is closer to the ADAC members' publication than to the alternative IDV, mentioned above.

In its first year (1980), at Bremen, the ADFC started a series of international bicycle conferences called VELO CITY, a term with an encouraging double meaning, and initiated other conferences which helped to improve the exchange of ideas and the development of political strategies (BMV, 1981a; ADFC, 1988).

The ADAC has also concerned itself with pedestrian and cycle traffic, particularly in the field of transport safety. For this purpose several town competitions have been held. The results, and recommendations for practice, were jointly published with the BMV (BMV, no date, no date; ADAC, no date). Although many sensible suggestions were made, speeding car traffic was scarcely questioned and the potential for a change in means of transport sceptically evaluated. Moreover, the brochures on safety for the pedestrian and cyclist are not representative of the policy of ADAC, which is more generally one-sided and car-orientated.

In Switzerland in 1979, a 'Traffic Club of Switzerland' (Verkehrs-Club der Schweiz, VCS) was established in favour of an environmentally friendly traffic policy, embracing all forms of transport. Within 10 years it had 100 000 members and it now intervenes successfully in traffic policy discussions and in the launching of referenda, typical of the direct democracy of Switzerland. Following this example, and with the support of numerous environment protection associations, the Traffic Club of Germany (Verkehrsclub Deutschland, VCD), was founded in 1986 in the Federal Republic. By the middle of 1990 it had approximately 40 000 members. They were offered, as in other travel clubs, a broad spectrum of services in order to discourage anyone from becoming a member of a car-orientated club. In many cases the members joined first and foremost because of concern over environmental policy. In 1987 Austria followed with the VCÖ (Verkehrsclub Osterreich).

The most frequent triggers for traffic action are issues of environmental protection, next to which the danger of accidents plays a significant role. The traffic problems faced by children cause particular concern, so parents' initiatives are frequent. Amongst other things this has led to the German Children's Protection Society, which published a brochure in 1987 depicting the consequences of motorisation and the possibilities of traffic calming (Deutscher Kinderschutzbund, 1987). A special survey, initiated by the state of Baden-Württemberg, has demonstrated that the battle against child accidents is impeded in many ways by deficiencies in the regulations, which fail to ensure that accidents typically involving children (e.g. widespread locations, many different causes) are avoided in the future (Peter-Habermann, 1979).

In order to build an opposing force to the car orientation of the majority of academics and planners and the institutions which they dominate, others set up, in 1985, a forum for environmentally friendly traffic, 'Man and

Traffic'. The forum initiated working committees, conferences and information brochures. In 1987 the Union of Town, Regional and State
Planners (SRL), which had been in existence since 1964, incorporated this
forum as a special section which, by 1989, included 365 traffic and planning
experts from a variety of disciplines. An example of its understanding of
traffic problems is a conference which took place in 1987 in Erlangen on
'New strategies for traffic in the town' (Vereinigung der Stadt-, Regional-
und Landesplaner, 1988).

To date, the fragmentation of the initiatives concerned with environmentally friendly traffic has prevented any individual organisations from
having a really large membership. On the other hand, after certain initial
problems, there is now much reciprocally fruitful collaboration.

To conclude this discussion about institutions and initiatives, an important requirement for the success of a policy for the green modes should be
recalled: the commitment of individuals who have built up an increasingly
substantial network of reciprocal support. This commitment does not,
however, always bring recognition: indeed, in many authorities and
universities it often leads to serious conflicts. Despite many declarations of
goodwill for the environment, the main thrust of traffic research and
decision-making is still in favour of the car.

Are conclusions possible?

This analysis of political activies in the Federal Republic in support of the
green modes shows, above all, how confusingly stratified these are.
Efficient structures are missing, and in the political apparatus the will for
fundamental change is lacking. This is not rooted in a failure of the
population to accept a new traffic policy – on the contrary, all surveys show
their very wide agreement, a consensus which again and again surprises
and confuses politicians and administrators. The general opinion among
the citizens in favour of an environmentally compatible transport policy,
and the scepticism of most decision-makers, has been demonstrated very
clearly by several inquiries which were conducted to sustain a campaign for
a new public awareness concept by the public transport agencies (Verband
öffentlicher Verkehrsbetriebe, 1989). When consistent measures have
been carried out, they have almost always been considerably more successful than the 'experts' had predicted. A significant example is the 'environment ticket', with which one could travel as far as one wished on the
federal railways in 1989 on the 'Day of the Environment' for DM50. Whilst
market research had predicted 15 000 passengers and financial losses for
the railway, on the day 100 000 additional passengers came and brought the
railway a profit of DM five million.

The stubborn opposition to environmentally friendly traffic within the
planning and decision-making structures can only be gradually overcome

by persistent pressure. The initiatives shown in this account have certainly moved a great deal, but the decisive breakthrough has not yet been achieved. Just as with the environmental problems – dying woodlands, global warming or holes in the ozone layer – one wonders whether cata-strophic worsening is necessary to overcome the extremely influential, short-sighted, egotistically activated interest groups, in this case the car lobby. In the end, these offer no serious political alternatives. That is why there is no other choice for the way forward than the arduous one of continuing to take small steps and refusing to be discouraged by stumbles and setbacks.

References

Ahrens, G.A., and Beckmann, K., 1989, Verkehrsinfarkt: 'Chance für Stadt und Umwelt', *Bauwelt*, 12,554–7 (=*Stadtbauwelt*, 101).
Allgemeiner Deutscher Automobilclub e.V. (ADAC), 1986, *Zonen-Geschwindigkeits beschränkung, Erfahungen aus der Praxis, Empfehlungen und Hinweise aus der Sicht des ADAC*, Munich.
—— no date, *Fußgängerschutz in Städten*, Schriftenreihe Straßenverkehr 3, Munich.
Allgemeiner Deutscher Fahrrad-Club e.V. (ADFC), 1988, *Fahrrad Stadt Verkehr, Internationaler Kongreß 1987 in Frankfurt*, 2 vols, Darmstadt.
—— (ADFC), 1989, 10 Jahre ADFC, special issue, pedal, Bremen.
Allgemeiner Deutscher Fahrrad-Club e.V. (ADFC), 1989, *Tritt für Tritt, Zehn Jahre Allgemeiner Deutscher Fahrrad-Club 1979-1989*, Bremen.
——monthly, Radfahren, Bielefelder Verlagsanstalt, Bielefeld.
Apel, D., 1984, *Umverteilung des städtischen Personenverkehrs: Aus- und inländische Erfahrungen mit einer stadtverträglicheren Verkehrsplanung = Stadtverkehrsplanung Teil 3*, Deutsches Institut für Urbanistik, Berlin.
—— and Lehmbrock, M., 1985, *Modellvorhaben: Umweltschonender und sicherer Stadtverkehr: Entwurt: Verkehrsentwicklungspan Stadt Lahr/Schwarzwald*, Deutsches Institut für Urbanistik und Stadt Lahr (ed.), Berlin and Lahr.
—— Kolleck, B., and Lehmbrock, M., 1988, *Verkehrssicherheit im Städtevergleich: Stadt- und verkehrsstrukturelle Einflüsse auf die Umweltbelastung = Stadtverkehrsplanung Teil 4*, Deutsches Institut für Urbanistik, Berlin.
Arbeitsgruppe Fahrradforschung in Fachbereich 8 der Universität Oldenburg, 1985, *Bibliographie aktueller Fahrrad-Literatur*, Bibliotheks- und Informationssystem der Universität Oldenburg, Oldenburg.
Arbeitskreis Verkehr im Bundesverband Bürgerinitiativen Umweltschutz e.V. (BBU), 1980, *Bürger für das Fahrrad*, Berlin.
—— and Ernst, K., 1980, *Mobilität, Grunddaten zur Entwicklung des städtischen Personenverkehrs = Stadtverkehrsplanung Teil 1*, Deutsches Institut für Urbanistik, Berlin.
—— 1981, *Gehwege in Städten*, Berlin.
Arbeitskreis Verkehr und Umwelt e.V. 1985, *Neue Stichworte, Fakten und Argumente zum Stadtverkehr*, Berlin.
—— no date, *Informationsdienst Verkehr IDV*, periodical, Berlin.

Baron, P., Brilon, W., Hoffmann, G., Leutzbach, W., Retzko, H.-G., Ruske, K,-H., Scharchterle, G., Steierwald, G., and Stolz, M., 1988, Stadtplanung und Verkehrsplanung: Verkehrsberuhigung auch für Hauptverkehrsstraßen? Ein Diskussionsbeitrag einer Gruppe von Hochschulprofessoren der Stadt-und Verkehrsplanung, *Internationales Verkehrswesen*, 40, 3, 151–7.

Bracher, T., 1987, *Konzepte für den Radverkehr: Fahrradpolitische Erfahrungen und Strategien*, Bielefelder Verlagsanstalt, Bielefeld.

Brög, W., 1985, 'Changes in Transport users' motiviations for modal choice: passengers transport, Germany', *Report of the Sixty-eighth Round Table of Transport Economics*, Paris, 8 and 9 November 1984, European Conference of Ministers of Transport (ECMT), OECD, Paris.

—— 1985, Verkehrsbeteiligung im Zeitverlanf-Verhaltensänderung zwischen 1976 und 1982, *Zeitschrift für Verkehrswissenschaft*, 56, 3-49.

BUND für Umwelt und Naturschutz Deutschland e.V., Arbeitskreis Verkehr, 1983, *Verkehrspolitisches Grundsatzprogramm,*, Bonn.

Bundesanstalt für Straßenwesen (BASt), 1977, *Grundlagen zum Zweiradverkehr*, Unfall- und Sicherheitsforschung Straßenverkehr 9, Cologne.

Der Bundesminister des Innern, 1983, *Fahrrad und Umwelt: Programm zur Umweltentlastung durch Förderung des Fahrradverkehrs*, Umweltbrief 26, Bonn.

Der Bundesminister für Raumordnung, Bauwesen und Städtebau (BMBau), 1974, *Die Rolle des Verkehrs in Stadtplanung, Stadtenwicklung und städtischer Umwelt*, Seminar der Europäischen Wirtschaftskommission der Vereinten Nationen, Munich, 1973, Schriftenreihe 'Städtebauliche Forschung' 03.023, Bonn.

—— 1978, *Mit welchen Maßnahmen kann eine stärkere Benutzung des Fahrrads im Nahverkehr unterstützt werden?*, Schriftenreihe 'Städtebauliche Forschung' 03.066, Bonn.

—— 1979, *Verkehrsberuhigung: Ein Beitrag zur Stadterneuerung, Schriftenreihe* 'Städtebauliche Forschung' 03.071, Bonn.

—— 1980, *Wohnstraßen der Zukunfr: Verkehrsberuhigung zur Verbesserung des Wohnumfeldes*, Bonn.

—— 1982, *Planungsfibel zur Verkehrsberuhigung*, Schriftenreihe 'Städtebauliche Forschung' 03.090, Bonn.

—— 1983, *Kostenhinweise zur Verkehesberuhigung*, Schriftenreihe 'Städtebauliche Forschung' 03.098, Bonn.

—— 1984, *Städtebauliche Integration von innerortlichen Hauptverkehrsstraßen: Problemanalyse und Dokumentation*, Schriftenreihe 'Städtebauliche Forschung' 03.107, Bonn.

—— 1985a, *Straßen in Stadt und Dorf: Planen + Entwerfen mit den neuen Empfehlungen für die Anlage von Erschließungsstraßen* (EAE 85), Schriftenreihe 'Städtebauliche Forschung' 03.113, Bonn.

—— 1985b, *Verkehrsberuhigung und Stadtverkehr: Textsammlung zu einem städtebaulichen Verkehrskonzept*, Schriftenreihe 'Städtebauliche Forschung' 03.111, Bonn.

—— 1986a, *Neue städtebauliche Aufgaben, Zukunftsaufgaben der Erneuerung, der Wirtschaft, der Ökologie und des Verkehrs in unseren Städten und Gemeinden: Umrisse, Lösungsansätze, Perspektiven*, Schriftenreihe 'Städtebauliche Forschung' 03.115, Bonn.

—— 1986b, *Stadtverkehr im Wandel*, Bonn.

Der Bundesminister für Verkehr (BMV), 1981a, *Dokumentation 1. Internationaler Fahrradkongreß VELO/CITY 1980, Bremen* (including translation into English), Forschung Stadtverkehr, Sonderreihe, 9, Kirschbaum Verlag, Bonn.

—— 1981b, *Mitteilungen über Forschungen zur Verbesserung der Verkehrsverhältnisse in den Gemeinden*, Forschung Stadtverkehr 29, Kirschbaum Verlag, Bonn.

—— und Allgemeiner Deutscher Automobilclub e.V. (ADAC) no date *Sicherheit für den Fußgänger: Vorschläge für die kommunalen Bemühungen um die Verkehrssicherheit: Ergebnisse und Schlußfolgerungen aus dem Städtewettbewerb 1975*, Bonn and Munich.

—— no date, *Sicherheit für den Fußgänger: Ergebnisse und Schlußfolgerungen aus dem Städtewettbewerb 1980, Empfehlungen für die Praxis*, Bonn and Munich.

Bundesverband Bürgerinitiativen Umweltschutz e.V. (BBU), 1980, *Die Fahrradfibel: 'Steig um auf's Rad!'*, Umweltwissenschaftliches Institut e.V. (UWI), Umweltmagazin Verlag für Bürgerinitiativen GmbH, Berlin.

Burghof, A. and Stolterfoth, B. (eds), 1985, *Vorfahrt für das Rad, Konzept einer umweltgerechten Verkehrspolitik*, Das Mandat, Arbeitshefte zur Kommunalpolitik, Vorwärts Verlag, Bonn.

Clarke, A., 1988, 'A comparison of European experimental cycling projects in Nottingham (UK), Delft (NL) and Detmold (FRG)', *Proceedings Velo City 87 International Congress 'Planning for the Urban Cyclist'*, Netherlands Centre for Research and Contract Standardization in Civil and Traffic Engineering C.R.O.W., Record 2, Ede, 123–30.

Deutscher Kinderschutzbund e.V., 1987, *PlanungsgröBe: KIND – für einen menschenfreundlichen Straßenverkehr*, Hanover.

Deutscher Städtetag, (DST) 1984, *Verkehrspolitisches Konzept der deutschen Städte*, DST-Beiträge zur Wirtschaft- und Verkehrspolitik, Reihe F, H. 5, Cologne.

—— 1989, *Tempo 30, Materialien zur Verkehrsberuhigung in den Städten*, Bearbeitet von F. Kiepe, DST-Beiträge zur Wirtschafts- und Verkelospolitik, Reihe F, H.7, Cologne.

Eichenauer, M., von Winning, H.-H. and Streichert, E., 1988, 'HauptverkehrsstraBen: ungenutzte Reserven für städtebauliche Integration', *Der Städtetag*, H.1, 2–8.

Fiebig, K.-H., Horn, B. and Krause, U., 1988, *Umweltverbesserung in den Städten, H. 5: Stadtverkehr: Ein Wegweiser durch Literatur und Beispiele aus der Praxis*, Deutsches Institut für Urbanistik, Berlin.

Forschungsgesellschaft für Straßen- und Verkehrswesen, Arbeitsgruppe Verkehrsplanung, 1985a, *Leitfaden Für Verkehrsplanungen*, Cologne.

Forschungsgesellschaft für Straßen- und Verkehrwesen, 1985d, *Empfehlungen für die Anlage von ErschließungsstraBen – EAE 85*, Cologne.

Garbrecht, D., 1981, *Gehen: Ein Plädoyer für das Leben in der Stadt*, Beltz Verlag, Weinheim and Basel.

Gersemann, D., 1982, *Sachexpertise 'Fahrradrecht'*, Modellvorhaben Fahrradfreundliche Stadt, Werkstattberichte Nr. 1., Umweltbundesamt (ed.), Texte 31/32, Berlin.

—— 1984, *Fahrradrecht heute und morgen*, Reihe VELO, Bd. 1, Bauverlag, Wiesbaden and Berlin.

Grebe, R., 1982, *Leben in der Stadt: Mensch–Umwelt–Natur–Gärten. Inform-*

ationen zu Grün in Erlangen 1982, Graphische Betriebe, Lippstadt.

DIE GRÜNEN, 1985, 'Verkehr auf dem Land und in der Stadt', *Alternative Kommunalpolitik, Fachzeitschrift für Grüne und Alternative*, special issue No. 5, Bielefeld.

—— im Bundestag, no date, *Vorrang für Fußgänger, Radfahrer, Bahn*, Bonn.

Institut für Kommunalwissenschaften, Konrad-Adenauer-Stiftung e.V., 1983, *Fahrradinfrastruktur in Innenstädten?!*, Arbeitshilfen und Programme für die praktische Kommunalpolitik, Kommunal-Verlag GmbH, Recklinghausen.

Institut für Landes- und Stadtentwicklungsforschung des Landes Nordrhein-Westfalen (ILS), 1977, *Raum für Fußganger: Ein Beitrag zur Stadtplanung*, Materialband I/II, Verlag für Wirtschaft und Verwaltung, Essen.

—— 1979, *Raum für Fußgänger: I Wohnbereiche / II Wege durch die Stadt / III Straße und Stadtgestalt*, Schriftenreihe Stadtentwicklung–Städtebau, vol. 2.023, Verlag für Wirtschaft und Verwaltung, Essen.

Kiepe, F., 1989, 'Der DST-Vorschlag zur Verkehrsberuhigung: Kritik und Gegenargumente', *Der Städtetag*, H. 3., 211–14.

Klewe, H. and Weppler, H., 1982, *Bürgerbeteiligung und Verkehrsberuhigung: Auswirkungen einer unterschiedlich intensiven Bürgerbeteiligung auf Planung, Durchführung und Nutzung von Verkehrsberuhigung*, Diplomarbeit, Dortmund.

Kommunalverband Ruhrgebiet (KVR), 1986, *Gesamtstädtische Verkehrsberuhigung Dorsten*, Planungshefte Ruhrgebiet P O 17, Essen.

Kuhn, C., Autorenkollektiv Fachgruppe Forum Mensch und Verkehr in der Vereinigung der Stadt-, Regional- und Landesplaner (SRL) and Menke, R., 1988, 'Stadtplanung und Verkehrsplanung: Leserbriefe', *Internationales Verkehrswesen*, **40**, 5, 346–9.

Landesverband Bürgerinitiativen Umweltschutz Niedersachsen e.V. (LBU) and Verein für Umweltschutz e.V. (VfU), 1985, *Verkehr in Niedersachsen*, special issue, Umwelt informationen für Niedersachsen, Zeitschrift der Niedersächsichen Bürgerinitiativen, 11/12.

Ludmann, H., 1972, *Fußgängerbereiche in deutschen Städten: Beispiele und Hinweise für die Planung*, Cologne.

Der Minister für Landes- und Stadtenwicklung, 1982, *Wohnumfeldverbesserungen in der Städtebauförderung*, MLS Kurzinformation 982, Düsseldorf.

—— 1984, *Ruhiges Wohnen: Sichere Straße. Ergebnisse ders Landeswettbewerbs 1983*, MLS informiert, Düsseldorf.

Der Minister für Stadtentwicklung, Wohnen und Verkehr des Landes Nordrhein-Westfalen, 1988a, *Grundsätze zur besseren Integration von Stadterneuerung und Stadtverkehr*, Runderlaß vom 17.03.1988, Ministerialblatt für das Land Nordrhein–Westfalen Nr. 41, 835–7, MSWV Kurzinformation, Düsseldorf.

—— 1988b, *Sicher auf dem Fahrrad*, Düsseldorf.

—— no date, *LandesstraBenausbauplan 1988–1992*, Schriftenreihe 23 Düsseldorf.

Der Minister Für Wirtschaft, Mittelstand und Verkehr des Landes Nordrhein-Westfalen, 1979 *Verkehrsberuhigung in Wohngebieten, Schlußbericht über den Großversuch des Landes Nordrhein-Westfalen*, Kirschbaum Verlag, Bonn.

Monheim, R., 1985, 'Analyse von Tätigkeiten und Wegen in der Stadt. Neue Möglichkeiten für den modal-split', *Verkehr und Technik*, H. 8, 267–70 and H. 9, 324–31.

—— 1989, 'Verkehrswissenschaft und Verkehrsplanung im Spannungsfeld von Trends und Zielen', *Der Städtetag*, H. 11, 691–6.

—— 1990, 'Verkehrsplanung in Erlangen: Konzepte, Maßnahmen und Ergebnisse von Planungen für einen stadtverträglichen Verkehr', *Verkehr und Technik*, 43, 5.

Muthesius, T., 1984, 'Städtische Verkehrspolitk in den achtziger Jahren. Ein Hintergrundbericht zum verkehrspolitischen Konzept der deutschen Städte, *Der Städteteg*, H. 1, 3–8.

Der Niedersächsische Sozialminister, 1983, *Untersuchungen des Fahrradverkehrs in Fußgängerzonen unter Berücksichtigung der Struktur und Bebauung*, Berichte zum Städtebau und Wohnungswesen, Hanover.

OECD, 1975, *Better towns with less traffic*, Paris.

Peter-Habermann, I., 1979, *Kinder müssen verunglücken: Von der Aussichslosigkeit, bei uns Kinder zu schützen*, rororo aktuell, Rowohlt Taschenbuch Verlag, Reinbeck.b. Hamburg.

Der Rat von Sachverständigen für Umweltfragen, 1973, *Auto und Umwelt*, Gutachten, Bonn.

Schwerdfeger, W., 1979, 'Wer geht denn heute noch zu Fuß . . . Ein Beitrag zur Korrektur eines Planer-Weltbildes', Verkehrsberuhigung: Ein Beitrag zur Stadterneuerung. Schriftenreihe des Bundesministers für Raumordnung, Bauwesen und Städtebau 03.071, Bonn, 61–74.

—— and Küffner, B., 1981, *Analyse der Verkehrsteilnahme: Art und Häufigkeit motorisierter und nichtmotorisierter Verkehrsteilnahme*, Unfall- und Sicherheitsforschung Straßenverkehr 33, Bundesanstalt für Straßenwesen (ed.), Cologne.

Stadt Erlangen (ed.), 1977a, Stadtentwicklungsplanung Erlangen, Untersuchungen zum Generalverkehrsplan, Dorsch Consult, Erlangen.

—— (ed.), 1977b, *Stadtentwicklungsplanung Erlangen, Fachplan Verkehr, Leitlinien zur Generalverkehrsplanung*, Erlangen.

Umweltbundesamt, 1980, *Umweltgerechte Stadtverkehrsplanung: Das Fahrrad in der Stadt*, Texte, Berlin.

Verband öffentlicher Verkehrsbetriebe, 1989, *Einschätzungen zur Mobilität, Grundlagen für ein Public-Awareness-Konzept*, SOCIALDATA, (research institute in charge) Cologne.

Vereinigung der Stadt-, Regional- und Landesplaner e.V. (SRL), 1988, *Neue Strategien für den Verkehr in der Stadt, Bericht über die Jahrestagung 1987 in Erlangen*, SRL Schriftenreihe 24, Bochum.

Wacker, H. and Wolters, G., 1989, *Programm fahrradfreundliche Stadt Münster*, Oberstadtdirektor der Stadt Münster–Stadtplanungsamt (ed.) Stadtplanung Information Dokumentation Nr. 29, Münster.

10 A systematic approach to the planning of urban networks for walking
Anthony Ramsay

Historical context and professional perceptions

Ever since the industrial expansion of towns in the nineteenth century, pedestrian traffic has been treated as second-rate by the public authorities. For instance, the provision during the era of kerbed footways to each side of the busier streets of British towns implied that vehicles had a prior right to use the carriageways (Martin, 1961; Webb and Webb, 1920). Since the carriageways were interconnected at every street junction, drivers were thus provided with a town-wide route network with continuity of surface throughout. By contrast, any pedestrians who wanted to go farther than the next street corner had to step down to cross the carriageway at every junction, having judged when the various streams of vehicles had sufficiently abated to allow safe passage.

To add insult to injury, proper parking spaces for motor vehicles are now so scarce in the older and more central parts of many towns, and locally owned vehicles so numerous, that motorists have tended to usurp the footway as well for parking, so creating inconvenience or obstruction for pedestrians. The exceptions in the urban world to today are a few medieval cores such as Dragr, Dubrovnik, Siena and Venice (where the street network is so delicate in scale and geometry as to be totally unsuitable for use by motor vehicles) and a larger number of new towns planned from the start on a basis of traffic segregation.

The very strict control of vehicular speeds in Great Britain in the early years of this century was soon relaxed under fierce political pressures brought to bear by people of influence, many of whom constituted the car-owning (Plowden, 1971). Equally, the 'scientific' tradition of traffic engineering established in the United States in the 1930s treated pedestrians in an essentially negative way. For example, a formula was given which converted the flow of pedestrians crossing the street (in persons per hour) into average resultant delay to automobiles (in seconds per vehicle) (Matson et al., 1955). Thus pedestrians were regarded merely as a hindrance to motor traffic, without any reciprocal consideration of how cross-flows of vehicles might hinder the progress of pedestrians, or of the hazard posed to people on foot by the need to cross the street so frequently at surface level in the face of fast-moving streams of vehicles.

The rapid growth of vehicular traffic in the 1950s prompted in turn:

— ambitious plans for high-capacity roads by municipal authorities (e.g.-
    Coventry, Glasgow, Nottingham);
— the first motorway plan for Great Britain by the Ministry of Transport
    and Civil Aviation (Starkie, 1982);
— research on theories of traffic generation and on theoretical traffic
    capacity of urban streets and junctions by Smeed, Wardrop *et al.* at the
    Road Research Laboratory (RRL, 1965).

Sensing that there was no adequate strategy for handling the mounting pressure of traffic or equally the clamant demands for additional capital to invest in roads, the Transport Minister appointed a special group led by Buchanan (with a steering group under Crowther) to review the long-term problems of traffic in towns, a formidable task at that time.

This was the first significant attempt to deal with traffic in a town-planning context, i.e. as part of urban structure, relating it to land-use patterns and building densities. The report was permeated by the strategic approach of segregating traffic, and in particular the physical separation of pedestrians and vehicles (Crowther and Buchanan, 1963).

The government acclaimed its recommendations and proceeded to:

— require municipalities of 50 000 population or more to submit 'traffic
    and transport plans' (later superseded by 'transport policies and
    programmes');
— increase the roads budget;
— introduce a standard procedure for the comparative evaluation of
    major road schemes (Reynolds, 1960); and
— produce new manuals on the prediction of road traffic, on traffic
    engineering techniques, and on the design and layout of roads.

Unfortunately, it failed to remove at the same time the bias of government grant schemes towards trunk roads and hence towards vehicles rather than pedestrians.

Since the mid-1960s, remarkable progress has been made in north-west Europe, notably in West Germany, Denmark and the Netherlands, in making special provision for pedestrians in towns. Extensive zones of pedestrian priority have been established in most towns of any size. The precedent of separate tracks for trams and for cycling have made it fairly easy and natural for them to contemplate substantial routes and networks for walking. The *Woonerf* notion of restricted vehicular access to older

streets of terraced housing, first conceived in Delft, has been enthusiastically adopted, and the concept elaborated, in Denmark and West
Germany (Tolley, 1990).

Progress in the United Kingdom has been very much less, and achieved
mainly in other directions. This has been at least partly due to the fragmentation of responsibility amongst different professions and to inertia by
central government politicians and civil servants. The most significant way
in which safety and comfort for pedestrians in the United Kingdom has
been improved is through the formation of 'planned' shopping precincts,
either as city-centre redevelopments or as new peripheral development.
Many such schemes have been instigated by the private sector, almost (one
could say) by default of the local planning authority. Only a few progressive authorities (e.g. Coventry, Durham, Norwich and Nottingham) with
unusually enthusiastic officials and fortuitous circumstances have achieved
recognisably comprehensive facilities for pedestrians, in programmes led
by municipal initiatives.

Examination of traffic growth trends suggests that car ownership in the
United Kingdom may double over the next 30 years. Unless there is a
radical change in government policy, the implications of this for pedestrians are horrendous. Although there is much we can learn from our sister
countries in north-west Europe, they themselves recognise that their traffic
problems are far from completely solved and that much scope remains for
enhancing the walking environment. The following sections suggest how
this might be approached systematically.

Definitions and basic requirements

An important reason for the historical neglect of pedestrians has been the
tendency to think of communications in the town-planning context as
'transport' rather than 'travel' or even 'traffic'. Such a conceptualisation
emphasises 'arranged movement' and hence mechanisation as distinct from
travel (which includes autonomous movement such as walking) or traffic
(which again includes pedestrians since they are moving and hence 'traffic'). The American term 'transportation', increasingly adopted in the
United Kingdom, emphasises the 'arranged' aspect of transport even
more. In spite of its universal practice, walking somehow seems to be
regarded not only as inevitable (which it largely is) but also as mundane
(which it need not be) and unimportant (which it is not).

The significance of this choice of terminology applies equally in the fields
of municipal engineering and associated research. Local authorities typically have a department of highways/roads/transport, again stressing
assisted forms of movement. The relevant government ministry is referred

to as 'Transport' and, comparably, its research wing as the Transport and Road Research Laboratory. Moreover, research units in British universities and similar institutions for the most part prefer to use the term 'transport' in their title.

Although 'walking' when used in ordinary speech connotes a moderate speed and particular gait, in this context it is intended to cover all movement on foot in public places, whether sprinting, jogging, romping, striding out or ambling; or indeed any of the more or less stationary poses such as standing, sitting, crouching or lying down.

Especially in the traffic philosophy prevalent in Scandinavian countries, pedestrians along with pedal-cyclists are categorised as 'weak traffic' or 'soft traffic'. This is to highlight the features which distinguish them, namely, non-motorised (hence relatively slow-moving) and lacking a protective envelope (the vehicle chassis). The situation is more complicated in countries where draught animals are still widely used on the roads.

This tendency to treat pedestrians in combination with cyclists can lead to much confusion. It ignores, for example, the great difference in their respective scale and pattern of flow, pedestrians typically being much more numerous and much more highly concentrated than cyclists in and around important commercial and social centres. Typical journey lengths are also significantly different.

To describe pedestrians as 'soft traffic', however, helps to throw up another basic distinction from motorised traffic – the organic and sensuous nature of the pedestrian in contrast to the inorganic and insensitive machine (Ramsay, 1977). More tenuously, cars are manufactured to discrete sizes, with engine performance, etc. clearly specified. The size and properties of individual humans are much more varied, and vary continuously throughout their life (Pheasant, 1986).

In the framing and executing of travel surveys, the difficulty arises of the informal and incidental nature of much walking. Many journeys on foot cover only very short distances and many of them are within buildings, or moving only within or very near curtilages of buildings. Again, every journey by car, bus or train generates its own walking trips to and from the vehicle – what could be termed ancillary walking. Should these trips be recorded? If not, huge gaps will exist in the deduced traffic pattern, for they almost certainly constitute the great majority of movements on foot in town centres. Surely the criterion should be that all movements in streets, paths and associated surfaces open to the public for travel are included as far as this may be feasible.

Ramsay (1986) explains the terms used to define various types of route or other special facilities for pedestrians. Of these, the most basic are:

— the distinction between a footway (part of a highway for walking, alongside the carriageway) and a footpath (route exclusively for walking away from the carriageway); and

— right-of-way (a legal term referring to the public's right of passage, and by extension, to the track or path itself which is usually in the countryside or on the edge of a settlement).

The lack of widely agreed definitions reflects how poorly developed are the concepts and practices relating to positive provision for the pedestrian. The basic requirements for walking in acceptable conditions are:

— availability: the system must be accessible by right to all users within reason;
— negotiability: the routes, surfaces, etc. should not present a real barrier to any significant group;
— safety: the pedestrian must be able to use the system with a good prospect of traffic safety and personal security;
— economy: pedestrians should not be subject to congestion and undue delay, whether caused by lack of footpath capacity or obstructing streams of vehicles;
— convenience: any implied detours should be very limited;
— comfort: users should not have to suffer distressing conditions (climatically or socially); and
— amenity: every effort must be made in planning, design, construction and management to provide as pleasant and enjoyable an environmental experience as possible.

The parameters and standards under each of these headings would be relatively easy to establish if the relevant characteristics of all pedestrians were identical. In fact, however, pedestrians vary greatly; furthermore, the characteristics of any individual pedestrian change significantly with age.

One has to decide, therefore, which group of pedestrians exhibits the critical characteristics in respect of each determining factor, e.g. chairbound persons need the greatest width of even surface in which to circulate, and (since seated) have a very low eye height which restricts their visibility more than most, whereas adult males tend to be tallest and so require the greatest headroom. To cover most generalities, one can say that standards should satisfy the needs and preferences of the very young, and the very old and the seriously disabled as the three groups with the most critical characteristics from a planning point of view. (See Ramsay, 1977, for a detailed exposition on such factors.)

Urban networks and the planning process

In practice, networks for walking are only part of a wider physical environment, comprising:

- buildings, gardens and open areas lying between routes, and
- travel/transport routes traversing the town.

Hence the possibilities and conditions for walking are critically influenced by town planning decisions on policy and zoning, and to some extent also by those on programme. Within Great Britain, the process of plan-making recognised by statute since the late 1960s assumes two stages – structure plans followed by local plans. The structure plan is far-ranging in space and time and defines only broad strategies. Local plans elaborate these for particular areas, in accordance with the principles laid down in the structure plan.

Any policy aiming for the creation of a town-wide travel network would be strategic by its very nature, whether the network consists of railways, roads or footpaths. Conversely, the common assumption in the preparation of plans that walking routes are not a strategic matter implies (as a corollary) rejection of any notion of setting up a separate or special route system for pedestrians. In essence, this is why most urban authorities have failed to establish walking routes substantial enough for these to constitute a reasonably comprehensive system.

The municipality of Bordeaux has recently adopted a radical strategy relating to the city's existing road network, designating each route into one of three tiers in a hierarchy, namely:

- 'red': priority for motor traffic at a maximum speed of 50 km/h;
- 'blue': for delivery vehicles and public transport at 30 km/h; and
- 'white': for pedestrians and cyclists.

In the plan, which is to be achieved within 10 years, around 25 per cent by length of all routes will be red, 25 per cent blue and 50 per cent white. This is essentially a scheme for traffic management, aiming to adapt the traffic to suit the city rather than vice versa. While such a dramatic change will undoubtedly achieve a major improvement in conditions for pedestrians and cyclists, to achieve a well-planned system for walking will take much more thought, time and resources.

Traditionally, it has been seen primarily as the role of the municipal engineer rather than the town planner to analyse existing traffic patterns, assess deficiencies in the present routes and junctions, and formulate proposals for extending and improving the network. Hence town planners with positive ideas about providing independent networks for pedestrians tend to lack the necessary knowledge and skill with which to pursue such ideas, either by themselves or in collaboration with other professionals. Even municipal engineers, while they may be familiar with the calculative routines for planning a road network of sufficient capacity for the vehicles it is expected to have to carry in the future, have in general only the vaguest or crudest notion of how to do the equivalent for pedestrian traffic.

Truth to tell, pedestrian traffic patterns are as yet insufficiently under-stood for anyone to tackle this job with any degree of confidence. Only in the last few years has the TRRL seemed, by its budget allocation and research programme, to attach any significance to such problems. Even then, it has concentrated on low-cost measures to improve road safety marginally rather than adopting a holistic approach to planning for pedes-trians. Predictably, then, government manuals give only the slightest ad-vice on the location and dimensioning of facilities for pedestrians (e.g. the Institution of Highways and Transportation with Department of Transport, 1987).

So how should networks for walking be planned? For areas already developed, it approximates to the maze problem – how to select, mainly from the existing street system, routes which are suitable for conversion/a-doption as part of the primary footpath system. In the main, these will be longish stretches of secondary through-roads carrying volumes of vehicular traffic well below their capacity, especially if the readiest alternative routes for the main diverted flows possess spare capacity too. Another basic aim should be to provide, as far as possible, traffic-free routes from all residen-tial addresses to local schools, especially primaries and nurseries; to the nearest district centre for shopping, etc.; and to any sizeable employment areas within, say, two kilometres of the group of dwellings under consideration.

For areas still to be developed, the task should be one of trying to weave the network into the proposed urban structure in such a way as to give adequate capacity, feasible routes topographically and a reasonable enough choice of route to avoid undue detours.

In either case, the network topology is highly constrained by the main networks of roads, railways and waterways (where applicable), in that grade-separated crossings would be desirable at all places where these would (otherwise) intersect the footpath network. Since the main road network is bound to be the most extensive of those 'interlocking' with the footpath system, the problem then becomes one of deciding how many primary routes for walking should be provided between each adjacent pair of main roads running in broadly the same direction.

If only one such is deemed necessary, it should be located roughly midway between the enclosing roads so as to give the best potential traffic-free ambiance. If, say, three such are thought to be required, then the zone should be divided approximately into three equal strips and each path located along the middle of a strip. The above procedure assumes a relatively even density of development. If certain parts of the zone are more heavily developed, the alignment of paths should be skewed so as to reflect this spatial bias, thus giving a tighter network in the densest areas.

There are other common factors, e.g. the need for 'service' equipment such as benches, toilets, phones and shelters *en route*, for wayfinding aids (signing, etc.), and for servicing staff to provide casual food and drink, local information, surface cleansing and maintenance and security patrols. Arguably, there are also less tangible but equally crucial needs for aesthetic treatment of the pathscape and for casual opportunities to socialise and enjoy artistic displays and performances of various kinds.

Pedestrian service points should be located at the busiest intersections of primary footpaths. In these would be the largest concentrations of service facilities and personnel, e.g. as transfer points from roads they could offer electrically driven wheelchairs for hire to disabled people to be used for travel between such service points.

Another practical consideration is the relationship to utilities networks. These represent as big a complication as the road, railway and waterway networks. They are not normally visible (being buried), but the public became aware of their existence when excavations are made for repair or replacement. Official policy needs to be urgently revised so that utility mains, at least in new areas of development, are placed in a special verge, clear of the walking surface. Only then will it be possible to contain the continually growing problem of disruption of pedestrian routes caused by street works.

Geometrical aspects

Those who advocate a ring-and-radial geometry for footpath networks suppose that all towns conform to the concentric model of urban growth, and that the road network should also assume a similar geometry (but displaced by rotation). Where rectangular grids of roads or supergrids of main roads have been established or proposed, one would rather expect a rectangular grid to be suggested for the footpath system also, displaced on each main axis by, say, half the module. In practice, the geometry of the primary or macromodular path network must relate to both general town shape, and scale, regularity and orientation of other principal transport networks.

Since the shape of towns and the geometry of such other networks are never entirely regular (often being distorted to reflect, for instance, a coastal location or siting astride a winding river), it is most constructive to consider all networks as topological grids, with the footpath net interwoven and interlocking with each and every other transport system. Overbridges or underpasses would then obviate surface intersections of the footpath links with any others, as far as feasible.

Motor and pedestrian traffic both tend to concentrate radially towards town centres, so that the layout module should reduce in sympathy. With main road networks, however, the scope for doing this is strictly limited by the corresponding reduction in throughput capacity of major junctions as they become closer to one another. Primary walking routes on the other hand are handling traffic of a quite different dynamic character – the speed regime is considerably lower, weaving is much easier and lateral acceleration is appreciably greater. The minimum interval for these to retain their efficacy is much less, say 50 metres compared with one to two kilometres for main vehicular routes.

Likewise, frontage access is normally prohibited or heavily discouraged on primary through-routes for vehicles, whereas frequent direct access to primary footpaths is not only tolerable but indeed almost essential if they are to perform efficiently in that role.

Visibility from the driver's viewpoint (literally) is a basic parameter in the planning and design of roads, particularly those intended for high-speed operation. Visibility from the pedestrian's stance is equally crucial for their safety but is not provided for formally in the conventional design process. This needs to be urgently reviewed for equity's sake.

An associated problem for the pedestrian in traffic is the discrepancy between actual speeds of vehicles using a road and its official design speed. Because visibility standards are related to speed of travel, motorists who exceed the design speed deprive themselves of sufficient visibility for safe stopping. Since the relationship is an exponential one, greatly excessive speeds create much more than proportionate risks. Pedestrians must be protected against this by the installation of physical barriers which prevent vehicles travelling at speeds substantially above the assumed limit.

Aesthetic, social and psychological aspects

Paradoxically, the 'street schemes' promoted by the Civic Trust in the 1960s covered everything but the street surface. In their approach to civic design, architects have been preoccupied with elevations of buildings, and with changes of level in the street scene, as demonstrated by standard texts such as Cullen's (1961). This could be likened to designing an interior without considering the choice of floor-covering. The 'floorscape' scheme carried out in Durham City is one of the notable exceptions. Town planners are at last beginning to recognise the scope for integrating inputs related to elevations, horizontal surfaces and street furniture in the widest sense.

Municipal engineers have seen it as their responsibility to arrange service equipment such as street lighting, even if sometimes seeking the advice of landscape architects regarding planting, seating, etc. Moreover, all these designing professionals have a tradition of formulating their designs within tightly conceived territorial boundaries. Municipal engineers in particular tend to adopt this 'project' approach, signified by the practice of defining the project's extent with a red line on a map and then never looking beyond that. Considering ideas for change in a wider perspective is a proper concern of the town planner, and some planners are now insisting on their right to contribute in this way or indeed to lead a multidisciplinary team in deciding the form to be proposed.

There is no highly developed and universally accepted theory of visual composition, merely conventions within various regions which reflect a culture tradition. Thus the *beaux-arts* tradition in France is obsessed with 'le grand axe', symmetrical compositions around a long axis, often consisting of monumental architecture and avenues of trees, whereas Camillo Sitte advocated a constantly curving vista with frontage irregularities in order to create variety and so maintain visual interest.

More specifically, there are very different attitudes and circumstances regarding what permanent fixtures should be put in the street. The Japanese tradition demands a bare street so that the view of the street and its buildings is uninterrupted. In India, by contrast, the objection to substantial provision of seats and so forth is that the pavements, in city centres at least, are already heavily congested by beggars living on the street and by hawkers and craftsmen occupying pitches for their stalls and workshops. Naturally, the priority there is to clear the pavement rather than fill it with extra items of street furniture.

Social factors should be taken into account too. First, members of households without a car walk more often than others. They also depend more on public transport so that any ancillary walking trips they make are typically longer than for those using cars. Hence there is a prima-facie case for according them more resources proportionately and a higher priority in schemes.

Badcock (1984) draws attention to the inequities built into how most cities are structured. In the normal configuration, people living in the 'inner ring' suffer very badly in that they have to put up with heavy flows of lorries, buses and cars through their locality, with all the associated pollution, noise and intrusion; whereas their generally low level of car ownership means that most are then all the more exposed to traffic-related danger, dirt and discomfort. Hence there is a social argument for prioritising such areas for action to improve safety and amenity.

The response of local authorities to this problem has tended to concentrate on low-cost schemes aimed at improving traffic safety within residential areas, such as the recent TRRL-sponsored experiments (Grime, 1987). A much more comprehensive and resolute approach must be taken if there is to be any hope of massive reductions in pedestrian casualties. Considering the spatial distribution of accidents in towns, this would imply making an impact also on the present situation on main through roads, where the bulk of pedestrian casualties occur and where the presumption has always been that the interests of motorists must be given precedence over those of pedestrians.

Lower speed limits (say, 25 or 30 km/h) need to be introduced on stretches of main road as they pass through busy town centres, shopping parades and other important civic areas. Means of physically ensuring compliance with these limits are essential, such as humps (as recently authorised on public roads in England) and waltzer-type waves (such as those installed in one or two French towns (Loiseau van Beurle, 1988).

In many districts of American cities, due to the very high rates of car ownership, anyone walking is suspected of being delinquent. If, as expected, car ownership continues to increase until in 30 years it has approximately doubled, it is likely that such a situation will also obtain in the United Kingdom unless deliberate attempts are made to counteract this tendency, e.g. by major investment in decent facilties for pedestrians, thus according implicit approval to walking.

Psychological factors are arguably the most important of all in the planning of walking routes. In their choice of places to be and routes to travel on foot, people have been observed to behave in compliance with the 'prospect-refuge' theory, i.e. to seek positions which afford some sort of protective backdrop while enabling at the same time the observation of one's surroundings.

Coleman's research (1985) into London housing estates was based on the general hypothesis that all anti-social behaviour by residents is at least partly prompted by a poorly designed environment. A complication here is that people react differently to their environment, depending on their culture and personality. Nonetheless certain general principles obtain. For example, walking surfaces should be wide enough to enable people walking in a social group to proceed side by side and so maintain their integrity. Again, pathscapes should reflect or transmit the identity of their locality. This can be achieved by ground modelling, choice of vegetation (scale and species), provision of outdoor sculpture in the vernacular, use of local materials and methods in construction, securing views of well-known landmarks and so on.

Particularly for strangers, aids to way-finding help to convey a sense of security. Government directions and regulations on traffic signs treat pedestrians scantily and shabbily, e.g. most direction signs are conceived for the benefit of motorists, listing destinations which for the most part are well beyond practical walking distance. Further, the 'no through road' sign is sometimes inaccurate in that a path for walking may emanate from the head of what is a cul-de-sac only in respect of the carriageway. Braille signs indicating the sequence of shops have been installed in the pedestrianised sections of Sauchiehall Street, Glasgow as part of the recent upgrading scheme. There is great scope for such aids to the blind, as well as for the commoner 'talking pelicans', tactile strips and the like.

Footpaths should all bear a name of their own, which could then be used in the addresses of all properties having direct access to them. If street nameplates carried the first part of the postcode plus the next character, pedestrians searching for an address could confirm that they had arrived in the correct vicinity, provided they knew the postcode of the address being sought.

Similarly, street and path maps are especially valuable to pedestrians in that detours are particularly wearing when on foot. Street maps seldom show footpaths systematically: doubtless this is partly because of the typically sparse provision of such routes in towns, and the absence of official names for the few that do exist. If paths are to be fully used, the potential users must be made aware of their existence.

The value of indicating compass directions should not be overlooked. This can most readily be done by embedding a compass diagram in the paving, as done so attractively at Basildon town centre.

Summary: character of the ideal network

As a kind of summary of the ideas discussed within the previous sections, the following portrayal of the ideal network is proffered:

- All citizens, but particularly those most vulnerable to traffic, should have direct and easy access at all times to the primary system.
- To achieve maximum safety, the network itself should be separate from, but interlocking with, the main road and rail systems. This will necessitate regular grade-separated crossings in order to sustain the coverage and continuity of the network for walking.
- To achieve the optimum conditions for security, paths must be wide and well serviced with phones, good lighting, etc. and patrolled regularly. Their alignment must be such that people can see far enough ahead to be able to anticipate potential danger and take avoiding action.
- The basic geometry of the path net should reflect the pattern of land uses and building densities, so that normally as one approaches the town centre of any large district centre an intensification of the route density and services for pedestrians should be expected.
- To accommodate changes in land use and intensity of pedestrian movement related to building densities, any urban network of footpaths must be planned in a flexible way so that it is capable of extension into expanding suburbs and of adjustment within areas of major redevelopment or changes of use.

For these goals to be achieved, the European Charter of Pedestrians' Rights, included in full as the frontispiece to this book, must be adopted and enacted.

While one could have hoped for less ambiguous wording of Clauses V and VI(g), the Charter as a whole is fairly comprehensive and succeeds in making a plausible and inspiring statement of ambitions for the European Community. Let us hope that the governments of the Member States are bold enough to take up the challenge without delay.

References

Badcock, B., 1984, *Unfairly structured cities*, Blackwell, Oxford.

Coleman, A., 1985, *Utopia on trial: vision and reality in planned housing*, Hilary Shipman, London.

Crowther and Buchanan Groups *pro* Minister of Transport, 1963, *Traffic in towns*, HMSO, London.

Cullen, G., 1961, *Townscape*, Architectural Press, London.

Gehl, J., 1960 (tr. J. Koch, 1987), *Life between buildings: using public space*, Van Nostrand Reinhold, New York.

Grime, G., 1987, *Handbook of road safety research*, Butterworths, London.

Institution of Highways and Transportation with Department of Transport, 1987, *Roads and traffic in urban areas*, HMSO, London.

Loiseau van Beurle, F., 1988, *'Pedestrian safety in European towns'*, paper to the Planning Exchange conference 'A better deal for pedestrians', Glasgow, 12–13 May.

Martin, G., 1961, *The town: a visual history of modern Britain*, Studio Vista, London.

Matson, T.M., *et al.*, 1955, *Traffic engineering*, McGraw-Hill, New York.

Pheasant, S., 1986, *Bodyspace: anthropometry, ergonomics and design*, Taylor and Francis, London.

Plowden, W., 1971, *The motor car and politics 1896–1970*, Bodley Head, London.

Ramsay, A., 1977, *'Scope and criteria for pedestrianisation'*, M.A. research thesis, University of Manchester, Department of Town and Country Planning.

—— 1986, *Planning for pedestrians*, topicguide 3, 2nd ed, Capital Planning Information, Stamford, Lincs.

Reynolds, D.J., 1960, *The assessment of priority for road improvements*, RR TP 48, Road Research Laboratory, Harmondsworth.

Road Research Laboratory (RRL), 1965, *Research on road traffic*, HMSO, London.

Starkie, D., 1982, *The motorway age: road and traffic policies in post-war Britain*, Pergamon, Oxford

Tolley, R.S., 1990, *Calming traffic in residential areas*, Brefi Press, Tregaron.

Webb, B. and Webb, S., 1920, *The story of the King's highway*, English Local Government, Longmans Green.

11 Why you can't walk there: strategies for improving the pedestrian environment in the United States

Rich Untermann

Introduction

All the problems planners face today in adapting our communities to serve pedestrians and cyclists have emerged in the last half of this century. Our communities were pedestrian friendly prior to the Second World War, but then over the last 45 years we have rebuilt them to accommodate the automobile, leaving pedestrians few opportunities to walk or bike.

Until the end of the Second World War, most people lived in communities where walking was a necessary part of getting to work, play, school or shop. Many towns in both Europe and the United States had a bus or transit system that was used and supported by residents. Land uses were mixed and compact with houses located reasonably close to goods and services. Business and retail centres were concentrated and mixed to include a variety of activities: it was possible to satisfy most of one's daily needs on foot or with a bicycle. Beyond that, there were few motor vehicles, cars had limited reliability, and driving was a somewhat restricted activity. Even when people drove, walking formed a substantial portion of the trip.

Communities were organised to support walking and cycling. Residential neighbourhoods were adjacent to retail districts. They had sidewalks, kerbs and gutters and street trees. Though laid out to serve cars, American towns and cities were safe and pleasant places to walk in. Downtown had wide sidewalks, awnings for rain or sun protection, on-street parking to shield pedestrians from the traffic, and narrow-fronted shops with attractive window displays orientated to shoppers. Each business district had a convenient mix of shops so it was possible to use a bank, drugstore, hardware store, coffee shop, or restaurant and still visit the doctor – all on foot. Often there was a strong 'sense of community' as people shopped weekly in the same stores so as to meet friends and to be a part of a community. The 'socialness' of the setting was important and that 'socialness' was enhanced by people being able to meet friends because they were on foot.

Following the war, there were dramatic changes in the form and land use of communities, changes that drastically reduced the safety and ease of walking and cycling. The changes were obviously different in Europe from those in the United States: Europe was rebuilding its cities,while the United States was expanding into suburban and rural areas.

American community developments since the Second World War

Suburban development had been occurring in the United States for many years before the war, but the pattern of development was appropriate for walking. Railroads, street cars and in some places the automobile extended housing opportunities a short distance out from the cities into small new neighbourhoods. Each important trolley or train stop became the focus of a small retail district, and neighbourhoods developed around them. Most of these districts were compact, mixed-use neighbourhoods organized with a traditional pedestrian-orientated Main Street. While the main wage-earner commuted by trolley to town during the day, the family remained behind and carried out many of its activities on foot or bicycle.

The wholesale expansion into suburban areas following the war was a very different phenomenon. Prior to the war, development *followed* infra-structure: rail and trolley lines organised development patterns. Residents had to live close to stations for convenience, as flexibility to settle else-where was limited by access to goods and services. The war changed all that. Returning GIs needed housing and employment. Automobile tech-nology was vastly improved and retired 'war production' factories began producing automobiles inexpensively. The gasoline and oil industry was booming, and the road-building and construction industries were hungry for new challenges.

The policy-makers in Washington, DC saw this energy best employed in suburban expansion. The government provided low-cost loans for subur-ban housing and subsidies for massive road construction projects. Many of these initial roads were wider than necessary in order to transport military vehicles. The roads all combined to create a federal highway system, and eventually similar state and local road building took on a scale and pace that was never before imagined.

The important change was that development was no longer infrastructure-bound. It could occur *randomly* in the landscape, prior to completion of any trolley or railroad lines. Even if roads were poor, development could occur, with farm land converted to housing, shopping, schools or parks. Development sought the least expensive land, since people could drive to wherever they needed relatively easily and inexpensively. Distances between home and market or work grew and stores began to locate in a random fashion. The resulting pattern of auto-orientated development no longer worked for pedestrians or cyclists, for it was impossible to reach needed destinations on foot, since they were all randomly placed and separated by long distances.

The ensuing years were spent expanding the road network. 'Transportation' planning became reactive, allocating funds to build roads to meet the overwhelming demand of more cars operating in increasingly decentralised regions. To stretch the road-building dollars, pedestrian facilities were reduced and eventually eliminated. New roads were constructed without sidewalks, kerbs or other pedestrian amenities. Roads became wider and wider over time. Widening a road often meant eliminating the sidewalk. Walking alongside roads or crossing streets became dangerous and uncomfortable. Parking was prohibited on many streets to increase the flow of traffic, and that further reduced pedestrian comfort and opportunity. The conversion of streets from social places to channels of traffic was becoming a reality.

Hierarchical road patterns replaced the multidirectional grid and pedestrian opportunities were further decreased. Hierarchical roads channelled cars in increasing numbers to wider and wider roads. With an incomplete road network, pedestrians no longer had easy access to many facilities and activities.

Land uses began to change to serve the automobile. 'Strip' commercial developments lined major roads, with large parking lots separating the street from the buildings. Shopping centres appeared on the corners of every major intersection. With their wide driveways, pedestrian safety was compromised. Pedestrian-orientated facilities in narrow 'Main Streets' were converted to windowless façades with wide frontages to match the size requirements of larger parking lots and the higher speeds of automobile travel. Fences separated properties, so walking between stores became impossible. Shopping and jobs continued to move to strip locations on the busiest arterials. These roads were strictly auto-orientated,with unsafe and unpleasant walking conditions, and soon stores and jobs became inaccessible to pedestrians.

Auto-orientated shopping created entirely new ways of merchandising, and these slowly replaced older pedestrian shopping precincts. High-volume discount 'carry home' retail sales became the trademark of the newer strips and shopping centres. Small-town 'pedestrian' business districts and corner neighbourhood stores could not compete. One by one, individual stores went out of business and soon the last vestige of true pedestrian environments – 'Main Street' – disappeared.

Some may argue that the shopping mall became the new pedestrian precinct. While these were internally pedestrianised, the isolation created by vast parking lots and surrounding freeways meant that reaching them required a car. Isolated strips and mini-malls developed around every shopping mall, each with its own large parking lot. Streets were widened to handle increased traffic,and soon crossing them on foot became dangerous and uncomfortable. In fact, crossing a street to reach another store often required driving there, even though the time taken on foot was far less. Fewer safe pedestrian places meant fewer pedestrians and as there were fewer pedestrians, there was less need to serve them; the downward spiral continued.

Suburban development occurred in outlying counties and rural communities with unsophisticated planning processes and little public participation. Promises of a better tomorrow were commonplace. Political processes were controlled by the development and road-building community. Questions of environmental degradation, resource depletion, loss of 'sense of community' and pedestrian safety were unimaginable. Everything 'suburban' seemed positive and better than ever before. Professional planners were busy learning their new reactive role and trying to keep up with traffic. There were new 'auto-orientated' theories on community form. Traditional ideas of community organisation were abandoned and the universities produced three or four generations of planners who were only able to think and act in auto-orientated terms.

In the United States, engineers who were skilled at moving cars and building places that served the automobile were advanced and rewarded. In many traffic departments, the person planning for pedestrians and cyclists was the least skilled auto transportation engineer, relegated there by default. These people were not forceful advocates for pedestrians and their passive approach missed many opportunities to develop good pedestrian environments.

Meanwhile, vehicles were becoming cheaper and more reliable. Families needed two or three to do all their chores, plus a recreational vehicle. Congestion increased, roads grew wider and with better roads the speed of travel increased. Drivers, in their quest to accomplish more and more by car, travelled faster and faster, and stopped less frequently for pedestrians. Fights between drivers over simple rights caused pedestrians to be less willing to demand their rights. For a driver to ignore amber traffic lights has become routine, while the number running red lights is alarming.

Police officers have grown noticeably supportive of cars over pedestrians or cyclists. In city after city police have been transferred from 'foot beats' to patrol cars, leaving them less supportive of a walking population. Police hassle jay-walkers in many cities, when in fact jay-walking is a safe activity that marks a successful social street. Fewer and fewer tickets are given for speeding or running traffic signals or stop signs. In Seattle police ticket jay-walkers seven times more frequently than they ticket drivers of cars who violate pedestrians' rights.

Many traffic rules have been altered to serve automobiles at the expense of pedestrians. A typical in-town speed limit of 35 mph (55 km/h) is far too fast for pedestrian safety. It is even worse given the tendency of Americans to drive faster than the posted limit. A 30 km/h speed limit, observed and enforced, is the maximum that encourages walking. Allowing free right turns to speed up traffic creates real hazards for pedestrians crossing the street. The Uniform Traffic Code rules for crossing streets gives vehicles a major advantage, one that is wholly uncalled for.

Suburban problems have spilled over into the cities. Most jobs were located downtown and facilities were poor, so transit workers commuted from the suburbs by car. Traffic build-up followed and soon the city centre was widening its roads, eliminating sidewalks, tearing down buildings to create parking lots and generally reducing the quality of pedestrian environments. Large parking garages located under high rises allowed workers to remain all day inside their buildings, never using the sidewalk. Downtown housing was razed to build parking lots and high rises, further reducing the pedestrian viability of downtown. Street life in many downtowns diminished, as did the city's walking facilities.

All of the recent auto-orientated development leaves us with two kinds of planning problems that complicate the development of pedestrian and bicycle facilities. They are:

— an existing land-use and transportation pattern that is not appropriate for walking and cycling; and
— auto-orientated attitudes, ideas and beliefs that are thoroughly embedded in the minds of the planners, decision-makers and population.

These attitudes have led to the development of high levels of funding for new road construction and auto-orientated standards for street design that make cycling and walking difficult.

European community development since the war

Needless to say, this author has greater familiarity with American than European town planning; however, some comparative observations may be helpful. Europe had a far greater task following the war than the United States, that of both rebuilding its cities and housing its war-ravaged population. It had one advantage that benefited pedestrians – Europeans were urban-orientated, with much of their development at higher densities and of greater mixed uses than in the United States. In time, though, with increased prosperity, improved communication and the availability of the automobile, Europeans sought 'higher' standards of living, fell in love with the automobile, moved to suburbia, and walked less.

Even though many European people still walk and use public transportation, there has been a decrease in pedestrian comfort and safety in most European communities. Build-up of cars has left many unsafe walking places. Preserving the delicate balance necessary to sustain older, pedestrian-orientated districts against the impacts of the automobile is difficult. The slightest increase in the number of automobiles in a community where cars were never part of the original layout offsets the balance very quickly. European streets were easily clogged with a few additional cars and as that occurred the quality of the air decreased, noise increased and pedestrian safety and comfort tumbled.

Cycling is an even riskier activity than walking in much of Europe, except perhaps in Holland. Cyclists are compromised by too many cars on narrow roads, so that while there are always a few hardy souls willing to risk a dangerous and unpleasant situation, the majority of potential cyclists are wisely timid and, if they have one, use their car instead.

Suburban communities began to emerge around many European metropolitan areas. Some of these were developed in an urban spirit, i.e. dense, connected to older cities by public transportation and perhaps laid out to encourage walking. Even so, they were designed to accommodate cars and were more spacious than older cities. Maintaining short distances between activities is a critical factor to encourage walking and even the slightest increase can cause busy people to drive instead of walk. Residents soon purchased automobiles and began to use them more frequently.

This subtle build-up in the use of the automobile has had a major impact on the pedestrian viability of many small towns and the larger cities. Over time, the newer commercial facilities began to employ land use and transportation forms that catered to automobiles, with larger parking lots, deeper building setbacks, reduced pedestrian facilities, poorer public transportation, and so forth.

Many Europeans experienced the same lifestyle change as was occurring in the United States, a shift from neighbourhood orientation to regional identity. People lived in one community and worked or shopped in another. People had extra income, increased leisure, travel and time away from their home, but life was busier and families needed a car to accomplish all their tasks. Many families bought two cars, further congesting the roads. All this fostered a life with little time for walking or bicycling.

Europe did recognise the drawbacks of 'automobility' early on and many cities took some form of evasive action. With more planning authority than in the United States, many suburban communities were able to develop co-ordinated plans and land-use patterns that were pedestrian friendly. Some older cities restricted cars by constructing 'pedestrian zones'. Many 'High Streets' now cater exclusively for pedestrians, with networks of pedestrian-friendly paths leading back into the neighbourhoods. Car-free areas work and have been readily accepted by small and large towns over the last 25 years. People walk safely and comfortably as they carry out their shopping, work and socialising activities, while residents live in relative peace and quiet. The air is fresher and merchants again use personal sales techniques appropriate for pedestrian shopping.

Some car-free zones have their own set of problems. To create the zones, planners developed peripheral bypass roads, modelled after those proposed by Colin Buchanan. Unfortunately, these roads degraded their immediate surroundings and prevented pedestrians living in outlying communities from reaching the town centres, pinching off some pedestrian potential.

In terms of opportunities for enhancing pedestrian facilities, Europe is better off than the United States in many ways, but worse off in others. On the one hand, its citizens are urban-orientated, and still maintain an attitude and awareness of the needs and opportunities that pedestrian circulation offers. The planners and policy-makers are also urban-orientated and familiar with the ingredients necessary to create community form that serves pedestrians. So the *attitudes* supporting walking are more in place than they are in America.

On the negative side, European cities do not have as much space as the United States does to introduce adequate pedestrian and bicycle facilities. Most communities are compact, the streets narrow and land-use patterns more fully and permanently developed. There will be hard political choices in allocating space between the competing demands of car and pedestrian.

The American scene

In the United States, the two principal changes necessary to create positive pedestrian environments are:

— educating planners, decision-makers, and populations of the needs, opportunities and techniques necessary to enhance pedestrian and bicycle circulation; and
— changing land-use patterns and transportation facilities the better to accommodate pedestrians.

These two tasks necessitate unravelling almost 50 years of bad development practices. Some of the solutions are quite obvious. We need more sidewalks, creating a network of comfortable access between home, school, work and play. We need improved safety at all street crossings, better street lighting, reduced speed limits for cars, and myriad other adjustments that make it possible to walk and ride bicycles as part of our daily activities.

Building new communities

Other changes, like adding housing and offices to 'strip' and shopping centres, or reducing the amount of parking, are more complex and will take time. As a start, it may be easier to develop *new communities* that are responsive to pedestrian needs than it is to refit existing communities. We know how to create new communities that reduce the need for excessive reliance on the automobile and how far residential commercial districts can be from one another and still be reachable on foot. We know something about the best arrangements to support pedestrian and bicycle activity. However, we have had little success developing new, pedestrian-orientated communities in the United States over the last 25 years. Part of the problem lies in the very expensive start-up costs and environmental problems associated with large-scale development. But a more pressing problem is the unwillingness of developers to build 'walking' communities at a time when potential residents are so entrenched in auto-orientated lifestyles.

One inexpensive policy planning approach is to require new development to be in medium-density, mixed-use, large-scale, planned communities. These communities would presumably be developed on land selected for its transit connection to other employment opportunities, and planned using arrangements that reduce the impact of, and need for, automobile travel. They would be denser than most suburban projects, with a compact business community located near residential districts. Residents could stay healthy by walking or biking to work, or use public transportation. Narrow roads with safe sidewalks for pedestrians would be the norm. Roads or trails would be planned for bicycles and good public transportation should be adequately funded.

Such developments might require subsidies to offset the initial costs of long-term development. They most certainly would require political support during the community-involvement phase and assurances that the planning and design teams were skilled in designing pedestrian and bicycle communities. Responsibility for developing pedestrian environments would be assigned to the most skilled and capable transportation and land-use planners. This is by no means easily done, as most planners have limited knowledge of what is necessary to develop pedestrian friendly places (though many think they can learn quickly). It would also be necessary to curtail adjacent low-density developments so that the new planned communities would have a real chance to function. Overall, there would be a conscious shift from our current decentralised, random pattern of development to centralised, compact communities similar to medieval cities. In such new communities, cars would seem out of place for normal day-to-day activities.

One can imagine a number of new pedestrian-orientated communities constructed across the United States that repeat some of the early British

New Town models. They might be nestled within 35 kilometres of down-town, on up to 5000 acres of land, and with populations ranging from 20 000 to 50 000 people. They would presumably be located near public transportation routes, near employment, and adjacent to open space. They should also be sited in attractive locations so residents could recreate near home, further reducing automobile dependence.

That scenario is easier to discuss than it is to accomplish. It would require federal or state legislation to help offset the substantial costs of initial development. Legislators would need to be educated on the import-ant environmental, health, energy and balance-of-payment problems that might be reduced by this type of development. It would also require regional allocation of growth areas and restriction of development on other lands. The history of growth controls and regional land use planning in the United States is uneven, and down-zoning land is complicated as land owners adamantly demand their right to develop their land. Whenever a new road is constructed, 'For Sale' signs immediately appear, and the suburban phenomenon begins anew.

Adjusting existing communities

Americans have fully adopted a lifestyle centred around the automobile with virtually every activity – shopping, work, play, romance, learning, etc. – all requiring using a car. There are generations of adults who have never walked to school or to the grocery store. They value the freedom made available to them by owning cars and are going to be very unwilling to give it up. Furthermore, we have created a landscape that supports the car; most of our communities are single-use instead of mixed, spread out instead of compact, low- instead of high-density, with extensive roads instead of a variety of transportation facilities.

Changing existing land-use and transportation patterns to meet pedes-trian needs will involve considerable education. It may not be fully possible until the costs of automobile travel climb drastically. That, of course, may soon be a reality, given the world's unstable oil supply, and our better understanding of the pollution and environmental damage caused by cars. However, we do not know some of the conditions and many of the development directions necessary to recycle existing communities the bet-ter to accommodate pedestrians. These include: improved public transpor-tation; mixed land uses; changing zoning ordinances; setting new road standards; developing comfortable pedestrian facilities; more research; and adjusting values through education.

Improved public transportation. There is beginning to be less resistance to discussing public transportation and improved pedestrian and bicycle facilities. Some cities have improved their transit, but there is still not much support for funding new projects on the scale that is necessary to support pedestrian activity. Moreover, there is considerable neighbour-hood resistance when it comes to locating actual routes. Residents even complain about proposed bike trails, arguing that their quality of life would decrease drastically. Meantime transit operators are all too willing to cut services on less frequently used routes, a policy that is completely contrary to supporting pedestrian friendly places.

Mixed land use. There is considerable resistance to mixing land uses and increasing density in existing American neighbourhoods. Americans be-lieve that higher density means more cars, worse traffic, parking problems, increased noise and crime, and all the horrors of urban life. They have many misconceptions about what a good community is, and so people use catch-phrases to describe good and bad environments. 'High density' means 'bad', 'low density' means 'good'. 'separate land uses' are 'good', 'mixed land uses' mean 'bad'; 'single-family houses' mean 'good', 'apart-ment developments' mean 'bad', and so on. Unfortunately, many recent auto-orientated developments in the United States reinforce this view, so that all people need to do is to look around to see that it is so.

We might select specific 'auto' places and convert them to serve pedes-trian needs. Converting linear strips and shopping centres to compact patterns so that pedestrians are better served will require changes in zoning and funds to improve the environment of these new special pedestrian districts. Adding housing, multi-storeyed offices and medical and dental services are all in order.

It is difficult without good examples to convince people that overall environmental quality and individual quality of life can be enhanced by places which support pedestrian activity, i.e. compact communities with mixed uses and sufficient density. Planners need to work carefully to produce selected 'role model' environments that are unique, safe and comfortable because of their adherence to good pedestrian and bicycle planning techniques. These models can then be used to educate deve-lopers, politicians and residents in other neighbourhoods.

Changing zoning ordinances. Many zoning ordinances produce environ-ments that are not pedestrian friendly, and they need to be rewritten. Zoning that encourages single, isolated land uses is incompatible with pedestrian and bicycle travel: to support pedestrians, planning land uses through zoning should require the integration of residential, commercial, retail and recreation uses.

Zoning ordinances that require deep setbacks from the street encourage parking lots between the sidewalk (if there is one) and the building. This results in an unattractive and unsafe sidewalk and a disjointed shopping arrangement. A minimal setback (at most 1.5 metres) would force the parking to be in the rear and refocus the street to serve pedestrian and other social purposes.

Moreover, zoning regulations that require high parking ratios make walking unpleasant because of the large areas of asphalt. Limiting the number of parking spaces or the size of parking lots may force people to carry out their activities on foot. Zoning regulations requiring parking for each store should be altered so people have less opportunity to park easily. Drive-in businesses should not be allowed as they compromise pedestrian safety and detract from the visual quality of the urban environment.

New 'road standards'.   As well as the need for new state or federal policies to redirect funding for land and transportation uses, there is also much technical and detailed work that needs to be done. For example, the United States current 'road standards' produce roads that serve the automobile, and should be rewritten to create more pedestrian friendly streets (Untermann, 1984). These road standards were developed over the last 40 years by highway engineers at the federal and state level to support high-volume, fast-moving, inter-city travel. They were supported by institutions such as the road-building industries, auto manufacturers, insurance corporations and auto clubs, groups whose power to dictate road design and hence community quality is enormous.

Because of subsidised funding requirements these standards have been inappropriately applied to many local roads. Typically they require wide lane widths, generous curb radii and straight vertical alignments to support high-speed auto travel. Many residential roads are 10 metres wide, when 6 would be perfectly adequate. Business and retail streets are designed without on-street parking to speed up traffic, resulting in an unsafe pedestrian environment. These 30-year-old street standards are still practised, even though vehicles are smaller, air pollution persists, and the social life of streets has vanished. Indeed, designers can no longer design attractive walking streets because most American communities adhere to old-fashioned, inappropriate, auto-oriented road standards.

Sidewalk standards are, not surprisingly, inadequate. Sidewalks are often not required, or built too narrow, or without protection from vehicles. Pedestrian friendly standards would encourage configurations to slow the speed of cars, restrict automobile entry in places, ensure wide sidewalks, allow ease of street crossing, and encourage environments that are safe and attractive in which to walk.

Changing road standards may also increase innovation in transport planning. Planners have learned not to do creative transportation planning because of liability fears. There is the belief that any road constructed that does not conform to adopted road standards (for instance, one with a narrow traffic lane, or tight intersection geometry) will render the designer and the community legally liable for any accidents occurring there. This prevailing attitude has diminished the designer's ability and desire to be innovative and to develop streets and places that are more pedestrian friendly and less auto-orientated.

Developing comfortable pedestrian facilities. In the United States, most roads have been designed by engineers, and have a very functional feel about them. They were designed to be viewed at higher speeds, say 55 km/h, and when viewed closely at walking speeds, are seen to lack detail and embellishment. The sidewalks are often unattractive, and do not encourage pedestrian use. There is little protection from sun or rain, or benches to sit and rest. We need to understand more about what detailed development makes pedestrians feel safe and comfortable, and begin to construct our pedestrian places more sensitively. Street crossing places need to be carefully marked and attractively landscaped.

Separate bicycle trails need to be constructed to encourage increased ridership. Large numbers of potential cyclists are wary of the dangers involved with cycling and simply will not take chances. Routes must connect shopping, school and work places with some efficiency, but they must be safe and pleasant. The battle for space will intensify, for America's roadways simply do not have enough room for autos, pedestrians, bikes and parking.

More research. The information on what makes places safe, comfortable and functional for pedestrians is scarce, so that we need to embark on a long-term research effort. Most planners are not able to say with any certainty what conditions will make a pedestrian or bicycle environment attractive. We do not know enough about what extends the desire to walk, what retail uses need to be in close proximity to each other, how close they should be, or the effect of various types of environment and numbers of cars on pedestrian activity. It would be helpful to understand how much centralisation, how much compactness, is required. There needs to be as much rigorous research about pedestrian and bicycle safety as there has been about auto safety. Walking has to be viewed as a serious contributor to solving our traffic and transportation problems, as a positive force that could solve many national problems.

We have too few theoretical pedestrian friendly land-use models to rely on, and need to generate and test additional ones. We rely too heavily on the 'centralised, compact community' theory: are there any others that assume decentralised activities and are thus more appropriate for converting suburban communities? There is a need to study hierarchical and grid-road orientations and to investigate at what point they interfere with pedestrian and bicycle transportation. The list goes on and on.

Adjusting values through education. The 40 years we have been building auto-orientated communities have left us without 'pedestrian' leadership on all land-use and transportation planning fronts. We have very few people – planners, landscape architects, designers, policy-makers, politicians, or citizen activists – who are knowledgeable and practised in developing successful pedestrian environments. This represents a great obstacle for those few people who are in tune with pedestrian needs, as they have very little collegial support. There is a need for massive educational programmes at all levels – from kindergarten to the university, and for community leaders as well. We need to develop a network of advocates through seminars, symposiums, books (such as this one), new courses in universities, short courses on 'Community and Street Design', etc. For planners *au fait* with the need for pedestrian circulation the greatest task in the advocacy of pedestrian places will be the education of others.

Conclusions

The problems may sound insurmountable, but the United States has examples of bits and pieces of each solution. Pedestrian friendly New Towns were financed in America during the 1960s with the New Communities Act, so presumably it could be done again. Many communities are guiding development to minimise sprawl by purchasing development rights, or using zoning creatively, or limiting access and utilities. There has been discussion in America of increasing the gasoline tax and using the proceeds for purposes other than highway building. A few cities are introducing new categories of road standards – 'park' streets, 'pedestrian' areas, *Woonerven*, etc. to open new options to design innovative places.

Some older suburban communities now realise that new development brings few advantages and many problems. Residents are beginning to resist new development and demand involvement in the planning process. This is a new phenomenon for suburban communities, whose developers have maintained almost complete control over the land-conversion process. Most of these citizen groups are reactionary and non-discriminatory: they fight all projects, good or bad. But at least there is a slowdown in continued sprawl.

In the end, it may be that new coalitions of institutions that have previously competed, such as environmental groups and the various governments at metropolitan, city, county and regional level, must come together to give more direction to transportation and land-use planning. Without doubt, professional organisations can and should direct more of their efforts to support plans that rely less on fossil fuels.

Reference

Untermann, R., 1984. *Accommodating the pedestrian: adapting towns and neighborhoods for walking and bicycling*, Van Nostrand, New York.

12 Walking and public transport: two sides of the same coin

Dietrich Garbrecht

Introduction

We talk about pedestrians – and we talk about phantoms. We talk about riders of public transport – and again we talk about phantoms. Or do you know somebody who will only and always walk when he wants to get somewhere? Or somebody who will only and always use public transport?

Transport is all about getting from one point to another and, depending on circumstances and on distance, we use different means. For very short distances we will use our shoes. Longer trips will consist of a combination of trips by shoe and trips using public transport, i.e. bus, tram or rail. This chapter will advance the view that the familiar compartmentalised way of conceptualising transport – walking or pedestrian system here, public transport system there – has direct and very real consequences on the environment. In other words, many of the unsatisfactory situations we encounter when wanting to get from A to B are a result of inadequate system definition.

Being able to get from A to B means that B is accessible from A. It also means that the city is permeable between A and B. Accessibility focuses on the destination, permeability stresses the environment between, stresses experiencing this environment. As we know, accessibility and permeability facilitate executing our life plans, pursuing our everyday activities. However, accessibility without safety is not really accessibility (the same holds for permeability). Children and the elderly are particularly sensitive to this condition – which is a prerequisite for autonomous, self-determined movement in the environment.

Today the system that provides accessibility with a high degree of safety and comfort is the one based on the private car. However, access to this accessibility is only available to those who have access to a car. As for the other ones, consider this example. An elderly couple wants to take a walk through a park which cannot be reached by foot. The couple leaves the house and walks down a quiet residential street. To get to the bus stop they have to cross two dangerous roads. They wait for the bus. They take the bus. After getting off, the couple must cross another dangerous road before getting to the park. After their walk through the park, the couple crosses a road (not that dangerous this time, but still a potential risk). They reach the bus stop. They wait. They board the bus and enjoy the scenery along the trip. They get off, cross two pretty heavily trafficked roads and reach the quiet residential street. The couple returns home.

Things are different in My City. In My City, planners and politicians and people think in terms of a Walking Transit System. In view of the fact that the technology that goes with public transportation is so dominant and so prevalent, one might have expected Transit Walking instead of Walking Transit. However, in My City people felt other criteria were even more important, such as autonomy (i.e. not depending on some technological system); conservation of energy; and harmlessness to other people, as well as to the natural, the urban and the architectural environment. For My City dwellers these were reasons enough to opt not for TWS, but for WTS.

In My City, transportation policy is embedded in a strategy of ecology-orientated city development. And it is aimed at securing safe accessibility and permeability to the population without car-access. In fact in My City WTS is supplemented by BTS, the bicycle transit system, though this is beyond the scope of this chapter.

Objective and principles

My City's premise is: 'make the whole to be more than the sum of its parts'.

The objectives of My City are to:

— give maximum freedom, autonomy and self-determination of move-ment to children, youngsters, housewives, mothers, the elderly, the handicapped and other no car-access people;
— make WTS as perfect as possible to make it comparable in safety and comfort with private car driving;
— make WTS a symbol for the values that are held high in My City.

To reach its goals, My City transportation policy follows several principles:

— provide a safe, comfortable and pleasant walkway system;
— provide an efficient and comfortable public transportation system;
— provide safe and pleasant connections between the two systems, i.e. public transit stops;
— give equal attention to all three sub-systems of the WTS.

Much has been written about desirable properties of walkway and of public transportation systems and does not need repeating here. However, with respect to walking, there are three properties for which My City stands out:

— specified levels of service are secured for all those parts of the walkway system which are part of WTS;
— in particular, getting to a transit stop quickly and unimpeded by obstacles or barriers is an essential prerequisite of an attractive WTS. From this principle follows the third one:
— whenever a walkway and a road cross, and whenever this walkway is part of the WTS, walking has priority over car driving.

My City Council has drawn far-reaching organisational consequences from its innovative approach to providing accessibility and permeability without basing it on the private automobile. The Council has established a Public Access Authority (PAA). The Authority consists of three major subdivisions:

— The Department for Non-Mechanised Access (walkways);
— the Department for Mechanised Access (transit); and
— the Department for Interfaces (transit stops).

Public transport stops

Among the many features that distinguish My City's WTS from almost any other city's transportation system, the stops are some of the more striking ones. The underlying philosophy is that the transit ride does not start when the customer boards the vehicle, but when he or she gets to the stop. Hence when people arrive at the interface they are, in a figurative sense, welcomed. The authorities apologise that the future passenger has to wait, they ask him or her to take a seat, to make themselves comfortable.

This is not simply rhetoric. The attitude of welcoming people is expressed by the amenities and the conveniences that are offered at the stop. The connection between the walking and the transit systems is interpreted, and designed, as a gesture of welcome.

In My City the main purpose of a transit stop (that of connecting walkway and transit systems) is taken seriously and priority is given precisely to this purpose. All interface areas are areas where public transport and pedestrians have priority over private car driving. Private traffic is not excluded, but tolerated. The car driver drives through the interface area as a guest. The traffic scheme is similar to the one in the Dutch *Woonerven* or to the one during delivery hours in pedestrianised areas. It is expressed in the layout and by the materials chosen: the road surface is interrupted and material used for walkways dominate.

Anyone visiting My City is struck by the structures which shelter walking transit interfaces. They are bigger than in other cities; they are small buildings in their own right, light, airy, well designed. They provide an amenity unheard of in most other surface transit systems: they protect you from the rain or snow not only once you have reached the shelter, but even when, stepping out from the shelter, you board the vehicle.

Sure enough, there has been a public debate about these pavilions. Conservationists argued that these structures destroyed traditional public spaces. But then the modernists prevailed. Their view was that the inter- face structures can be used to structure longitudinal, corridor streets. Here, as on piazzas, the decisive criterion is not the structure itself but the degree of integration, of connection, with surrounding buildings. Proportions and design quality are decisive. The modernists also claimed that there was no reason not to develop and modify public space according to today's necessities, especially in the light of the tremendous damage inflicted upon the cityscape by private car driving.

Many surface transit lines in cities run along major roads. These are roads difficult to cross for people who walk. In My City the interface areas, by giving priority to the pedestrian, provide points where one may cross major roads safely and conveniently. Hence interface areas are not only important points in the sense that they connect walkway and transit systems. They are also important points in the walkway system itself. As a matter of fact they may be interpreted as those areas which connect, in a near perfect way, walkway systems on either side of a major road.

The walkway system

Without going into the details of performance and design standards that the walkway system in My City satisfies, it seems appropriate to mention the following that are adhered to by the municipality.

First, whenever a walkway constituting a link in the WTS crosses a road (be it minor or major), the walking mode has priority over the (private car) driving mode. This applies to WTS walkways that provide access to a transit interface. It also holds for WTS walkways that do not provide direct access to a transit stop (e.g. WTS walkways running parallel to a line of mechanised access as described below). The main considerations behind this rule are:

— safety;
— attaining a high average walking speed (which is considerably lowered in conventional cities because of barriers and interruptions);
— convenience; and

— symbolic significance.

Second, the walkway system of WTS is not primarily a system of feeder walkways leading to walking transit interfaces. Rather, it is a city-wide, ubiquitous, continuous network spanning all of My City. Restricting the WTS-classified walkway network to feeder walkways would run counter to the general principles of overall accessibility, permeability and choice.

Furthermore, a feeder-walkway network would not correspond to the overlapping individual life-spaces of My City inhabitants. Which is to say that hardly ever will anyone walk a 10-km-long walkway running more or less parallel to a mechanised-access line. However, the many sections of this walkway, each one between, say, 50 and 150 metres long, will be part of the life-spaces of many people, and hence will be indispensable for the carrying out of these people's everyday routines.

Therefore, in My City good non-mechanised access of two points towards each other is a requirement even if mechanised access between the two points is provided for.

My City's lesson

Obviously there are many things other cities can learn from My City. By no means the least important is that even if the responsibilities for walkways and for public transit are not under the same roof, the respective departments should work closely together, supporting each other's goals and activities. Those who fight for better walking conditions and those who fight for better public transportation are allies fighting for the same cause! This is true even if, by improving walking conditions, some short public transit trips will be substituted by walk trips. My City's experience is that this loss in ridership is by far offset by increased use of public transit due to its city-wide improved accessibility.

You haven't been to My City yet? Imagine something like a modern Venice, a Venice without water, a Venice at the turn of the twentieth century. Imagine a city which provides an accessibility and a permeability similar to the ones provided by cars for their owners in motorised cities, without all the negative ecological consequences of the private automobile, and all its socially discriminating consequences as well. My City leaves the car-dominated age behind. It uses latest technology and latest design. It is unique, but since its success is not based on a unique geographical situation it needn't be, for other cities can adopt what creative and courageous My City has pioneered.

PART 3

Practice

13 The Delft bicycle network
Jan Hartman

The background to cycle planning in the Netherlands

One of the things visitors from abroad are astonished about when they visit Holland is the great number of cyclists. In fact 14 million inhabitants own 12 million bicycles. The bicycle is a very popular means of transport thanks to rather favourable geographical conditions; the country is flat, it has a high density of population so that distances are short, and it has a dense road network.

At present bicycle use seems to have stabilised at a fairly high level. However, in the early 1960s the use of the bicycle declined in the face of the very fast growth of motor-vehicle mobility. Bicycle paths were even removed in favour of extra lanes for motor cars. After the energy crisis, though, the unlimited growth of motor-car use had to be curbed. Subsequent traffic and transportation policy was thus aimed at a change in the modal split, in favour of less energy- and space-consuming modes. The use of public transport and the bicycle were encouraged. In 1975 the Ministry of Transport and Public Works introduced a fund for the construction of bicycle paths beside roads outside built-up areas. Financial support from the state for the construction of infrastructure for traffic in towns (bicycle facilities included) was already provided for.

Up to 1985, the sum spent on bicycle facilities by the Ministry of Transport was 500 million guilders (£160 million), though the total cost was three times as high (Wilmink, 1988). At this stage the funds were cancelled because it was felt that the backlog in the provision of bicycle facilities had been overcome. From this point onwards, state, provinces and municipalities had their own responsibility for the construction of bicycle facilities in their domain. The role of the Ministry from here on was to develop a policy to integrate the bicycle in transportation planning and to acquire specific knowledge on the effectiveness of various bicycle facilities.

Transportation planning

Long-term, integrated traffic and transport policies are laid down in the Structure Scheme for Traffic and Transport (SVV). In November 1988 the

SVV, issued in 1981, was renewed. The SVV is the starting point for all traffic and transportation planning and has impacts, too, in the field of physical planning. Within the SVV the priorities for the implementation and research planning of road projects are established in a Multi-Year Plan for Passenger Transport (MPP). In this MPP incentives are given for evaluation studies of, amongst others, bicycle facilities.

Research

Within the Ministry, the Transportation and Traffic Engineering Division conducted three different major evaluation studies concerning bicycle traffic. Firstly, in 1975 a Demonstration Project on Urban Bicycle Routes was introduced. Two high-standard routes were established in The Hague and Tilburg (Ministry of Transport and Public Works, 1979, no date). The studies showed that there was a gain in traffic safety, and in particular the subjective feeling of safety improved. The cycle routes caused a reallocation of cycle trips, but a growth in the total number of cycle trips did not occur. The overall conclusion was that single urban cycle routes do not have a clear, large-scale effect.

The second Demonstration Project concerned cycle routes outside built-up areas. Along two main roads in the Provinces of Gelderland and Limburg a fairly large number of cycling schoolchildren formerly could only use a narrow strip on the edge of the carriageway. Separate cycle paths were created together with various kinds of facilities at junctions. All the people in the near vicinity of the cycle routes and the schools were kept informed of the developments that were made. The public participated enthusiastically. One of the effects is that people use their bikes more often, especially in their spare time,although there is no modal shift from the use of the car to the bicycle. Practically all the users of these routes are of the opinion that the new situation is safer, more agreeable and more comfortable (Kropman and Pas, 1988).

The follow-up to these projects was the idea to create an urban bicycle network. This network was created in Delft and is described below.

The Delft bicycle network

The Delft bicycle network, so far, consists of:

— two large tunnels;
— three bridges;
— 3.3 km of new bicycle tracks;

— 2.6 km of streets that are bi-directional for cycles but one-way for cars;
— 8.5 km of bicycle lanes and tracks; and
— 10 km of new asphalt pavement.

A comprehensive evaluation study was set up to determine the effect of the network improvements. This study was aimed at three targets:

— to evaluate the effectiveness of the bicycle plan with respect to stimulating bicycle use and improvement of comfort and road safety;
— to test the traffic engineering principles; and
— to monitor the behavioural changes of road users to be able to obtain general insight into mobility.

Therefore the evaluation study focused on the following five aspects of mobility:

— changes in modal split;
— changes in origin–destination patterns of cyclists;
— changes in route choice in relation to the network;
— changes in subjective feelings of comfort and road safety; and
— changes in road accident patterns.

The study was carried out as a before-and-after study with a study area and a control area. The various 'before' studies were carried out in 1982 and 1983, the 'after' studies in 1985 and 1986 (Ministry of Transport and Public Works, 1986, 1987). Furthermore, two large and expensive projects were evaluated separately, namely a cycle bridge and a cycle tunnel. The tunnel was not opened until September 1987, so the results of the after study are still (1989) being analysed. Finally, a comparative study was carried out with respect to the mobility patterns of medium-sized Dutch cities. It showed that Delft is a representative city within this group, so that the research findings may be generalised for these cities.

Results obtained from the evaluation study

Mobility and modal split

Overall mobility in Delft did not change between 1982 and 1985. In the control area, where no pro-cycling measures were taken, the modal split changed in favour of the motor vehicle, with an increase of 10 per cent at the expense of public transport. This is a general trend in these medium-sized cities.

On the other hand, in the study area and in Tanthof, another district benefiting from the cycle network, there has been a decrease in motor vehicle trips in favour of bicycle trips: the share of the bicycle in all trips increased by six to eight per cent depending on the district.

The increased number of trips is mainly attributed to males making more bike trips to school or work. Another interesting result is that the distance travelled also increased, whereas the travel time did not change. This means that the mean travel speed also increased. On the other hand, it means that destinations further away came within the reach of the bicycle. For example, in the Tanthof district the bicycle trips were six per cent longer, and the travel speed increased by 15 per cent. This result also explains why the number of trips which were formerly felt to have an excessively long travel time by bike decreased from 28 per cent to 18 per cent.

The attitude towards cycling

A panel was asked its opinion about the comfort, continuity and road safety of the network. In general it was felt that the cycling climate had improved considerably in Delft. Only 10 per cent of the road users still consider the comfort and continuity of cycle facilities negatively, whereas they thought that the circumstances for cars had worsened.

This more positive opinion of cycling can lead to more bicycle use. In particular, inhabitants of the peripherally located district (Tanthof) experienced a strong improvement in cycling comfort. This positive opinion can be attributed to some expensive measures, such as two tunnels and separate bicycle tracks, which provide a fast and direct link with the city centre.

Potential for cycle trips

In 1982 it had been found that the potential decrease in bicycle use was much bigger than the potential increase. After the measures were taken the potential use of the bike increased considerably. This increase is most predominant for car and public transport users. The analysis showed that the position of the bicycle in the modal split has improved towards a balanced situation. For example, about 41 per cent of all trips in Delft are made by bike and, moreover, 32 per cent of all trips made by foot might be lost to cycle trips, amounting to seven per cent of all trips in Delft. The change-over potential between cycle trips and car trips is now evenly balanced, for since the measures were taken, 10 per cent of cycle trips could potentially be lost to the car and 11 per cent of car trips could potentially be lost to the bike. It is remarkable that this balance has been reached in a situation where, before the pro-cycle measures were enacted, the chance of a decrease in bicycle trips was much greater than the chance of an increase. Therefore the bicycle network has definitely had a positive effect on the actual usage of the bicycle as well as on the circumstances which influence the use of a bicycle. Perhaps even more important is the conclusion that the bicycle network has avoided an increase in motor vehicle trips. In this way, the position of the bicycle compared to the car has improved.

Changes in route choice

One of the studies investigated whether cyclists would choose other routes for their trips as a result of the new network. An inventory of the network was made as well as route surveys around the study area (before and after). The study showed an increase in the number of bicycle trips entering or leaving the study area from 25 000 to 28 000 (a rise of 10 per cent) per day. It also showed that the mean trip length increased by 6.5 per cent from 3.7 to 3.9 km, in spite of the fact that shorter routes were available.

Important changes in route choice were noticed at spots where a new link became available. For example, the proportion of trips that passed through the Barbarasteeg increased from 4 to 28 per cent after its reconstruction specifically as a cycle path.

There is no clear evidence with respect to the effect of new or improved traffic signals at intersections. It seems that travel time is the most important factor whether traffic lights are successful or not.

Changes in the usage of the network

In Delft the bicycle network is hierarchical, with an urban, a district and a neighbourhood level (Figure 13.1). Does the network function as it is supposed to? The study shows that 60 per cent of all bicycle kilometres are travelled on the urban level, whereas this level represents only 30 per cent of the total network length. After the completion of the network a strong concentration of bicycle traffic has occurred on the urban level network. The high quality of these facilities which, in general, consist of separate tracks, has a positive effect on feelings of road safety.

It may be concluded that, in spite of the fact that many parts of the network existed before, the improvements in the coherency and quality of the network have caused many positive changes in route choice. As a result it has been possible to detour cyclists from busy and dangerous routes to more comfortable and safe routes. For example, cycling on separate bicycle tracks increased from 30 to 35 per cent of the total bicycle kilometres. On the other hand, cycling on a normal street (with mixed traffic) decreased from 45 per cent to 40 per cent of the total.

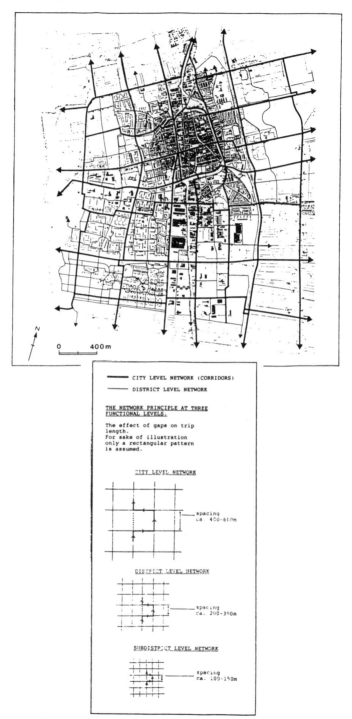

Figure 13.1   The Delft cycle network

Conclusions and recommendations

The first policy target of the bicycle network was to promote cycling. All the individual studies indicate that bicycle mobility (in terms of bicycle kilometres) has increased by at least six per cent. The increase due to other factors is not included in this figure.

A second policy target was to limit car use by promoting bicycle use. The study shows that car use in the study area has remained stable and indeed car use for internal trips in Delft even decreased. A part of this decrease is a result of the network. Overall it can be concluded that the modal split changed in favour of the bicycle, with the contribution of the bicycle increasing from 40 to 43 per cent.

A third policy target was to improve road safety for cyclists. A before-and-after study has yet to be completed, but the preliminary results indicate that less bicycle accidents occur. Statistically speaking there is no *evidence* of an improvement, but all changes point in the same direction. It has already been concluded that cycling on comfortable separate bicycle tracks increased by 40 per cent, whereas the total growth of this network is much less (17 per cent).

Summarising, it may be concluded that the Delft network concept has proved to be successful. Five recommendations may be made. First, the construction of a coherent and consistent hierarchical network of bicycle facilities does promote cycling considerably. This is not only a short-term benefit but it also provides the bicycle with a good competitive position in the long run. A network with a fine grid and good continuity serves many purposes: because cyclists do not like detours, short as well as long trips are made by bike and origins and destinations of trips spread over the whole city become within easy reach. Local authorities should keep this in mind when they design a network.

Second, it is not necessary for measures to be expensive and on a large scale, for small-scale inexpensive measures also have a positive effect if they aim at improving the continuity of a route. In particular, measures which cut down travel time are effective. However, all measures should fit into a masterplan which has hierarchical levels. These levels must be clearly distinguished by geometrical features and grid. Expensive measures should be focused on the highest level. These measures are cost-effective because of the concentration of high volumes of bicycle traffic on comfortable and safe routes.

Third, a black-spot approach does not promote cycling. Measures dealing with black-spots should fit into a masterplan. Traffic safety is not the most important factor cyclists in the Netherlands take into account when choosing a route.

Fourth, a logical, consistent network makes it easier to create a mental map. In this way road users can easily assess distances and travel times. This mental map influences the decision-making process with respect to the modal split, for the chance of using a bike increases when the mental bike map is better. Therefore local authorities should frequently publish an overview of the new facilities.

Last, local authorities play an important role in the promotion of the bicycle. The positive attitude of the Delft municipality during this project has contributed much to the success of the network. It is not enough to build bicycle tracks, it is also vital to market them. Delft has set a good example by giving information during public participation sessions, a permanent exhibition, frequent publications in the local press, dissemination of leaflets, and a map with cycle routes. Local authorities should pay prominent and continuing attention to promoting the positive image of cycling. There is no doubt this recommendation is valid for many other countries besides the Netherlands.

References

Kropman, J.A. and Pas, B., 1988, 'Cycling facilities in rural areas: planning and design', in de Wit, T. (ed.), *Planning for the urban cyclist*, 171–4, proceedings of Velo City 87 international congress, 22–6 September, Netherlands Centre for Research and Contract Standardisation in Civil and Traffic Engineering, Ede.

Ministry of Transport and Public Works, no date, *Demonstration route Tilburg*, The Hague.

—— 1979, *The Hague cycleway pilot project 1975–79*, The Hague.

—— 1986, *Evaluation of the Delft Bicycle Network: summary report of the before study*, The Hague.

—— 1987, *Evaluation of the Delft Bicycle Network plan: final summary report*, The Hague.

Wilmink, A., 1988, 'The effects of state subsidizing of bicycle facilities', in de Wit, T. (ed.), *Planning for the urban cyclist*, 209–12.

14 Planning for the bicycle in urban Britain: an assessment of experience and issues
Hugh McClintock

The revival of interest in planning for the bicycle in urban areas in Britain dates from the energy crisis in the early 1970s. The 1977 Transport White Paper recognised the importance of cycling and introduced the Department of Transport's (D.Tp.'s) Innovatory Cycling Scheme budget to encourage local authorities to adopt special facilities (see Figure 14.1).

This commitment was restated in 1981 in *Cycling: a consultation paper* and in 1982 in the *Statement of cycling policy* (Department of Transport, 1981, 1982). Both of these excluded Scotland, an omission rectified only in 1985. In England several local authorities were encouraged to make cycling provision. This chapter discusses this experience, particularly in the implementation of cycling facilities.

The provision and use of cycle facilities

The effect of cycle facilities on the pattern and volume of cycle traffic

Cycle sales grew steadily during the late 1970s and most of the 1980s, with a virtual doubling of sales in 10 years (Morgan, 1988). There was also, however, a marked lag between this and the more modest increase in cycle usage. Nevertheless, this increase in cycle use has still been very significant, after about 30 years of decline. The introduction of special facilities has been a common official response in order to cater for this increased number of cyclists as well as to help reduce the increasing cycling accident toll.

Facilities have been commonly advocated as a way to encourage more people to ride bikes, as well as to make existing cyclists feel safer. The term 'cycle facilities' is most often understood to mean cycle tracks or cycle

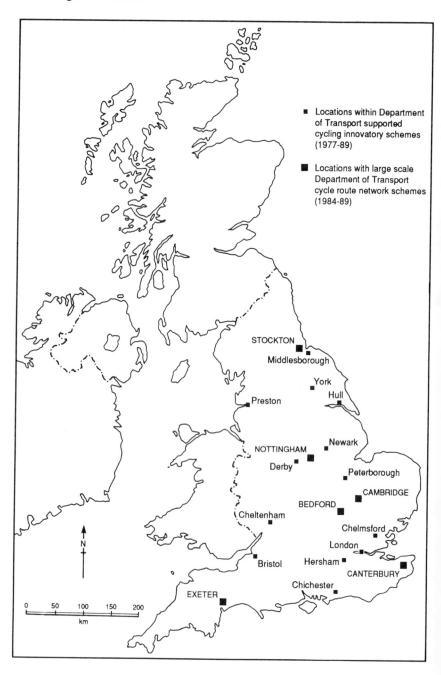

Figure 14.1   Location of the Department of Transport experimental schemes, 1977–89

paths. It can also involve paths shared with pedestrians (with or without segregation), special cycle crossing arrangements (often with special signs), or other measures. Some facilities are modest, such as cycle gaps, while others may be much larger, such as cycle subways or even cycle bridges. By far the largest of these is the cycle and pedestrian bridge completed late in 1989 across 16 railway tracks near Cambridge station.

The provision of facilities has often resulted in a significant increase in cyclists. This may result not just from the generation of new cyclists but also from the diversion of existing cyclists from more dangerous routes. Cycle facilities are more likely to be regarded as a safer alternative where they form part of a continuous route. Fragmented stretches of cycle path, which abandon cyclists at dangerous points or are hard to reach safely, may in fact increase overall dangers. Such fears were particularly expressed by Brian Oldridge at a D.Tp. conference (Department of Transport, 1985). His comments helped to direct attention not only to the effect of cycling schemes on safety but also to the importance of careful phasing in the implementation of such schemes as well as to the benefits of whole networks of cycle routes and other facilities. These are designed to link major generators and attractors of cycle traffic and include major routes and feeder links. They can include quieter roads as well as specific facilities. The best plans for such networks will aim to penetrate right into and across city centres and to provide safe, attractive and convenient routes right out into surrounding countryside.

Achieving a comprehensive cycle route network should involve specific attempts to overcome major barriers for cyclists, such as providing special crossings of railways and rivers as well as main roads. Although one or two good examples are to be seen in this country, as in Cambridge, they are very few compared to the numerous examples built in Delft in the Netherlands as part of its major cycle route network demonstration project in the early 1980s, described in the previous chapter.

The best example in England of an attempt to identify a long-term comprehensive network of cycle routes was the 1600km plan adopted by the former Greater London Council soon after the setting up of its cycle planning project team in 1981. The GLC was committed to spending one per cent of its capital expenditure on cycling. This target was in fact recommended to other councils by the D.Tp. in 1982, although financial cutbacks since then have helped discourage many from such commitment.

Momentum in the implementation of the London cycle network slowed down in all but a handful of London Boroughs (such as Hammersmith) after the abolition of the GLC in 1986. However, an attempt to revive the network in 1988 was made by the London Cycling Forum and this has been backed by the London Planning Advisory Committee.

In Nottingham, the Greater Nottingham Cycle Route Network Project is being implemented between 1986 and 1990 (Figure 14.2). This is a joint venture of Nottinghamshire County Council and the D.Tp., and is the

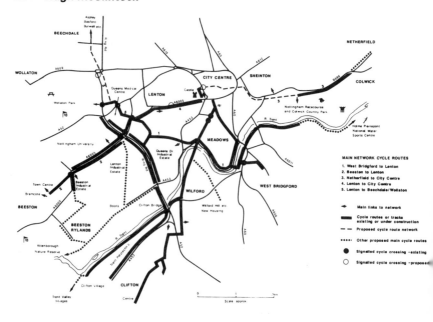

Figure 14.2 Diagrammatic map of the Greater Nottingham Cycle Route Network Project (1986–90), showing implementation progress as at spring 1989

largest of the five large-scale Urban Cycle Route Network Projects promoted by the D.Tp., and selected in 1984. The others are in Bedford, Exeter, Stockton, Canterbury and Cambridge (a recent addition), with the Canterbury scheme now effectively abandoned through a weakening of local political support.

In the Nottingham conurbation, the total length of the cycle route network is already much more extensive than the 20 kilometres in the official D.Tp. network project, and several more routes are planned. This is the result of a commitment over several years now by the D.Tp. and local councils rather than the fruits of any special cycling project team as in Lothian. More recently in Greater Manchester there have been impressive efforts to identify routes in which – as in London under the GLC – there has been a close association with cycling groups. Other councils, at county and district level, have designated cycling officers, planners or engineers who spend at least a substantial proportion of their time on cycling matters.

The number of local authorities providing facilities has grown steadily. The local authorities' Cycle Planning Liaison Group started in 1984 and is flourishing, meeting twice a year to discuss experience of planning and implementation of facilities, as well as to exchange information. It is maintaining a data base of relevant reports, including material from abroad.

However, financial commitment by councils to cycling has been discouraged, not only by the financial cutbacks required by central government but also by the rather ambivalent attitude of the D.Tp. For example, only £160 000 was spent in 1987–8 on its programme of experimental cycling facilities, a very meagre sum when compared with the costs of individual road schemes, or with the £900 million a year spent on the national roads programme. It is also very small compared with the amount spent to help cyclists in the major Dutch project in Delft, as the previous chapter has shown.

Apart from continuous networks, even isolated facilities can at times be well worthwhile in their own right, particularly when they give cyclists some clear advantage. Contraflow cycle lanes, for example, can open up very useful safe short-cuts, as can cycle gaps in road closures and certain special cycle crossings. Dutch-style advanced stop-line schemes, where cyclists are given their own special waiting area at traffic signals in advance of motor vehicles, have proved very helpful in making cyclists feel safer when turning at junctions (see Department of Transport 1986a, 1986b, 1989).

Special facilities are also more likely to be appreciated when they open up more direct routes and reduce cyclists' journey times. This is more likely to be the case with off-highway routes than cycle paths parallel to main roads. The creation of direct links across parks and other open spaces hitherto not (legally) available has often been particularly appreciated by cyclists, and opposition from Parks Departments has become less common.

However, the creation of direct off-highway links can still face other opposition and needs to be handled carefully. This may arise because of fears about security and vandalism. It may also be the result of concern by other agencies that 'low status' cycleways may undermine the prestigious appearance of new developments like science parks and high-tech industrial areas. Routes away from highways can also arouse security fears among some cyclists, especially women worried about cycling after dark on poorly lit paths.

Nonetheless, such paths may still offer great net benefits in terms of avoiding busy traffic and saving time. Often no easy alternatives are available. The provision of lighting and care with landscaping can in any case help to reduce risks. Moreover, the safety of all path users may be enhanced by upgrading an existing path to make it suitable for shared use and more attractive to users.

Some new direct links may well shorten distances and some may reduce journey times as well. However, other routes, especially those with signalled crossings, may actually increase overall journey times. For more hardened and confident cyclists, the value of facilities can be much undermined by the much greater journey times in using them. Long delays at special traffic lights may encourage some cyclists to ride thorough without waiting, increasing not decreasing the likelihood of accidents. There can,

Figure 14.3   A two-way cycle path near the Silverdale roundabout in Nottingham, helping cyclists avoid heavy traffic on the main road and roundabout

in other words, sometimes be a dilemma in deciding how far to emphasise safety rather than speed and convenience (Figures 14.3 and 14.4).

The problem has been complicated by the D.Tp.'s insistence, at least up to 1989, on relying on detector loops rather than push-button signals, as found on pelican crossings. With loop detectors it is easy for cyclists to feel that their presence has not been registered. The possible hazards are increased further by the tendency of some cyclists, including adults, to ride recklessly and to use facilities in very different ways to those intended by their designers.

The quality of facilities

The underlying issue of quality has come more to the fore in the late 1980s, so that discussion of the effects of facilities is difficult without some consideration of their quality which, it is clear, varies widely. For example, Bracher (1988), comparing cycling policy and provision in different European countries, commented that facilities in Britain, although rarer, tended to be of better quality. With that said, by no means all facilities offer the distinct advantage over other modes or routes that is important if they really are to be attractive to cyclists.

Figure 14.4 Signalled cycle crossings can open up safer and more direct links for cyclists, despite constraints of space in city centres: Canal Street, Nottingham

It is not difficult to find cases of facilities being provided but little used because of poor quality. Perhaps the best publicised example of poor provision in Britain is the Redway system of Milton Keynes. These shared cycle- and footpaths were grafted on to the basic grid road layout some years after the adoption of the master plan. With the rather undulating terrain in the new city it then became particularly difficult to provide Redways of no steeper gradient than roads. The basic defects of alignment have been compounded by poor details, such as priority markings, sight-lines and visibility (Franklin, 1984). These have led many cyclists, especially more confident ones and those making longer journeys, to neglect the Redways in favour of the roads, despite their many roundabouts and other hazards. It was only in 1989 that the Development Corporation finally embarked on a comprehensive programme to remedy the Redway defects. However, it is very questionable whether this will greatly improve the Redways' poor image and accident record, especially with the poor maintenance of many of the paths.

There have been other cases of poor facilities, with narrow paths, sharp bends, ramps too steep to ride over comfortably, poor surfaces and paths obstructed by lamp-posts or other protruding street furniture. Adjoining fences, walls and railings may be sited too close to the path, reducing its effective width, as well as visibility near bends. The value of cycle paths is also reduced by a requirement for cyclists to give way frequently to other traffic, and where routes are substantially longer without any compensating safety benefits.

Some cycle facilities in older urban areas consist largely of advisory cycle routes, designated on existing roads, without separate provision. These are easily provided, enabling the creation of fairly long routes at relatively low cost. However, traffic volumes may be high, especially if the road is subject to 'rat-running', or is close to major new developments such as new industrial estates or superstores, which increase volumes of heavy traffic in particular. This is especially discouraging for less confident cyclists.

This increase in traffic is of course less likely where the streets in question are closed to through motor traffic, with cyclists exempted. However, it is on these roads that parking is more likely to be allowed, increasing the risk of obstruction of cycle gaps and of car doors being opened in the path of passing cyclists. Road surfaces also tend to be worse on such routes. Riders may have to give way more often than on main roads, disrupting their momentum. Cyclists' journey times on such routes may also suffer from the inclusion of pinch points, such as narrow openings and bridges, particularly if they are obliged to dismount at these to lessen the risk of conflict with pedestrians. Cyclists may try to get round such restrictions, or avoid the route altogether.

Variations in attitudes towards facilities between different cyclist sub-groups

Discussion of the effects of facilities also has to be related to variations in attitudes among different cyclists, for this affects the way in which facilities are used. There is some evidence that it is women, in particular, who appreciate their safety benefits. Children, even more, can benefit enormously from routes that are largely or wholly traffic-free. This is clear from the popularity of the paths now created in several places on disused railway tracks, as in Avon and the Lothian areas.

There is some evidence that women are more inclined to take up cycling when it seems safe and generally accepted, such as in places like

Cambridge, Peterborough and York with particularly high cycle use. Women's security can, in general, be much assisted by encouraging them to cycle on safe streets and safe paths, helping them to feel less vulnerable than when walking or waiting at bus stops, or when using public transport late at night.

Different cyclists clearly have different priorities which affect their decisions on whether or not to use facilities and, if so, how. More confident ones are inclined to give higher priority to time-saving and convenience, keeping up their speed and momentum. In contrast, less confident cyclists will be more prepared to take a longer route if it makes them feel safer. However, there is some evidence to suggest that most cyclists are unwilling to take a route that involves more than about 10 per cent extra distance, especially if it is less flat, unless it offers overwhelming safety advantages. Time-saving and directness are probably less important to recreational cyclists than those using their bikes to get to work, education or shops, whereas the attractiveness of the route as a whole is probably more important for those cycling in their leisure time.

Because of the constraints of space and finance, it is often impossible in older urban areas to create high-standard facilities. Nevertheless, facilities that are less than ideal can still yield significant benefits, especially in areas with significant cycle flows. It may indeed still be worthwhile to introduce facilities even if only about half the theoretical potential use is met. For instance, new and less confident cyclists may be attracted who would not cycle on the carriageway. Again, particular facilities may be used by only some of their potential users, depending on their route origins and destinations, as well as their level of riding skill and confidence.

British cycle planning has much to learn from Dutch experience but, in assessing this, it is important to remember that most bikes in Britain tend to be lighter, faster and less well sprung. This means that smoother surfaces and better visibility at junctions are all the more important in the layout of facilities in Britain.

Facility construction and maintenance standards

Cycle facilities that have good basic design features may be spoiled by poor detailed construction and maintenance, with a consequent detrimental effect on their attractiveness to cyclists. Kerbs at junctions are often not properly flush, barriers to help reduce conflict with pedestrians are sometimes poorly sited, curves are too sharp, and gradients or ramps too steep. Surfaces may never be smooth, even when the path is first built. Drainage may be poor on some stretches.

Even facilities that are well-designed and built, with good details can fast lose their appeal if surfaces are not regularly swept, potholes not promptly and smoothly filled, or if they become obstructed by overhanging vegetation or damaged signs and other street furniture. The very absence of motor traffic on cycle paths means there is less likelihood of debris such as broken glass being cleared by 'natural' sweeping, making regular brushing important.

The desirability of combining cycle and pedestrian facilities

A much-aired issue is the advisability of allowing some kind of shared provision with other users, especially pedestrians. There have been particular fears expressed by groups representing the blind and the disabled. The D.Tp. has recommended councils to undertake close consultation with these groups, as well as with cyclists, when shared-use schemes are first proposed. It has also given advice on the need for segregation and its form, particularly where there are likely to be substantial numbers of disabled and visually handicapped pedestrians in subways and on other shared paths. Finding solutions acceptable to all parties is still often difficult.

Segregation by kerb is usually more popular with both cyclists and pedestrians, encouraging both users more effectively to keep to their respective sides. However, it is of course also more expensive, and can also be more inflexible. White-line segregation, or shared paths without any form of segregation, can work better where relative numbers of pedestrians and cyclists fluctuate, giving both the opportunity to pass slower path users easily, and making it easier to dodge debris and puddles.

Proposals for sharing of paths often arouse intense fears which are not usually borne out by actual experience, although this does depend on the responsibility of path users. There are also variations in reactions in different parts of the country, depending on how accustomed local pedestrians are to seeing cyclists around. In some areas, like Cambridge and York, cycling is more a part of the local 'culture', so that public understanding of such issues is more widespread. Flatter terrain also diminishes the dangers of conflict. In any case, it seems that less opposition is likely to the creation of new shared paths than to the conversion of existing footpaths.

Special problems are presented by shared subways, and the particular need to ensure good visibility on the approaches to them. This potential, as well as the width of the 'barrel' of the subway itself, affects the practicality of converting pedestrian subways into shared facilities. The overall security of subways can sometimes be increased by attracting larger numbers of users, and barriers can be used to force cyclists to slow down.

The issue of cycle access in pedestrianised areas can be particularly controversial. The acceptability of cycle access in these schemes must depend on local factors, including the relative numbers of cyclists and pedestrians, the width of the street, and the amount and location of street furniture, as well as the need to make exemptions for other vehicles, such as service traffic and the practicality of combining that with cycle access. There also has to be recognition of related issues, such as the extent of dangers facing cyclists using alternative routes if riding through is banned; the proportions of cyclists having business in the street as opposed to using it just as a through-route; and the likely deterrent effect of the extra time required to push bikes through.

How far potential difficulties become problems in practice may depend greatly on the behaviour of the cyclists themselves. Reckless behaviour by a minority of cyclists is enough to encourage latent fears about cyclists from many pedestrians, especially the elderly. Inadequate signing and surface treatment for the cycle access arrangements, because of priority being given to other considerations such as aesthetic factors, can also exacerbate the risk of conflict.

The sharing of signalled crossings in Britain has, at least up to 1989, been resisted by the D.Tp., although providing separate cycle crossings and pelican crossings adds greatly to the costs. However, some experiments with shared signalled crossings might well be of great benefit to both pedestrians and cyclists. The provision of a signalled cycle crossing alone at a point where there is pent-up demand for a pelican crossing can be particularly frustrating for pedestrians. In the absence of any push-button they have to stand and wait for a passing cyclist to enable them to cross when it activates the detector loops and calls up the green cycle aspect.

There are indeed other ways in which pedestrians might benefit from more explicit consideration of their needs in planning cycling facilities. The provision of new cycle paths and crossings can encourage pedestrians to walk where previously this was impossible or difficult, because of barriers or rough surfaces, or because the criteria for the provision of pelican crossings were not met.

On the other hand, if the footway surface has been poorly maintained, pedestrians may stray into the cyclist part of the shared paths. Account should also be taken of pedestrians' likely desire lines and efforts made to reduce the need for them to have to cross the cycle path more than necessary to reach their destinations. Where some conflict is inevitable, such as near a bus stop, careful layout can minimise dangers.

Cyclists and pedestrians may benefit from the kind of 'traffic calming' schemes common in some continental countries (Tolley, 1990). In these the street layout is radically changed to slow down motor vehicles and to put motor traffic, cyclists and pedestrians on a more even footing. However, whether cyclists do in fact benefit, and whether motorists are really forced to slow down, depends on a number of factors, not least on the height of ramps and widths of carriageway narrowings. They may benefit more if there is room to provide a cycle lane around the obstructions, as is done in Buxtehude in West Germany (Chapter 19). Without these modifications cyclists may be replacing one form of risk by another, although there is now abundant accumulated experience to accommodate cyclists successfully in such calming schemes.

Combining cycle access with access for other users, such as horseriders and motor cyclists

Proposals for sharing rights of way with other users can also be controversial. Cyclists are legally entitled to use bridleways but these often have rough surfaces, preferred by horseriders. Asphalting the surfaces to reduce likely damage from horses may result in an outcry from their riders while still not avoiding damage. However, lack of space may make it hard to provide separately surfaced tracks for different users.

Motorised two-wheelers are generally banned on cycle paths in Britain. However, the creation of new paths, or the improvement of existing paths, for cycle as well as pedestrian use has often aroused fears from local residents of motor-cycle abuse. Experience has now been gained with several different designs of barrier to deter motor-cycle access at the ends of routes, but it can still be hard sometimes to prevent access from the side of the routes. It has not always proved easy, furthermore, to exclude motor bikes while still permitting wheelchair users and pedestrians with prams and buggies.

The context for pro-cycle planning

The balance between special cycling facilities and provision for cyclists' needs in everyday highway planning and traffic management

Even where good facilities have been provided and well used, they have been seen by some cyclists as a way of avoiding the real issue, that is the fundamentally motor-car orientated bias of most highway planning and traffic management. New roads do not, of course, necessarily create extra problems for cyclists, who can derive substantial benefits from the removal of through traffic, especially heavy vehicles, on to bypasses and other relief roads. However, new roads and road improvement schemes continue to appear with dangerous features for the cyclist, such as roundabouts and slip roads designed to accommodate fast traffic. Roundabouts have a generally beneficial effect on the accident rate, but are very dangerous for two-wheelers and experiments to make them safer for cyclists have had only limited success. The situation is aggravated by the recent practice of providing 'free-flow' entry lanes on roundabouts for motor traffic turning left. Indeed, separate turning lanes at any junction tend to make them more dangerous for cyclists.

Cyclists' safety has also suffered from the installation of central refuges to assist pedestrians' safety, without careful assessment of the extra risks these can pose for cyclists. Similar problems can result from another general safety measure, the increasing use of speed humps.

The wider disparity in speeds between motorised and non-motorised road users, which is often encouraged by road 'improvement' schemes, tends generally to increase cyclists' sense of danger and discomfort. There is one view that this problem should be addressed not only by fundamental changes in road design but also by 'vehicle calming' rather than 'traffic calming', i.e. deliberately making cars' acceleration (and even braking) slower and using speed governors to enforce lower speeds.

In the absence of such measures, cycling facilities can be seen as mere tokens, mainly intended to get cyclists out of the way of drivers. In any case facilities are of limited value in promoting the general safety of cyclists in urban ares where most cycling is likely to continue to have to take place on roads. Examples are still rare of the practice of the former West Yorkshire County Council requiring a paragraph outlining the likely impact of road schemes on cyclists and pedestrians to be included in each Highways Committee report.

The work of the D.Tp.'s Traffic Advisory Unit in promoting innovatory cycling projects has in theory been reinforced since 1981 by the designation of regional cycling officers in each of its eight regional offices. These posts, designated after the Cycling Consultation Paper, were intended not only to ensure that cyclists' needs were fully considered in the D.Tp.'s own trunk-road schemes but also to advise the local authorities about cycling provision. In many cases it appears that the officers have lacked both the time and the inclination to do this job effectively, being officials with many other (higher priority) responsibilities than cycling.

Despite this lack of support, cyclists can still benefit greatly from 'cell-type' traffic management systems that prevent traffic from crossing city centres by confining movements to particular 'cells', accessed from an inner ring road. Movements by cyclists and buses can be exempted from such restrictions.

More generally, cyclists can benefit too from exemptions from road closures and turning bans, and from measures to combine cycle access with exemptions for buses, as in Sheffield and Derby. Even such small-scale measures can usefully open up much shorter and safer links, despite the sometimes inflexible attitude of the D.Tp. on authorisation for variations to existing signs.

With steadily increasing traffic congestion, a combination of cycle priority measures, cycle friendly road layouts and continuous routes can help reinforce the advantage of the bicycle in achieving faster journey times. This could add much to its attraction as a means of commuting in the peak periods. This might be further strengthened by another real increase in the price of petrol.

The potential for the promotion of cycling through town planning

Cycle use, and that of other transport modes, is greatly affected by land-use patterns and the distances involved. The recent spate of developments of large superstores and retail parks, usually on peripheral sites, has tended further to undermine local facilities like small shops and thus the attractions of the bicycle and walking, which are of most value over short distances. The growth of new employment areas at peripheral locations tends to result in greater distances to work for most people and, along with easier car parking than in city centres, again effectively encourages motorised travel. It tends to discourage cycling, walking and especially the use of public transport, which still tends to be geared to radial movements. On the other hand, any policies which produce more concentrated urban form, although unpopular in the current planning context, would tend to encourage non-motorised travel, as Hillman and Whalley (1983) have stressed.

The context for travel patterns, especially to work, is changing now with pressures for new settlements and looser settlement forms, on surplus agricultural land, encouraging lower density living and increased commuting distances. However, some of these pressures may be countered by increased trends towards homeworking and telecommuting in the labour force, as well as greater concern for energy conservation, which may help to increase the importance of local travel and the significance of walking and cycling. Increased consciousness about health and the environment are also of course very relevant in this changing context.

On a day-to-day basis cycling can be promoted by a constant awareness among planners and engineers of opportunities to encourage it as part of other schemes such as environmental improvement, derelict land reclamation, and major development and redevelopment projects. Such opportunities can be used as steps towards the eventual development of a network of cycle routes in an urban area and policies can be adopted to safeguard such routes, once identified, for ultimate development.

At a more detailed level there can be conflict between cycle planning and other, aesthetic, planning requirements, largely because of the clutter of signs and equipment that the D.Tp. often insist on for relatively simple cycle schemes. These can be seen as a threat to the character of attractive buildings and streets.

The balance between planning/engineering measures, road safety/ education and legal/enforcement provisions

Standards of riding behaviour vary widely. Engineering-type measures can yield only limited benefits without close co-ordination with educational measures and road safety publicity. Indeed, as Oldridge pointed out, the extra usage encouraged by publicity for new facilities can well lead to an increase in the local pedal cycle accident rate (Department of Transport, 1985). Partial improvements at locations with a very dangerous reputation among cyclists may result in accidents where none previously was recorded. In any case, it is important that publicity for new facilities contains clear advice on how they should be used, and that this is under-lined by road safety officers. New facilities will certainly not increase safety if they are used by careless riders, or by riders with poorly maintained bikes.

Publicity also needs to be encouraged by efforts to make many drivers more respectful of cyclists, when, as must often be the case, they are riding in ordinary traffic. Bracher (1988) remarked that cyclists in the United Kingdom seem to be given less respect than many of their continental counterparts. This may have something to do with the lack of (recent) cycling experience of many drivers since, as Speed (1988) found, there is evidence of the more respectful attitude in people who are both drivers and cyclists. She suggested that respect for cyclists would be much greater if all drivers had to ride a bicycle as part of their driving test! Better law enforcement among cyclists and drivers, as recommended by the North Committee review of traffic law in 1988 might also help mutual respect (Department of Transport, 1988).

Cycling and other transport policies

Another wider issue is the appropriate balance between cycling and other transport policies, and how far cycling's potential is constrained by the general bias in transport policies towards private road traffic.

Attempts to link cycling provision and public transport have been rare anywhere but particularly rare in Britain. At a basic level they include combining provision for buses and cycles in traffic management schemes and secure cycle parking at railway and bus stations. Promoting combi-nations of cycling and public transport also means encouraging arrange-ments for the carrying of bikes on trains and on or behind buses. Cycle carriage on trains has been made much more difficult by the greater financial constraints on British Rail which have resulted in scarcer provi-sion for bikes on most new rolling stock.

A recent issue has been the potential impact on cyclists of the light rail rapid transit systems now being planned in several British cities. In Avon and Edinburgh these appear to threaten some of the cycle paths success-fully established on disused railways. However, they do also offer more positive prospects, particularly if they help to reduce congestion and if they result in some streets being closed to road traffic, but not to cyclists. LRT schemes also permit the encouragement of various 'bike and ride' travel combinations, as Brunsing shows for Germany in Chapter 16. There are differing local constraints and opportunities.

Cycling and wider environmental policies

Cyclists are much more exposed to toxic substances in busy traffic than drivers. Depending on changes in the level of traffic, they therefore stand to gain particularly greatly from measures like the widespread use of lead-free petrol and catalytic converters.

A significant increase in cycling use could do much to help reduce congestion and pollution. Conversely, a serious deterioration in the environment would ensue in places like York and Cambridge were there, for any reason, to be a decline in their current high levels of cycling. The Dutch, for these sorts of reasons, have been very conscious of the importance of maintaining cycling's position in the modal split.

Conclusion: the perception of cycling as 'a problem'

A final issue is whether cycling can ever be further encouraged in the absence of a more comprehensive attempt at creating a cycle friendly atmosphere. Such a policy, as described by Hülsmann for Germany in the next chapter, should include widespread publicity for new schemes, aimed at different sections of the population, and events, like guided rides, to help publicise them and cycling in general. The effect of these can be much enhanced if well-known local people, in addition to councillors and officials, are encouraged to take part, and, indeed, to cycle regularly!

As Finch (1985) has remarked, cycling in much of Britain is still not seriously considered as a mode of transport by most people, once they get beyond childhood. Some official efforts to provide for cycling seem to be motivated more by a perception of cycling as a problem to be tackled rather than as a serious mode of transport, with many positive attributes, that should be positively promoted. Fundamental attitudes of this kind can be very hard to change: it is indeed little wonder that, with few exceptions, cycling conditions in the United Kingdom are worse than anywhere else in Europe, except for Belgium (Bracher, 1988).

Policies to encourage greater use of cycles need not necessarily be anti-car use *per se*, so much as directed at discouraging inappropriate car use. Given a context of greater public and political concern about the environment, a comprehensive cycling strategy that is effectively implemented might do much to encourage a more positive image for cycling. It could thereby increase the likelihood of even habitual car users being persuaded sometimes to ride a bike!

References

Bracher, T., 1988, *Evaluation of policy and provision for cyclists in Europe*, report produced for the European Cyclists' Federation, IVU-Gmbh, Berlin.

Department of Transport, 1981, *Cycling: a consultation paper*, HMSO, London.
—— 1982, *Statement of cycling policy*, HMSO, London.
—— 1985, *Ways to safer cycling: conference report*, D.Tp., London.
—— 1986a, *Local transport notes 1/86: cyclists at road crossings and junctions*, HMSO, London.
—— 1986b, *Local transport notes 1/86: shared use by pedestrians and cyclists*, HMSO, London.
—— 1988, *Road traffic law review report*, HMSO, London.
—— 1989, *Local transport notes 1/89: making way for cyclists: planning, design and legal aspects of providing for cyclists*, HMSO, London.
Finch, H., 1985, *Attitudes to cycling*, Transport and Road Research Laboratory Report RR14, Crowthorne, Berks.
Franklin, J., 1984, *Cycling in Milton Keynes: a user's view*, Milton Keynes Cyclists' Users' Group, Milton Keynes.
—— 1988a, *Compendium of cycle path design standards and guidelines*, Milton Keynes Cyclists' Users' Group, Milton Keynes.
—— 1988b, 'Design at the crossroads', *The Surveyor*, **170**, 5007.
Hamer, M., 1987, *Wheels within wheels: a study of the road lobby*, Routledge and Kegan Paul, London.
Hillman, M. and Whalley, A., 1983, *Energy and personal travel: obstacles to conservation*, Policy Studies Institute, London.
Morgan, J., 1988, *How many cyclists and how many bicycles are there in Great Britain*, Working Paper 35, Transport and Road Research Laboratory, Crowthorne, Berks.
Speed, L., 1988, 'Road user attitudes and the safety of cyclists', *Friends of the Earthy Bicycles Bulletin*, 44, April/May/June.
Tolley, R.S., 1990, *Calming traffic in residential areas*, Brefi Press, Tregaron.

15 The 'Bicycle-Friendly Towns' Project in the Federal Republic of Germany

Wulf Hülsmann

Promoting bicycle transport as a means of environmentally conscious planning

Free choice of mode for short-distance transport presupposes that the transport user has the possibility of making daily journeys of different distances safely and rapidly, and at the same time in a way which does not harm the environment. In many places this freedom of choice does not exist. Transport policy and planning in recent decades have been mainly orientated to the needs of motorised traffic. This has led not only to a deterioration in the quality of life in the cities and the environment in general (caused by high noise levels and pollution, use of land and paving over of land, for instance), but also to the fact that streets and squares have become increasingly less attractive and more dangerous for other transport users. Settlement structures which have been predominantly designed with the motor car in mind have contributed to the fact that it has become increasingly difficult to reach certain public amenities such as shops, schools and recreation facilities without making recourse to some form of transport.

The problem cannot be expected to solve itself. On the contrary, although there have been some isolated improvements, the increase in motorisation means that an intensification of the conflicts must be expected. In order to reverse this trend, more transport concepts will be necessary in the future which influence traffic behaviour, create compatible transport systems, reduce the one-sided approach which has reigned until now, and abolish intolerable forms of pollution and nuisance. Bearing in mind the order of priorities set in environmental policy-making ('*avoidance* is better than *reduction* is better than *compensation*'), it is not sufficient to rely solely on measures related to vehicle technology. It is crucial here to influence the choice of modes of transport in favour of environmentally benign ones, wherever this is possible. Areas for possible action could focus, for example, on:

— increasing the attractiveness of public transport, or
— creating settlement and access structures which are designed to be pleasant for pedestrians.

In this connection *bicycle transport* is gaining particular significance among German local authorities as an increasing number of towns and cities recognise its benefits. The aim of promoting bicycle transport is to remove it from the rather peripheral status it has occupied to date in urban and transport planning and give it its appropriate status as an environmentally benign alternative in local transport (Schulte, 1986). If one seriously wants to ensure equal opportunities for every citizen, everyone who cannot drive – and those who are not allowed, or simply do not want, to drive – should have the possibility of using the bicycle to be mobile in a manner which does not harm the environment. This does not mean a desire to replace the motor car by the bicycle. It is simply a question of co-ordinating the different kinds of transport to the best possible degree and promoting certain means of transport in places where their advantages can best be developed (Deutscher Bundestag, 1985; Bundesminister für Raumordnung, Bauwesen und Städtebau, 1986).

Advantages of the bicycle as a means of transport

The basic advantages of the bicycle as a means of transport are as follows (Bundesminister des Innern, 1983):

— The bicycle is an environment-friendly means of transport: it causes neither noise nor harmful exhaust fumes. If those journeys which would have been by car are made instead by bicycle a considerable reduction in motor vehicle emissions can be achieved. Bicycle traffic uses up relatively little space on the street. In many cases space can be created for bicycles in traffic by changing or narrowing existing roads. Another characteristic of the bicycle as a mode of transport is its low use of raw material and energy.
— The bicycle is a flexible and time-saving means of transport; it facilitates door-to-door transport. On short distance and inner city journeys of up to five kilometres the bicycle can compete on equal terms with other means of transport. The bicycle is ideal as a feeder for public transport.

- The shift to the bicycle has positive effects on the quality of the local environment in urban areas. It facilitates environmental traffic management schemes and the redesigning of streets, to provide sufficient space for planting, for pedestrians, for residents to sit in pleasant surroundings, and for children to play.
- The bicycle is a social means of transport. It costs relatively little to buy and enables people who do not have access to a car to be mobile.
- Bicycle transport concepts and schemes are also sensible from an economic point of view. In many cases a carefully focused promotion of bicycle transport can avoid the necessity for investments in motor traffic.
- Bicycles have a positive influence on health. Regular daily bicycle rides are a good form of exercise, beneficial to the heart and circulation.

Principles and aims of promoting bicycle transport

In order to accentuate the advantages of the bicycle in a suitable way, federal, regional and local government will have to engage in bicycle-promoting transport policies using whatever instruments are at their disposal. This involves the assumption of a high degree of responsibility on the part of the towns and cities. Promoting bicycle transport in environmental politics, urban planning and transport planning on a local level cannot be confined to merely looking after the safety and comfort of today's cyclist. Far more than this, promotion of bicycle transport must bring about a change in the habits of transport users so that an increased number switch from the environmentally polluting motor car to the environmentally benign bicycle, thus making a contribution to improving the quality of life and the environment (Otto-Zimmermann, 1986). Noise levels and pollution from exhaust gases must be reduced and urban streets must once more accommodate different functions and activities. It is therefore essential that a consistent promotion of bicycle transport be incorporated into an ecologically orientated overall transport planning policy which should include the following features:

- equal treatment of the needs of the bicycle in all decisions made in transport planning;
- comparisons of different modes of transport which are based on facts, not prejudices;
- consideration of the side-effects and consequences of the individual means of transport, including their effect on the environment; and
- consideration for 'weaker' forms of transport when planning and designing the street and regulating traffic.

Under these conditions the bicycle can take on an important function in the urban transport system. The existing potential for bicycle transport has not yet been exhausted in most towns and cities. For example, results of investigations show that on average the bicycle is used at present for about 11 per cent of all journeys in the Federal Republic of Germany and that this figure could be increased to 20 or 40 per cent (Brög and Erl, 1985). Conducive to this are the facts that over half of all citizens have a bicycle and that half of all local journeys carried out by the population are under three kilometres, i.e. a typical cycling distance.

The 'Bicycle-Friendly Towns' pilot project

When the Federal Environmental Agency carries out a pilot project it is with the aim of setting a signal; it wants to acquire a general overview of a subject, transfer the knowledge acquired to other similar cases and encourage similar action. The aim of the 'Towns for cyclists' pilot project was to encourage the use of the bicycle in urban transport and to have the bicycle generally accepted as an environmentally benign means of mobility. It was hoped that this would be reflected in greater acceptance of the bicycle by the public and in the financing and planning policies of local authorities. The task of the pilot project was to convey the idea of a bicycle-friendly town as a town with higher environmental quality, both in the demonstration towns and on a broader basis.

The pilot project was conceived and announced in 1979. Over 130 towns from all over West Germany applied to participate. Detmold (Nordrhein-Westfalen) and Rosenheim (Bavaria) were chosen as demonstration towns because, although they had practically no bicycle infrastructure, they showed good potential for developing one and declared that they would like to place emphasis in their urban and transport planning policies in the 1980s on promotion of bicycle transport. Both towns agreed to develop a programme over the course of several years with the theoretical, planning and organisational support of the Federal Environmental Agency, with a broad objective of creating a user-friendly bicycle infrastructure with a climate which was generally conducive to cycling. The aim was to increase the proportion of bicycles used as means of transport *vis à vis* other vehicles, thus improving the quality of urban life and the environment in general. Taking into consideration the different social functions of urban streets, it was necessary to pay particular attention to pedestrians, public transport and the needs of disadvantaged sectors of the population, such as the disabled, children and elderly people.

To accompany the projects in the demonstration towns, a programme of subsidiary pilot projects was set up in the towns of Bad Oeynhausen, Böblingen and Sindelfingen, Landshut, Marburg, Norderstedt, Offenburg,

Pforzheim and Trier. These towns were also interested in creating conditions more conducive to cycling. They were in contact with the pilot project and participated in exchanges of information and experience. In each town a specific problem was studied. In Landshut, for example, the focus was on 'Bicycle transport schemes in historic inner-city areas of high architectural value'; in Trier, 'Linking up bicycle traffic and the public transport system'; and in Bad Oeynhausen, 'Promotion of the bicycle in a spa resort'.

There was also an informal association consisting of the towns of Basle (Switzerland), Chambéry (France) and Graz (Austria) which were connected with the pilot project. The co-operation took the form of an exchange of reports and studies and the organisation of joint events.

The pilot project was served by an advisory committee of some 50 representatives of the demonstration towns, subsidiary demonstration towns, federal and federal state authorities, local authorities, cyclist and environmental protection associations and other institutions. The task of the committee was to inform those involved in the project about progress, plans, successes and problems, and to advise the demonstration towns and those actually in charge of the project. It was born of the idea that promoting and planning bicycle transport requires harmonisation and co-ordination between different levels of government and different authorities. In general, the characteristics of an ideal bicycle-friendly town were stressed, thus providing a horizon for which the towns could aim. The main areas of specific advice came under the headings

'Financing possibilities, funding programmes and guidelines';
'Personnel and organisation aspects';
'Environmental traffic management and bicycle traffic'; and
'Junction design'.

The Federal Environmental Agency provided financing totalling DM2.5 million over a period of six years for the planning, advisory and accompanying research work by commissioning three research and development projects. The towns were responsible for implementing any measures proposed and could claim subsidies under existing funding programmes run by the federal government and the governments of the *Länder* Nordrhein-Westfalen and Bavaria.

The Federal Environmental Agency appointed the following institutions to carry out the project:

— The Socialdata Institute (Munich) was responsible for the overall co-ordination of the project, the necessary sociological and transportation research, the acquisition of expert reports on particular themes, the organisation of planning seminars and the supervision of the subsidiary demonstration towns;

— The Arbeitsgemeinschaft Fahrradfreundliches Detmold (Working Group for the Promotion of Detmold as a Town for Cyclists) and the Planungsbüro Eichenauer – Dr von Winning – Streichert in Munich were responsible for the towns of Detmold and Rosenheim respectively, with particular emphasis on the development of a network of bicycle paths, exemplary individual schemes, and a programme of activities to promote the use of the bicycle. They also advised the towns and carried out public relations work.

Evolution of the project: development in the demonstration towns

When work began in 1981, both towns provided rooms in the town centres where the planning consultants could set up bicycle offices. They were used as local offices for the planners, as a contact point for the public, and as a venue for meetings, discussions, seminars and exhibitions.

A comprehensive study and analysis of the existing infrastructure and organisational aspects available for bicycle transport was undertaken and used to develop a programme of immediate measures for improving bicycle infrastructure. Those measures implemented included marking out bicycle 'fords' across major roads, marking separate bicycle lanes at junctions to facilitate left turns, or rectifying shortcomings in existing bicycle transport facilities.

The central task was the planning of the urban bicycle network. This was not undertaken using conventional methods (i.e. counting bicycle traffic, forecasting, identifying particular stretches of road with sufficient bicycle traffic to warrant building cycle paths), but using destination network planning methods. This involved analysing the potential origins and destinations for bicycle traffic and laying down direct connections (desired routes) according to specific traffic or access functions. In a second phase the ideal connections between destinations had to be co-ordinated with existing urban structures and transport systems. The bicycle transport facility appropriate to each section and its potential volume of bicycle traffic had then to be selected in each case, for example, separate bicycle paths away from the road or bicycle lanes marked out on the carriageway. In connection with the network plan, locations were earmarked for bicycle parking facilities.

Special solutions for individual sections were developed such as closing up gaps in the network, eliminating danger spots or repairing cycle paths within the annual financial programme of the local authorities. It was not the task of the planners commissioned by the Federal Environmental Agency to take over the continuous detailed planning for normal cycle paths but to present model solutions for problem situations (Figures 15.1 and 15.2). The idea was to put the demonstration towns in a position to be

Figure 15.1 Waiting areas for cyclists making indirect turns on crossroads in the 'Bicycle-Friendly Towns' Project

Figure 15.2 Cycle route with right of way for the cyclist in the 'Bicycle-Friendly Towns' Project

able to use these examples in the future to draw up their own plans. Some examples of demonstration bicycle facilities which were set up in Detmold and Rosenheim are:

— introduction of a signal-controlled 'bicycle lock' (in the sense of a canal lock) and a waiting area for making indirect turns;
— construction of a cycle route away from the road along a former tram track, with raised track where it crosses over roads, with right of way for the cyclist at some locations;
— extension of bicycle routes linking up different districts of a town using quiet residential streets and new cycle paths; proper signposting of these routes;
— creation of leisure routes connected up to the main cycle path network with a signpost and information system;
— marking out cycle lanes on the carriageway of one-way streets to enable bicycles to go along them in the 'wrong' direction;
— opening of bicycle offices as a contact point for the local people;
— setting up of a bicycle rental centre near the railway station;
— acquisition of bicycles for local authority employees;
— public relations activities such as poster competitions, information weeks.

(See Dammann, Hänel and Richard, 1987, for Detmold; and Eichenauer, von Winning and Streichert, 1987, for Rosenheim.)

The success (or otherwise) of the projects cannot be measured solely on the basis of short-term results but has to be seen in the mid- and long-term process of development. It was not the aim of the pilot project to conclude by having created a perfect infrastructure for bicycles, but to have increased the consciousness of local authority planners and those responsible for decision-making for promoting bicycle transport. Incorporating bicycle transport promotion into local authority commissions, establishing it firmly as an important local authority responsibility and making adequate financial backing and personnel available in order to implement concrete measures are all more important for lasting success than simply building more kilometres of cycle paths.

Parallel to local measures to promote bicycle transport, a transport and sociological survey was undertaken (Bróg and Erl, 1987). This survey was designed to identify the basic potential which can be activated for bicycle transport and ascertain the changes which have taken place in the choice of means of transport by comparing the present situation with the previous one.

In Rosenheim there was a 13 per cent increase in bicycle traffic between 1981 and 1986 and a rise in the modal share from 23 to 26 per cent. It should also be noted that although more people owned motor cars in 1986 than in 1981 there was not an increase in use of individual motor traffic.

Promotion of bicycle transport has proved here to be an appropriate strategy for limiting the modal split percentage occupied by the motor car and the motor cycle. The Rosenheim figures also show that it is perfectly possible to sustain the high proportion of mainly environmentally benign modes of transport in the overall transport system: 57 per cent of all trips in Rosenheim are made on foot, by bicycle or using public transport and only 43 per cent by individual motor traffic.

In Detmold, it was still possible, despite unfavourable trends in age patterns and car ownership, to stabilise the level of bicycle traffic. This was very important in view of the sharp increase in bicycle traffic in the second half of the 1970s.

In both demonstration towns there were also structural improvements in bicycle transport. For example, the bicycle could chalk up gains in the number of people using it to go to and from work. Use of the bicycle in this way as an everyday means of transport was one of the main aims of the pilot project.

It should also be noted that in both towns the numbers of car owners using bicycles as a means of transport has increased since 1981. This shows clearly that an increase in car ownership does not necessarily lead to a drop in the proportion of bicycles used for transport.

Interim results from the pilot project were announced to the advisory committee and the interested public at planning seminars, and open discussions were held. In addition to this, workshop reports and information sheets were published regularly and provided extensive information on virtually all aspects of bicycle transport. An expert report on bicycle transport in different European countries was also drawn up. The pilot project was therefore able to provide impulses for increased promotion of bicycle transport in towns and cities in the Federal Republic of Germany whilst it was still in progress.

The way forward: towards the bicycle-friendly town

On completion of the pilot project in 1987–8 the Federal Environmental Agency published a brochure 'The way forward: towards a bicycle-friendly town' which contains recommendations for the implementation of aims and measures to promote the bicycle in administrative practice (Umweltbundesamt, 1987).

In general it has become clear that promoting bicycle transport must not be confined to building cycle paths. Attempts must be made to dismantle the obstacles to the use of the bicycle with the help of a comprehensive package of aims and measures. Promotion of bicycle transport should therefore encompass the following points:

— The basis for promotion of bicycle transport in a town should be a programme run by the local authority, in which aims, measures, approaches, responsibilities and investment requirements are laid down. As well as urban and transport planning schemes (e.g. extension of the cycle path network) it must also include 'soft' promotion methods such as public relations campaigns.

— A working group comprising participants from different civil service departments would facilitate the work of the administration in implementing the policies. It should include representatives from departments involved in planning and implementation of bicycle transport promotion, i.e. the planning department, civil engineering department, environment department and road transport department, and in certain cases the real estate office, parks and gardens department, treasurer's office and public relations department (Habermeier, 1988).

— In order to be tenable, the bicycle transport promotion policy must be backed by adequate financing and staff. As a rule of thumb the formula

$$\frac{\text{Inhabitants}}{2.5} \times \text{DM}1000 \ (\pounds 350)$$

can be taken to establish the investment requirement in towns with little bicycle infrastructure.

— A 'bicycle-friendly climate' is essential for the acceptance of the bicycle by the local inhabitants of a town. The cyclist must have the feeling that he/she is welcome there. Bicycle promotion measures which raise consciousness and influence behaviour play an important role in this.

— A 'bicycle office' has proved to be very useful as a centre for people to meet and seek advice. Different kinds of models for the organisation and financing of this can be imagined but some kind of funding from the local authority is essential. There are numerous possibilities for public relations campaigns, such as the opening of leisure routes, organised group bike rides, poster competitions, and bicycle 'MOT'-testing. The role-model function of local authority personalities should not be underestimated, for it can give important incentives to the public to use bicycles more often. Of paramount importance is that any improvement in the bicycle climate of a town keeps pace with the extension of the bicycle infrastructure and vice-versa.

— As far as bicycle infrastructure is concerned, the central aim must be to create a large-scale, self-contained bicycle traffic network. A bicycle traffic network can consist of the following components:

* bicycle routes
* bicycle streets
* separate cycle paths or paths parallel to the road
* cycle lanes on the carriageway

    * residential streets with low traffic volume, if possible in areas with a 30 km/h speed limit

    * areas with traffic restraint schemes in operation.

From this it follows that it is not necessary to build cycle paths everywhere. Often simple but imaginative solutions are sufficient, such as joint use of bus lanes, lanes for bicycles to go along one-way streets the 'wrong' way or marking of bicycle 'fords; over major traffic roads.

— Paths for bicycles must be user-friendly, that is:

    * as direct as possible without diversions

    * of adequate width, taking into account an appropriate turning radius

    * safe at junctions where conflict situations are likely. This can be ensured by marking out waiting areas in front of other traffic, for example

    * continuous so that uninterrupted cycling is possible and the paths are always visible

    * attractive, i.e. in pleasant surroundings.

— Bicycle traffic networks should be planned on the basis of the destination network system. Bicycle parking facilities and a signposting system are essential additions to a bicycle traffic network.

— The green modes of transport should be co-ordinated in a linked system. The aim of this is to create a large-scale, local transport system as an alternative to motor car traffic. The measures required to implement this *green network* include:

    * linking up path infrastructures

    * erecting secure, sheltered parking facilities for bicycles at bus and tram stops and train stations

    * bicycle hire centres, particularly at railway stations

    * introduction of a green travel pass for commuters (a monthly season ticket for the local transport network which includes bicycle hire at the traveller's destination).

Promotion of bicycle transport in this 'green network' can, however, only have a limited effect if environmental traffic management schemes are not implemented and motorised traffic is not generally reduced. There are different possibilities for doing this:

    * speed limits, introduction of 30 km/h zones

    * introduction of large-scale environmental traffic management schemes in urban areas and re-routing and narrowing of roads

    * limitations on street parking

* and, in addition to this, increased mixing of urban functions and activities.

Conclusion

The 'Bicycle-Friendly Towns' pilot project was an important step towards creating towns in West Germany which are more bicycle-friendly and thus have increased environmental quality. It has shown that promotion of bicycle transport is an important component of an urban transport concept which seeks to influence choice of mode of transport in favour of transport systems which do not harm the environment. The Federal Environment Agency is convinced that the activities initiated in the demonstration towns will be continued and extended. The results of the pilot project will motivate other towns and cities to set up local concepts and programmes for promoting bicycle transport, taking into account state programmes and subsidies.

The aim must be to achieve a co-existence between the different transport systems which is compatible with the environment and therefore with society. The further extension of the 'green network' for pedestrians, bicycle and public transport, along with large-scale environmental traffic management, will be central measures towards reaching this goal. The Federal Environmental Agency will continue in future to follow the development of bicycle transport in the Federal Republic of Germany with particular attention and will support it with research in the field of 'The town, transport and the environment'.

References

Brög, W., and Erl, E., 1985, 'Fahrradnutzung in der Bundersrepublik Deutschland: stand und perspektiven', *Bau intern*, **5**, 78–80.
—— and Erl, E., 1987, *Abschliessender bericht zum modellvorhaben 'Fahrradfreundliche Stadt': Teil A: Begleituntersuchung und übergreifende aspekte*, Reihe TEXTE 18/87 des Umweltbundesamtes, Berlin.
Bundesminister des Innern, 1983, *Fahrrad und umwelt-programm zur umweltentlastung durch förderung des fahrradverkehrs*, Umweltbrief 26, 58–63, Bonn.
Bundesminister für Raumordnung, Bauwesen und Städtebau, 1986, *Städebaulicher bericht 'Umwelt und gewerbe in der Städtebaupolitik'*, Schriftenreihe 'Städebauliche Forschung' (Sonderheft), 76–8, Bonn.
Dammann, F.J., Hänel, K. and Richard, J., 1987, *Abschliessender bericht zum modellvorhaben 'Fahrradfreundliche Stadt: Teil B: Fahrradverkehrsplanung in der modellstadt Detmold*, Reihe TEXTE 19/87 des Umweltbundesamtes, Berlin.
Deutscher Bundestag, 1985, *Antwort der bundesregierung auf die BT-Anfrage zum thema 'Stadtökologie: umweltschutz in städten in gemienden'*, Drucksache 10/4208, 13–15.

Eichenauer, M., von Winning, H.H., and Streichert, E., 1987, *Abschliessender bericht zum modellvorhaben 'Fahrradfreundliche Stadt': Teil C: Fahrradverkehrsplanung in der modellstadt Rosenheim*, Reihe TEXTE 20/87 des Umweltbundesamtes, Berlin.

Habermeier, D., 1988, 'Der weg zur fahrradfreundlichen stadt am beispiel Erlangen', in Walprecht, D., *Fahrradverkehr in stadten und gemeinden: planung, ausbaur, förderung*, Carl Heymann Verlag KG, Cologne, 47–59.

Otto-Zimmermann, K., 1986, 'Umwelt-verbund im nahverkehr', *Städte- und gemeindebund*, **2**, 55–62.

Schulte, D., 1986, 'Pladöyer für das fahrrad: eine alternative im nahverkehr', *Verkehrsnachrichten*, **9**, 5–6.

Umweltbundesamt, 1987, *Wegweiser zur fahrradfreundlichen stadt: erkenntnisse und erfahrungen aus dem modellvorhaben Fahrradfreundliche Stadt des Umweltbundesamtes*, Reihe BETRIFT des Umweltbundesamtes, Berlin.

16 Public transport and cycling: experience of modal integration in West Germany

Jürgen Brunsing

Introduction

Using the slogan 'The family on tour would like a nature trip with bus and bike', the Bremen transport system has been advertising its bike–bus idea, trying to make it attractive. What is the reason for wanting to transport bikes in buses? The aim of this chapter is to explain, using examples, the current situation of bike transport in German buses and trams, and to examine other possibilities of a connection between the bike and public transport. Clearly, the successful combination of these transport modes could stop the decline of public transport and speed up urban journeys without using cars.

Since the beginning of the discussion about the environmental damage caused by motorised vehicles through their emissions and the space they take, walking, cycling and the use of public transport have gained more and more importance for planners, politicians and, of course, for the population. 'Integrated traffic planning' means a reorganisation of local traffic with the aim of reducing the transport user's dependency on motorised individual traffic. It creates the circumstances in which the combination of bike and public transport is one possibility for an attractive joint traffic system. In such conditions, there would be greater opportunity for using these complementary means of transport, because of better road conditions for bikes on the one hand – e.g. 30 km/h zones and abolition of free on-street parking – and, on the other, new suburban rapid rail systems as an improvement of the existing local transport. The new rapid trains require longer distances between stops. Since it is rarely the case that you can get to those stops directly by bus it thus becomes attractive to go the 800–4000 metres to the stations or stops by bike. That makes it necessary to cater for bike-and-ride movements at these stops and stations in addition to providing the more usual park-and-ride and kiss-and-ride facilities.

In the past, using the bike in order to reach a public transport stop was a common thing to do, particularly by school children and further education students. However, coping with prosperity and increasing levels of car ownership have been the basic objectives of urban planners in recent decades. The result has been 'cities for cars'. The consequent widening of roads and the obliteration of cycle paths made cycling less attractive, whilst for public transport the opportunities for efficient service were reduced by the decentralisation of population due to mass motorisation. A competition began between bike and public transport to try to get the non car-driving/riding on their side, a phenomenon difficult to understand. In Germany in 1982, 17.1 per cent used the bike as their main means of transport for distances up to three kilometres, whereas the equivalent figure for public transport was 6.8 per cent. For distances over four kilometres the position was reversed, with only 6.1 per cent using the bike and 17.3 per cent public transport (Bracher, 1985). As these distances and modes are complementary, it is obvious that the co-operation of these two systems would be more effective than competition between them.

Such co-operation would imply connecting the advantages of public transport – high capacity over longer distances at higher speeds – with the independence of the bike from schedules, lines and stops. The combined modal split for both means of transport is approximately 25 per cent in West Germany. Only five per cent – mainly pupils and further education students – combine the bike with public transport. For other users, though, this could also be an attractive combination. The advantages for the users of such a combination are the possibilities of more flexible arrangements, lower costs and improved connections. The disadvantages of the use of non-motorised means of traffic alone cease to exist. Moreover there would be more stops or stations in most traffic systems that could be reached by the user within an acceptable time. For the first leg of a journey up to 1.7 km in length, such as that from home to a railway station, a cyclist has a time advantage of at least 10 minutes in comparison with the foot/bus mode. These advantages have been known in the Netherlands for a long time: about 50 per cent of the cyclists there use both bicycle and public transport.

Potential combinations of bicycles and public transport

There are three possibilities of combining the bike with public transport:

—   The bike is used *to reach public transport facilities* and is left there. The customer is now taken to the stop where she or he wants to get off and then walks to the final destination. The emphasis here is on bike-and-ride parking facilities.

— The customer walks or drives to the first stop or station. At the end of the coach or train ride the bike is used *to get to his/her final destination*. This is especially interesting for leisure activities. The emphasis here is on marketing.

— The bike is used *to get to, and away from, the stop or station*. During the journey by rapid train or by bus it can be transported in specially designated areas. The emphasis here is on facilities for travelling with bicycles.

Table 16.1 Evaluation of the combination of bike/public transport and likelihood of use

Combination	Commuters	Shopping/personal business	Leisure and recreational
Bike-and-ride	+	+	−
Bus and rail with bike	0	0	+
Bike hiring	−	−	+

Note: + = well suited; 0 = suitable; − = not suitable.
Source: MSWV, 1986.

The suitability for different ways of travelling is listed in Table 16.1 and the principal combinations are discussed in the following sections.

Bike-and-ride

The largest user group of the bike/public transport combination consists of commuters, pupils and students. Here, the main emphasis should be on the constructive establishment of parking facilities. These have to make sure that it is possible to lock the bike against theft even when the next bike-stand is occupied (each stand being 70 cm apart from the next) and must be designed in such a way that they blend into the surroundings but still are in full view of the public (Forschungsgesellschaft für Strassen- und Verkehrswesen und HUK-Verband, 1982). An evaluation of different bike-parking facilities is provided in Figure 16.1.

In the area of the Rhein-Ruhr transport system 8000 bike-parking facilities are at present available, mainly at suburban rapid rail stops, although they do not necessarily fulfil the above criteria. For example, older ones do not allow the whole bicycle to be secured. With the installation of new bike-parking facilities more of the so-called Rhein-Ruhr-Bügel are being used. These combine bicycle security with economical use of covered parking. Meanwhile, urban planners are taking more account of the architectural integration of bike-parking facilities. At a few suburban rapid rail stops like Düsseldorf-Hilden more customers are sought by

		Ease of use	Theft protection	Weather protection	Luggage storage	Use of space	Costs
	Clip	good	bad	bad	bad	good	good
	Frame	good	good	bad	bad	good	good
	Saddle-stand	good	good	satisfactory	bad	good	good
	Clip & box	good	bad	bad	good	satisfactory	satisfactory
	Vertical stand	satisfactory	good	good	bad	satisfactory	bad
	Bike cage	satisfactory	good	good	good	bad	bad
	Attendant	good	good			satisfactory	bad

good   ○ satisfactory   - bad

Figure 16.1 Evaluation of bike-parking facilities

Figure 16.2 Bicycle cages

offering bicycle cages for hire (Figure 16.2). These guarantee safe parking, shelter and they reduce the possibility of damage. If potential users can depend on a bicycle stand being available they are more likely to become regular users of local public transport. Due to the lack of parking facilities people still use fences and lamp posts on the pavements and station squares to park their bikes, very much to the displeasure of the local inhabitants and pedestrians. In Münster, one of the cities with the largest number of bikes in Germany, thousands of bikes block the station square daily to the extent that they have to be taken away by local council workers and put elsewhere.

Ride-and-bike

Apart from the small number of commuters who leave a (second) bike to be used after they have got off the train, this sort of combination is rarely used. For recreational traffic, bicycle-hire services close to stops offer an alternative to walking. German railways hire out bikes at about 250 stations as an attractive additional offer for people travelling by train. Even so, German railway marketing departments have not exploited this as a promotional opportunity. An attempt made by Bremen to 'hire out', free of charge, bikes owned by local government was unsuccessful. Many of the 60 bikes that were available were stolen in a much shorter time than anticipated. The bikes which were not stolen are now hired out for a charge.

Bicycle transport in suburban rapid rail

The most interesting solution for using the bike as a means of getting to or from the suburban railway station is carrying it in the luggage compartment of regular trains. However, this is unattractive because the standards of price, availability and value for money clearly lag behind those of suburban rapid rail where, since the end of the 1970s, the carriage of bicycles has been first tolerated, then allowed experimentally, and finally officially approved. Now suburban rapid rails which operate in the Rhein-Ruhr, Rhein-Main, Berlin, Hamburg, Munich, Stuttgart and Nuremberg networks carry bicycles during the week – excluding peak hours – and all day at weekends (Figure 16.3). The fares for bicycles lie between those charged for children and adults depending on the area. This facility varies from place to place. For example, in the area of Hamburg, 500–700 bikes are transported daily. The Rhein-Ruhr Transport System, on the other hand, only carries about 100 bikes a day, though paradoxically this is actually a good sign because the high accessibility of railway stations means that commuters and students do not need a bike to be transported. However, traffic forecasts show that in the next few years this use of integrated public transport will decline. Because of the decreasing number of customers the

Figure 16.3 Bicycle transport facility in suburban rapid rail

transport companies will be forced to concern themselves more than ever with recreational traffic as an extension of their services, the only growth area for the future. The projected rate of increase is five to six per cent p.a. to the year 2000.

Bicycle transport in buses and trams

According to the conditions of carriage of city transport companies in the Federal Republic of Germany, passengers are not entitled to carry goods, including bicycles. The main arguments against the transportation of bikes in regular line traffic concern the lack of storage facilities on buses and trams, inadequate entrances and the potential annoyance caused to other passengers.

In order to attract new customers, German transport companies have tested various facilities which would overcome these difficulties (Karl, 1986).

— The redesign of buses and trams for the transportation of bikes, e.g. Bremen.
— Seasonable variations in layout for a more flexible use of the vehicles. For example, bike buses can be used for driving lessons when not in use for bikes, e.g. Wuppertal.
— Scheduled buses or trams equipped with trailers that carry the bicycles, e.g. Hanover, Stuttgart.

— Interior space for a limited number of bicycles in buses and trams in regular line traffic, e.g. Münster area, Bonn, Bochum.

In this context Zürich City Transport in Switzerland serves as a model, for it offers a monthly season ticket which allows the transport of bicycles on all off-peak buses and trams. In the following sections the opportunities and limitations for transporting bicycles by bus are illustrated by reference to several German cities.

Examples of bicycle transport by bus and tram in German cities

Bremen: traffic with redesigned buses

In 1986, co-operation between the German Bicycle Association (ADFC) and Bremen City Transport resulted in the introduction of the 'Bike-and-Bus-Traffic' system on summer weekends. The low fare of DM1 for a return ticket to a recreational area and a well-organised advertising campaign led to great success. The bus could carry 25 bikes, but high levels of demand made it necessary to put on a second bus from time to time. During the first year, the buses operated nine times on each weekend and carried 2500 passengers with their bicycles. The cost of only DM5000 (£1800) for the redesign proves that there is no inevitable contradiction between 'cheap' and 'attractive'. A further stimulation is undoubtedly the city's general support for bicycle and short-distance traffic. An example of this support is the transferable 'Environment Ticket' for all public transport which costs DM40 per month. Furthermore, bikes are repaired and can be rented at the bicycle service station near the central station.

The fact that the bus did not operate in 1989 was a disappointment to those who were satisfied customers during the previous years. Nowadays the bus can be rented only by groups. A similar organisation for the transport of bikes – which was free of charge in some cities – could be found in Saarbrücken, Kassel, Wiesbaden, Heinsberg, Herne and Braunschweig (Figures 16.4 and 16.5).

Wuppertal: combined operation of redesigned buses

Wuppertal is an agglomeration of several cities situated in the Bergisches Land region, which is characterised by its steep hills. In order to facilitate the journey to the cycling trails, Wuppertal City Transport introduced the 'Bicycle Express' in 1986. It ran on weekends and on public holidays, transporting passengers who wished to cycle for recreational purposes to the elevated plateaux north and south of the valley. Wuppertal City

Figure 16.4   Bike bus in Braunschweig

Figure 16.5   The interior of a re-designed bus in Braunschweig

Figure 16.6   A bicycle trailer

Transport invested DM 100 000 (£360 000) for the redesign of the Bendi-buses (which offered space for up to 16 bicycles), the reconstruction of nine bus stops, and for the repair and signing of the cycling trails.

In 1986 two buses were in operation. Each of them ran five times a day at a frequency of 90/120 minutes. It was not necessary for the bicycle passengers to notify the bus in advance. The low degree of utilisation (20 per cent) and receipts of only DM5000 were the causes for the suspension of this service. The buses were redesigned in order to run the normal service again.

In 1988, the service was re-installed, but with a reduced service. One bus with a trailer operated ten times each weekend and served three stops. The fare per passenger was the same as on the regular lines, monthly season tickets were valid and reductions were offered. As in 1986, the fare per bicycle was DM1.50. The wet summer and the irregular schedule put an end to this project too. The cost for each bicycle that had been transported amounted to DM60 (£21).

Hanover: regular line traffic with trailer

In contrast to Wuppertal, Hanover City Transport used trailers to carry the bicycles from the very start (Figure 16.6). The buses that ran on the regular service to the Steinhuder Meer, a recreational area, had a trailer attached that carried up to 20 bikes. But the transport company set obstacles for those interested in this service: the customers had to register and the only stop at which they could load their bicycles into the trailer was at the central bus station. They had to arrive 15 minutes before departure and had to go to the end of the line. Inconsistent operation did not help the potential consumers to get used to the new service: for example, in the space of four months, one trailer operated on five different lines. Even the fact that bicycles were transported free of charge did not encourage the project. In 1988, the service was extended: up to three bikes were allowed to be taken on the regular lines on Sundays. One year later the trial run ceased to operate. Equally unsuccessful were the projects in Aachen, Detmold and Stade.

Stuttgart: regular line traffic with the trailer in front of the tram

The cog tramway in Stuttgart is exceptional in every respect. It is the only cog tramway operating in any German integrated transport system. Normally, it carries up to 10 bicycles from the valley station to the mountain station, though carriage of bicycles to intermediate stops is not possible. The trailers were built by the apprentices of the Stuttgart City Tramway for DM25 000 (£9000) each: one advantage is that the passengers can load and unload their bicycles without assistance (Bracher, 1985).

Münster area: independent lines

The KML transport company has tried a new approach, sponsored by funds from the state of Nordrhein-Westfalen. The project is called 'Leisure bus line with bicycle transport facilities'. The eastern part of the Ruhr area is linked with the Munsterland by a service that was especially installed for this purpose and which runs once on Fridays and six times at the weekends. This year (1989) the coach serves 22 stops on several routes, carrying up to 40 bikes in a closed trailer. By combining different stops to get on or off the bus, passengers can go for day or weekend trips on their bikes. The fares for passengers depend on the distance they intend to travel plus DM3 per bicycle; there are several family reductions. Co-operation with tourist agencies helps the passengers to get information about the countryside and objects of interest, and guided tours are organised. All in all, this project promises to be an economic success.

Bonn: regular line traffic

Whereas redesigned buses and trailers always generate various disadvantages, it seems to be less problematic to take along bicycles in regular line

Figure 16.7 Bicycle transport in Bonn

traffic in off-peak times such as at the weekends. In connection with the project 'Bike on the Bus', in 1984 Bonn City Transport offered more space for bicycles in five buses running on regular line traffic. Only three seats were lost in this reconstruction (Figure 16.7). While the bus was in motion the bicycles were strapped by rubber belts, so the owners did not have to stand close to their bikes. These buses operated on Saturdays, Sundays and public holidays but during the week they ran the normal service. But the expectations on this line from Bad Godesberg to the Siebengebirge were not fulfilled: in 1985 only 265 bicycles were transported. This project was further undermined by passengers complaining about the lack of seats and about the rubber mats which covered the floor in order to protect the bikes. So this experiment – which had half-heartedly been introduced during an election campaign – was abandoned (ADFC/BIS, 1988).

Bochum: regular line traffic on the whole net

The Bochum-Gelsenkirchener Tramway Company started a new campaign on 1 May 1989 to improve the attractiveness of public transport on Saturday afternoons, Sundays and public holidays. Bicycles can be transported in all buses and trams. Interchange to suburban rapid rail and trains with luggage compartments is also possible. Operating until Autumn 1989, this experiment allows the transport of up to four bikes per vehicle in the space which is marked with a pram symbol. Delays that result from the loading of several bicycles can be compensated by shorter halts at other stops. The fare does not depend on the length of the journey; cyclists pay DM1.50 per trip and only DM1 when using a travel ticket. First reports show that such a combination of passengers and cyclists with their bikes causes no annoyance. It agrees with similar reports in the area of Ravensburg and Reutlingen, where bicycle transport has been introduced every summer month for five years. During the summer holidays Essen and Dortmund City Transport will experimentally follow the Bochum model. It is to be hoped that this trend-setting offer is going to fulfil the expectations of the company as well as those of the passengers.

Munich: prospects for the future

The Munich integrated transport system is a good example of how bicycle facilities can be improved as a by-product of the redesign of both vehicles and stops to assist the handicapped. Unfortunately this development has occurred rather late: all subway stations that do not have ramps will be equipped with ramps and/or lifts before 1991. This will be advantageous for the transportation of bicycles, as well as of use to the handicapped. If all of the subway stops and most of the tramway stops can be reached comfortably with the bike, this will certainly have a positive effect on the number of passengers. Although at the moment the possibilities for taking along bicycles are limited on subway and tramway lines, the use of low-floor buses would be useful for the transport of bikes. The entrances are broad and without steps, since the floor is only about 10 cm above the height of the kerbstone. According to the StadtBahn 2000 plan, whose aim it is to increase the attractiveness of public transport, the service offered will be extended in favour of all passengers. This will have a positive effect on the future possibilities for the transportation of bicycles in buses and trams (Bonk and Hilsenbeck, 1989).

Prospect

The possibilities for carrying bicycles are often complicated, inadequate or limited to certain times or days. Thus the potential passenger–rider must put a lot of effort into the preparation and planning of a combined journey by bicycle and public transport, so much so that the potential passenger is often deterred from making the trip at all.

One aspect must not be forgotten: the aim is to enable all passengers of public transport to reach a stop by walking an acceptable distance. The bicycle as a means of transport to and from the stops should not be a substitute for a good public transport system with facilities convenient for pedestrians. However, bicycles have a role to play where circumstances are unfavourable for pedestrians or special demand factors are concerned: these potential consumers should have the chance to choose.

The integration of bicycle and public transport leads to a transport system that is ecologically acceptable, healthy and helps to save energy. The consumer can choose from a variety of combinations in order to find a quick link that does not require the use of a car. For the transport firms it brings various opportunities to enlarge their clientèle, though whether or not they will be proved successful will have to be decided by the market. However, the likelihood of success can be increased by public activity in matters concerning the built environment, whether through infrastructure to overcome the specific disadvantages of bicycles and public transport or through measures to limit urban sprawl and thus keep trip lengths down. These are necessary steps to developing the integration of bicycles and public transport as a serious alternative to motorised individual traffic.

References

ADFC/Büro für integrierte Stadt und Verkehrsplanung (BIS), 1988 *Materialsammlung zum Thema Fahrradbeförderung in Bussen*, Bonn.

Bonk, R. and Hilsenbeck, O., 1989, 'ÖPNV für Behinderte dient allen Fahrgasten', *Verkehrsnachrichten*, Heft 4, 7–11.

Bracher, T., 1985, 'Fahrradverkehr: Ein Markt für den ÖPNV?', *Verkehr und Technik*, Heft 2, 47–52.

Forschungsgesellschaft für Strassen- und Verkehrswesen and HUK Verband, 1982, *Empfehlungen für Planung, Entwurf und Betrieb von Radverkehrsanlagen*, Cologne.

Karl, J., 1986, 'Mit dem Fahrrad in Bus und Bahn'. *Verkehrszeichen*, Heft 3, 46–50.

Minister für Stadtentwicklung, Wohnen und Verkehr (MSWV) des Landes Nordrhein-Westfalen, 1986, *Radfahren, aber sicher: Radverkehrssicherheit in NRW*, Düsseldorf.

17 The evolution and impact of pedestrian areas in the Federal Republic of West Germany

Rolf Monheim

Pedestrian areas are one of the most controversial measures for habitable cities. They are idolised by their advocates as an ideal; on the other hand, their critics see them either as sounding the death-knell for the city centre or as a consumer-orientated trick to merchandise it. Often they fundamentally change the impression which a city centre makes on its visitors.

Such areas have been widely introduced in the Federal Republic of Germany (Monheim, 1975, 1987), as well as in the German Democratic Republic (Andrä *et al*, 1981). Many have reached exceptional proportions, are often lavishly laid out and have become universally famous, as in Munich. However, the development of the pedestrian area in the Federal Republic has by no means ended and the ideal one does not exist. The repercussions of the provision of pedestrian areas stretch out beyond the city centre into the entire region and even into the lifestyle of the society.

Conceptual and spatial expansion of pedestrian areas

The development of pedestrian areas began in most towns with single sections of streets being reserved for pedestrians, where the streets were too narrow and the high density of pedestrians made car traffic scarcely practicable. The first two German pedestrian streets – Hohe Strasse in Cologne and Limbecker Strasse in Essen – are typical examples of this. However, where the shopping streets were wider than 15 metres it seemed that their change to pedestrian areas was not only unnecessary, since the main object was the elimination of traffic conflicts, but was also not practicable because pedestrians would feel lost in such a space. The retailers for the most part rejected the notion of pedestrianisation.

Pedestrian streets in no way signified a reorientation of traffic planning in the interests of the pedestrian; rather they were part of a car-preferential modification of the city centre, with new central ring roads (often along the medieval town walls), multi-storey car parks and rear-access streets for goods delivery. This often required profound intrusions into the stock of historical buildings. This type of pedestrianisation followed the model of new, free-standing, shopping centres. In the larger cities with about half a million or more inhabitants, the installation of underground railways at the end of the 1960s and beginning of the 1970s formed an important impetus for urban redevelopment. They not only improved accessibility but also made the installation of bigger pedestrian streets more economical, such as in the main shopping streets of Frankfurt and Munich.

In the first half of the 1970s the conception of pedestrian areas changed as a result of their economic success. This resulted from a self-reinforcing process: the improved accessibility and urban design produced investments from traders and landlords, which attracted more visitors, which again acted as an incentive to investment potential. Success of the downtown was eased by the fact that the establishment of new out-of-town shopping centres, which had begun in the mid-1960s and reached a peak in the early 1970s, was slowing down after the mid-1970s due to widespread opposition and to planning restrictions.

For further development, changes in the standard of living and lifestyle became important (Gehl, 1987). Downtown trade changed its emphasis from convenience to comparison goods: many visitors valued an attractive shopping area with a casual atmosphere and were stimulated to buy goods that they did not really need. Indicators of this changed reaction were the rising numbers of visitors who left a shop without having bought anything: in large department stores these amounted in 1988 to 41 per cent on Thursdays and 39 per cent on Saturdays; and in large textile chain stores as many as 67 and 58 per cent respectively (Bundesarbeitsgemeinschaft der Mittel- und Grossbetriebe e.V., 1989).

These shopping and recreation functions led to a revival of arcades. Some of these were quite remarkable developments which improved the image of the town centre. Such an agreeable, relaxed environment is especially important for the success of spa and holiday towns, which are mainly small in size. In response to this they have adopted large measures for traffic calming in the centres much earlier and more intensively than other towns (Heinze and Schreckenberg, 1984; Monheim and Sonntag, 1989).

An important element of this new assessment of city centres was the rediscovery of historical heritage. Whilst up until the beginning of the 1970s buildings had been torn down to make way for the putative require-ments of the time, they were now being lovingly restored. In part, even rows of houses destroyed during the war were re-erected according to historical models, the most striking example being the Frankfurt Romer. These trends culminated in the town centres. They gave pedestrian areas important impulses, since the new feeling for life could develop much better in car-free or mainly traffic-calmed streets. A town without rep-resentative pedestrian areas now appears hopelessly antiquated.

The extended function of pedestrian streets led to more pedestrianisation in parts of town centres which were less strongly commercially orientated and even in streets and squares without any retail function, where they formed important parts of the historical and social identity. Representative examples are the new developments on the banks of the Rhine in Cologne and those planned in Düsseldorf, with spacious promenades freed from traffic, which in each case is concealed in a tunnel.

Traffic-calmed shopping streets, especially in small and medium-sized towns

In many small and medium-sized towns retailers and the car lobby rejected pedestrian areas even though the populace, on the contrary, wanted them. One way out of this conflict between citizens and business was to introduce traffic-calmed shopping streets using the traffic regulations which were originally developed in residential areas. They are indicated by a special traffic sign, which gives equal rights to all forms of traffic: pedestrians can use the whole street for walking or standing around while cars must travel at walking pace and park in specially designated parking spaces. All road users must be considerate to one another. These traffic-calmed streets can also be introduced where car access must remain, for example, to industrial enterprises. Traffic-calmed shopping streets are preferred in smaller towns because parking is still used in the immediate vicinity of the destinations. The greatest disadvantage, however, is the disturbance by car traffic, but at least pedestrians are no longer in danger, whereas previously there were many accidents.

There was a boom in the development of traffic-calmed shopping streets in the 1980s, but nevertheless many planners and politicians are still unfamiliar with them. Due to different local situations, many transitional forms were developed. Often traffic-calmed streets were introduced as peripheral extensions of pedestrian areas: the opposite could also occur by pedestrianising the narrow side-streets which lead to an extensive traffic-calmed market place. By using time-banding during the day, the shopping street as a traffic-calmed area can remain accessible to the car whilst offering the necessary peace to shoppers and residents in the afternoon and at night. Compromises of this sort make tailor-made solutions possible. In any case, as a general rule the kind of compromise is decided less by practical necessity than by local political conditions.

The traffic-calmed shopping street is a considerable improvement on the shopping street with unrestricted access to traffic and a separation of carriageway and sidewalk, but for many downtown visitors it does not fulfil their expectations of a city centre. This can be seen from investigations which show critical attitudes from many visitors on the quantity and speed of car traffic (Monheim *et al*, 1989).

The significance of the possibility of getting to the shopping area by car is frequently overestimated. Most car users do not think it important that they can park in traffic-calmed areas, only a few try to park there very often and many never do. One result of this 'reasonable' attitude is that only a few fail to find a parking space (Monheim *et al.* produce data from three towns in 1989).

The pedestrian friendly street with separate road and sidewalk

Where main streets have developed into a commercial strip there are still functions which need to be protected and numerous pedestrians who must frequently cross the street. Thus recently the conditions for pedestrian movement and shopping have been improved even on main traffic roads (Der Bundesminister für Raumordnung, Bauwesen und Stadtebau, 1984; Monheim 1987; Eichenauer *et al.*, 1988). To this end, sidewalks are widened, aids to the pedestrian to cross are provided – such as the narrowing of roads and provision of central reservations at crossing points – and trees, benches, flowers and street lamps, all carefully in proportion, are installed. A decrease in the speed of traffic is also important. In spite of this remodelling, these main roads can cope with considerable amounts of traffic since the capacity is limited by the road junctions and not by the streets between the junctions.

Traffic-calmed main streets typically fit into two different situations. First, in the main centres of larger towns, they extend the pedestrian-friendly space along roads mostly designed as boulevards, or lead from pedestrianised areas to important destinations on the edge of the inner city, such as the railway station (as in Frankfurt, Nuremburg and Munich) or locations characterised by representative functions (e.g. Cologne). Even in those situations where pedestrianisation seems not to be possible because main shopping streets cannot be completely closed to car traffic, the streets are laid out as boulevards (e.d. Düsseldorf and Hamburg).

Second, in the district centres of large towns and centres of smaller towns, main traffic thoroughfares have frequently developed as commercial strips, which present the most important point of reference of their respective catchment areas. Here a pedestrian-friendly arrangement is important to prevent any devaluation of the district.

Number and size of urban centres with pedestrian streets or traffic calming

In the Federal Republic today there are well over 1000 pedestrian areas and traffic-calmed town centres. All cities and almost all medium sized towns with more than 50 000 inhabitants have central pedestrian areas. Amongst towns with 20–50 000 inhabitants, almost three-quarters have a pedestrian area or traffic-calmed shopping area. In towns with 10–20 000 inhabitants, up to one-third follow this model. In smaller settlements the share is smaller still, but here and in the independent district centres which occur in larger towns, traffic-calmed shopping streets (or less frequently pedestrian areas) are being introduced.

Just as important for the increasing significance of pedestrian areas is their growth in size. Most towns began with closing off short stretches of streets; newly established pedestrian areas and traffic-calmed shopping streets nowadays mostly cover 100–300 metres. After their successful introduction pedestrian areas are almost always extended. The older ones embrace several kilometres of pedestrian streets, principally in larger cities, but also even in medium sized and smaller towns. In towns such as Aachen, Frankfurt, Hanover, Cologne, Munich, Nuremburg and Stuttgart the more or less closed-off pedestrian streets and arcades form a network of four to seven kilometres in length with, in addition, boulevards or pedestrian friendly streets. The growth process which led to these complexes has been documented for several cities by Monheim (1975, 1980) and in more detail for Nuremburg (1986).

An unpublished survey by the Ministry for Urban Development,

Table 17.1   Pedestrian areas in Nordrhein-Westfalen according to municipality size, 1988

	Inhabitants in '000s						
	<10	10–25	25–50	50–100	100–150	150–500	>500
Municipalities with pedestrian areas	6	48	57	33	7	16	5
Per cent of all municipalities	8	30	74	89	100	100	100
Mean total length per municipality in km (including district centres)	0.2	0.4	0.7	1.2	1.2	2.8	6.6

Source: Unpublished documentation on the position of traffic calming in settlements in Nordrhein-Westfalen, drawn up by the study group Plan-local and Akoplan, 1989.

Housing and Traffic for the state of Nordrhein-Westfalen gives, for the largest federal state, the most up-to-date documentation on the development of pedestrian areas and traffic calming. Though the extent of traffic-calmed shopping streets is not clear, the widespread development of pedestrian areas is confirmed (Table 17.1). In the small centres the extent is mostly modest, but in the large to medium sized towns and cities, including all pedestrian streets in district centres, it is considerable, with average lengths ranging from 1.2 to 6.6 kilometres.

In Bavaria there is a similar scale of development when one takes into

Table 17.2 Pedestrian areas and traffic-calmed shopping streets in centres in Bavaria according to municipality size, 1985

	Inhabitants in '000s						
	*<10**	*10–20*	*20–50*	*50–100*	*100–150*	*150–500*	*>500*
Municipalities with pedestrian areas/ traffic-calmed shopping streets	7	27	17	11	3	2	1
Per cent of all municipalities	11	21	52	100	100	100	100
Mean total length per municipality in km (including district centres)							
Pedestrian centres and traffic-calmed shopping streets**	0.2	0.6	0.9	1.3	3.7	4.3	5.0
Pedestrian areas only	0.2	0.5	0.7	1.0	1.6	4.3	5.0

* All municipalities with the title 'town' or 'spa', as well as those 'market towns' with over 7500 inhabitants were surveyed
** Excluding traffic calming in residential areas
Source: Author's survey.

consideration the investigation terms from three years previously (Table 17.2). The traffic-calmed shopping streets have a mostly supplementary function so far, yet strong growth is evident, especially in smaller areas. In towns with 10–20000 inhabitants, one-quarter have only traffic-calmed and no pedestrianised shopping streets. In the two largest cities, Nuremburg has 1390 metres of pedestrian and traffic-calmed shopping streets located in district centres (19 per cent of the city total), whilst Munich, with 1280 metres, has 26 per cent.

Consequences of pedestrian areas

Pedestrian areas and traffic calming should serve the achievement of specific goals. The decision as to whether and where these measures are to be used depends, therefore, on the assumption of their effectiveness. This political dimension is often forgotten, and many discussions are limited to the question of whether or not sales in the shops have increased. (The Forschungsstelle für den Handel (1978) has published a detailed study

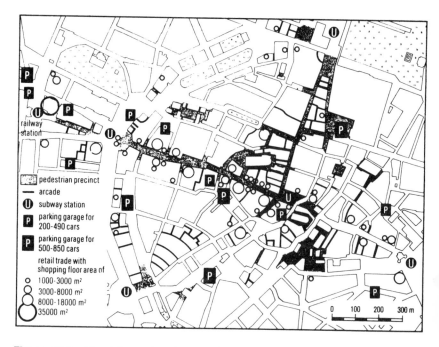

Figure 17.1   Munich: pedestrian precincts, traffic arrangements and retail trade

about this aspect, and there is discussion of the effects of traffic calming on the retail structure in Kanzlerski and Monheim (1987) and Kanzlerski (1988).) In spite of there being well over 1000 pedestrian areas and traffic-calmed shopping areas, in spite of their sometimes considerable size, and despite many years of experience, it is nonetheless difficult to judge their success, even though planning policy decisions are often made as if one knew exactly. There are several reasons for this.

Since pedestrian areas normally cannot be introduced as isolated measures but tend to be a part of a bundle of measures taken to improve the attractiveness of the inner city, such observed changes can scarcely be ascribed to single causes. When, for example, between 1960 and 1983 the number of passers-by in the pedestrian area in Munich increased by 44 per cent throughout the day and by 68 per cent in the afternoon, the effect of the introduction of successful U- and S-bahn rail systems had to be taken into consideration because, as Figure 17.1 shows, all the lines are connected to the pedestrian areas. (Hall and Hass-Klau (1985) show the effects of public transport on the success of pedestrianised city centres in British and German cities.) Furthermore, the increasing number of inhabitants and visitors to the Greater Munich area has to be taken into account.

Moreover, the effect of the measures is not a direct one. Rather they are triggered, as it were, as catalytic chain reactions, for they give impulses to the increase in value of buildings and their exploitation. Through them more people are attracted, which again becomes the basis for further improvement in facilities. Only when business people and house owners are unable to take up the opportunities offered to them do pedestrianisation initiatives fail.

Many analyses of results pay too little attention to unintentional and possibly unwelcome side-effects. (This aspect has been criticised among others by a study edited by the Bundesminister für Raumordnung, Bauwesen und Stadtebau, 1978.) The increased attractiveness of shopping facilities has, as a consequence, raised shop rents. This accelerates the replacement of old-established and less rentable uses by branches of national chain stores, so that many principal shopping streets are threatened by standardisation and trivialisation. Moreover, the establishment of many pedestrian areas has followed too slavishly the contemporary ruling fashion of urban design and they have thus become streets like living rooms furnished according to the latest whim. Though these problems of urban design can arise without the introduction of pedestrianisation, nevertheless committed planners have specifically warned against the 'nightmare pedestrian areas'. (For further discussion on this, see Garbrecht, 1977, on Hanover and the response by Monheim, 1978. For the more technical design principles, see Boeminghans, 1977.)

Another problem is the fact that as a result of an increase in visitors and sales turnover in a pedestrianised location, generally other locations do less business. The immediate peripheries of pedestrian areas are affected by this because their attractiveness is taken away relatively or even absolutely through more traffic, delivery vehicles and unattractive exploitation. (Monheim, 1980, 92–118; 1986).

This redistribution also concerns the district centres in the principal cities and the towns in the surrounding countryside, which mostly introduced pedestrian areas later and therefore have, at least relatively, lost attractiveness. Meanwhile they could win back customers through better design and retail standards. The large department- and chain-stores have analysed these shifts through regular studies since 1965 (Bundesarbeitsgemeinschaft der Mittel- und Grossbetriebe e.V., 1989).

In terms of the numbers of visitors and turnover in town centres, many processes threaten historical centres and in the United States have led to their extensive destruction. These include population suburbanisation and the establishment of car-orientated shopping centres in the periphery of the town and in the surrounding countryside, which affects mainly the less specialised department stores. This was of great importance for the city centres in earlier times, as shown in a study by Meyer and Monheim (1988) of Erlangen, where this sector of retailing lost visitors, whereas specialised retailers realised significant gains. The increased car orientation of the customers is a further trend which in the old-established areas is not matched by the road capacity or by its potential for expansion. If this challenge is considered, then the traditional town centres in the Federal Republic can be seen to have held their own outstandingly well. If together with the inhabitants a part of the buying power (especially for basic necessities) is transferred to the surrounding areas, this can even be seen as positively beneficial for traffic relief.

Whilst numbers of visitors and business turnover play their central role in the arguments of the interest groups, the citizens evaluate the experience much more in terms of the increased liveability of the town centre. As the town centre to date is the most important orientation and identification point in German towns, this improvement, in general, makes living in the town more worthwhile. This is important for planning policy, for the economic development of a region depends fundamentally on high-tech industry and quality services, whose entrepreneurs, executives and qualified workforce lay great stress on the liveability of their town. An attractive inner city fundamentally promotes a good image, which is an essential factor of production. This is the opinion of decision-makers in places like Cologne, Munich and Frankfurt and in leading cities in other countries.

The growing appreciation of a 'liveable' city is connected with changes in lifestyle. The single family home is 'out' and an apartment in town is 'in', especially because the number of children and marriages are declining. This results in a strong demand for dwellings in the centre, whose inhabitants play an intensive part in urban life. They emphatically demand better living conditions than the previous inhabitants, who are increasingly being pushed out. To this lifestyle belong street cafés, culture and public squares, noble arcades and museums.

Although there are good examples of the re-creation of habitable town centres in the Federal Republic, this point of view plays a surprisingly small role in German specialist literature. In contrast there are several English-language publications which give special attention to this point of view, with reference to European, and particularly to German, examples. Brambilla and Longo (1977); Crowhurst-Lennard and Lennard (1984, 1987); Gehl (1987); Whyte (1980); and Wiedenhoft (1981) are representative.

Pedestrian areas have contributed fundamentally to the fact that streets and squares have been rediscovered as areas for everyday life. A strong motivation has arisen to recapture even those urban street areas that lie beyond pedestrian oases and to turn the car back to its serving role. That means that the pedestrianised area has become an important learning place for urban life.

References

Andrä, K., Klinker, R. and Lehmann, R., 1981, *Fußgängerbereiche in Stadzentren*, VEB Verlag für Bauwesen, Berlin.

Boeminghans, D., 1977, *Fußgängerzonen*, Arbeitsblätter zur Umweltgestaltung 3, Institut für Umweltgestaltung Aachen, Karl Krämer Verlag, Stuttgart.

Brambilla, R. and Longo, G., 1977, *For pedestrians only: planning, design and management of traffic-free zones*, Whitney Library of Design, New York.

Bundesarbeitgemeinschaft de Mittel- und Großbetriebe e.V. (BAG) (ed.), 1989, *Mittelzentren im Aufwind: Ergebnisse de BAG-Untersuchung Kundenverkehr 1988*, Cologne.

Bundesminister für Raumordnung, Bauwesen und Städtebau, 1978, *Siedlungsstrukturelle Folgen der Einrichtung von verkehrsberuhigten Zonen in Kernbereichen*, Schriftenreihe 'Städtebauliche Forschung' 03.065, Bonn.

— 1984, *Städtebauliche Integration von innerörtlichen Hauptverkehrsstraßen: Problemanalyse und Dokumentation*, Schriftenreihe 'Städtebauliche Forschung' 03.107, Bonn.

Crowhurst Lennard, S.H. and Lennard, H., 1984, *Public life in urban places: social and architectural characteristics conducive to public life in European cities*, Gondolier Press, Southampton, NY.

— 1987, *Liveable cities: people and places: social and design principles for the future of the city*, Gondolier Press, Southampton, NY.

Eichenauer, M., Von Winning, H.H. and Streichert, E., 1988, 'Hauptverkehrsstraßen: ungenutzte Reserven für städtebauliche Integration', *Der Städtetag*, **I**, 1–8.

Forschungsstelle für den Handel (FfH), 1978 *Die Bedeutung der Füßgängerzonen für den Strukturwandel im Handel*, Bearb. R, Spannagel, Berlin.

Garbrecht, D., 1977, 'Fußgängerbereiche: ein Alptraum? *Baumeister*, fasc. 11, 1052–53.

Gehl, J., 1987, *Life between buildings: using public space*, Van Nostrand Reinhold Company, New York.

Hall, P. and Hass-Klau, C., 1985, *Can rail save the city? The impacts of rail rapid transit and pedestrianization on British and German cities*, Gower Publ. Co., Hants and Brookfield, Vermont.

Heinze, G.W. and Schreckenberg, W., 1984, *Verkehrsplanung für eine erholungsfreundiche Umwelt: ein Handbuch verkehrsberuhigender Maßnahmen für Kleinstädte und Landgemeinden*, Veröffentlichungen der Akademie für Raumforschung und Landesplanung, Abhandlungen 85, C.R. Vincentz Verlag, Hanover.

Kanzlerski, D. (ed.), 1988, *Verkehrsberuhigung und Entwicklung von Handel und Gewerbe: Materialien zur Diskussion*, Seminare–Symposien–Arbeitspapiere 33, Bonn.

— and Monheim, H., 1987, *Verkehrsberuhigung und Entwicklung von Handel und Gewerbe, Grundüberlegungen, Ergebnisse und Folgerungen einer Expertenumfrage*, Seminare–Symposien–Arbeitspapiere 25, Bonn.

Meyer, G. and Monheim, R., 1988, 'Erfordernisse und Probleme einer regelmäßigen Erfassung der Entwicklung von Einkaufsstraßen', in Kanzlerski, D. (ed.), *Verkehrsberuhigung und Entwicklung von Handel und Gewerbe: Materialien zur Diskussion*, Seminare–Symposien–Arbeitspapiere 33, Bonn, 102–26.

Monheim, R., 1975, *Fußgängerbereiche: Bestand und Entwicklung*, Reihe E, DST, Beiträge zur Stadtentwicklung 4, Deutscher Städtetag, Cologne.

— 1978, 'Müssen Fußgängerzonen ein Alptraum sein? Eine Antwort an Dietrich Garbrecht', *Baumeister*, fasc. 2, 162–3.

—— 1980, 'Fussgängerbereiche und Fussgängerverkehr in Stadtzentren in der Bundesrepublik Deutschland' *Bonner Geographische Abhandlungen*, 64, Dümmters Verlag, Bonn.

—— 1986, 'Der Fußgängerbereich in der Nürnberger Altstadt: ein Beispiel wechselnder stadtentwicklungskonzepte', in Hopfinger, H. (ed.), *Franken, Planung für eine bessere Zukunft?*, Verlag H. Carl, Nuremburg, 89–112.

—— 1987, *Entwicklungstendenzen von Fußgängerbereichen und verkehrsberuhigten Einkaufsstraßen*, Arbeitsmaterialien zur Raumordnung und Raumplanung 41, Bayreuth.

—— and Sonntag, R., 1989, *Verkehr in der Kurstadt Bad Kissingen*, Arbeitsmaterialien zur Raumordnung un Raumplanung 71, Bayreuth.

——, Sonntag, R. and Westrich, P., 1989, 'Parken in verkehrsberuhigten Einkaufsstraßen: Erfahrungen aus Günzburg, Marktredwitz, Selb und Miltenberg' in Monheim, R. (ed.), *Parkraummanagement und Parkraumbewirtschaftung in Stadzentren*, Arbeitsmaterialien zur Raumordnung und Raumplanung 75, Bayreuth, 120–41.

Whyte, W.H., 1980, *The social life of small urban spaces*, The Consevation Foundation, Washington, DC.

Wiedenhoeft, R., 1981, *Cities for people: practical measures for improving urban environments*, Van Nostrand Reinhold Company, New York.

18 Safe routes to school in Odense, Denmark
Ole Nielsen

Introduction

During the period 1955–71 Denmark had the highest rate of child mortality due to road accidents in Western Europe. Reaction to this situation has taken several forms. Most importantly, a new Road Traffic Act was implemented in 1976, incorporating the statement: 'It is the responsibility of the police and the road administration, upon consultation with the schools, to make provisions for the protection of children against the dangers of motorised traffic on their way to and from school.' There was also an increasing demand from schools and parents for traffic restraint measures to protect children against the dangers of traffic. However, it was apparent that adults did not normally appreciate that children are handicapped in traffic, considering them merely as small adults, despite the studies such as those by Stina Sandels in Sweden (Sandels, 1975–7). These have shown that children have hearing problems in detecting traffic, understanding the meaning of signs and signals, judging speed and anticipating manoeuvres. To combat these disadvantages, children are now given a better understanding of traffic through education. From the age of three, children can join a nationwide traffic club, run by the Danish Road Safety Council. In schools children – by law – must have five or six lessons on road safety a year.

A further reaction to the lack of child safety was the formation of a working group, with representatives from the Accident Analysis Group (AAG) at the University Hospital, school authorities and planning and road authorities. Background information about children in traffic was collected and analysed (AAG, annually).

The statistics showed that while most accidents to cyclists occur at junctions, most accidents to pedestrians occur elsewhere. From Table 18.1 it is clear that until the age of seven most of the children that are injured are pedestrians. The most significant drop in the number of accidents for

Table 18.1 Number of accidents in Odense between motor vehicles and children aged 0–14 years, on foot or bicycle, measured over a three-year period (1975–77)

Age	Foot	Bicycle	Total
		The child was on:	
1	3	0	3
2	9	0	9
3	12	0	12
4	16	3	19
5	25	9	34
6	22	15	37
7	22	18	40
8	15	25	40
9	12	24	36
10	14	13	27
11	5	21	26
12	6	28	34
13	8	41	49
14	6	39	45
Total	175	236	411

Source: AAG, 1975–7.

pedestrians occurs from 10 to 11 years and thereafter it is at a stable, low level. The older the children the higher is the number of accidents as cyclists.

Table 18.2 shows the bias introduced if figures are based on the official (police-reported) statistics only. In general the police only know about 41 per cent of pedestrian and 35 per cent of cyclist accidents. The more severe the accident, the higher will be the percentage recorded by the police.

Most accidents, approximately 50 per cent, happen in the afternoon, long after normal school hours. The AAG statistics from the 1970s also show that only one out of six accidents occur on trips to and from school. More recent AAG statistics from the 1980s give no reason to believe that the percentage of accidents known by the police is higher and confirm that most accidents still happen mostly in the afternoon.

The Odense 'Safe Routes to School' Project

In addition to action at a national scale, there have been initiatives in individual cities. This chapter describes a project, started ten years ago, which has had a great impact on attitudes towards children in traffic in Odense, an old but small city, with a population of 150 000. The study has been carried out in all of the 45 schools in Odense, with a total of more than 5800 children (aged between 9 and 15) participating. The study not

Table 18.2 Number and percentage of accidents in Odense to child pedestrians and child cyclists, recorded and not recorded by the police, 1975–77

	Number recorded by police	Number not recorded by police	Total	Percentage known by police
Pedestrians				
Category 1	16	58	74	22
Category 2	3	14	17	18
Category 3	3	4	7	43
Category 4	43	28	71	61
Category 5	6	0	6	100
Total	71	104	175	41
Cyclists				
Category 1	19	82	101	19
Category 2	1	31	32	3
Category 3	3	9	12	25
Category 4	56	31	87	64
Category 5	4	0	4	100
Total	83	153	236	35

The accidents are grouped in 5 categories by increasing severity:
Category 1: Emergency-room treatment
Category 2: After treatment the patient is referred to general practitioner
Category 3: After treatment the patient is referred to out-patient clinic
Category 4: Admitted to hospital
Category 5: Died.
Source: AAG, 1975–7.

only included routes to and from school but also routes to and from organised activities such as different types of sport, clubs and so forth. Two types of questionnaire were used, one to cover transport to and from school and the other for social activities. Aerial photographs of a scale of 1:5000 for urban areas and 1:10 000 for rural areas were used for mapping each child's routes (Odense Magistrat, 1979).

The results of the study are shown in Table 18.3. Cycling is the most common mode of transport to and from school, and is even more dominant for trips to and from organised activities. The only group with a majority walking is that of the youngest children (9 years old). The use of cycling increases with age, whereas walking and car use (by parents) decline over the same time period.

For each school, maps of the area have been drawn, showing where the children actually move around and the places which they consider danger-ous. Additionally, the parents' association and the teachers at each school were asked to point out places which they considered dangerous for the children. Based on the study, proposals to improve the traffic environment

Table 18.3   Mode of transport in Odense of children of different ages from both school and other activities

| Age | Walking | From school (per cent) | | Bus | Number of children |
		Cycle	Car		
9	47	32	4	17	2080
12	30	53	1	16	1930
15	24	63	1	12	1800
Mean	34	49	2	15	5810

| Age | Walking | From activities (per cent) | | Bus | Number of children |
		Cycle	Car		
9	23	38	27	12	1662
12	14	63	8	15	1553
15	10	73	3	14	1650
Mean	15	58	13	14	4865

Source: Traffic Department of Odense.

for children were worked out. All results and proposals for each school were included in a report which was sent to the school and to any authority involved. Figure 18.1 illustrates how the process of co-operation takes place.

Physical measures and their effects

Since 1981 a total of 185 proposals have been worked out and 65 of the proposed changes have been implemented. Approximately £100 000 annually has been earmarked for improvements in children's safety. The most common measures have been slow-speed areas, road narrowings, traffic islands and separate foot and cycle paths. These are discussed in turn below.

Slow-speed areas

In the slow-speed areas the roads are reconstructed with raised areas and raised crossings, humps and road narrowings (Figure 18.2). The raised areas and raised crossings are usually given a completely different surface, normally using concrete flagstones. Typically, the carriageway is narrowed, trees are planted and humps, constructed as a segment of a circle installed. The recommended speed is usually 30 km/h.

Children in standard 3, 6 and 9 fill in questionnaires about routes to school and social activites, and point out the dangerous places.

A report is sent to each school. It describes the results and proposals are made to improve children's safety.

Teachers and parents comment on the findings and proposals.

A draft proposal for each project is made and discussed with the school and the police.

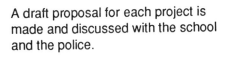

The project is carried out.

The project is evaluated.

Figure 18.1 The process of developing safe routes to school in Odense

Figure 18.2 A raised area and soft landscaping on a safe route to school in Odense

Normally it is the roads just outside the school which are rebuilt as slow-speed areas, provided they are not primary schools. The 30 km/h zone around a school will usually only cover 200–300 metres of the road, but the indirectly affected part of the road will be much larger in most cases, and in general the whole road will change its character because it will be avoided by through traffic.

Seven slow-speed areas constructed in 1981–3 have been evaluated. The speed around schools in these areas has declined from an average of about 50–5 km/h (approximately 33 mph) before traffic restraint measures were implemented, to 20–5 km/h (about 15 mph) afterwards. The number of lorries passing schools has dropped considerably in a number of areas. In some cases the number of cars has dropped too.

Accidents reported by the Accident Analysis Group for at least three years before and after reconstruction, have been collected. The effect on the total number of accidents has been tremendous. There were 9.65 accidents per year before the reconstruction, but only 1.5 afterwards, a reduction of 85 per cent. Furthermore the accidents are now less serious.

Road narrowings

Different types of road narrowings have been tried in six cases (Figure 18.3). In general, there has been no effect on accidents and only a minor

Figure 18.3 An example of road narrowing in the 'Safe Routes to School' Project

and temporary effect on speed. Road narrowings to only one lane cannot be recommended and are no longer used in Odense. Road narrowings to two narrow lanes make crossing the road easier, and for that reason this measure will still be used in some cases.

Traffic islands

Traffic islands have been used in a number of cases (Figure 18.4), usually on more heavily trafficked roads. Very few accidents have happened at these places, both before and after treatment; the main benefit is that children, parents and teachers will find the crossing much easier and safer after the construction of the traffic island.

Separate foot and cycle paths

In some cases new, separate foot and cycle paths have been constructed (Figure 18.5). The purpose is to give children an alternative – preferably a better alternative, such as a short-cut – to the use of major roads that have heavy and fast traffic but no provision for cyclists. Up to now five alternative paths have been constructed. They are indeed used by the children and in such cases a safer route to school has been achieved.

Figure 18.4   An example of a traffic island in the 'Safe Routes to School' Project

Figure 18.5   Separate foot- and cycle-paths for schoolchildren in the 'Safe Routes to School' Project

Other measures

Around one school a larger area has been regulated using traffic islands, a road closure, a raised crossing and restraint on lorries in the area. The effect on accidents has been very good, the number has dropped by 85 per cent.

Road closures have been used in two instances in the older urban areas. In both cases the closed road passes a school, and its junction with the primary road was very close to dense traffic crossings with traffic lights. One of the roads is now a foot and cycle path. The other closure has stopped through traffic and the area around the school is now much quieter.

Risk to cycling children

As an integral part of a Nordic study on traffic accident risks to children cycling in urban areas, research has been carried out in Odense in 1982–3 (Odense Magistrat, 1988). The study consists of six investigations into

— accidents, based on hospital statistics;
— parents' attitudes to the risk of bicycling children;
— children's behaviour in traffic;
— classification of roads according to their risk;
— analysis of the children's use of the bicycle; and
— the condition of children's bicycles.

Table 18.4 The use of bicycles in Odense

	Percentage using the bike	Number of trips per day	Distance per day (motroo)
Standard 1 (age 7)	51	2.5	1910
Standard 3 (age 9)	60	2.8	2790
Standard 5 (age 11)	75	3.2	3380
Standard 7 (age 13)	80	4.3	5040
Average	68	3.4	3580

Source: Odense Magistrat, 1988.

Similar studies have taken place in Linköping, Sweden and to a certain extent in Stavanger, Norway and Kuopio, Finland.

The studies are not yet fully completed, but at this point the following conclusions can be drawn.

— The accident risk is 2.3 times higher in Odense than in Linköping. This is the case both for light and severe accidents.
— Swedish parents are more restrictive than Danish parents. In general, a Swedish child must be about two years older than a Danish child before it is allowed to move around in traffic. Table 18.4 shows how much children in Odense use their bicycles.
— More than 90 per cent of all trips are either started at, or end at, the child's home. The greatest number of trips are made between 07.00 and 08.00 hours and in the afternoon between 13.00 and 17.00.
— Boys use bicycles more than girls and make longer trips, resulting in traffic exposure approximately 20 per cent greater for boys than for girls.
— Most accidents take place in the afternoon and in the early evening hours (between 13.00 and 17.00 hours). However, if accidents are related to cycling distances, a somewhat different picture appears. By far the largest (relative) risk is found in the evening (after 19.00 hours), but also the late morning hours (10.00–12.00) are rather dangerous.

Conclusions

For more than ten years Odense has been working determinedly to make the roads safer for children. The 'Safe Routes to School' Project has given very valid information about the problems children face in traffic. Moreover, the process has been very important. The co-operation with schools, parents, authorities and the press has been excellent, and a general awareness of the children's problems in traffic has been achieved. Furthermore, it has been accepted that something should be done to improve children's safety. The Nordic study, too, has given very valid information about cycling children and parents' attitudes.

But the most important point is that the projects have had the desired effect. In the slow-speed areas the number of accidents has been reduced by 85 per cent and the accidents are less severe. In general, schools and parents are very satisfied with the projects and consider the routes to school safer than before.

References

AAG (Accident Analysis Group), annually, *Reports of traffic accidents registered at the University Hospital*, Odense.
Odense Magistrat, 1979, *Born pa skolevejen- Born i trafikken (Safe Routes to School Project)*, 2, og 4. afdeling, Odense.

—— 1988, *Cyklende borns trafikrisiko i byomrader (Traffic accident risk to bicycling children in urban areas)*, 2. og 4. afdeling, Odense Syfehus, Odense University, Odense.

Sandels, 1975–7, *Skandiarapport* I, II and III, Skandia, Stockholm.

19 Environmental traffic management strategies in Buxtehude, West Germany

Alice Döldissen and
Werner Draeger

The German interministerial research programme on environmental traffic management schemes

In 1980 three German federal ministries (Town Planning, Transport and the Interior, now Ministry of the Environment) and their research institutes/agencies agreed to carry out a joint research and demonstration programme on large scale environmental traffic management strategies. The aim of these strategies was, without simply diverting the traffic to other areas, to improve

— traffic safety;
— the mobility of non-motorised persons;
— neighbourhood recreation and development possibilities; and
— the local environmental situation.

Apart from the relatively large size of the proposed environmental traffic management areas (up to 3 km² and 30 000 inhabitants) and the attempt to give equal priority to safety, mobility, urban development and environmental aspects at all stages of the planning and research process, this programme differed from previous traffic restraint programmes in that

— main thoroughfares were included;
— public, pedestrian and bicycle transport were to be particularly encouraged; and
— great importance was laid on lowering costs by achieving area-wide effects with fewer and simpler measures.

From over 200 towns wishing to participate and over 100 detailed applications, six towns were chosen for intensive studies. Details of these towns and the areas in question are shown in Table 19.1.

The chosen study areas are representative of a wide selection of town and village situations throughout the Federal Republic of Germany in terms of their size; their structures of traffic, population and land use; and their geographical positions, political representation and administrative organisations.

The time plan for the programme was as follows:

1981	Selection of the six model areas
1982–3	Analysis and development of environmental traffic management strategies for each of the areas (under contract to the federal ministries)
1983	'Before studies' on the traffic, urban development and environmental situation (under contract to the federal ministries)
1983–7/8	Detailed planning and implementation of the strategies (by or under contract to the towns)
1987–89	'After studies' (see 1983 'before studies')
1989–90	Analysis and comparison of the results in all six towns; drawing up of conclusions and recommendations.

In two of the towns (Berlin and Buxtehude) 'intermediary studies' were carried out after the first building phase was completed.

For each area investigated an individual traffic restraint strategy was worked out by the appointed town and transportation planners. Despite their many differences all the strategies proposed measures aimed at

– making public, pedestrian and bicycle transport safer, quicker, more comfortable, and generally more attractive;
– concentrating through traffic on main thoroughfares; and
– slowing down all motor traffic to 50 km/h on main thoroughfares and to 30 km/h or less on other roads.

As could be expected, not all of the proposals have been implemented and in some cases the towns developed alternative strategies for particular aspects. As far as costs and financing are concerned, there have been different arrangements in each of the towns, some of them financing all measures by themselves, others receiving support from a federal and/or state level.

Of great – if not decisive – importance for the results were the publicity and public participation activities that accompanied the building, planting and traffic-signing measures. Apart from the usual public meetings, leaflets, press coverage and information stands, provisional or experimental building phases proved to be an important and very successful instrument

Table 19.1 The German interministerial research programme on environmental traffic management schemes: the six project areas

Town (population)	State	Type of area	km²	Population of area	Costs (DM millions)
Berlin (1 900 000)	Berlin	Large town, edge of city	1.2	30 000	5.5 (1)
Borgentreich (2 300)	Nordrhein-Westfalen	Village, whole area	2.5	2 300	6.5
Buxtehude (33 000)	Niedersachsen	Medium-sized town centre and surroundings	2.5	10 000	5.0
Esslingen (87 000)	Baden-Wurttemberg	Medium-sized town, edge of central area	1.5	11 000	15 (2)
Ingolstadt (91 000)	Bayern	Medium-sized town, central area	1.2	5 500	18 (2)
Mainz (105 000)	Rheinland-Pfalz	Large town, suburbs, old village	2.5	12 000	3.2

(1) without main roads
(2) estimated

for the participation both of the public and of other relevant interest groups and official bodies (e.g. local businesses, police and the fire brigade).

A summary of the six proposed strategies and the implemented measures, their costs and effects, is to be found in Bundesforschungsanstalt für Landeskunde und Raumordnung (1983, 1988); Umweltbundesamt (1985); and Döldissen (1988). This chapter will, however, focus on one example of the six model areas, that of Buxtehude.

The project area in Buxtehude: the planning process and overall concept

The town of Buxtehude is cut into two almost equal sections by the railway line from Hamburg to Cuxhaven. In the northern part, the project area, there are approximately 10 800 inhabitants, schools for 3000 pupils and the historic town centre with its shopping and other facilities. The area measures 2.2 km from east to west and 1.2 km from north to south (Figure 19.1).

As far as distances and topography are concerned, Buxtehude is actually ideally suited for pedestrian and cycle transport, whether to the schools,

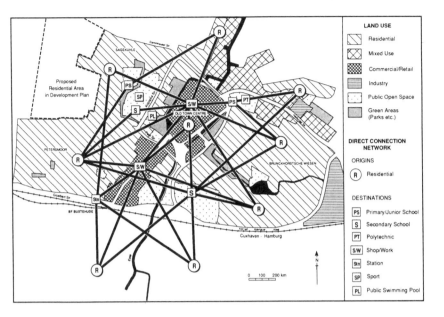

Figure 19.1 Environmental traffic management in Buxtehude: land use and the 'direct connection network'

the sports facilities, the old town centre, the main shopping street (Bahnhofstrasse) or the railway station. Therefore, one of the most important aims of the 'preparatory planning study' for Buxtehude was the improvement of conditions for pedestrian and cyclist transport (Bundesforschungsanstalt für Landeskunde und Raumordnung, 1983).

Taking account of the existing and planned land use of the area, lines of direct connection between all important origins and destinations of existing or potential pedestrian and bicycle traffic were drawn on the map. The result was the 'direct connection network' (Figure 19.1). The next step involved superimposing this on to the existing streets and paths and working out approximately the traffic loads, considering pedestrian and cycle traffic together.

For shopping traffic the west–east connections and the main north–south shopping street, Bahnhofstrasse, are the most important. For school pupils several north–south and west–east connections are necessary. For people on their way to work it is mainly the station with its trains to Hamburg that is of most significance for cyclists and pedestrians. According to an analysis at the beginning of the project the proportion of journeys to work carried out by bicycle or on foot was much lower (18 per cent) than the average for all journeys (52 per cent) (Table 19.2).

Table 19.2   Percentage modal split according to journey purpose, Buxtehude project area

	All trips	Work	Education/ training	Shopping	Recreation	Others
Walk	35.4	12.6	50.7	49.6	40.5	9.1
Cycle	16.4	5.5	29.0	23.7	16.3	4.6
Walk or cycle	51.8	18.1	79.7	73.3	56.8	13.7
Moped/ motorbike	1.7	1.6	2.7	2.7	0.9	–
Car passenger	7.6	4.1	7.2	3.0	14.0	7.7
Car driver	27.9	43.2	5.0	17.7	25.7	61.1
Public transport	11.0	33.0	5.4	3.3	2.6	17.5
Total	100.0	100.0	100.0	100.0	100.0	100.0

Source: Institut für Stadtforschung und Structurpolitik, Socialdata, 1985.

The journey speed by bike was only 8 km/h. This was low compared to the national average of 10.1 km/h and showed that measures were necessary to allow cyclists to reach their destinations more quickly. The 10 800 inhabitants of the project area carried out about 2000 journey chains (journeys with intermediate destinations) by bicycle per day. These journey chains were made up of about 4500 cycle journeys per day, including the journey to and from home. On average each inhabitant left home 1.11 times and had 1.40 outside activities per day.

On top of this there are, of course, many journeys from the southern half of Buxtehude with destinations in the project area with all its infrastructure and attractions. In order to find out the real pedestrian and cycle loads on the most relevant routes, the traffic was counted. The greatest loads were found to be on the roads with the heaviest motor traffic (calculated from Heusch and Boesefeldt, 1985). These were:

—   Bahnhofstrasse (the main shopping street), with 4500 pedestrians, 1700 cyclists and 10 000 motor vehicles per day;
—   the level crossing (connecting the project area with the southern half of Buxtehude), with 5000 pedestrians, 2800 cyclings and 14 500 motor vehicles per day;
—   Konopkastrasse (main collector with schools and sports centres, formerly the western ring road around the town centre), with 1100 pedestrians, 1200 cyclists and 6000 motor vehicles per day;

In a problem analysis the shortcomings of the existing pedestrian and cycle network were found to be:

— no direct connections for shopping and school traffic in a west–east direction;
— insufficient protection for pedestrians and cyclists at points where autonomous pedestrian and cycle paths crossed roads for motor traffic;
— serious breaks in cycle connections by pedestrian-only bridges, one-way streets and the pedestrian precinct;
— bad routing and marking of priority cycle paths at cross-roads and junctions;
— indirect cycle and pedestrian routing over right-turn lanes with triangular centre islands;
— no direct left-turn for cyclists at cross-roads with traffic lights, even if motor traffic load was low;
— cycle paths not paved across private drive-ways;
— insufficient width of the communal pedestrian and cycle path along the northern ring road;
— lack of a cycle path on one side of the main shopping street, leading to conflicts with pedestrians.

Taking account of all the aims of the research programme, especially the cost aspect, a concept was proposed with a large-scale introduction of 30 km/h limits on all subsidiary roads in the area, together with a package of specific measures to improve pedestrian and cycle transport. The 30 km/h speed limit in two large zones was to be supported by a general 'right before left' priority rule and occasional speed restricting measures for motor traffic (e.g. road narrowings and raised paving) as deemed necessary. In the next section some of the particular measures used in the project area are described.

Individual measures to improve conditions for pedestrian and bicycle transport in Buxtehude

Creation of an acceptable route network for pedestrians and cyclists

Gaps in the cycle and pedestrian route network were gradually closed with new bridges, cycle paths against one-way streets (Figure 19.2), well -designed subways under the eastern 'ring-road' and the opening of the pedestrian precinct for cyclists. From 1983 onwards cyclists and pedestrians started benefiting from routes to the town centre and other important destinations that were shorter and quicker than those open to motor traffic (Figures 19.3–19.5).

More than anything else it was the opening of the pedestrian precinct for cyclists that caused the greatest immediate improvement to the cycle route network. Thanks to good campaigning, to a clever signpost design asking

Figure 19.2   A cycle path against a one-way street in Buxtehude

Figure 19.3   A well-designed cycle- and pedestrian subway under the railway in Buxtehude

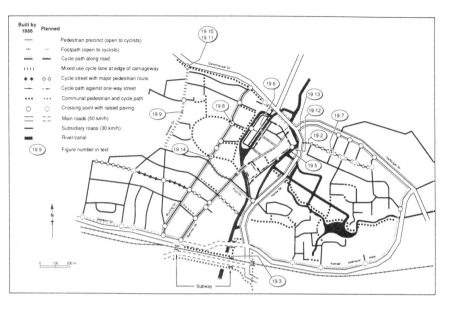

Figure 19.4 Environmental traffic management in Buxtehude: the cycle-and pedestrian route network

Figure 19.5 A pleasantly designed direct pedestrian route to Buxtehude town centre

Figure 19.6 A pedestrian precinct open to cyclists ('Radfahrer frei'). The hare and the hedgehog are well known figures in a famous Buxtehude fable

Figure 19.7 A bicycle street in Buxtehude with limited access for cars and lorries

cyclists to be considerate, and to the street lay-out (with a central 'carria-geway'), conflicts do not arise between pedestrians and cyclists (Figure 19.6).

Bicycle streets

Particularly important routes for shopping and school traffic were designed as 'bicycle streets' (Figure 19.7). Cars (and lorries) are only allowed to enter these streets if they belong to or are visiting residents there. Sign 237 of the German Highway Code (cycle path) has been set up with additional signs allowing cars and lorries with a destination in the street to enter too. The original distance between the pavement kerbstones (usually about 6.5 m) was not changed, but on one or both sides of the road flower beds were installed every 30 to 50 km so that the remaining carriageway was only 3.5 m wide. Taking account of the results of a research project (Ruwenstroth, 1984), a path 3.0 m wide was marked in front of the flower beds. The width was chosen very carefully with the aim of slowing down motor traffic to a cyclist's speed. Had it been wider, cyclists would have moved to the edge, allowing cars to overtake. Car drivers may even have tried to overtake with cyclists travelling in *both* directions. Parking needs are below average in these streets because of the low population density and presence of private garages, so that, in fact, even lorries can usually pass each other at a slow pace, though this is a very infrequent necessity. In the stretches without flower beds cars can pass each other despite there being parking on one side of the street.

Cross roads are raised so that vehicles crossing the bicycle street have to drive over a 10 per cent ramp. Along the bicycle street the ramp is hardly noticeable. The pictograms painted right in the middle of the crossing warn drivers that they are crossing a bicycle street and that they must reckon with cyclists coming in both directions. After much discussion it was decided not to give the bicycle street priority at cross roads in order not to introduce exceptions to the general right-before-left priority system in the 30 km/h zones.

The bicycle streets have been well accepted. Since the only building measures were the flower beds and the raised crossings, they were not an expensive measure.

Introduction of cycle paths in the main shopping street

Prior to the project, the Bahnhofstrasse had the normal 50 km/h speed limit and carried heavy traffic, with daily flows of 10 000 motor vehicles, 4500 pedestrians and 1700 cyclists. The great number of shops caused many people to cross the road, and this, together with cars constantly trying to

Figure 19.8 A road narrowing on the Konopkastrasse in Buxtehude with raised paving of crossing point of main pedestrian and cycle route

park or leave parking spaces, made it necessary to build cycle paths on both sides of the road. The space needed was taken from the main carriageway, reducing it to 6.5 m. However, since the space for pedestrians, cyclists and shop displays is not really wide enough on the western side, it is possible that the cycle path on this side of the road will be given over to pedestrians. This follows from the view that cycle paths are generally only thought suitable for roads with heavy traffic and/or high speeds. Traffic on the Bahnofstrasse has been considerably reduced since a tunnel has been built under the railway and the road has been incorporated into the 30 km/h zone.

Protection of cycle and pedestrian traffic in collector roads and at entrances to 30 km/h zones

Measures such as road narrowings and raised paving were designed in the first place to reduce the speed of motor traffic. As pedestrian and cycle traffic was to be made safer and generally encouraged, the positioning of these measures was particularly recommended at points where pedestrians and cyclists need to cross flows of motor traffic. This is the case where, for instance, autonomous pedestrian or cycle routes cross the carriageway, or in fact, at all cross roads and junctions where cyclists have the right of way to go straight ahead before motor traffic can turn (e.g. at the entrances to

Figure 19.9 Speed-reducing paving design in Buxtehude (optical 'narrowing' and 'shortening' of the carriageway) and road narrowings allowing cyclists to pass freely

Figure 19.10 The junction of Altländerstrasse with Dammhauserstrasse in Buxtehude with provisional narrowing of entrance using large flower pots (1984)

30 km/h zones where the 50 km/h road along the outside edge of the 30 km/h zone is always a priority road).

Example 1: Konopkastrasse (a collector road with 6000 vehicles per day before redesign and 4500 vehicles per day afterwards). To reduce motor vehicle speeds road narrowings of 4.5–5.0 m were introduced and the carriageway raised with a 10 per cent ramp at crossing points for pedestrians and cyclists. Since there were already cycle paths on both sides of the Konopkastrasse there were no problems for cyclists travelling *along* the road to pass these points (Figure 19.8).

Example 2: Altländerstrasse (a collector road with approximately 4500 vehicles per day before and after redesigning). Since this road needed total repaving before the project even began, it was decided to introduce a speed reducing design when doing the repair work. On both sides of the carriageway and along the whole length of the road, 0.8 m strips of red concrete paving stones were laid. Next to this there was a white boundary stone on each side, leaving a central carriageway in grey of 4.0 m. This carriageway was then interrupted at approximately 15 m intervals by a 1.0 m cross-band (again red stones with a white boundary). This optical 'narrowing' and 'shortening' of the 6 m-wide carriageway was supported by actual road narrowings to 3.5 m with tree islands at approximately 50 m intervals.

Apart from slowing down the motor traffic, the red side strips are meant to give cyclists more protection without, however, being cyclist-only lanes.

Figure 19.11   The junction of Altländerstrasse with Dammhauserstrasse in Buxtehude after final redesigning had been completed (1987)

With their white boundary they are 1.0 m wide and continued straight ahead behind the tree islands along the whole length of the road (Figure 19.9).

Example 3: Junctions of Altländerstrasse and Konopkastrasse with Dammhauser Strasse (main through road). Generally, all entrances up to the 30 km/h zones were narrowed and given a raised paving in the red and white pattern described above. The extent of the redesign work depended upon the original entrance width and curve radius. In the cases of Altländerstrasse and Konopkastrasse the original entrances were extremely wide and were therefore almost halved in width (Figures 19.10–19.11). Apart from slowing down motor traffic, the new design shortened the crossing distance for cyclists and pedestrians. At the same time the joint cycle and pedestrian path along the main road was brought forward, raised and paved through in the same colour, making it safer and more direct.

Particular improvements at cross roads (collector and main roads)

Free right-turn lanes allow motor traffic to drive faster and thus make it more difficult to notice pedestrians and cyclists wanting to cross the traffic flow and continue straight ahead. Despite the fact that they should have the right of way, pedestrians and cyclists not only have to slow down and be very cautious, they are also highly endangered. In order to improve the situation three typical cross roads with free right-turn lanes were redesigned.

Example 1 can be seen in Figures 19.10 and 19.11 already described above. The free right-turn lane from the main road into the 30 km/h zone was given over to plants and the triangular island became the new carriageway. As already mentioned, the joint cycle and pedestrian path was made very much safer and more direct.

In *Example 2* (Figure 19.12) the cycle path via the triangular island used to make quite a detour to cross over the then free right-turn lane at right-angles and thus, of course, lost its right-of-way. It has now been replaced by a marked cycle lane as part of the carriageway which makes no detour at all. The lane starts directly behind a road narrowing so that motor traffic is both slowed down and moved to the left. It is now the motor vehicles that have to cross the cyclists' route and not vice versa.

Example 3 (Figure 19.13) shows a different solution in a different situation. Here there is a free right-turn lane from one main road into another. The crossing point for pedestrians and cyclists to and from the triangular island has been raised and repaved in the new Buxtehude manner (red concrete

Figure 19.12   Viverstrasse in Buxtehude, with the cycle lane crossing the free right-turn lane (right) and a cycle path against the one way street (left)

Figure 19.13   Raised and redesigned paving for pedestrians and cyclists crossing the free right-turn lane at a junction of two main roads in Buxtehude

Figure 19.14   A direct left-turn cycle lane in Buxtehude

paving with white boundary stones). Because of large lorries, etc. it was not possible to tighten the curve, but there is quite a steep ramp (eight per cent) and the paving design gives the illusion of narrowing the carriageway to three metres.

Another measure to increase the speed and security of cyclists at cross roads is the direct left-turn cycle lane as seen in Figure 19.14. Again it starts immediately behind a road narrowing to give it better protection at the crucial point of leaving the cycle path and moving out into the middle of the carriageway. (With the removal of the traffic lights at this crossing, the direct left-turn cycle lane has now been painted over.)

Other measures

If a general atmosphere conducive to the green modes of transport is to be developed, it is important that publicity measures are carried out, in addition to physical measures such as cycle paths, lanes and tracks, wider pavements and modifications to the pedestrian precinct. In Buxtehude these publicity measures were an integral part of the whole environmental traffic management project. There were several public meetings, many articles in the local newspapers and a special leaflet was printed explaining the various new measures for cyclists and pedestrians. It is also planned to install a pedestrian and cyclist signposting system, not only to show the quickest or most pleasant routes but also as a publicity measure, subtly advertising the green modes of transport to inhabitants and tourists alike.

Up until now the renting out of bicycles by the local tourist office has not been very successful. However, now that these bicycles have been handed over to the town-planning and building department, perhaps we will at least have the pleasure of seeing town employees and the mayor using them more frequently – a publicity activity for the green modes that should not be underestimated!

Effects and outlook

The final figures are not yet available for the effects of all these measures on modal split and therefore on pollution. However, it is certain that at least cycle traffic has increased considerably. As far as traffic safety is concerned, more detailed figures are available. Accidents involving pedestrians have been reduced by 46 per cent. In streets with raised carriageways at pedestrian (and cycle) crossing points there have been no accidents at all (Institut für Verkehrswesen, 1987).

Accidents involving cyclists have, in contrast, increased by 32 per cent from 37 for 1982–3 to 49 for 1986–7. Taking account of the increase in cycle traffic of 40 per cent (Heusch and Boesefeldt 1985), the cyclist accident risk has, however, been reduced. Of particular interest is the fact that the number of light and serious cyclist casualties has not changed despite the increase in cycle traffic, indicating that the relative casualty risk has actually fallen considerably (Figure 19.15). About 70 per cent of the accidents also show no connection with the new measures for cyclists or with the environmental traffic management measures at all.

Conclusions

Environmental traffic management can be a very successful instrument by which to encourage and improve conditions for pedestrians and cycle traffic if both the whole scheme *and* the individual measures are planned and designed with the green modes in mind.

The more important precondition is that the measures planned to slow down motor traffic and to keep through-traffic on the main roads do not cause hindrances and dangers for cyclists and pedestrians. Typical traffic restraint measures of the past, such as one-way street systems and (diagonal) road blocks, should only be used where absolutely necessary, and they should be made passable for the green modes. Humps, road narrowings and other measures must be so designed as to allow cyclists to pass easily and without danger. In other words, measures should, if possible, be planned so that at the same time as reducing the speed of motor traffic,

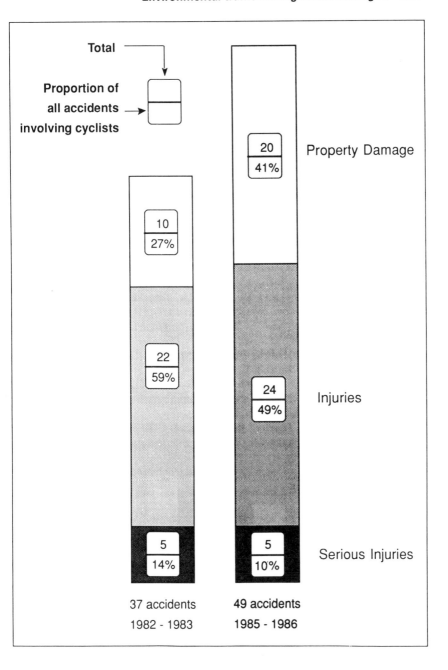

Figure 19.15 Accidents involving cyclists in the Buxtehude project area, before and after environmental traffic management

they give particular protection to cyclists and pedestrians and thus provide them with additional priority and advantage.

References

Bundesforschungsanstalt für Landeskunde und Raumordnung, 1983, *Flächenhafte Verkehrsberuhigung, Zwischenbericht, Informationen zur Raumentwicklung,* heft 8/9, Bonn.

—— 1988, *4. kolloquium: Forschungsvorhaben Flächenhafte verkehrsberuhigung,* Bonn.

Döldissen, A., 1988, 'Environmental traffic management: German interministerial research programme, *Proceedings,* Vol. M., PTRC Summer Annual Meeting, Bath.

Heusch and Boesefeldt, 1985, *Beratende Ingenieure: Forschungsprojekt 'Verkehrsverlagerung durch Verkehrsberuhigungsmassnahmen'* – Buxtehude – *Ergebnisse der Vorherhebung,* Bericht zu FE-Nr. 70114 im Auftrag des Bundesministers für Verkehr, Aachen.

Institut für Stadtforschung und Structurpolitik, Socialdata, 1985, *Flächenhafte Verkehrsberuhigung: Auswirkungen auf Entwicklung de Boden-und Mietpreise, Investitionsverhalten und Modernisierungstatigkeiten, sowle auf Standortverhalten von Haushalten und Betrieben, Vorher-Untersuchung Buxtehude,* Bericht im Auftrag Bundesministers für Raumordnung, Bauwesen und Städtebau, Berlin/Munich.

Institut für Verkehrswesen, Ruhr-Universitat Bochum, 1987, *Flachenhafte Verkehrsberuhigung: Unfallanalyse,* Forschungsprojekt im Auftrag der Bundesanstalt für Strassenwesen, Bochum.

Ruwenstroth, G., 1984, *Fuhrung des radverkehrs im Innerortsbereich: Teil 5, Radwegtrassen, Forschungsberichte der Bundesanstalt für Strassenwesen,* Bereich Unfallforschung, Band 106, Cologne.

Umweltbundesamt; 1985, *3. kolloquium Forschungvorhaben: Flächenhafte Verkehrsberuhigung,* Berlin.

PART 4

An Overview

20 Summary and conclusions for policy
John Roberts

Introduction

Twenty years ago, this book would have been considered to consume a large number of trees to proclaim an insignificant message. It is often said that technology rushes ahead out of sync with social progress. Arguably, these processes are slowly being reversed: the car has changed little since it first started to diminish the quality of life, back in the nineteenth century, but human awareness of its multiple capabilities for damage has increased to an extraordinary extent. Moreover, action follows awareness, in many cities throughout Europe and other parts of the world.

It is very important that this should be happening, for we constantly see the effects of ever-increasing car ownership and use, and we are promised positively horrendous levels of both by the first decade of the twenty-first century.

We are all to blame. We have allowed ourselves to be conned by manufacturers, road constructors, their admen and their tame politicians. We have seen our neighbours buy one and believed we should too; we have absorbed, in the blotting paper of our minds, sufficient myths to fill as many pages as Hans Christian Andersen, to the effect that mobility is good for us, when all the time it was accessibility we really wanted. For accessibility the car is often not needed at all, and is rarely required if other transport facilities are good enough, or the things we want are easily accessible.

The fine collection of essays in this book should stimulate the minds of policy-makers in Britain, though at least three problems arise for that country. First, how much policy is actually being made, and is it transport policy, or car and commercial vehicle policy? Second, why should a market-orientated administration support modes of transport like walking and cycling that are deemed to make little contribution to the economy? Third, Britain has different obsessions from mainland Europe: it is polarised, apathetic, self-centred, money-manic, and has every appearance of lacking consensus.

Are these unfair things to say about a country whose government or its agents raise fares with the explicit aim of stopping people using public transport; undermine its bus system by granting market hegemony; believe each (financially impoverished) local authority should determine whether or not it should accommodate cyclists and provide little national policy support; have different evaluative systems for road and rail investment which disadvantage rail; ignore constituents, a majority of whom advocate car restraint; believe in road building when there is abundant evidence that it simply allows suppressed demand to crawl out of the woodwork; consider the function of railways is to make a profit; subsidise car users but not public transport users . . . ?

In the face of such a mixture of marketable ideology and sanitised intervention, is it not unreasonable first to ask: whose policy are we trying to influence? A future, alternative, government's? The people's, acting together through a fear of environmental holocaust or experiencing an accession to power as happened in Eastern Europe during 1989? Or the European Communities' – for in their better moments they countervail excesses of British *laissez-faire*?

These opening paragraphs may appear overly doom-laden, and in fact attitudes towards transport in Britain *are* changing in order to meet the requirements of the Environment White Paper, proposed for the mid-1990. If these judgements seem harsh, they are based on a longer timescale during which the pro-road activists determined policy, public transport was under-funded and under-recognised, walking and cycling were seen as matters of road 'safety', not as vital modes that needed proactive policies, and when involvement in transport itself was politically equivalent to Siberian exile. It is not possible at the beginning of 1990 to see what fundamental shifts may take place in British transport thinking in order to tackle the undeniably formidable problems of environmental destruction – for which transport is primarily responsible. As we shall see, the Dutch are tackling this problem head-on, with important support from Switzerland, Denmark, Germany and France. Even Britain is beginning to make encouraging noises.

This suggests that the role of this book is to try to see the future through a wide-angled lens, though there is still some uncertainty whether the British government will become innovative in its transport thinking, or learn from its mainland European neighbours, or . . . do nothing. What do the authors say, individually and corporately, and how should that be progressed? The book's structure – of principles, strategies and practice – cocoons the main issues, though often ideas in one section overlap those in another. This structure will be used in this chapter, with the addition of a final section on implications for policy.

Principles

This section makes clear the obvious (though misunderstood or ignored), vital contribution that walking and cycling make to the need, want and desire to move around urban areas. The lack of a truly supportive policy in Britain (and the United States) is compared to the greater realism of mainland Europe. Evidence for this state of affairs is not hard to find: simply consider the mismatch between demand and supply for walking and cycling. It has been estimated that if one were to combine present-day cycling in London with suppressed demand, and with mode-changing given better facilities, then one should be considering a modal split containing 20–40 per cent cycling. At the time of this book it is little better than one to two per cent of the commuting modal split (Department of Transport, 1989), and probably not greater than five per cent for all purposes. Hülsmann shows that in Germany about 11 per cent of all journeys are made by bike and the Germans also believe that this could rise to between 20 and 40 per cent.

In towns outside London the contribution of cycling is sometimes much better and the level of activity is often supply-led. 'Supply' here does not just means segregated cycleways or special signals at road crossings – the term can be stretched to include roads that have been managed or 'calmed' so that there are fewer other vehicles.

In terms of walking, there *are* pedestrian precincts in Britain (I conclude that there might be 1500 single streets or enclosed shopping centres in 1981 (Roberts, 1981), which could well have risen to 2000 today), though numbers of precincts, extent and quality tend to fall short of the provision in, say, West Germany. But areas like the City of London and London's West End, milling with large numbers of pedestrians, have few pedestrian streets and the narrow footways are cluttered with the impedimenta of the carriageway (meters, parked cars, motorcycles, bicycles, signals, signs, lighting, grit bins, etc.). Crossing facilities are inadequate. The pedestrian system, if you can call it that, is discontinuous – unlike the carriageway (TEST, 1985). Similar malfunctions can be found in most provincial cities and towns.

Who gains and who loses?

Preston discusses danger to pedestrians and cyclists, using the standard euphemism of 'safety'. In fact it would be difficult to find two groups more exposed; Adam's (1985) risk compensation theory has argued that the danger to them has increased since the added feeling of security conferred on vehicle drivers by seat belts; he has also shown how the mobility of pedestrians, particularly the young and old, has been reduced through fear of crossing heavily-trafficked roads. Preston's explanation of the difficulties in standardising accident data is salutary, and heaps further caution on those of us wishing to make international comparisons. While it would be satisfying to dwell further on her chapter, just three findings will be reinforced here: that recent British safety measures have largely benefited those in vehicles; that Dutch cycle and pedestrian accidént rates per 100 million km travelled were about half those in Britain (she also notes that, per distance travelled, it is much safer to be in a vehicle than on foot) and that severity and frequency of casualty accidents appears to be directly related to the speed of vehicles. Therefore the German 30 km/h speed restriction in many parts of their urban areas is an improvement on the British 30 mph.

If pedestrians and cyclists lose in terms of accidents on all-traffic streets, when special measures for them are introduced they gain immediately in terms of quality of environment, greater safety and in opportunities for relaxed movement, which allows for standing and staring. Simultaneously, shopkeepers, office employers, landowners and lessors also usually gain when areas are set aside for pedestrians and, probably (I do not have supportive evidence), when special provision is made for cyclists. The reason, as I try to show in the second chapter, is that making special provision for these modes has to be at the expense of other vehicle users, just as one of the attractions of bus lanes is that they remove a road lane from other vehicle users. Such space won back from the car can be improved environmentally, so that people will want to be there. In its turn, this enhances not simply its attraction, but its economic performance too.

Public transport operators usually also gain from pedestrianisation or cyclist priority measures, *provided the resultant facilities are large enough*, and the public transport service is of high quality. It is no good pretending that Alf Jones's clapped-out single-decker, fiercely contending for a share of the most profitable route, is going to activate a transfer from cars.

Whitelegg, in a wide-ranging presentation, makes the point that management and technological gains – introduction of traffic calming, pedestrianisation, catalytic converters, lead-free petrol – are nullified by the increased ownership and use of cars, and many now forecast increases over 1990 emissions despite cleaning-up programmes. Some technologies act as a kind of aphrodisiac, heightening the demand for energy or producing even more carbon monoxide. Whitelegg also shows speed reductions achieved through the Tempo 30 (km/h maximum) regulations: in one street a reduction of 19.3 per cent in those travelling over 30 km/h was achieved, but generally the reductions are inconsequential. The other vital point he makes concerns the need for a package of measures – one on its own is likely to be ineffectual, ignored or difficult to enforce, for there will be no new alternative to one's current behaviour. His advocacy of *Verkehrsentwicklungsplanung* (VEP) is timely for it demands integrated transport, a concept not particularly visible in Britain, but upon which cycling and walking policies should be based. It may entail a walk to the bus stop or station, or carrying one's bike on light rail (Oslo) or heavy rail (virtually all mainland European railways), or even on buses (Bremen and Bonn, for example), sometimes with special trailers, as in Germany and the United States.

Hanna and Hillman focus more on the pedestrian. Hanna credits me with saying pedestrianised shopping streets are a minute proportion of road space, 'mere islands in an ocean of motor traffic'. Much the same could be said about calming devices, and about cycling provision in Britain. Hanna considers that improved *access* for pedestrians is a key criterion and, connectedly, that most journeys people make are short, and that most short journeys are on foot. But, as Hillman points out, the journeys of under 1.6 km are pushed into a late chapter of the 1985–6 *National travel survey* as the Department of Transport seems to be more concerned with length of journey (mobility) than number of, and/or ease of making journeys (more related to accessibility). Their data also show the large proportion of all journeys which are between 1.6 and 8.0 km, a similarly high proportion of which are in cars. If these are joined up with the car journeys of under 1.6 km (which are not adequately recorded), the potential for additional walk trips – given safe and pleasant conditions – must be quite large.

For me, Hanna's main contribution to this book's debate is on the question of facility location. She points out that the Department of Transport's COBA road-building model is crucially dependent on time savings for the motorist, to justify new roads. And yet out-of-centre shopping, as well as health care, education and leisure facilities placed on a broad mesh network which almost requires car use and lengthened journeys and time, is scarcely questioned. Yet such facilities, permitted through the relaxation and/or inadequacy of planning controls, are a direct expression of mobility, and against rationalism and an efficiently working society. Reaching them virtually excludes the pedestrian and places significant new demands on the cyclist.

Hillman shows, from the 1975–6 and 1985–6 *National travel surveys*, that walk and cycle journeys, as a percentage of all journeys, fell from 43 per cent to 37 per cent in 10 years. Why has this happened? There are several reasons, among which have to be the increase in car ownership, the centrifugal spread of communities, and perceived danger to the vulnerable green modes. Hillman notes the paucity of references to walking and cycling in official publications on transport, so that these modes are deliberately (if sometimes unconsciously) downgraded among policy-makers and planners. Furthermore, if public costs can be reduced by the encouragement of cycling and walking, the lack of such encouragement in the government's expenditure plans could be seen as an irrational bias towards roads, supported merely by the power of the road lobby.

Hillman then suggests that there is discrimination against the green mode users. He detects this in the pollution of their environment by motor vehicle exhausts, in the danger to pedestrians both from vehicles and from their own deteriorated environment, in discounting walkers and cyclists when saying the alternative way to the car is public transport, and so forth.

Ullrich takes a holistic perspective. He is probably even more critical of the adversities of the car than I am, though one can learn. Ullrich contrasts the endlessly destructive capabilities of the car while simultaneously asking what these offensive outputs mean in constitutional terms. While he is lucky to have a constitution, permitting such questions to be asked, there does appear to be a mismatch between initial promises and eventual fulfilment. Undoubtedly, the emission levels he catalogues in no way coincide with an acceptable environment in which to live, pursue whole-some existences, and nurture children: he then establishes some thresholds of tolerance. These cover fundamental rights of undisturbed sleep and clean air, though his maximum sound level would soon be exceeded by a child crying or modestly disturbing neighbours. Thus one cannot always legislate for one sector of society's activities.

An interesting concept of Ullrich's is of 'socially critical sizes of buildings and developments', which would follow an ending of the trend towards widely separated, massive concentrations of function: the large health-, shopping-, educational- and leisure-campuses inflicted on the countryside. In terms of spatial demands, Ullrich notes that a stationary car occupies one-third of the average German's residential space, and over twenty times that average person's public open space. These figures lead him to suggest spatial redistribution, with much greater amounts being allocated to bicy-cles, pedestrians and trees. Public transport is exalted on the bases of spatial economy and low emission per capita.

Strategies

Kroon provides invaluable data concerning air pollution and politics in the Netherlands, which he describes as 'the most polluted country in Western Europe'. The Dutch have examined past and existing pollution levels and projected these to the twenty-first century. They have been dismayed at their findings and resolute in starting to deal with them. Not only are they instituting measures that will reduce noise and air pollution emissions, they are also determined to reduce car use and effect transfers to public transport and cycling. Kroon says little about pedestrians.

The Dutch experience is of great importance to us all. Proposals to curb motor-vehicle impact on society brought down the Centre–Right coalition in May 1989. The facts were clear, but it is as if those ignoring them were intent on *auto-da-fé*. A Social Democrat–Christian Democrat alliance followed, and is responsible for implementing the present measures, par-ticularly the National Environmental Policy Plan (NMP) for 1990–4. Kroon shows that road traffic is 'the largest single source of air pollution and noise nuisance'. Air pollution means CO, CO_2, HC, NOx, particu-lates, asbestos, and SO_2. While Kroon does not specifically say this, it is ironic that Western societies spent perhaps 100 years eradicating or con-trolling the worst pollutant excesses of the industrial revolution, only to replace them, from the middle of this century, with road-vehicle pollution. There is some progress and some retrogression: Kroon shows that road-traffic emissions in the Netherlands, 1970–88, decreased by 64 per cent for lead, and by 47 per cent for CO. NOx increased by 123 per cent and HC stayed the same. While there are no comparative data for CO_2, it has almost certainly increased over the period. So, both forests and the ozone layer are threatened by the Dutch (and everyone else's) motor vehicles.

It is not necessary to repeat much of Kroon's chapter, only to encourage its absorption by as wide a range of people as possible. However, two final points must be made: first, reducing car use came from a policy balancing 'individual freedom, accessibility and the environment. It has been con-cluded that the only way of doing sufficient justice to all these aspects is to control the use of cars'. The Dutch are attempting this incrementally, and 'within the last three years the issue of "automobility" has developed from a taboo into a political battleground and a widely recognised problem'. It follows that 'Government papers on traffic and physical planning reveal a steadily developing set of policy goals and decisions, the latest . . . always more elaborate than its predecessors'.

Second, Table 8.4 shows expected trends in car-km from 1986 to 2010: with an unchanged policy there would have been a 72 per cent increase; applying the NMP makes the increase fall to 48 per cent. This should be compared with the British forecasts of a range of 83–142 per cent increase in vehicle-miles by 2025, for which no policy leading to a reduction was suggested at the time of the announcement in 1989.

Monheim also helps us understand mainland European policy, if it can be grouped over such a large area. Its unifying characteristic is that it differs so much from Britain in many areas, though there are some connective threads. Monheim is interested in the political struggles in-herent in making proper provision for walking and cycling, and opposing the all-powerful car lobby. He is the first to admit that progress has been slow, and a re-evaluation of urban transport structure is far from complete. Nevertheless, the Kontiv data show some groups with a bias towards the green modes, though they tend towards the disadvantaged: old and young, women, no-car households. It is a shame these data do not embrace modal use by occupation or income.

There are some surprising similarities with Britain. For example, the common belief that 'everyone has a car these days': in 1982, 32 per cent of all households and no less than 68 per cent of one-person households did not have a car. Monheim follows this with 'given the importance of green modes, it is clear that traffic policy should always incorporate social policy'. There are also, with up to 10–15 year time gaps, biases towards provision of facilities for the car, and, among research projects, towards motor vehicles. In time terms, however, we must recognise that the first federal publication about traffic calming was published in 1978, about ten years before a flimsy leaflet was produced by the British Department of

Transport. The other comparison that should be made concerns the initiative taken by the West German Federal Environment Ministry towards proper recognition of the green modes. The British Environment Department in 1990 is prodding the Transport Department to understand the environmental implications of an unchecked growth in car use.

Monheim takes us through the ministerial policies of state and region, singling out Nordrhein-Westfalen as the most adventurous and innovative. Yet this region still has undertaken a massive motorway-building programme over the last twenty years or so. As Monheim says, 'car-orientated forces have maintained a dominant influence', though he believes 'decisive opposing forces could emerge from environmental policy in the future'. This is what redeems the gloom of transport futures in Britain in early 1990: it is the environment that will dictate policy far more than the manufacturer or his advertising agency. As in Britain, the most powerful opposition to the pre-eminence of green mode planning comes from car owners in rural areas: this begs the question of whether those with largely self-chosen special environments should be clamouring for special attention.

Ramsay, Untermann and Garbrecht are complementary, but they also span between the poles of day-by-day reality and poetry. Ramsay provides a comprehensive review of action upon and for the pedestrian in Britain, with a sideways look at the new Bordeaux, starting from the convenient misreading of the Buchanan report (in that it spawned massive road schemes, rather than terrifying people with their likelihood or bringing about a segregation of modes and far fuller provision for the pedestrian). Ramsay's extensive knowledge is useful to us at this point in the book, and I like the way he compares machine unfavourably with man. Such a view, which I share, risks having 'Luddite' labels attached to one's lapel though even the machine *aficionado* tends to become human once s/he has climbed out of it, and become dependent again upon her or his own devices. What is alarming is the way the machine has been granted a decree absolute to confirm its separation from, and superiority over, mere unmechanised humans.

Ramsay and Garbrecht, each in their own way, consider how pedestrian networks should be established, Ramsay carving them rather formally from the all-traffic networks we have now, Garbrecht dreaming about My City almost from the standpoint of a lover. Each in their own way symbolises the sheer inadequacy of what we have now, as if traffic planners regard the pedestrian as little more than contemptible, in powerful contrast with Pushkarev and Zupan's (1975) eulogy:

Pedestrians comprise the greater part of humanity . . . created the world . . . built cities, paved streets, spread civilisation throughout the world. When everything was finished . . . motorists appeared on the scene. One should note that the automobile itself was invented by pedestrians but somehow the motorist forgot that very quickly.

There is more.

Ramsay glances at the negative treatment of pedestrians in the 1930s United States of the 1930s, a situation which has improved little since then. Untermann goes into much more detail on the decline of the walking city through to the low density sprawls of today – partly a response to the apparently inexhaustible supply of land, and partly to the inexorable rise of the automobile. Untermann's message is very timely for contemporary Europe, paradoxically: while the space is not available the growth in car ownership and use is painfully insistent . . . and little if anything is done about it. A number of contributors touch on the *parallel* growths in public transport, pedestrian and cycle facilities on the one hand, and freeway and parking construction on the other; one could also note that air travel is also growing rapidly, and that high-speed rail is climbing to the top of political agendas. All of these trends suggest an urgent need to question *mobility*, whose current status makes it seem as if it was delivered by special messenger from God.

But, to return to Untermann, his discussion of the worsening of pedestrian facilities in the United States led to a point where the *need* to walk became questionable. In some cities you would be regarded as a vagrant, in others you would be encouraged to walk within the new in- and out-of-town mega shopping centres, each with its own mall. But you could not *reach* these places on foot, for each was surrounded by a sort of porridge of parked cars, itself contained within multi-lane freeways. Given the pedestrian-as-nadir, it is brave of Untermann to suggest ways of bringing her/him back into prominence. His two changes centre on education of the planners, decision-makers and populations (they could be the same people, though he does not acknowledge this), and on different land-use patterns and transport facilities. The first clearly has to precede the second.

Garbrecht's delightful integrated green mode system, with preference over the automobile at the system's interface, supposes a city of sophisticated and sensitive people, where quality of life is more important than quantity of death, where non-motorists live until they are 150 – as most of the *car*cinogens and other mortal outputs of the motor vehicle will have been channelled away from seekers after truth. It really sounds positively Elysian. Unfortunately I haven't yet come across it – have you? Have you found a body of people willing to implement such a concept? But Garbrecht also recognises the here and now when he points to the rigours facing an elderly couple wanting nothing more complicated than a walk in the park. Bringing these two strands together makes a formidable indictment of our present way of being.

Practice

This section devotes more space to cyclists than to walkers, so that previous imbalance is corrected. Notable are the contributions of Hartman,

McClintock and Hülsmann, for they cover three countries: the Netherlands, Britain and Germany. Hartman notes that the Netherlands has 14 million inhabitants and 12 million cycles – not just a geographical accident, but also a result of careful planning for the cyclist. It has not always been this way, he tells us. In the 1960s there was a decline in cycling as motorisation rose and some bike paths were removed to make way for more cars. In the energy crisis of the early 1970s this was reversed, when public transport and cycling were encouraged. Since then the state has been consistent in its support of cycling.

Hartman's piece is mainly about a demonstration project which originated in The Hague and Tilburg as early as 1975; this flowed into the Delft project. This incurred substantial capital investment – two large tunnels, three bridges, all specially for cyclists, and about 14 km of special tracks of one kind or another. While evaluation continues (because infrastructure was not completed until 1987), findings are necessarily tentative. One is that while overall mobility did not change in Delft between 1982 and 1985, in a control area without special cycling measures the modal split changed in favour of motor vehicles, public transport losing 10 per cent. In the areas with special measures, motor trips have decreased in favour of cycle trips, which increased by six to eight per cent. Significantly, the increase was mainly male, to do with school or work trips, and the trip length increased without a corresponding rise in journey times.

McClintock's view of British achievement, while comprehensive, is necessarily much narrower than Hartman's. Special provision for cycling seems mainly to have happened in the 1980s – the Greater London Council's identification of a 1600 km network is said to be the 'best example in England' – and this was also the period when the Department of Transport produced a policy document and five 'large-scale urban cycle route network projects'. The Canterbury project collapsed through a weakening of local political support, the GLC one by the simple expedient of abolishing the Council, and other schemes elsewhere have foundered because of local authority expenditure cutbacks. A further reason, according to McClintock, was the 'rather ambivalent attitude of the D.Tp.'. He compares the 1987–8 expenditure on cycling of £160 000 against the £900 million a year spent on the national road programme.

McClintock is critical of the Milton Keynes network, 'shared cycle and footpaths grafted on to the basic grid road layout some years after the adoption of the master plan', which was heavily car-biased. He discusses the possibility of combining cycling and pedestrian facilities, a characteristic of some German towns, particularly Bonn, and is not too supportive, mainly because of the problems for disabled pedestrians. As for signalled crossings, apparently their shared use is resisted by the Department of Transport, though there are many, which seem to be working well, in Vienna. When he comes to the promotion of cycling in Britain, McClintock notes that it is 'greatly affected by land-use patterns and the distances involved' – similar phrases to this recurring within this text. And there is the peculiar British attitude to cycling first as something children do, and second as a problem to be solved, rather than a happy solution to be nurtured. Cycling conditions in the United Kingdom, he cites, 'are worse than anywhere in Europe, except for Belgium'.

Hülsmann wafts fresh continental air into our muddled heads, discussing the West German 'Bicycle-Friendly Towns' project. It is tempting to quote his chapter in its entirety, but the reader can do this, so I will have to hold myself in check. In his second paragraph he reminds us that the problem of motorisation cannot be expected to solve itself; its increase means an intensification of the conflicts between, shall we say, 'red' (environment-enemy) and 'green' (environment-friendly) modes.

One fascinating insight is that it was the Federal Environment Agency, not that of Transport, which initiated the 'Bicycle-Friendly Towns' Project. We should pause here to reflect that the British Department of the Environment is similarly suggesting environment-friendly policies. Two studies were set up in Detmold and Rosenheim, together with a number of subsidiary studies in other towns, and a looser link with Basle, Chambéry and Graz. The reader will have to refer to Chapter 15 for a list of innovations and new experiences gained from this project: it is very impressive. As to results, Rosenheim experienced a 13 per cent increase in bicycle traffic between 1981 and 1986, and a rise in the modal share from 23 to 26 per cent. The comments on Detmold in the text are less clear. The other result that deserves mention is that promotion of cycling is not just a matter of building cycle paths, but of dismantling 'the obstacles to the use of the bicycle by a comprehensive package of aims and measures' detailed in the text. Changing the attitudes of local authority staff is a key require-ment, as is the provision of adequate money, and the need for the popu-lation of a pro-bike town to be supportive and welcoming the macho-aggressiveness of many British car drivers towards cyclists would need treating with some kind of adrenalin-reduction technique, or perhaps there has to be a maximum segregation of the modes.

Brunsing provides a detailed view of the potential for integration of cycling and public transport. Again in Germany we find experiments and detailed study of this, when in Britain bikes are gradually being excluded from Intercity trains, were rarely permitted on commuter trains, may never have been on London underground trains, and . . . buses? Unthinkable. The German rail systems nearly all accept bikes, and most of their experi-ments have concerned buses; not all have been successful, but the argu-ment for trying is quite potent. Brunsing cites Germany in 1982 when, for distances up to 3 km, 17.1 per cent used a bike, and 6.8 per cent public transport as their main modes of transport; for distances over 4 km the position reversed. He deduces that for relatively low distances the two modes are complementary and they should cooperate rather than compete.

In Chapter 17 we return to the topic of walking, and one of its leading researchers, Rolf Monheim. This chapter is surprisingly cynical and eminently readable for the insights it gives into Germany's elaborate pedestrian networks. Particularly illuminating is the direct relationship between urban population and pedestrian facility: in small towns of less than 10 000 people in Nordrhein-Westfalen, only eight per cent have any pedestrianisation, and then only a mean length of 200 metres. Proportion and length both increase with town size until all towns with over 100 000 population have a pedestrian area, whose mean length increases from 1.2 km to 6.6. km in towns greater than 500 000 population.

The second illumination that Monheim switches on is in the change from the original concept of full-scale pedestrianisation, whereby on-street servicing of zones might be permitted up to 11.00 a.m. after which, for the rest of the time, they would be virtually the exclusive province of the pedestrian. Today, he points out, urban centres are much more likely to be an amalgam of a substantial pedestrian area with associated streets that have been traffic-calmed. The smaller the town, the more likely its shopping street is to be the latter type, thus providing a degree of access to car users directly to the shops rather than to an adjacent car park. This seems to be the sort of compromise that increasing car ownership and use are likely to bring, but which ought to be strongly resisted, for traffic calming is a far from perfect device, and this compromise can be seen as extendible to the time when we revert to all-traffic shopping areas once more. Monheim's chapter is thus a welcome extension of our knowledge of pedestrianisation, its causes and effects, and the types of warning signals which are beginning to emerge.

In Chapter 18 the topic changes again, this time to a matter of crucial importance – safe routes to school. In Britain it is not more than a few decades since most children above infant age found their own way to and from school. They might walk or cycle, and some might have had to take the bus or tram. All of these were possible because the levels of other traffic were still modest and there was little conflict. Today many parents will not permit their children to go on their own to and from school, so we have the emergent phenomenon of parental cars ferrying the kids, adding to traffic congestion, and increasing risks of accident- and pollution-damage to the green mode users.

Neilsen discusses some attempts to solve these problems in Odense, in a comprehensive study of 5800 of the town's schoolchildren aged from 9 to 15. The study showed that the youngest children walked, with cycling becoming increasingly used as the children grew; parental car use declined over that period. A large number of changes followed surveys of the children's movement through the town, and of places where they were most at risk from other traffic. Of the £100 000 spent annually, the most common measures to benefit are: slow-speed areas, road narrowings, traffic islands, and separate foot and cycle paths. The results are heartening. The slow-speed areas (described in the text, but achieving 30 km/h) have been most effective, and accidents involving children have been reduced by 85 per cent there. A similar reduction was achieved by applying a package of measures to the surroundings of one school. New cycle paths which have effected short-cuts have also been successful, but road narrowings and traffic islands have made little change.

The final chapter is apposite, for here we learn about a variety of measures used to enhance both walking and cycling in Buxtehude, one of the six West German special studies of environmental traffic management strategies which have been under way throughout the 1980s. The four aims for the six studies were to improve traffic safety, the mobility of non-motorised persons, neighbourhood recreation and development possibilities, and the local environmental situation. Following a careful study of Buxtehude's transport shortcomings, a range of measures was established and applied to the town. These were: creation of an acceptable route network for pedestrians and cyclists; bicycle streets; cycle paths in the main shopping streets; protection of cyclists and pedestrians in collector roads and at entrances to Tempo 30 zones; and publicity measures to help pedestrians understand what was being done and why, though it is not clear to what extent the public participated more actively in the study.

Döldissen and Draeger say final data are not yet available on the effects of these measures on modal split and therefore on pollution, though they feel that it is certain that cycling has increased considerably. On safety, the picture is clearer: accidents involving pedestrians have decreased by 46 per cent; in streets with raised carriageways at pedestrian and cycle crossing points 'there have been no accidents at all'. While the *number* of cycling accidents has increased, the *rate* has decreased.

Policy

This book is supportive of walking and cycling (and public transport), and less happy about the car. But control of excess car use is a first requirement in improving conditions for walking and cycling. This might appear anomalous when one recalls that there are nearly 20 million cars in Great Britain and that 61 per cent of all trips under 8 km were made by car in the mid-1980s (Department of Transport, 1988). But the car needs a government health warning: it devours precious urban and rural land, it is far from being available to all who might want to use it, and it actually aborts opportunities for movement of those without it. Kroon shows how the Dutch, at government and local levels, have categorised the dangers to health and proposed a rigorous programme to deal with these. The Swiss are keenly aware of the problems of excess motorisation and are acting to curb them; Bordeaux has turned its transport policies on their head, offering far better conditions for the green modes; Stockholm contemplates a variety of actions; and Berlin and Frankfurt have elected *Die Grüne* politicians who want much of their cities to be traffic-calmed. The movement towards a sophisticated green transport policy, attractive to all countries, is therefore under way.

What, then, might future policy do for people walking and cycling? A number of contributors have quoted the European Charter of Pedestrians' Rights, but that is only part of the story. This book has focused upon walking and cycling, the so-called 'green modes', but it has had much to say also about (perhaps 'dappled-green') buses, trolleybuses, streetcars and light rail. Looked at this way, the policies derive from two polarised groups: the 'red' modes of cars, taxis, motor cycles and most commercial vehicles, versus the coalition of 'green' modes. Some policies of significance which have emerged in this chapter, mainly from the contributors and partly from me, are summarised below.

Goals and concepts

* Sensible transport planning should evolve from the need to move people and freight from one place to another. It should reflect personal freedom, constrained only by a requirement that freedom should cause minimal damage to others and the environment. In other words, a kind of 'market' operates, but it is not concerned with financial profit.
* To influence policy, we need to understand who makes it. In much of Europe policy-makers range from the Community through national governments and local authorities, to people and special interest groups; often one level will act against the interests of another until democratic activity attempts to cancel the damage done. This means that transport policy has to include social policy, and that people, rather than machines, should be central to that policy.
* Transport policy should be holistic. It should therefore derive from *integrated government departments* (transport, land use, environment and energy are crucially interrelated); these interests should then be transferred to the transport planners and providers. But there must also be *integrated transport systems* so that modes interconnect and are genuinely supportive of each other (for example, park + ride is well established but bike + ride + bike is not).
* Understand that the 'red' modes have to be checked to allow the 'green' modes to function. Note that the Dutch, with perhaps the most comprehensive set of objectives, have recognised that the only way of meeting them is through control of car use (short-term) and car ownership (longer-term). Consequently, car-orientated forces should not be allowed to dominate either environmental, or general transport, policy.
* Question the concept of 'mobility' and support 'accessibility.'

Communicating concepts

* Introduce special educational programmes for high-level decision-makers, urban and transport planners and the population at large. Concepts like 'everyone has a car these days', 'we are producing a green car', 'buses are downmarket', 'lead-free petrol solves the air-pollution problem' and so forth need to be demolished authoritatively.
* Undertake substantial demonstration projects in environmental traffic management to examine and correct deficiencies, monitor the results and widely disseminate the findings.

Land use

* In terms of space, note that land use dispositions and urban density are vital factors in creating or controlling trip generation.
* Recognise that there are socially critical sizes of buildings: no megaliths.
* Act on the excessive spatial demands of the car, per person carried per km travelled, compared to the green modes.
* Publicise the minute proportion of urban movement space allocated to traffic-calmed, pedestrianised and cycle-route areas.

Emissions

* In terms of pollution, publicise the fact that in the Netherlands (and probably elsewhere) road traffic is the largest single source of air pollution which severely damages forests, cuts holes in the ozone layer and creates the greenhouse effect.
* Be aware that the growth in vehicle ownership and use nullifies efforts to control vehicle exhaust pollution.

Economic benefits

* Note the economic benefits of good, green mode facility provision and its correlate, an improved urban environment: increased trade, better conditions for employees, counters to out-of-centre developments, etc.
* Consider the savings in not providing excessively for vehicles in reduced health-care costs, in extended economic activity, in improved quality of life.

Propagating the green modes

* Counter discrimination against green mode users.
* Recognise walking and cycling as legitimate modes of transport requiring their own policies, funding and *connectivity* with other modes.

* Note that recent safety measures have benefited those in vehicles, while cyclists and pedestrians experience a higher level of risk.
* Act on the fact that casualty accidents are directly related to vehicle speed and that the 30 mph concept should be abolished and replaced with 30 km/h.
* Facility provision for cyclists brings positive results at little cost. So examine the cost of provision of all transport schemes and opt for those which are truly cost-effective.
* Create simple facilities to get walking and cycling children to school.

Conclusion

At the end of this fascinating book, what is its pre-eminent message? It originates in the presentation of clear and unequivocal evidence that shows a gross imbalance in spatial provision for the greenest modes, walking and cycling, in virtually all of the countries considered here. While most of them are busily creating pedestrian-only spaces, providing bike routes, applying speed limits and calming traffic, two problems emerge. The first is that these laudatory efforts occupy only a small fraction of the total urban movement space, and the second is that they are placebos – they divert attention from the real sickness, which is the continuing growth in owner-ship and use of the private car. I have suggested elsewhere (Roberts, 1989) that some measures, like traffic-calmed residential streets, can actually increase the likelihood of car use by providing more space in which to park – whether legally or illegally – than was there before the street was restructured. So the greater the supply of parking, the more is car owner-ship sanctified.

It is necessary continually to remind ourselves of an early policy state-ment among those drawn from this book: 'understand that the "red" modes have to be checked to allow the "green" modes to function'. I hope that there is someone out there listening and acting.

References

Adams, J.G.U., 1985, *Risk and freedom*, Transport Publishing Projects, Cardiff.
Department of Transport, 1988. *National travel survey 1985/1986*, HMSO, London.
—— 1989, *Transport in London*, HMSO, London.
Pushkarev, B. and Zupan, J.M., 1975, *Urban space for pedestrians*, MIT Press, Cambridge, Mass.
Roberts, J., 1981, *Pedestrian precincts in Britain*, TEST, London.
—— 1989, *User-friendly cities: what Britain can learn from mainland Europe*, TEST, London.
TEST, 1985, *The accessible city*, a report for the Campaign to Improve London's Transport, and the Greater London Council, TEST, London.

Index

Note: Numbers in italic refer to figures or tables

accessibility, as distinct from mobility 94,
    105–6, 287, 291
  see also trip length
acidification 2, 24, 114, *115*, 116, 123
  see also forest dieback
air pollution 76, 97, 113–33, 138, 145–6,
    219, 301
  ammonia 116
  carbon dioxide 7, 24, 76, 98, 101, 114,
    117, 123, 130, 292–3
    see also global warming
  carbon monoxide 65, 84, 114, *120*, 124,
    130, *131*, 292–3
  hydrocarbons 84, 99, 114, 116, 122, 124,
    130, 292–3
  in the Netherlands 113–33
  Luxembourg agreement on 119, *120*
  nitrogen oxides 65, 76, 84, 101, 114,
    116, *120*, 121–4, 129, 130, *131*,
    292–3
    see also acidification
  ozone layer 154, 293, 301
  photochemical 114, *115*, 123, 293, 301
  soot 101, 108, 122
  sulphur dioxide 114, 116, 130, 292
    see also acidification, traffic pollution
  maps 131
airy fairies, who disagree with Margaret
    Thatcher 2
ammonia 116
Amsterdam *22*, 128
animals, killed on roads 98
area-wide traffic restraint 27, *30*, 77, 86,
    266–84
  see also environmental traffic
    management, traffic calming, traffic
    restraint
automobility 122–30, 177, 293

  see also motorisation

Barn Owls, cars as prime cause of death
    98
Basle, Switzerland 222, 297
Bavaria, FRG 143, 151, 222, 248–9
benzene 99, 130
Berlin 79, 151, 235, 300
Berlin Wall 132
Bicycle Friendly Towns Project 139–40,
    218–30, 297
bicycles see cycles
Birmingham, UK 37–8
Bochum, FRG 237, 241, 242
Bonn, FRG 43, 237, 240, *241*, 290, 296
Bordeaux, France 164, 294, 300
Borgentreich, FRG 84
Bottomley, Peter 72
braking distance 19, *21*
Braunschweig, FRG 237, *238*
Bremen, FRG 41–3, 151, 231, 235–7, 290
Britain 1–3, 13–33, 34–46, 64–74, 88–96,
    201–17,
  cycling 22–6, 64–73, 201–17, 288–9, 291,
    296–7
  Department of Environment 2, 294, 297
  Department of Transport 2, 3, 7, 25,
    35, 72, 94, 291, 294, 296–7
  Innovatory Cycle Scheme 201, *202*
  motorisation 2, 36, 90–1
  pedestrianisation 1, 289
  promotion of green modes 1–3
  retail location policy 36–9, 94
  road safety 18–21, 47, 45–59, 75, 93–4,
    159, 289–90
  transport planning 88–96, 163–5,
    201–17, 288–9
  Transport Policies and Programmes 160

transport policy 7–8, 64–74, 88–96,
    287–8, 291, 293–4
Urban Cycle Route Network Projects
    204, 296
walking 14–21, 24–6, 65–73, 88–96,
    159–61, 163–5, 167–70, 288–9, 291
White Paper on the Environment 288
Buchanan, Colin 26–8, 160, 178, 294
buildings, socially critical size of 104, 292,
    301
    see also trip length
bus stops *see* public transport stops
buses 35, 108, 215, 231–3, 236–7, *238*,
    239, 240, *241*, 242, 288, 297–8, 300
Buxtehude, FRG 79, *82*, 84, 211, 266–84,
    299

Cambridge, UK 203–4, 209–10, 216
Canterbury, UK 204, 296
carbon dioxide *see under* air pollution
carbon monoxide *see under* air pollution
car ownership (*see also* car use,
    motorisation) 3, 54, 137, 226, 293,
    300–2
    trends 7, 8, 85, 125, 161, 169, 287–8,
    291, 295, 302
cars, killing animals and birds 98
car lobby *see* road lobby
car parking 78, 103, 172, 174–7, 182, 208,
    229, 231, 245, 247, 275–6, 295, 298,
    302
    effect on retail trade 42, *43*
    obstruction by 40, 85
    on footways *see* footways
car pooling 127
car use (*see also* trip length)
    advantages 99, 124
    external costs 69, 71, 103
    inessentiality 34, 76, 106, 124
    reduction 8, 124–6, 199, 293, 299–300
    see also traffic calming
    trends 2, 7, 40, 129, 148, 257, 287, 293,
    295
    see also car ownership, motorisation
catalytic converter *see* clean vehicle
    technology
Chalker, Lynda 72
Chambéry, France 222, 297
chicanes 90
child safety (*see also* safe routes to school,
    traffic vulnerable people)
    accidents 18, 47, 56–8, 152, 255–65,
    298–9
    at play 24, 40, 56, 220
    in residential areas 25, 56
    in traffic-calmed areas 82–4, 282
    risk to cycling children 23, 263–4, 208
city centre 34, 39–41, 44–5, 86

pedestrianisation of *see*
    pedestrianisation
Civic Trust 167
clean vehicle technology 7, 97, 101–2, 108,
    118–19, *120*, 121–3, 126, 216, 219,
    290
climatic change *see* global warming
COBA 94, 160, 291
Cologne, FRG 41, 76, 85–6, 144, 244,
    246–8, 252
Coventry, UK 17, 37, 160–1
cycle facilities 3, 22, 76, 84–5, 128,
    193–200, 201–17, 218–30, 231–44,
    255–65, 266–84, 289, 301–2
    construction and maintenance 209, 211,
    224
    cost 71, 193, 199, 205, 227, 296
    networks *see* cycle networks
    parking 107, 215, 224, 228, 232–3, 234,
    235
    streets 272, 275, 279
    tracks *see* cycle tracks
cycle networks (*see also* cycle facilities,
    cycle tracks) 43, 57, 72, 107, *149*,
    193–200, 203–5, 223–4, 228,
    266–84, 299, 301
    Delft 193–200, 296
    hierarchical structure 197, *198*, 199
    marketing 199–200
cycle tracks (*see also* cycle facilities) 40,
    62, 72, 160, 179, 181, 183, 193–200,
    201–17 *passim*, 261, *262*, *280*, 2981,
    299, 302
    networks *see* cycle networks
    Redways 207–8, 296
    shared with pedestrians 203, 205, 207–8,
    210–11, 263, 279, 296
    signing 239, 282
cycles
    Bicycle Friendly Towns Project 139–40,
    218–30, 297
    bicycle service stations 237
    for lcoal authority employees 225, 282
    hire 225, 228, 235, 237, 282
    ownership and use 65–6, 105–7, 134–7,
    148, 193, 201, 226, 257–8, 263–4,
    270, 282, 289, 296
cycling
    advantages 3, 13, 22, 219–20
    and environmental policy 215–16
    and public transport 215, 222, 231–43,
    297
    attitudes towards 23, 196, 216, 297
    bicycle offices 140, 223, 225, 227
    cycling law 140
    discrimination against 68, 70–1, 140
    effect of facilities on 201, 203–6
    exclusion from traffic forecasting 66
    facilities for *see* cycle facilities. cycle
    networks, cycle tracks

for recreation 224, 236–7
impact on by motorised traffic *see under* green modes
in Netherlands *see under* Netherlands
in pedestrian areas 43, 145, 210–11, 271–2, *274*
latent demand for 69
lobby groups 107, 144, 151–2, 204, 222
on footways 17, 210–11
planning 193–200, 201–17, 218–30
problems 22–6, 176, 227, 291
promotion 4, 139–40, 199, 218–30, 266–8, 297, 302
publicity 146, 199–200, 215–6, 223–5, 227–8, 282
speeds 270
cycling safety (*see also* child safety, pedestrian safety, road accidents, safe routes to school)
accidents 22–3, 49–54, 145, 199, 201–17 *passim*, 282, 290, 299, 302
death and injury rates 22, 49–54, 147, *283*
fear of accidents 23, 65, 201, 255, 264, 289
risk to cycling children 23, 208, 263–4

Delft, Netherlands
Woonerven *27*, 160–1
cycle network 5, 193–200, 203, 205, 296
Denmark
pedestrianisation 43, 160
road safety 59
safe routes to school 58, 255–65, 298–9
speed limits 59
traffic calming 26, 161
Detmold, FRG 139–40, 221, 223–4, 226, 240, 297
developments, socially critical size of 104, 292, 301
see also trip length
disabled *see* traffic vulnerable people
Disabled People's Transport Advisory Committee 92
domesticating the car *see* traffic restraint
Dortmund, FRG 79, 82, *83–4*, 85, 242
Durham, UK 161, 167
Dusseldorf, FRG 235, 246–7

East Germany 49, 244
elderly people (*see also* traffic vulnerable people)
fear of assault 93
mobility handicapped 92, 185, 222
susceptibility to accidents 18, 65, 289
electric vehicles 108, 122
energy consumption 1, 13, 99, 184, 219, 243, 290
environmental areas 26, 28
environmental awareness 2, 97, 137, 151, 214

environmental impact
of green modes 3, 15, 22, 64, 215–16, 219, 243
of motorised vehicles 3, 31, 34, 75, 98–102, 113–6, 130, 180, 288, 293–4; on green mode users 13–14, 24–6, 65, 70, 107, 182, 218, 290–1, 298
environmental policy 5, 100–9, 113–33, 145, 292, 294, 301
in the Netherlands 113–33
reducing automobility 122–30
technical vehicle standards 119–22
'three-track approach' 119–32
urban traffic measures 130–32
environmental traffic management (ETM)
(*see also* area-wide traffic restraint, traffic calming, traffic restraint) 7, 27–30, 32, 75–87, 266–84
cycling and 220, 228–9
West German research programme 79, 82, 142, 266–84, 299
Erlangen, FRG 148, *149*, 153, 252
Essen, FRG 41, 144, 242, 244
European Charter of Pedestrian's Rights *xvi–xviii*, 73, 170, 300
European Commission 126
European Community 119–22, 170, 288
European Council of Ministers of the Environment 119
European Parliament 72
exhaust emission control *see* clean vehicle technology
exhaust emissions *see under* air pollution

'feet first' campaign 88, 92
Finland 52, 57, 263
footpaths 162, 261, *262*, *see also* footways
footways (*see also* pedestrian facilities) 162, 172, 174, 176, 179, 182, 247, 289
car parking on 17, 20, *22*, 24, 71, 85, 159
cycling on 17, 210–11
dog fouling of *17*
shared with cyclists 203, 205, 210–11, 263, 279, 296
widening of 40, 104, 281
forest dieback 98, 115–6, 154, 293, 301
see also acidification
Fowler, Norman 72
France 168–9, 288
Frankfurt, FRG 86, 245–8, 252, 300
Freiburg, FRG *30*, 36, 41–2
freight transport 108, 118, 126, 128
FRG *see* West Germany

GDR 49, 244
global warming 2, 24, 76, 98, 114, 116, 154, 301

Godfrey, C.V. 56
Graz, Austria 222, 297
green modes (*see also* cycling, walking) 3,
    34, 300
    impact on by red modes 13–14, 22–6,
        65, 70, 107, 182, 218, 290–1, 298
    promoting 134–58, 302
greenhouse effect *see* global warming
GRUNEN, DIE 86, 150, 300

Haarlem, Netherlands *28*
Hague, The, Netherlands 128, 194, 296
Hamburg, FRG 41–3, 151, 235, 247, 268,
    270
handicapped *see* traffic vulnerable people
Hanover, FRG 36, 41–4, 236, 239, 248
health
    effect of pollution on 13, 24, 65, 70, 76,
        98–100, 114
    promotion of, through cycling and
        walking 64, 220, 243, 302
Highway Code 91
hydrocarbons *see under* air pollution

integration
    of government departments 300
    of modes *see* modal integration
    of pedestrians and cyclists 27–8
    see also Woonerven, *see under*
        pedestrianisation

Japan 49, 61–2, 119
junction narrowing 90

kilometre reduction plans 127
Kuopio, Finland 263

land use planning 40–1, 103–5, 128, 160,
    163–6, 178–84, 194, 213–4, 229,
    269, 300
lead, in petrol 99, 121, 130, 216, 290, 301
light rail transport (LRT) 3, *30*, 41, 108,
    160, 173–4, 298, 300
    and cycling 215, 236–7, 240–2
Linköping, Sweden 263–4
London 35, 38–9, 43–4, 65, 67, 91, 93,
    169, 203–4, 289, 296–7
LRT *see* light rail transport
Luxembourg agreement on exhaust gas
    standards 119, *120*

Manchester, UK 85, 204
Milton Keynes, UK 207–8, 296
Mitchell, John 92
mobility, as distinct from accessibility 94,
    105–6, 287, 291
    see also trip length
mobility impaired *see* traffic vulnerable
    people
modal integration 102, 109, 185–9, 219,
    229, 231–43, 290, 295, 297, 300

motorcycles 212
motorisation (*see also* car ownership, car
    use, red modes) 97–109, 122–30,
    177, 231, 243, 293, 301–2
    accident effects *see* road accidents
    effect on cycling and walking *see* green
        modes
    environmental effects *see* environmental
        impact, environmental policy,
        pollution
    traffic effects *see* road construction,
        traffic demand, trip length
motorised individual transport (MIT)
    98–109
mugging 93
Munich, FRG 41–3, 102, 148, 235, 242,
    245, 247–8, 250, *251*, 252
Münster, FRG 145, 235, 237, 240

National Consumer Council 16–17, 20–1,
    70, 89–90, 92
Netherlands
    air pollution in 113–33
    Clean Car Research Programme 120
    cycling 5, 43, 47, 49, 124, 177, 193–200,
        232, 296
    Demonstration project on Urban
        Bicycle Routes 194
    emission reduction targets 116, 119–22,
        288
    environmental policy 113–33, 292
    National Environmental Policy Plan
        (NMP) 113, 116, *117*, 118, 125–6,
        292–3
    pedestrianisation 160
    political parties 113, 116, 292
    road safety *21*, 49–50, 52, 57–8, 61
    Second Traffic and Transport Structure
        Scheme (SVVII) 123, 129, 193–4
    sustainable development 8, 116, 125
    traffic calming 7, 26, *27*
    traffic policy 113–33
    traffic pollution maps 131
    Woonerven *27*, 57, 140, 160–1, 187
Niedersprockhövel, FRG 77, *80–1*
nitrogen oxides *see under* air pollution
noise pollution 24, 65, 70, 75–6, 98, 100,
    102, 108, 114, 119–22, 130
Nordrhein-Westfalen, FRG 140–1, 143–5,
    222, 240, 249, 298
Nottingham, UK 160–1
    Greater Nottingham Cycle Route
        Network 203, *204*
Nuremberg, FRG 148, 235, 247–8, 250

Odense, Denmark 6, 30, 255–65, 298
Oldridge, B. 203, 214
out-of-town shopping
    effect on trip length 35, 213–4, 245, 252,
        292, 295

ozone *see* air pollution, photochemical
ozone layer 154, 293, 301

Parkinson, Cecil 2
pavements *see* footways
pedal cycling *see* cycling
pedestrian facilities (*see also* pedestrians,
    walking) 15, 16, 76, 85, 183, *274*,
    295
  footbridges 71
  footways *see* footways
  maintenance 16, 166
  maps 170
  networks *20*, *30*, 57, 70, 72, 88, 105,
    159–71, 185–9, 271, *273*, 294, 298–9
  obstacles to using 16, 85, 176, 289
  precincts *see* pedestrianisation
  services 165–6
  underpasses *15*, 71, 91, 105, *273*
pedestrian lobby groupa 16–17, 20–1, 72,
    88–92, 150–53
pedestrian safety (*see also* death and
    injury rates, road accidents, traffic
    vulnerable people) 282, 288, 291,
    302
  and crossing roads 17, 160, 168, 175,
    178, 182–3, 186–8, 247, 258, *260–2*,
    263, 275, *276*, 277, 279, *280*, 289,
    299
  and speed limits 58–60
  death and injury rates 18, 50, 54–60
  pavement accidents 19
pedestrianisation (*see also* walking) 31,
    32, 41–2, 178, 244–54, 301–2
  and cycling 43, 145, 210–11, 271–2, *274*
  and historical heritage 245–6
  and public transport 35, 249, 290
  and retailing 42, 88, 161, 245–6, *251*,
    290
  arcades 245
  consequences 44–5, 250–3
  in Britain 1, 32, 161, 289
  in West Germany 244–54
pedestrians (*see also* walking)
  definitions 14, 91, 134–8, 161–3, 258
  discrimination against 68, 70–1, 291,
    302
  environments of 16, 172–85, 291
  facilities for *see* footways, pedestrian
    facilities
  needs 16, 163
  precincts *see* pedestrianisation
  rights *xvi–xviii*, 73, 170, 300
  safety *see* pedestrian safety
  town for 103–5
Pedestrians' Association 72
petrol, consumption of 13, 99, 184, 219,
    243
  increasing costs of 126, 213
  lead in 99, 121, 130, 216, 290, 301

photochemical air pollution *see under* air
    pollution
physical planning *see* land-use planning
play streets 56
Policy Studies Institute 71–2
pollution, *see* air pollution, noise
    pollution, visual pollution
  see also environmental impact,
    environmental policy
pollution maps 131
public policy, towards green modes 64–74
public transport (*see also* buses, light rail
    transport, public transport stops,
    rail transport, U-bahn)
  and cycling 215, 222, 231–43, 297
  and walking 185–9, 242–3
  bike and ride 215, 232–5, 290
  fares and tickets 29, 127, 228, 237,
    239–40, 242
  improving service 40, 77, 84, 107–8, 181
  integration with other modes 40, 76, 85
  Motorised Public Transport (MPT)
    107–8
  park and ride 91, 231
  promoting 29, 127–8, 219, 267
  ride and bike 215, 235
public transport stops 186–8, 231–43
  bus stops 93, 209, 211, 215, 228, 290
  railway stations 216, 228, 247, 269–70,
    290

Radburn layouts 26
Rail transport 41, 173–4, 250, 297
  and cycling 215, 231–3, 235–6, 241
  underground *see* U-bahn
railway stations *see under* public transport
    stops
red modes 3, 297, 300, 302
  impact on green modes 13, 14, 24–6, 65,
    70, 107, 182, 218, 290–1, 298
residential areas (*see also* traffic calming)
  calming 26–7, 76, 78, 84, 88, 147,
    160–1, 228, 302
  environmental problems 24
  safety of children 56
Rhein-Ruhr, FRG 143–4, 233, 235
right of way 163
risk compensation theory 60, 289
road accidents 47–63, 71, 138, 147
  speed 19, *21*, 58, 290
  speed limits 59–60, 176, 302
  braking distance 19, *21*
  death and injury rates by age 18, 52–3;
    by race 61; international
    compar[]s[]n 47–62; children 57,
    82–4, 98, 255–7; cyclists 22, 49–54,
    147, 283; pedestrians 18, 50, 54–60;
    under-recording 256–7
  exposure to 93, 263–4
  fear of 23, 65, 255, 264, 289, 298

in traffic-calmed areas 82–4, 144, 282
in West Germany 75, 98
risk compensation theory 60, 289
animals 98
children 18, 47, 56–8, 152, 255–65,
   298–9
   see also child safety
cyclists 22–3, 49–54, 145, 199, 201–17
   passim, 282, *283*, 290, 299, 302
   see also cycling safety
elderly 18
   see also traffic vulnerable people
pedestrians 18–20, *21*, 282, 290, 299
   see also pedestrian safety
road construction 2, 3, 7, 88, 137, 173–6,
   178, 212, 231, 245, 288, 291, 293
road lobby 2, 7, 85, 107, 124, 138, 141–2,
   148, 154, 182, 246, 287–8, 291,
   293–4, 301
road pricing 126
road safety *see* road accidents
Rosenheim, FRG 139–40, 221, 223–4,
   226, 297
Rotterdam, Netherlands 115, 128

safe routes to school (*see also* child safety)
   58, 255–65, 298–9, 302
SCAFT 26
Scandinavia 42, 61, 114, 162
schools, safe routes to *see* safe routes to
   school
segregation of pedestrians and cyclists 27,
   93, 159–60
shopping (*see also* trip length)
   and car parking 42, *43*
   and cycling 275–6
   and pedestrian networks 165, 169,
      270–2
   and pedestrianisation 42, 88, 161,
      172–5, 178, 245–6, 248–50, *251*,
      252–3, 290
   and public transport investment 41
   and traffic calming 246–50, 275–6, 298
   arcades 245
   concentration 40, 94, 103
   modal splits 36–8, 69
   out-of-town 35, 213–14, 245, 252, 292,
      295
   spending by mode 35, 37–9
sidewalks *see* footways
Sitte, Camillo 168
slow-speed areas 258, *259*, 260, 264
   see also traffic calming
Smeed, R.J. 48, 160
soft traffic 162
   see also green modes
soot 101, *108*, 122
space consumption by cars 99, 102, 104,
   292, 301–2

speed (*see also* speed limits, Tempo 30,
   traffic calming) 13, 19, 71, 167,
   175, 182, 212–3, 247, 268, 282, 284
   and accidents 19, *21*, 58, 290
   in traffic calmed areas *82*, 260
speed humps 90, 169, 212, 258, 282
   see also traffic calming
speed limits (*see also* speed humps, traffic
   calming) 40, 167
   influence on accidents 58–60, 302
   low speed zones 76, 105–6, 143, 147,
      178, 228–9, 231, 258, 271, 275–6,
      277, 279, 290
   poor enforcement 19, 71, 130
Stavanger, Norway 263
street car *see* light rail transport
Stuttgart, FRG 41, 43, 235–6, 240, 248
subways, rail *see* U-bahn
sulphur dioxide 114, 116, 130, 292
   see also acidification
sustainable development 8, 116, 125
Sweden 13, 26, 49, 61
   child safety in 47, 57–8, 263–4
Switzerland 58, 288, 300

Tempo 30 77, *83*, 84, 106–7, 143, 146,
   266–84, 290, 299
   see also speed limits, traffic calming
TEST 34–6, 38, 42
Tilburg, Netherlands 194, 296
town planning *see* land-use planning
traffic calming 7, 26, *27–8*, 103, 130, 152,
   160–1, 289–90
   benefits 26, 78–9, 81–4
   concepts 77
   in Netherlands 8, 26, *27*
   in West Germany 60, 75–87, 140–3,
      146–7, 266–84
   large areas *see* area-wide traffic
      restraint, environmental traffic
      management
   measures 76–8, 90
   main streets 78, *80–1*, 141, 247–8
   residential streets 26–7, 76, 78, 84, 88,
      228, 302
   safety 82–4, 144, 182
   shopping areas 42–3, 246–50, 275–6, 298
   slow speed areas 258, *259*, 260, 264
   speed *82*, 260
      see also speed limits, speed humps
   Tempo 30 *see* Tempo 30
Verkehrsentwicklungsplanung 84, 290
traffic clubs 152
traffic degeneration 30
traffic demand 7, 30, 90–1, 94, 160, 174,
   301
   see also motorisation
traffic generation *see* traffic demand, road
   construction
traffic management 26, 130, 164, 212–13

see also environmental traffic
   management
traffic restraint (*see also* area-wide traffic
   restraint, environmental traffic
   management, traffic calming) 3,
   26–30, 32, 90, 101, 106, 108, 255,
   260, 266–84
   effects 41–5
traffic-reducing town planning *see* trip
   length
traffic vulnerable people 17–18, 92–3, 163,
   169, 210, 222, 242, 296
   see also women, child safety
trams *see* light rail transport
Transport and Road Research Laboratory
   160, 162, 164, 168
Transport 2000 88, 91–2
travel demand *see* traffic demand
trip length
   increasing 2, 40, 65, 71, 94, 106, 177,
   214, 218, 291, 297
   need to reduce 29, 94, 103–4, 117–8,
   180–1, 243, 301–2

U-bahn 242, 245, 250
United States 4, 47–9, 52, 119, 252
   cycling and walking 5, 55, 159, 172–85,
   289–90, 295
   urban renovation 1, 252
urban sprawl *see* trip length

vehicle calming 213
vehicle emissions *see* air pollution
vehicle technology *see* clean vehicle
   technology
VELO CITY 152
Verkehrsberuhigung see traffic calming
Vienna 44, 297
visual pollution 24, 99, 130
visually impaired *see* traffic vulnerable
   people

walking
   advantages 3, 13, 64
   ancillary and primary 14, 162, 168
   and public transport 185–9, 242–3
   decline 16, 65, 289

discrimination against 68, 70–1, 291,
   302
   facilities *see* footways, pedestrian
   facilities
   impact of motorised transport 13, 24–6,
   65, 70, 182, 218, 290–1, 298
   jay walking 175–6
   not a strategic matter 164
   omission from public policy 66–70
   precincts *see* pedestrianisation
   problems 13–32, 64–6, 88–90, 288–9
   requirements for 16, 162–3
   safety *see* pedestrian safety
   taken for granted 15, 66, 288–9
walkers *see* pedestrians
Walking Transit System 186–9
West Germany
   Bicycle Friendly Towns Project 6, 139,
   218–30, 297
   consumer groups 150–3
   German Automobile Club (ADAC)
   143, 151–2
   German Children's Protection Society
   152
   German Cycling Club (ADFC) 144,
   151–2, 237
   Green Cyclists 151
   pedestrianisation 244–54
   political parties 150–1
   Verkehrsentwicklungsplanung (VEP)
   84, 290
   Winkelerven 42
   see under traffic calming
women (*see also* traffic vulnerable people)
   as travel escorts 6, 92–3
   as mobility impaired 92
   fear of assault 93–4
   safety when cycling 205, 208–9
Woonerven (Woonerf) 27, 57, 140, 160–1,
   184, 187
   see also traffic calming
World Health Organisation 65
Wuppertal, FRG 236–7, 239

York, UK 44, 209–10, 216